FIVE PLAYS

Also by Ben Travers

Novels

THE COLLECTION TODAY
A CUCKOO IN THE NEST
THE DIPPERS
MISCHIEF
ROOKERY NOOK
VALE OF LAUGHTER

Plays

A BIT OF A TEST
BANANA RIDGE
CHASTITY MY BROTHER
CORKER'S END
A CUP OF KINDNESS
THE DIPPERS
DIRTY WORK
MISCHIEF
A NIGHT LIKE THIS
NUN'S VEILING
OUTRAGEOUS FORTUNE
SHE FOLLOWS ME ABOUT
SPOTTED DICK
TURKEY TIME
WILD HORSES

FIVE PLAYS

A Cuckoo in the nest
Rookery Nook
Thark
Plunder
The Bed Before Yesterday

BEN TRAVERS

W. H. Allen · London
A Howard & Wyndham Company
1977

Printed and bound in Great Britain by Butler & Tanner Ltd,
Frome and London
for the publishers, W. H. Allen and Co. Ltd,
44 Hill Street, London W1X 8LB

ISBN 0 491 02132 1

CONTENTS

A CUCKOO IN THE NEST

A Play in Three Acts

CHARACTERS

This play was first produced at the Aldwych Theatre, London, on July 22nd, 1925, with the following cast:

Rawlins (maid at the Wykehams' flat)	Miss Ena Mason
Mrs Bone	Miss Grace Edwin
Major George Bone	Mr Tom Walls
Barbara Wykeham	Miss Madge Saunders
Gladys (maid at the 'Stag and Hunt')	Miss Rene Vivian
Alfred (barman at the 'Stag and Hunt')	Mr Roger Livesey
Marguerite Hickett	Miss Yvonne Arnaud
Peter Wykeham	Mr Ralph Lynn
Noony (a villager)	Mr Gordon James
Mrs Spoker (landlady of the 'Stag and Hunt')	Miss Mary Brough
Rev. Cathcart Sloley-Jones	Mr J. Robertson Hare
Claude Hickett, M.P.	Mr Hastings Lynn
Chauffeur	Mr Joe Grande

ACT I
    Scene 1 At the Wykehams' flat, Kensington. Tuesday evening.
    Scene 2 Parlour of the 'Stag and Hunt' Inn, Maiden Blotton, Somerset. Tuesday night.

ACT II
    Number Two Room of the 'Stag and Hunt'. Tuesday night.

ACT III
    Parlour of the 'Stag and Hunt'. Wednesday morning.

ACT I

SCENE I

Sitting-room in the Wykehams' flat in Kensington

The curtain rises on an empty room in darkness. There is a sustained ringing of an electric bell heard off

It is a small room not extensively furnished. What furniture there is is modern and new. A door D. R. *Another door in back wall* C. *Window* L. *in alcove. A writing-table and telephone* L. *of door. Fireplace* R. *with club fender, easy chair* L. *of fireplace. A small bookcase with lamp on top* R. *of fireplace, a table with silver salver and telegram* D. R., *and chair* L. *of table. Settee* D. L. *and parallel with alcove. Pouffe cushion* D. L. *of settee and chair* D. L. *Standard lamp in front of alcove, stool* L. *of door up* C., *and close against writing-table. 'Phone book on top of writing-table and an A.B.C. time-table in pigeon-hole. Backcloth behind door when opened should suggest a fairly wide main passage leading from front door down the length of the flat*

Rawlins crosses hastily from door D. R., *which she closes, switches on lights* D. R. *and crosses to door* C., *which she leaves open. Her attitude suggests that she has been waiting for the bell and that it means something important. Mrs Bone's voice can be heard off immediately afterwards*

Mrs Bone (*off*) Is Mrs Wykeham here?
Rawlins (*off*) No, madam.
Mrs Bone (*off*) No?

Mrs Bone enters. She is a tall and commanding lady of about forty-five with an overbearing manner. She comes into the room quickly and suspiciously with a quick turn of the head right and left. Rawlins follows her

Where is she then? (*Crosses* D. R.)
Rawlins (*up* R. C) I don't know, madam. I had a telegram to say she was coming back this evening. Alone, she said; but she hasn't come yet.
Mrs Bone Coming back *alone*?
Rawlins Yes, madam.
Mrs Bone Where did she wire from?
Rawlins Bristol, madam.

Mrs Bone M'yes. (*As though to herself*) I should like to know what's happened.

Rawlins Yes, m'm; but what have *you* heard, 'm?

Mrs Bone I and Major Bone—— (*Breaking off and turning up* C. *in front of Rawlins*) Where is he? (*Going to door* C. *and calling*) George! George! Come in, don't mooch about in the passage.

Mrs Bone D. R. *Rawlins crosses down* R. C. *just above* L. *of Mrs Bone.*

Major Bone enters up C.

Major Bone is a middle-aged man of military bearing, rather a sporty type with an eye for a pretty girl and a good judge of port. He is in evening dress with overcoat and opera hat. He takes off opera hat as he enters. He comes down L. C., *spots Rawlins; she is a pretty girl, and he seems to be very interested, keeping his eyes on her*

Mrs Bone I and Major Bone had been out all day. When we got home just now we found a telegram, also from Bristol. (*To Bone*) Where is it? (*Crossing* C.) *George!*

Major Bone (*pulling himself together*) What? Oh—yes. (*Searching*) All right.

Mrs Bone Well, where is it?

Major Bone (*still searching*) Half a minute.

Mrs Bone (*controlling herself in front of the servant*) Come along, do, something very serious has evidently happened.

Major Bone Yes, that's what you've been saying all along.

Mrs Bone Well, where is the wire?

Major Bone (*after contortions*) I know where it is all right. Don't be in such a hurry. (*Finds it in trousers pocket*) Here you are—here it is. Don't snatch at the thing. You're always snatching at everything. (*Sits on settee down* L.)

Mrs Bone (*taking telegram from him*) Now, listen. (*Reads to Rawlins*) 'Be at my flat at seven, have had most startling and terrible experience, Barbara.' That's what it says, and that's all we know. (*Pause. To Rawlins*) Do you know any more than that?

Rawlins (*after a moment's hesitation*) W—well yes, 'm, in a way I do. (*Slight movement to Mrs Bone*)

Mrs Bone (*looking at her closely*) Yes—what? (*Slight pause*) Come along now, you needn't be afraid. Does what you know concern my daughter's husband?

Rawlins Yes, 'm, it does.

Mrs Bone I sensed it. (*Looks meaningly at Major Bone. To Rawlins*) Go on.

Rawlins Well, madam, in the first place, Mr and Mrs Wykeham left here this afternoon for Paddington station as arranged.

Mrs Bone Together?

Rawlins Yes, 'm. They were going to Somerset—to Lady Bunter's.

Mrs Bone Yes, yes, *I* know. They left together for Paddington as arranged. Well?

Rawlins Some time later Mr Wykeham came back here to the flat.

Mrs Bone Alone?

Rawlins Well, without Mrs Wykeham, 'm. But not alone. There was another person with him.

Mrs Bone (*warming to it*) Who?

Rawlins I don't know who she was, 'm. A strange young lady, a foreigner it struck me—with a little dog.

Major Bone A little what?

Rawlins Dog.

Mrs Bone Dog! Dog!

Major Bone Dog!

Mrs Bone Go on!

Rawlins Mr Wykeham didn't wait to explain anything to me. He seemed in a great hurry. He went straight to the telephone.

Mrs Bone Were you here when he telephoned?

Rawlins Well—I was just outside the door, madam.

Mrs Bone Yes? And who did he ring up?

Rawlins Gamble's Garridge, madam, for a car at once for a long journey.

Mrs Bone (*to Major Bone, with an intake of the breath*) You see! (*to Rawlins*) Go on.

Rawlins They stayed here for some time. Then the hall porter rang up to say the car was below. And they went down together, 'm.

Mrs Bone (*nodding to her thoughts and speaking them aloud to Bone*) I knew something of this sort would happen.

Major Bone (*to Rawlins*) What happened to the little dog?

Rawlins Oh, she took the dog with her, sir, thank goodness. It was here too long as it was.

Mrs Bone (*still ruminating*) I sensed it. (*Sniff—pause*) Can the hall porter throw any light?

Rawlins No, 'm. He said there was luggage. That's all he knew.

Mrs Bone Luggage? And Mr Wykeham told you *nothing*? (c.)

Rawlins Well, of course, when I first saw him, madam, I said, 'What, sir? Haven't you caught the train?' and he said: 'Mrs Wykeham caught it,' he said, 'and I reely caught it too, only I let it go again,' he said.

Mrs Bone And have you no idea where he and this person were bound for in the car?

Rawlins None whatever, madam.

Mrs Bone Nor has the hall porter?

Rawlins No, 'm, oh—but there's another telegram here, 'm. (*Crosses to table* R.)
Mrs Bone (*keenly and quickly*) Another? Where?

Rawlins takes salver with telegram from table. Mrs Bone makes a move to take it

Rawlins I didn't open it because it's addressed 'Wykeham,' but of course it may be from Mr Wykeham to Mrs Wykeham.
Mrs Bone I'll take it.

Rawlins hands it to her reluctantly

Very well, you needn't wait, Rawlins. I shall stay here until Mrs Wykeham returns. (*Crosses to* C.)
Rawlins Thank you, 'm.

Mrs Bone, C., *is reading telegram to herself as Major Bone and Rawlins exchange glances. Rawlins smiles cheekily at him as she goes out* D. R.

Mrs Bone (*reading, crosses* L.) 'Returning immediately. Wait for me at home. Very put out. Barbara.' Well, nobody can say that I am wise *after* the event.
Major Bone I'm afraid I'm not wise at all.
Mrs Bone (*crosses* L.) I know you're not.
Major Bone Thank you very much.
Mrs Bone If you'd been wise, you'd have forbidden this marriage. I disliked the man from the very first. I told you so.
Major Bone You did.
Mrs Bone (*crosses* C.) A dark horse and a loose fish.
Major Bone But you've nothing to go on yet, you know.
Mrs Bone (*turning to him*) Nothing to go on! He's *left* her. Don't tell me. A flash foreign woman with a little dog. (*Going* R.)
Major Bone (*rising and crossing to* C.) Very likely Barbara knows all about it.
Mrs Bone (*wheeling on him again and flourishing her own telegram*) This is what Barbara knows. (*Reads*) 'Most startling and terrible experience.' (*Reads from the other telegram*) 'Returning immediately. Very put out.' Oh, I don't suppose it's the first time since they've been married. I expect he's living with this woman.
Major Bone Oh, nonsense, Constance. (*He turns up stage*)
Mrs Bone (*puts telegram on table* R. C. *Wheeling round on him as before*) What do you mean? Here he is, in a car. With this woman.
Major Bone (*suddenly inspired*) By Jove! I have it! (L. C.) Don't you see?
Mrs Bone What?

Major Bone (*coming down*) He missed the train, so he took a car and went after Barbara.

Mrs Bone *After* Barbara? Oh, then why did he start by going *away* from Barbara?

Major Bone Oh, very likely he didn't on purpose.

Mrs Bone Now what d'you mean? How can he be living with another woman but not on purpose?

Major Bone He isn't living with her, Constance, whatever it is. You can't call it that.

Mrs Bone I prefer to call it that.

Major Bone But what evidence have you got? (*Sits* L.C.)

Mrs Bone (*pointedly*) Evidence! He gives Barbara the slip and packs her off in an express train. Then he goes off in a car with luggage, on a long journey, with a woman. That was several hours ago, and there's no news of him. That's enough for me. I know what men are. (*Cross* L., *with emphasis*) It's no good your telling me.

Major Bone turns hopelessly away

Major Bone (*sitting*) I know that. Well, we'll wait and see what *Barbara* has got to say.

Mrs Bone (*cross* R. C., *picks up wires, glances at them and replaces them on table, and cross again* L. C. *to Major*) Yes, and don't forget that you listened to Barbara from the first, and if you had listened to *me*——

Electric door-bell off

Thank goodness! Here she is. (*Up* C.)

Major Bone It may be him. (*Crosses to Mrs Bone.*)

Mrs Bone (*with sarcasm*) It *may* be, yes. You stop where you are— I'll let her in.

She goes out C.

Major Bone heaves a very deep sigh and sits L. *After a moment the voices of Mrs Bone and Barbara are heard in the passage*

(*Off*) My poor child!

Barbara (*off*) Oh, mother.

Mrs Bone (*off*) Come in.

Barbara (*off*) Is Peter here?

Barbara enters. She is a handsome woman of thirty; she can be as biting as her mother but she has something of her father's gentler, yearning nature

Mrs Bone No, dear, he is not. (*Reappearing*) It *is* Barbara. (C.)

Major Bone (*plaintively*) Yes, I guessed it would be.

Barbara Oh, so father's here, too. (*Crosses down* R.)

Major Bone Yes. Father's here all right.

Mrs Bone Yes, I brought him. (*Crosses* R.)

Major Bone You did.

Barbara (*coming down* R.) I've had a terrible time. Is Rawlins here?

Mrs Bone Yes. Never mind about Rawlins. (*Crosses* R. *to Barbara*)

Barbara But I left my luggage downstairs.

Mrs Bone Never mind about that, dear. Tell me all. Tell me all.

Barbara (*sits on seat* R. C) I'm absolutely fagged out. Father, there's some wine in the dining-room sideboard. Go and get some, will you?

Major Bone (*rising promptly, cross up* C.) Oh, thank you very, very much, my dear. That's very kind of you.

Barbara For me, I mean. (*Rising, takes coat and hat off. Puts coat on club fender* R., *hat and gloves on bookcase*)

Major Bone (*pausing at door* C) Oh, I see. (*Closes door*) Well—er— where are the glasses? (*Crosses* L. C.)

Mrs Bone (*swinging on him furiously*) Oh, don't fiddle and diddle! Get the wine!

He turns again to the door

(*To Barbara*) Now, my poor child.

Barbara (*sitting* R. C.) I hardly know how to start telling you what has happened. (*She pauses*)

Mrs Bone at Barbara's side R. *Major Bone still hovers up* C. *listening*

Mrs Bone (*shortly and practically*) Well, try, dear.

Barbara Peter and I went to Paddington. We got in the train, both of us. In an empty carriage, to ourselves, I mean——

Bone closes door C. *quietly*

Mrs Bone Yes? Yes? Yes?

Bone comes down R. C.

Barbara Peter got out and went to get some papers. I waited, and he came back, but he didn't get back into the carriage. He stood on the platform and fumbled and said the girl at the bookstall had given him the wrong change or something.

Mrs Bone Huh!—mh!—huh!

Bone looks at Mrs Bone

Barbara By this time they were shutting the doors and saying, 'Take your seats, please.' You know how they do.

Major Bone M'yes.

Mrs Bone (*turning her head*) Get the wine!

Major Bone But I'd like to hear this. Do you mind if I just listen for a moment? I shall keep very quiet.

Barbara Before I could stop him, Peter went back to the bookstall. And the next thing I knew was the train began to move. You know how the big express trains glide out. I could scarcely realize it for a moment. So I jumped up and put my head through the window.

Major Bone Good God!

Barbara (*severely to him*) The window was open.

Major Bone Oh, I see.

Barbara There in the distance I saw Peter. He was standing with his back to the train talking to a young woman. She was no one *I* knew.

Mrs Bone (*quite complacently*) And what did *you* do?

Barbara What *could* I do? I shouted to a porter who was apparently a deaf mute. I waved. No-one took the slightest notice, except one offensive looking man who waved back.

Mrs Bone And—your husband?

Barbara Peter never so much as turned his head.

Mrs Bone You should have rung the alarm bell.

Major Bone Oh, I don't suppose he'd have heard it.

Mrs Bone (*swinging round at him*) Will you get the wine? The wine!

Bone nods his head

Major Bone⎫
Mrs Bone ⎬(*to Barbara*) Go on, dear.

Major Bone Oh, sorry!

Barbara Well, there I was. I tried to control myself and think. I had all our luggage in the train, his and mine.

Mrs Bone Go on, dear.

Barbara The first stop was Bristol. I got out there. I wasn't going to Peter's friends in the country with a story like that. So I wired him and you and Rawlins and came back here. Now, mother, what does it all mean?

Major Bone (*advancing importantly*) Now you listen to me, my dear. I'm a man of the world. I'll soon put this right. Had the lady a little dog?

Mrs Bone The *wine*! The *wine*!

Major Bone Yes, I heard you say that before.

Barbara (*scornfully*) What lady?

Major Bone Peter's pal—gal, I mean! Well, damn it—the woman person we're discussing. I must call her something. Had she a little dog?

Barbara What difference does that make?

Major Bone Yes, but had she?

Barbara Yes, I remember she did have a beastly little dog.

Major Bone (*to Mrs Bone*) There you are, my dear, the plot thickens.

Mrs Bone George!

Major Bone The wine!

Mrs Bone Yes!

Major Bone Right!

He goes out hastily C., *leaving door open*

Barbara Mother, what does he mean? 'The plot thickens'? (*Rises, crosses* D. C.)

Mrs Bone Now, Barbara, let me tell *you*. I have seen Rawlins. Your huband came back to the flat here with a woman!

Barbara What? Who *is* she?

Mrs Bone That remains to be seen. But he brought her here and rang up for a car.

Barbara A car? Oh, then, perhaps——

Mrs Bone And took the woman and her luggage away with him in the car. We don't know where to. But a long way away. (*Sits* L.)

Barbara And he's not come back? (*Sits with Mrs Bone*)

Mrs Bone No. (*Cross to settee* L.)

Barbara (*breaking down*) Oh, mother!

Mrs Bone There, there! You mustn't break down. No, no. (*Calling*) George—hurry up with the wine!

Major Bone (*off*) All right, my dear; do you want the port or the hock? I can recommend the port.

Mrs Bone The port. Hurry. (*To Barbara*) There, my dear. Don't give way. (*Caressing her*) Of course, I always expected this, and said so.

Bone appears with wine C.

Barbara You think he missed the train on purpose?

Mrs Bone To be quite candid, I think he missed it by appointment.

Enter Bone

Barbara But why should he bring her back here?

Major Bone (*crosses to table with port and glasses*) There you are, that's what I say, that's a point in his favour. (*Places tray with wine on table*)

Mrs Bone (*turning on him*) Oh, you! Do something sensible. Ring up Gamble's Garage on the telephone.

Major Bone On the telephone? Why? What's the idea? I think he's with these people the Bunters by this time. I'll wire them and find out. (*Crosses up* c.)

Mrs Bone Yes, (*rising*) and lug it into the public eye. No, thank you.

Major Bone Well, naturally, I mean to say, a judiciously worded wire. (*turning over leaves of telephone directory, which he has taken from table up* L.) You know, sort of—'Wykeham missed train, wife caught; he wouldn't come, so she didn't go,' or words to that effect.

Mrs Bone Oh, stop! (*Crosses up* R. *behind settee*) Fiddling and fuddling! Have you got that number?

Major Bone Yes, here it is. What shall I do with it?

Mrs Bone Ask for it.

Major Bone Ask for it? Right. (*Closes book and replaces it on table up* L.) Ask for the number, eh? What is the damned number?

Mrs Bone tries to get 'phone book

Barbara Oh, father! (*Rises from settee*)

Major Bone (*sits at 'phone table*) All right—all right—I've got it. Ah—ah—Kensington 1040. (*Closes book*)

Mrs Bone I'll speak.

Major Bone Oh! That'll be a very nice change. (*Looks at Barbara knowingly*) But just for once in a way you let me have a say. I think we should wire, we ought to enquire——

Mrs Bone Are you trying to be funny?

Major Bone (*on 'phone*) Oh, Lord! There you are, you see, the same old story, when father suggests anything—what?—Yes, I'm here. Is that whatever the number is? Are you Thingamebob's Whatsaname? What is it?

Barbara The garage.

Major Bone (*stamps foot impatiently*) The garage.

Mrs Bone (*taking 'phone from him*) Give it to me—give it to me.

Bone crosses R. c. *and looks appealingly at Barbara.*
Barbara intently listening

Are you Gamble's Garage? I am speaking for Mrs Wykeham. Mr Wykeham engaged a car to-day. Where for? Do you know?

Major Bone The maid said that when they came—— (c.)

Mrs Bone (*to Bone*) Quiet! You do? What? Oh, you've just heard. Where? Where? What?

Major Bone What's he say?

Barbara What, mother? (*Rising*)

Mrs Bone Hush, darling! (*On 'phone*) Where, though? To *what* place? Maidens-*what*?

Major Bone What's that?

Mrs Bone (*to Bone*) George! (*On 'phone*) Blot? Blotton. Oh, Blotton. Where is that? Oh! Oh! Yes? Yes? Thank you. Yes. Yes. Thank you. Very well. (*Rings off*)

Bone crosses to table R. *and helps himself to port*

Barbara What, mother? Quickly!

Barbara comes down L. *of settee towards* C.

Mrs Bone (*deliberately*) The garage has just heard the car broke down on a lonely road. They went off together to find the nearest hotel. The chauffeur got a lift on a motor cycle and telephoned to Gamble's.

Barbara Where is the place where Peter's gone?

Mrs Bone They set out to walk to a place called Maiden Blotton.

Barbara Where's that?

Mrs Bone They think Somerset. But——

Major Bone (*rising, triumphantly*) Somerset! There you are! I told you so! He's gone after Barbara.

Barbara What?

Major Bone Of course. It stands to reason. You had all his things.

Mrs Bone Things?

Major Bone Yes.

Mrs Bone What things?

Major Bone Ah, clothes and things.

Mrs Bone What things?

Major Bone Oh, Lord, clothes and things, don't you see? He went after Barbara. He thinks she's at the Buntings.

Mrs Bone Then why didn't he go on to the Bunters?

Major Bone Well, very likely he did.

Mrs Bone With a woman?

Major Bone Well, I can't be supposed to know everything. I'm not a clairvoyant.

Mrs Bone Oh, be quiet!

Barbara I shall go down to this hotel. (*Crosses up stage*)

Bone is about to have another drink

Mrs Bone Yes, first thing to-morrow. (*She sees Bone with the decanter, crosses to* R. *above table*)

Barbara I can go to-night.

Mrs Bone (*takes wine from Bone, who is about to drink*) Oh, no, you don't, you've had quite enough of that!

Barbara (*to Bone*) I can get a train to Bristol and motor on from there.

Mrs Bone (*replaces wine decanter on table and crosses* c. *to Barbara*) Not to-night, dear.

Barbara has gone to writing-table and got an A.B.C.

Barbara (*looking up train*) If I wait till to-morrow and there's anything wrong—it might be too late. Look, Paddington, 8 o'clock. Arrive Bristol 10.20.

Mrs Bone Yes, and then you'll have to motor out to this place.

Major Bone 'M, yes. I should think you'd be too late even if you did go to-night.

Mrs Bone Oh, you seem very experienced!

Major Bone No—just an ordinary public school education.

Mrs Bone (*to Barbara*) Do what I advise, dear. What is the first train to-morrow?

Barbara 5.30 A.M. Bristol 8.27.

Major Bone smoothing wine decanter affectionately

Mrs Bone Then go by that. They'll still be there.

Barbara Oh, dear! How can I wait? Very well, mother, I will.

Mrs Bone Get some food and go to bed early.

Barbara Very well—I will—I am absolutely fagged out. (*Crosses to Bone*) Good-night, daddy.

Kisses him and hands him A.B.C.

Major Bone Good-night, Babsy darling. (*Kisses Barbara*) Don't you worry, everything will be all right. Is this for me? Oh, thanks very much. (*He keeps turning leaves over*)

Barbara (*crosses* L. c.) Oh, mother dear, I can't believe there is anything wrong. I do love him; we were so happy. Good-night, mother.

Mrs Bone Good-night, dear.

Barbara calls Rawlins as she goes out.

(*After closing the door, turns at once on Bone, crossing* L. c.) That's it! Now we must go at once. We've just time to change and catch the night train.

Major Bone Say that again.

Mrs Bone You'll take me down to this place tonight. (*Picking up cloak and gloves from settee* L.)

Major Bone What? I positively refuse. If you must go to-night, you go with Barbara.

Mrs Bone puts cloak and gloves down again

Mrs Bone And let this man wriggle out of it and get round her with

lies and excuses? Not likely! By the time Barbara arrives I shall
have caught him red-handed.

Major Bone What the devil do you intend doing?

Mrs Bone I intend to go to that hotel to-night and catch him.
(*Crosses* L.) I know that man, and I mean to know that woman.

Major Bone Catch them at the hotel? But they'll have gone to bed!

Mrs Bone I know they will—that's just the point! (*Picking up cloak
and gloves*)

Major Bone Oh! So that's where you intend to walk in and catch
them!

Mrs Bone Of course it is. (*Putting on cloak*)

Major Bone Do you mean to say you are going to burst into this
woman's bedroom?

Mrs Bone Yes!

Major Bone Oh, I see. Well, in that case, perhaps I'd better come
too. (*Rising, makes a bustling movement towards the door up* C.)

Mrs Bone precedes him

CURTAIN

SCENE 2

Parlour of the 'Stag and Hunt' Inn, Maiden Blotton. In the C. *background a
door giving direct access to the road through a porch. In the back wall and* L.
*of this door, windows. The backcloth seen through these windows and also
through the door when open represents a country road. There is a door up* R.
with glass panel, also door up L. *with glass panel-entrances to bar. Just
below bar entrance there is a swing door, not a complete door, leaving an
aperture at the top which is the entrance behind the counter. There is one
other door down* L. *Above front door is a window with inscription set so as to
be legible from without. It reads: 'Elizabeth Spoker, Licensed to sell by
retail Beers, Wines, Spirits, Tobacco and Cigarettes, on and off the premises'.
There is a window seat in alcove at back with a green baize table in front of it.
A fireplace in the* R. *wall and a hard wooden bench running out at right angles
to it. A plain deal table is* C. *of stage, at which are placed two stiff deal chairs
with rush bottoms, one* R. *of table and the other* L. *of table with its back to
the bar door. There are one or two similar chairs about, and a dresser with
drawers standing against the wall,* L. *The place is supposed to be illuminated
by lamplight. A lighted lamp on the wall* L. *and another larger lamp also
lighted hangs from the ceiling above the table. There is also a light in the
bar off* L. *All the blinds are down*

*Gladys is discovered at the sideboard. She is preparing a meal on a tray. She is
a village girl of seventeen with a chronic snort; the bar door swings open*

rather cautiously and Alfred comes into the parlour. He is an elderly youth.
He is evidently greatly attracted by Gladys. He crosses down L. C.

Alfred Gladys!

Gladys Now, Alfred! (*Turning and facing him*) Get back to yer bar.
You know Mrs Spoker she don't allow you not to come into the
parlour not when she's not here.

Alfred I reckon I'll risk she. If so be you be here.

Gladys (*crosses to* C.) It's no use your coming and making them
fish-eyes at me. (*Snorts*) They don't bear no result in my breast.

Alfred (*beseechingly*) Gladys, it ain't true that you be walking out
with that ther' pig-lad o' Puddy's?

Gladys (*snort*) Me own company's me own concern. (*Snorts—
crosses* R. *with her tray*)

Alfred A pig lad. Ther' be no future to he. (*Cross* C.)

Gladys (*at door up* R.) You get back to yer bar. I'm going up to the
old lady in Number One room.

Alfred *Gladys!*

Gladys (*looking towards* C. *door*) 'Ush! There be someone there now.
If it be Mrs Spoker—— (*Snorts*)

Alfred (*fearfully*) Oo! (*Scoots back to bar door*)

Gladys snorts scornfully and goes out R.

Alfred remains at bar door peering towards C. *door*

Marguerite enters C., *carrying Pansy, a little dog. She is a young woman,*
very smart and modern, and rather authoritative. She has a slight French
accent. At the moment she is very fatigued

Marguerite (*seeing Alfred*) Oh, are you the landlord?

Alfred Noo (*At bar door*)

Marguerite Where is the landlord?

Alfred At rest.

Marguerite Already?

Alfred Yes, 'e be the dead 'usband of the landlady.

Marguerite (*leaning on chair* R. C) Where is the landlady?

Alfred Out she be.

Marguerite Well, can you attend to me?

Alfred No, 'm, not unless so be what you want is in the bar. I ain't
allowed in 'ere.

Marguerite (*crossing* R.) Thank goodness you've got a fire, if there's
nothing else. (*Warming her hands*)

Enter Peter, who comes down R. C.; *she turns to him. Peter is a man in the*
thirties, good-natured, but rather distrait and happy-go-lucky. He is
carrying two bags, has a mackintosh over his shoulder and is wearing a cap

Peter (*sees Alfred in bar* L.) What's that?

Marguerite Don't be silly—it's the barman.

Peter (*crossing* L.) Barman, come out!

Alfred I ain't allowed out.

Peter Not allowed out of the bar?

Alfred No, sur.

Peter Oh, what a paradise! (*To Marguerite*) What have we come in here for?

Marguerite (*explanatory*) This is the *place*.

Peter The place?

Marguerite This is the place that farmer told us of.

Peter He said there was an hotel. (*Puts down bags* U. L. *and closes door* U. C.)

Marguerite Well, what do you expect at a place called Maiden Blotton? A seven-course table d'hôte and a dance band? Thank goodness there's a pub at all. I'm not going to walk any further to-night. (*Sits* R. C. *at table*)

Peter If you do you walk alone; on the other hand——

Marguerite What?

Peter Something's got to be done.

Marguerite That's very clever of you.

Peter Well, someone had to think of a thought. (*To Alfred*) Why is this pub here?

Alfred I dunno.

Peter Was the road built to the pub or the pub built to the road?

Alfred I dunno, sur.

Peter He dunno. (*Moves to behind table* C. *To Marguerite*) You ask him something. I can't cope with him, I'm too tired.

Marguerite Don't you think I'm tired? (*To Alfred*) We walked three miles and met nothing. Now, what do they use this road for?

Alfred I dunno.

Peter I think this chap's trying to be insolent. Leave this entirely in my hands. (*Authoritatively*) Now look here, I don't know who you think we are but we're not. We've been walking on this road for— (*Looks at Marguerite*)

Marguerite Three miles.

Peter Three miles. Look at my shoes.

Alfred looks at Peter's shoes

Don't look at them all the time like that. Just look and carry on with the conversation, You know there's a road out there, and we know there's a road out there. What happens on this road? Come, come, come, come, come!

Alfred Puddy's pigs pass by 'ere.

Exit into bar

Peter Anyhow it's used by the best people.

Marguerite Oh, I suppose we can get some food here.

Peter I doubt it—even the pigs pass by. (*Hangs up coat* R. C.)

Marguerite Anyhow, we can get some food of sorts, and then the chauffeur said he would pick us up here in the car.

Peter But not to-night, Josephine! (*Sitting* L. C.)

Marguerite Marguerite!

Peter I was just quoting Shakespeare.

Marguerite But why can't he pick us up?

Peter My dear good Mrs Hickett, did you see the radiator?

Marguerite It was only leaking, that's all.

Peter Leaking? It was pouring. It's dry! You don't suppose I'd have started to walk if the car could have been repaired to-night?

Marguerite But, Peter, I thought we were just sort of walking to this place to sort of have a meal and sort of wait until the car came. (L. C.)

Peter Then I take it you sort of gave me your luggage to sort of carry as a sort of joke.

Marguerite Well, you said I'd better bring a bag in case, so I gave you two, because I thought if you carried one in each hand it would sort of balance you.

Peter Balance me? Look here! (*Shows hands all stiff*) I can't unfold my hands now.

Marguerite Well, it's a good job I did bring them and Pansy too, if we're out for the night.

Peter Out for the night! But we can't stay here for the night. What shall we do? (*Crosses down* L. C.)

Marguerite Exactly. What shall we do?

Peter Ah, that's not fair. I asked you first.

Marguerite (*nodding towards bar*) There's that man in there—call him. Be polite to him this time.

Peter All right. Fellow creature! (*Turns to Marguerite*) That sort of brings us together.

Alfred enters from bar and stands close to Peter

Alfred Aye, sur.

Peter turns sharply L. *and is startled to find himself face to face with Alfred*

Peter Have you a 'phone?

Alfred What be that, sur?

Peter A thing you put to your ear.

Alfred Oh, a keyhole?

Peter This is a hotel all right. Have you any food or a sausage?
Alfred No, sur; not in the bar, sur.
Peter I don't care where it is. Can we eat?
Alfred I don't know, sur.
Peter Well, damn it! Can we try?

Noony, an old villager very disreputable and looking like a tramp, makes a sudden dart and cautious entry from c., crosses L. to bar

Noony Alfred!
Peter (*startled*) Oh! (*Steps back to R. of table c.*)

Peter and Marguerite look on curiously during the next few lines

Alfred Aye, Burrt! (*Coming out of bar*)
Noony Be Mrs Spoker in?
Alfred Noo, she be gone to Downblotton.
Noony Then I'll go in.
Alfred Be careful she don't see 'ee, Burrt.
Noony (*cunningly*) Aye, just a careful 'arf tankard.
Alfred You best keep out of the way of she. Ye mind what she called you last time. Satan's fruit, she say.
Noony Aye, she be always hankering after they scriptures.
Alfred Well, go in, Burrt. (*Taking his arm and half pushing him in bar up L.*) Only be careful.
Noony Aye, a careful 'arf tankard.

Exit u. L. into bar. Alfred dodges through swing door L. into bar

Marguerite What is all that? (L. c., *sitting*)
Peter (*looking off at them*) Some sort of secret society I think.
Marguerite It's rather frightening.
Peter I don't like that one at all. He looks like a very, very old boy scout. (*Indicates old Noony in bar*) I didn't want to come down this road at all. I suppose we'd better wait for the landlord.
Marguerite Yes, but if you hadn't been quite so vague and sloppy . . . What are we going to do now?
Peter My idea was to get to an hotel and ring up the Bunters.
Marguerite And get them to send out a car.
Peter Yes, or stay at an hotel for the night, having told the Bunters where we are.
Marguerite Only you're so haphazard and piffling.
Peter Of course I'm haphazard and piffling after what's happened, and there's poor Barbara worrying over me.
Marguerite Oh, she'll be all right with the Bunters.
Peter Yes, but without me she won't sleep a wink. She hasn't even got my photograph.

Marguerite She doesn't need your photograph, she couldn't forget a face like yours.

Peter You needn't talk, it's a case of six of mine and half a dozen of yours.

Marguerite Now we are going to be rude. It was you that got us into this mess, missing the train.

Peter If you hadn't taken that caterpillar for a walk on the platform, I should never have seen you.

Marguerite Well, you have known me long enough, you could have said 'hallo' and passed on.

Peter You're all right. Your husband thinks you are safe at the Bunters'.

Marguerite My husband doesn't think—he's an M.P.

Sound of horse and trap off

Anyway, let's get some food and then find a telephone or a conveyance. (*Rises,* R. C.)

Peter Conveyance? Where to?

Marguerite The Bunters', of course. What distance is it from here to the Bunters', do you suppose? (*Cross down* R.)

Sound of horse and trap stops

Peter I can't go on distance-supposing, I'm fed up with it.

Marguerite Well, find somebody and ask.

Voice (*off*) Goodnight to 'e, Mrs Spoker.

Mrs Spoker (*off at door* C.) Good-night, Mr Pillbutton.

Peter (*looking towards door*) Here's somebody.

Enter Mrs Spoker from C.

Sound of horse and trap off going away

Mrs Spoker has an eye which gleams with sinister calculating suspicion. She is steeped in primitive religious principles. She has on an outdoor costume and carries an umbrella and a bag

(*Pleasantly*) Can you tell me where we can find the landlord?

Mrs Spoker (L. C.) Not yet, I'm his widow.

Peter Delighted! I'm sorry. Can we stay here for a bit?

Mrs Spoker I am completely occupied.

Peter I'm sorry, of course, if you're busy. I suppose we must wait, but—er——

Mrs Spoker I tell you I'm completely occupied.

Peter Oh, you mean you're full up!

Mrs Spoker Completely occupied.

Marguerite Well—— (*She attempts to cross* L., *Peter stops her*) Can we——

Peter Where's the nearest hotel?

Mrs Spoker This is the only hotel within miles. (*Puts bag with things on dresser* L., *groceries, etc.*)

Peter Oh, hell!

Mrs Spoker starts, shocked.

Can we get some food?

Mrs Spoker Not if you blarspheme! (*Tin of cocoa in her hand*)

Peter I'm sorry, I didn't mean you to hear.

Mrs Spoker (*Crosses* L. C.) Whether I hear or not it all goes down in the Book.

Peter The Book?

Peter and **Marguerite** (*Together*) What book?

Mrs Spoker The Book from which there is no rubbing out! (*Crossing* L. C.)

Marguerite Oh, how dreadful!

Mrs Spoker (*to Marguerite*) I wonder you allow him to blarspheme!

Marguerite Oh, I don't; it's very disobedient of him.

Mrs Spoker I'm very strict here. Times may change and folks may get 'ccdlcss in their talk and ways, but not here. This is my hotel and in it I admit only such as meets with my approval.

Peter Then I'm surprised that you are completely occupied. (*Crosses* R., *swaggers up and down hearth with cap on*)

Marguerite That'll do, Peter. (*Crossing to Mrs Spoker*) Our car has broken down. We must find a night's shelter.

Peter takes off cap

Peter Where is the nearest town?

Mrs Spoker Downblotton. Five miles on.

Marguerite (*flopping on chair* L. C.) Five miles?

Peter Have you a cab or a cart or an ox, or anything that is yours?

Mrs Spoker No such thing.

Marguerite Is there a telephone? (*Sits* L. C.)

Mrs Spoker Yes, at Downblotton. (*Crosses down* L. C.)

Peter My God!

Mrs Spoker Oh! (*Drops tin of cocoa, which Marguerite picks up and hands to her*)

Peter My godmother lives there with some godchildren——

Marguerite (*desperately*) Well, can we get some *food*?

Mrs Spoker gives Peter a freezing look

Mrs Spoker (*crosses down* L., *taking things from her bag and placing them on the table* D. L.) I daresay there's a drop of soup left over.
Peter Left over from when?
Marguerite Soup! All right, better than nothing. And could I have a cup of tea?

Mrs Spoker takes off her gloves

Peter (*crossing to fireplace, sits*) And two cups of beer.
Mrs Spoker (*crosses to bar and calls*) Alfred!
Alfred (*off*) Aye, Mrs Spoker.
Mrs Spoker Come you here.

Alfred enters from bar L.

Where's Gladys?
Alfred Ooop. (*Indicating ceiling*)
Mrs Spoker Send her to me.
Alfred Aye, Mrs Spoker.

As Alfred moves away R., *Mrs Spoker glances in the bar, which makes her turn quickly to Alfred*

Mrs Spoker And, Alfred!

He halts

Mrs Spoker Is that Noony I see in the bar?
Alfred (*sheepishly*) Well, you see, 'e called in, you see, for——
Mrs Spoker Send him to me.
Alfred Aye, Mrs Spoker.

Exit into bar L.

Marguerite Who is Noony? Perhaps he could help us.
Mrs Spoker He? He's Satan's helper.

Noony with Alfred enters with an air of great plausibility from the bar U. L.

Alfred (*pushing Noony out of bar*) Go on, Burrt.
Noony Ah, good evening to 'ee, Mrs Spoker.
Mrs Spoker (*with forefinger quivering towards* C. *exit*) Out you go!
Noony But oi——
Mrs Spoker (*taking him by the scruff of the neck*) Last week you recommended this hotel to a couple living in shame. I'll teach you! Out you go!
Noony Well, I thought——
Mrs Spoker (*pushing Noony towards exit* U. C.) You thought! You knew! And I know now! Out you go!

Noony (*still protesting*) They told oi they was a-travelling together.
Mrs Spoker Well, if that ain't enough for you it is for me. Out you go!
Noony (*going unwillingly, at the door*) If all was like you young folks would never get to know whether they suited!

Marguerite and Peter go up C.

Mrs Spoker Out you go (*pushing him*), and out you stay!

Exit Noony C., *muttering,* 'Bain't no harm.'

Mrs Spoker R. *of door. Noony opens door again and calls out* 'Cat!'

There—— (*Coming down* R. *of table* C.) You see. (*Pointedly*) If undesirables come to my hotel, that's what they gets. (*Crosses* L. *to front of table* L. C.)
Peter (*crossing to Mrs Spoker*) What did happen on that disastrous occasion?
Mrs Spoker (*severe*) It is not a nice subject, but a couple——

Gladys appears at door U. R., *crosses to door* D. L. *and exits*

comes here, just as you have come here to-night; it was only later that I discovered that they wasn't married.
Marguerite (*crossing to Peter*) But perhaps poor Mr Noony thought they were only just travelling together.
Mrs Spoker Couples don't travel together not without shame. If I'd known it they wouldn't have stayed a moment in here. I wouldn't have risked that not in this hotel. (*Crossing* L.) I'll just see about that soup. (*Turns, pauses at door*)
Marguerite Thank you.
Mrs Spoker (*crossing* R. C.) I need hardly ask whether *you* are married?
Marguerite What? Of course we are married!
Peter Yes, both of us!
Mrs Spoker Thank you, you'll excuse my asking, but once bit——

Exit D. L.

Peter I wonder who bit her?
Marguerite What a dreadful old thing! Anyhow, Peter, do humour her until we have had some food, if it's only soup. (*Crosses* L. C., *sits*)
Peter (R. C.) We wouldn't even get that if she knew we weren't husband and wife.
Marguerite Just imagine if all the hotels were so particular.
Peter Yes, Brighton beach would be one large dormitory!

Marguerite I'm beginning to wonder where we shall sleep to-night.
Peter I'll investigate. I know his name now. (*Going to bar door*)
Albert!

Alfred appears at bar door

Alfred *Alfred*, sur!
Peter Are you sure? Oh, Alfred. (*To Marguerite*) Make a note of
that. (*To Alfred*) Tell me, is this a big village?
Alfred Noo, sur.
Peter Just an ordinary village. Is there anywhere where we could
put up?
Alfred Nowhere in the village, sur.
Marguerite Not a cottage or——
Alfred Cottage—noo, mum. There be only fower cottages, and in
them they already sleeps unhealthy in moi opinion.
Marguerite Unhealthy?
Alfred Aye, six and seven in a bedroom mostly.
Peter Sort of whist drive.
Alfred Aye, sir.
Peter Well, get me some beer.
Alfred (*turning to bar door*) Aye, sur.

Exit L.

Marguerite (*exasperated*) Oh, I can't walk any further to-night.
(*Flopping into chair* L. *of table*)
Peter When I've had the beer I shall go and see if there is a light
in a cottage.

Peter crosses L. *to bar. Alfred hands him a tankard of beer and Peter goes
out into bar*

Marguerite at table L. C. *nurses Pansy*

Mrs Spoker returns busily D. L.

Mrs Spoker Well, madam, I find much to my surprise that one of
my rooms is unoccupied.
Marguerite What, for the night? (*Rises*)
Mrs Spoker Yes. My maid Gladys tells me that while I was out
Mr and Mrs Love, who were staying here, got called back home.
Marguerite Oh, er—Mr and Mrs—Love.
Mrs Spoker They were staying here while their house was done up.

Mrs Spoker crosses R. *to fireplace and puts some logs on the fire. Marguerite
follows her* R.

But Mrs Love's mother she remained in the house, and this

evening she fell over a bucket. She was walking round a ladder and failed to observe the bucket.

Marguerite I see. That comes of being superstitious.

Mrs Spoker So Mr and Mrs Love were called 'ome 'urried, and my Number Two room is unoccupied.

Marguerite I see—just one room?

Mrs Spoker It's a double room. So I can manage you and your husband. The maid got the room ready, thinking that I should sleep there myself.

Marguerite Oh?

Mrs Spoker You see, I have an old lady bedridden in Number One. And the maid thought I might wish to sleep next door.

Marguerite I see. Well, I think I had really better decide to sleep here.

Mrs Spoker Oh, I have given orders. The maid is getting your soup and tea now. (*Crosses* L.)

Marguerite Thank you *very* much (*Sits* R. C.)

Mrs Spoker (*crosses* R. C.) And as for your little dog, I'll take it to the stables.

Peter enters from bar

Marguerite Oh! Can't she stay with me for the night?

Mrs Spoker What? Upstairs?

Marguerite Yes, of course.

Mrs Spoker Certainly not! (*Crosses to table*)

Peter crosses from bar carrying a pewter pot

Mrs Spoker (*to Peter*) That is a thing I cannot allow.

Peter changes beer into other hand

I have no beasts in my bedroom. (*Turning to him*)

Peter I congratulate you! (*Crosses up behind Mrs Spoker*)

Marguerite Peter, madam says she's got a room for us.

Peter What? (*Crosses to Marguerite above table*)

Marguerite (*grimacing at him*) Isn't it great?

Mrs Spoker Number Two room. It's a double bed!

Peter It is? Oh, but—I——

Mrs Spoker Well, what now, sir?

Marguerite It's all right. Quite all right. At home we occupy separate beds, but it's quite all right.

Marguerite nudges Peter and he nudges Mrs Spoker

Mrs Spoker Ah! Well, it is not for me to arrange people's tastes in such matters, *and* if you are in the habit of sleeping with the *dog*, madam, I don't altogether blame your husband.

Exit door R.

Peter I say, what is all this?

Marguerite (*rising and going up* R.) Didn't you hear her say she had a room completely unoccupied? Do you think I was going to lose the chance?

Peter That's all right for you; but what about me?

Marguerite Well, you can easily find somewhere to sleep. You can sleep in this room or in the stables with Pansy. (*Sits* R. C. *at table*)

Peter Why not the hen-house?

Marguerite Oh, the hen-house—don't be silly! It only means our keeping up our little deception for a night instead of a meal.

Peter We shan't keep it up very successfully if Mrs Spanker, or whatever her name is, finds the wife in the bedroom and the husband sharing the stables with the dog.

Marguerite She won't. You can come up to my room first, and after she's gone to bed you can creep down here (*indicates* L.), and in the morning you can go out early to the car. It's very simple.

Peter Oh, yes, without food and no bath.

Marguerite Don't raise trifling difficulties. There's sure to be a pump outside.

Peter (C.) A pump? Have you ever had a bath in a pump? (*Bus. of pretending to wash at a pump*)

Marguerite cuts him short. Peter stands by Marguerite above table as Gladys enters down L. *She carries a large tray on which are two plates of soup, a loaf of bread and knives, etc. She puts tray on dresser down* L.

Marguerite Are you Gladys?

Gladys Yes 'm. (*Snorts, crosses to table, takes cloth from drawer*)

Peter What's that? Oh, Gladys, how many bedrooms are there in this hotel?

Gladys Two, sur. Number One and Number Two. (*Laying cloth*)

Crosses to dresser L. *for tray*

Marguerite We're in Number Two.

Peter (*As Marguerite sits* R. *of table* C.) What's Number One doing?

Gladys crosses to table with tray and rests it on corner D. L.

Marguerite There's an old lady in there bedridden, isn't there?

Gladys Yes, 'm, she's got—— (*Snorts, putting soup on table*)

Peter That must be very painful.

Marguerite You're bringing me some tea, aren't you?

Gladys Yes, 'm, it's ready. (*Snorts*)
Peter (*looking after Gladys*) Sounds like her bed-time.

Exit Gladys down L., *leaving door open*

Marguerite Peter, don't ask questions that rouse suspicion. (*Takes mouthful of soup*) Oh, that's good!
Peter (*taking mouthful of soup*) Yes, mox-tail.
Marguerite Cut the bread and pass the salt.

Peter cuts the bread and hands a piece to her

I don't mind about deceiving this landlady. If people are so narrow-minded—— (*Taking bread*) Thanks.
Peter No, but I wonder what poor Barbara will think.
Marguerite You must explain, that's all. She'll understand. Salt, please.
Peter Got all you want?
Marguerite For the moment.
Peter See you later. (*Eats soup busily*)
Marguerite It does sound silly, I know, but with this completely occupied landlady——
Peter We daren't tell her anything. She'd turn us out like a shot. (*He puts a small piece of bread underneath his plate which tilts the soup to one side*)
Marguerite I hope your wife will be quite reasonable.
Peter My wife's a darling.
Marguerite I'm so looking forward to meeting her.
Peter But she has a mother.
Marguerite Oh! (*Laughing*)
Peter Oh, a beauty. She's the head of the Cross Word Mother-in-Law Society. Her father's all right. He's a great sport—a sort of wet accumulator.
Marguerite Well, your mother-in-law mustn't know, that's all.

Enter Gladys down L. *She snorts as she carries a cup of tea and places it down on table* R. *Alfred appears at swing door, watching Gladys*

Peter I never let her know a thing. What's that?
Gladys (*above table to Peter*) Will there be anything more, sur?
Peter (*thoughtfully*) Anything more. What is there?
Gladys Nothing!
Peter Oh, then there will be nothing more.
Gladys Oh, I believe there be some chaise.
Peter What kind of chaise?

Gladys snorts

Well, bring me some more beer.

Exit Gladys to bar with tankard

Marguerite I didn't know what chaise meant at first.

Peter She means cheese; it's a very old Cheshire word.

Marguerite (*annoyed*) Peter, do you want *all* your soup?

Peter I think so. Why?

Marguerite (*still drinking soup*) I wanted some for Pansy.

Peter What about yours?

Marguerite I need that. I walked three miles.

Peter I walked three miles and two bags.

Marguerite (*to Pansy*) Never mind, darling, you shall have some milk.

Peter What worries me about Barbara is——

Mrs Spoker enters from down L.

Marguerite (*hoarsely*) She'll be all right——

Mrs Spoker (*crossing to* L. C.) I think I'll take the dog now, madam.

Marguerite Oh, can't she stay with me until I go to bed?

Mrs Spoker Well, I take it you won't be long now. We keep early hours here.

Peter (*turning to Mrs Spoker*) Give us a chance, I've ordered some more beer.

Mrs Spoker You can't sit up all night drinking beer, sir!

Peter Can't I!

Marguerite I shall turn in quite soon. (*Looks at Peter meaningly and tries to conciliate Mrs Spoker*)

Mrs Spoker Very well. (*To Peter*) And there will be the register to sign.

Peter The what? (*Startled*)

Marguerite (*drinking tea, calmly*) Yes, of course.

Mrs Spoker I'll get the book. (*Crosses* L. *to table*) What name, please?

Marguerite Name?

Peter Oh, the name—you've got it! (*To Marguerite*)

Marguerite Hickett.

Peter Hickett, Hickett.

Mrs Spoker Rikki-Tikki?

Peter I've got hiccoughs. Hickett. I said so twice. (*Sits* L. *of table* C.)

Mrs Spoker But why say so twice? That's what I didn't understand.

Voice heard off

Sloley-Jones (*off*) Oh dear! Oh dear, dear!

Mrs Spoker (*turning sharply*) See who that is, Gladys!

Gladys goes up and investigates

Marguerite Very good soup, Mrs Spoker.
Mrs Spoker Thank you, madam.
Gladys (*from up stage* C.) The Rev. Sloley-Jones.
Mrs Spoker Oh, what a nuisance that man is!

Marguerite's face suddenly becomes animated, but not with pleasure. She glances at Peter and crosses R. *as Sloley-Jones enters. He is in cycling overalls, with waterproof cape, motor gloves, and cap, and wears a clerical collar*

Sloley-J. (*in a hearty voice*) By Jove! I've had a terrible time to-night. Good evening, Mrs Spoker.
Mrs Spoker And what do you want, sir? I'm completely occupied.
Sloley-J. Well (*coming down* L.), as a matter of absolute fact, I looked in to see whether I could get you to give me a little oil. I want oiling.
Mrs Spoker Well, you can't come 'ere this time of night and get oiled.
Sloley-J. (*suddenly seeing Marguerite*) Why, good gracious alive! How do you do?

Sloley-J. puts his hand out, and Peter, rising, attempts to shake it, but Sloley-J. crosses over to Marguerite. Peter goes up to bar and shakes hands with Alfred

Surely it is Mrs Hickett?
Marguerite (*cordially*) Why, Mr Sloley-Jones!
Sloley-J. It is Hickett, the name, isn't it? First time we've met, you know, since you got married. (*Shaking hands with Marguerite*) Awfully sorry I couldn't be at your wedding. But fancy meeting you here, though!
Marguerite Yes, we're on our way to the Bunters'. Are you staying at the Bunters'?
Sloley-J. No—oh, no! But I always spend my leave in these parts, you know. I'm just on a holiday.
Marguerite Our car broke down and we came here.
Sloley-J. Oh, bad luck! (*Turning to Peter*) And this, of course, is your husband!

Peter turns his back on Sloley-J. and crouches up L. *to bar and comes down again* L.

(*Wringing Peter's hand*) First time we've met, isn't it?

Peter I hope so!

Marguerite (*to Peter*) Peter, this is Mr Jones, you know.

Peter Oh, Jones, of course, I've heard the name.

Sloley-J. I'm so delighted to meet you. How do you do? Splendid! How are you? (*Shakes hands again*)

Peter Not at all, are you?

Sloley-J. Oh, I'm very well, thanks, except that I'm having a good deal of trouble with my motor-bike. That's why I stopped here. I'm very overheated. However, an ill wind, you know. I'm awfully bucked to come across you like this. Of course, I've heard a great deal about you.

Peter About me? Oh, surely not!

Sloley-J. Oh, yes, come now! (*Laughing*) A man like you can't hope to remain in obscurity.

Peter I never remain there long. I'm gone like a shot.

Peter and Mrs Spoker exchange looks

Sloley-J. I've followed your career in the House.

Peter Oh, you mustn't follow me about like that.

Marguerite But my husband's got a holiday from his politics just now.

Sloley-J. Mind you, I don't see eye to eye with all you preach. Over this question of housing, now, I can't say that I altogether agree with your attitude.

Peter No—er—I don't feel very happy about it myself. (*Looks at Mrs Spoker*)

Sloley-J. Aha! I don't suppose you'd admit that in the House.

Mrs Spoker closes up towards Peter

Peter No, not in the house. I just do it outside and come back again.

Sloley-J. (*gushingly*) Well, I suppose with all said and done there is an awful lot of deception goes on?

Peter Oh, rather! Yes, we have a lot of fun!

Bus.: Peter puts his hand round Mrs Spoker's L. shoulder, and before she has time to look round he has exchanged places with Sloley-Jones. Mrs Spoker looks very indignantly at Sloley-Jones, who cannot understand her attitude

Sloley-J. (*turning to Marguerite*) I'm delighted to meet your husband in such candid mood, Mrs Hickett. Well, I suppose I'd better be pushing off. (*Crossing L.*) That is, if you're sure I can't get what I want here.

Peter crosses R., Marguerite C.

Mrs Spoker Quite sure. It's after hours in any case. And you can't stay here. I have just let my last room to Mr and Mrs Hickett.

Marguerite (*crosses* L. C., *to Jones*) Where are you staying, Mr Jones?

Sloley-J. Downblotton's my headquarters. Of course I'd go on to the Bunters' at Rushcombe, and let Lady Bunter know about you——

Marguerite and **Peter** Oh, no, no thank you! That is very kind of you.

Sloley-J. No? Well, perhaps it's just as well, because I don't suppose I shall get even as far as Downblotton, let alone Rushcombe. I do wish I'd got thoroughly oiled before I started.

Mrs Spoker Well, you can't come back here, whatever happens.

Sloley-J. Dear, dear me, then we must hope for the best. Good-night, Mrs Hickett—good—— (*Breaking off*) Oh, I say, hallo, by Christopher! what a nice little dog. Your little dog, Mrs Hickett?

Mrs Spoker crosses up C. *to door*

Marguerite (*with forced politeness*) Yes.

Sloley-J. (*patting Pansy*) Dear little dog, nice little dog! (*Holding his right hand out in front of him*) Pretty little dog. Good-night, little dog!

Peter Good-night, little man! (*Taking his hand and crossing* L.)

Mrs Spoker has gone up to door, which she holds open, clearing her throat. It is obvious that everyone wants Sloley-J. to go

Sloley-J. (*turning to door*) Well, well, I suppose I shan't be quite so hot by this time. Good-night—er—all!

Peter crosses C. *in front of table*

With a final chuckle of sociability Sloley-Jones goes

Mrs Spoker closes the door and comes down R.

Mrs Spoker (*to Peter*) And so you are a member of the House of Parliament?

Marguerite (*readily*) Yes, my husband is in the House.

Mrs Spoker And which side may you be on?

Peter Well, you know, as you come in, I'm just on the right.

Mrs Spoker Yes, but are you for or against the brewers?

Peter I'm for the brewers!

Mrs Spoker Hum, well I'll get the register. (*Crosses* L.) Perhaps when you sign your name you'll kindly put M.P. after it, it may be an object of interest in these parts.

Exits down L.

Peter This is terrible! Who is the person? He knows you!

Marguerite Oh, his name is Sloley-Jones.

Peter I don't care whether it's Quickly-Smith.

Marguerite He is harmless. I'll make it all right with him when I see him again. He won't remember you.

Peter Won't he? I know those little fussy men. (*Pacing stage* L.) They never forget things they should forget. And what about this register? I can't sign your husband's name!

Marguerite Of course you can!

Peter But it's forgery, and that's a thing I very seldom do.

Mrs Spoker returns with register, also pen and ink-bottle, which she puts on the table L. C.

Mrs Spoker If you'll kindly make the entry now, sir?

Marguerite And are you going to take the dog? (*Rising*)

Mrs Spoker Certainly.

Marguerite I'm going up to my room now if you'll please take her at once.

Mrs Spoker Yes, give her to me.

Marguerite (*surrendering Pansy*) I hope she won't howl.

Mrs Spoker (*crossing in front of table* C.) It won't make any difference if she do howl. She won't be heard from the stables.

Peter crosses up R. C. *and opens door for Mrs Spoker*

She goes out up R. *with dog*

Marguerite What a sweet face!

Peter Whose?

Marguerite Pansy's.

Peter (*who has taken pen and is regarding register dismally*) Look here, Marguerite, this won't do—I mean about this book.

Marguerite That's exactly why I got rid of Mrs Spoker. I'll sign it.

Peter (*passing book, giving her pen*) I think you'd better.

Marguerite (*preparing to inscribe*) Mr and Mrs Hickett, you see. I'm Mrs Hickett, aren't I? You can't be run in for half a forgery, can you?

Peter Go on, then. Mr Hickett, M.P., remember.

Enter Gladys D. L.

Marguerite And Mrs Hickett.

While Marguerite is writing and he is looking over her shoulder at the book, Gladys comes in down L., *quietly, and crosses to sideboard, collects groceries and puts them inside bag*

Room number?

Gladys snorts

(*Glancing up at Gladys*) Number Two, isn't it?

Gladys 'Sright.

Gladys takes bag of groceries from sideboard L. *and exits* D. L.

Peter What's that?

Marguerite That is right.

Peter Oh, short cut.

Marguerite (*to him*) I'd better put my address.

Peter Put any address you like, only don't put mine.

Marguerite I shall put 'London'.

Door bangs off R. *Marguerite quickly passes book over to Peter, who starts to write. Marguerite spells 'London' for him*

Mrs Spoker re-enters R. *and comes straight over and examines his handiwork*

Mrs Spoker H'm, you don't write very clear.

Peter I've just had some very thick soup.

Mrs Spoker tries to see what is written

Mrs Spoker (*closing book and taking it with ink-pot, etc., and turning to Marguerite*) Would you care for a fire in your room? Mrs Love used to have one and it is laid.

Marguerite Yes, I think it would be very welcome.

Mrs Spoker Very well, then. (*At bar door, calling*) Alfred!

Alfred (*in bar off*) Aye, Mrs Spoker!

Mrs Spoker Come you here. (*Crosses* L. *of table* C.)

Enter Alfred L.

Take you those two bags up to Number Two and show Mr and Mrs Hickett the way. And put a light to the fire.

Marguerite (*taking her coat from bench*) I think I'll go up to my room now. Good-night, Mrs Spoker.

Mrs Spoker Good-night to you, madam.

Peter (*fatuously*) Shall I come up too, dear?

Mrs Spoker Yes, please.

Peter Er—I was talking to my wife.

Mrs Spoker And the sooner the house is quiet the better.

Marguerite Come along then, Peter.

Exit door U. R.

Peter All right.

Peter pretends to be in a great hurry. Feels seat of bench U.L., *then goes to fireplace and warms his* R. *hand, which he holds up as he goes towards door* U. R., *goes back to fireplace and warms his left hand which he also holds up, then attempts to go, but finds himself on the wrong side of the door. Mrs Spoker's attention is drawn to his foolishness*

Mrs Spoker (*cross to table* L.) You'll be wanting a candle.
Peter Yes, I expect I shall.

Mrs Spoker goes to sideboard and gets candle in a stick, which she hands to Peter

I shall take great care of it! (*Hugs candle*) The bedroom is on the next floor, isn't it? (R. C.) The one above this.
Mrs Spoker It is.
Peter And the bedridden old lady, is she also on the same floor? (*Closing register on table* C.)
Mrs Spoker Next door to you, so please observe as much quiet as possible.
Peter Oh, I shan't take any notice of her at all. Where do you sleep, Mrs Spicer?
Mrs Spoker And *why* do you want to know?
Peter Ah, did I say that? I don't want to know. I thought that the old lady next door might——
Mrs Spoker On the same floor, but up a different flight of stairs. Don't you try and find your way about because it is not easy. I shall hear you if you call.
Peter Yes, I'm not likely to call you, to—er—call on you, to—er—yes, all right.

Alfred returns R.

Alfred (*as Peter crosses*) Can you find your way, sur?
Peter I think so, Albert. Your mother has just told me.

During dialogue between Peter and Alfred, Mrs Spoker clears table of register, pen and ink and puts them on dresser, then—
Exit into bar with tankard

Alfred The door facing 'ee, sur, on the first landing.
Peter Ah, yes.
Alfred Good-night to 'ee, sur.
Peter What's that?
Alfred Good-night to 'ee.
Peter Oh, do that, will you?

Exit up R.

Mrs Spoker re-enters from bar to table c.

Mrs Spoker Well, Alfred, did you light the fire in Number Two?
Alfred Aye, Mrs Spoker.
Mrs Spoker And have you locked the bar door?
Alfred Aye, Mrs Spoker.
Mrs Spoker And seen to the bar windows? (*Getting on chair* L. *of table*)
Alfred Aye, Mrs Spoker.
Mrs Spoker And locked the cash drawer in the bar?
Alfred. Aye.
Mrs Spoker Where is the key? (*Gets on top of table*)
Alfred (*producing key from pocket*) 'Ere she be.
Mrs Spoker Have you done all those things that you ought to have done?
Alfred Aye, Mrs Spoker.
Mrs Spoker (*severely*) And have you left undone those things that you ought *not* to have done?
Alfred Aye, Mrs Spoker.
Mrs Spoker Then you can go to bed. (*Puts out hanging lamp*)

Mrs Spoker gets down from table

Alfred Aye, Mrs Spoker.

Alfred exits door L.

Mrs Spoker takes key and locks door U. C., *turns out lamp outside bar, exit to bar and puts out small lamp inside bar.*

The stage is now in darkness excepting for the glow from the fire.

Peter is seen on landing through glass door up R., *stealing quietly down the stairs carrying a lighted candle and a blanket over his arm. He opens the door cautiously and makes his way* D. R. *towards* C. *Mrs Spoker re-enters from bar carrying a small lamp. She sees Peter and at once shades the light from her lamp by putting her hand in front of it. She comes down* L. *in front of table, and taking her hand away from lamp confronts Peter. Peter, obviously surprised, exclaims*

Peter Hallo!
Mrs Spoker What are you doing here, sir?
Peter (*at a loss for what to say*) I'm looking for a melon.
Mrs Spoker (*incredulously*) A melon! (*Then seeing blanket*) What may you be doing with that blanket? (*Down* L. C.)
Peter Oh, the blanket! Oh, yes, it was *you* I wanted to see. I was going to ask you if you would slip out to the stables and wrap the little dog in the little blanket.

Mrs Spoker What? In my best blanket!

Peter Is this your best blanket? I thought it was the other one. Never mind. Good-night (*Blows candle out*) Oh! (*Lights candle again*) Sorry, I thought I'd gone; it doesn't matter.

Mrs Spoker Doesn't matter?

Peter I mean about the little dog. (*Moving slightly towards door* R.) He'll be all right.

Mrs Spoker He'll have to be.

Peter Yes, that's what I said to him the day before yesterday. I said you'll have to be all right. He only just barked, and I wagged my tail, and then we were both happy. Now you go straight to bed like a good little girl. We know what dogs are, so she'll be all right.

Mrs Spoker I thought you said it was a he.

Peter It was, but not now.

He goes out and closes door R. *He is seen disappearing up the stairs*

Mrs Spoker stands for a moment staring after him

Mrs Spoker Well!

She makes a movement towards door D. L. *She can be seen to have an inspiration. She goes to the door* R., *locks it on the inside, and takes the key. This with the key that Alfred has given her and the door key of the inn, she takes with her, crosses* D. L. *Pause, looks across to door* R. *and with a satisfied look exit* D. L.

Peter's shadow is again seen through the glass door, making his way down the stairs. He reaches the door, tries the handle gently, but of course the door will not open. He looks close into the lock, and realizes the situation. Rattling the handle furiously the silhouette of his head is clearly seen as he says 'Damn!'

CURTAIN

ACT II

*Number Two room of the 'Stag and Hunt'. The room is small. A large pro-
portion of it is occupied by a big double bed. This has its head up the R. wall
and with a small table up stage occupies the whole of this side of the stage.
The one door to the room is in the centre background. L. of the door a towel
rail, U. L. of the door the fireplace. A window up stage in the L. wall. A
washing-stand down stage against the L. wall. A roller-blind hangs over the
window. A lamp on a chair by the bed R. The jug is out of the basin on the
washing-stand, but has not been placed on the floor. A toothbrush in the
customary receptacle like a vase, on the washing-stand. A pair of bedroom
slippers is beneath the bed. On the wall above the bed a picture of lovers.
On the wall above small table a picture of a soul being escorted by angels.
Above the fireplace another picture of a sailor and little girl. A trunk at the
foot of the bed, suitcase alongside. A chair by the window. A suitcase on chair
L. of bed*

*Marguerite is sitting up in bed reading a novel. She is in a very pretty and
becoming negligée. There is a faint and nervous tapping at the door. Marguerite lowers her novel and looks in that direction*

Marguerite (*sits up*) Come in.

> *Knocking is repeated. Peter pushes his head through door C. He still carries
> a lighted candle and a blanket. He closes the door*

Oh, it's you. What's the matter with *you*?

Peter (*softly, in a voice of one keeping a firm control over his feelings*)
I cannot sleep in the parlour. (*At door*)

Marguerite Oh, nonsense, Peter; you can't have tried. You've
only *been* there ten minutes.

Peter I tell you I can't sleep in the parlour.

Marguerite Why not?

Peter Because I can't get in—it's locked.

Marguerite Well, come in. Where have you been all the time
then?

Peter comes down to foot of bed

Peter I haven't been anywhere all the time. But I've been everywhere one can, and where one can one can't sleep.

Marguerite What about the back door downstairs?

Peter (*heartily*) I've been through there.

Marguerite Where does that lead to?

Peter To the back. Hence the expression—back door. (*Crosses down* L.)

Marguerite Can't you sleep there?

Peter How do you mean, sleep *there*? In the aperture of the back door? *Behind* the back door. Swinging on the back door to rock myself to sleep?

Marguerite Isn't there anything through the back door?

Peter A sink. Oh, and a pump. You were quite right about the pump. (*Crosses to foot of bed*) But if I remember rightly, that was for the morning.

Marguerite What about the stables?

Peter I tested the stables.

Marguerite Did you go into the stables?

Peter (*crosses* D. R., *puts candle on the mantelpiece*) One doesn't have to. I tested them from the back door. (*Warms hands by fire. Has blanket over his arm*)

Marguerite I hope Pansy is all right.

Peter (*looking over shoulder*) Oh, she's all right. I think she's getting some ratting.

Marguerite Oh, Peter, was she howling?

Peter She's perfectly all right. We are not discussing Pansy. We are discussing me. And I am anything but perfectly all right.

Marguerite I suppose you can't sleep on the stairs?

Peter You're right. I've tried the stairs, and I cannot sleep thereon.

Marguerite Well, there must be somewhere.

Peter I've been through every door there is that isn't locked, even the bedridden old lady's.

Marguerits Good heavens! What happened?

Peter Nothing. She just cocked an eye at me and murmured 'Eno's'.

Marguerite My dear Peter, I'm frightfully sorry, but I really don't see what can be done.

Peter (*crosses* U. C., D. L., U. L., *and* D. C.) The architecture of this place is all wrong. The parlour's locked, the kitchen's locked; there's no way to the bar, otherwise I'd go and do a bit of moaning at the bar. I appear to be condemned to wander about the house all night, like a lost soul with a candle and a blanket. (*Pause, looks at Marguerite*) I'd give anything for a bed like yours.

Marguerite Then you can't be hard to please. It goes up and down in the middle like the hump of a camel. Only it does it twice. That's a dromedary, isn't it?

Peter I should think that must be rather restful, if you work yourself into the right position.

Marguerite I can tell you if you're keen on a bed like this you'd take to the stables like a duck to water.

Peter crosses L. *to window and looks out*

Peter It is raining, by the way.

Marguerite Is it?

Peter Oh, terrible night. It's pouring all over the place.

Marguerite Oh, I hope the stables are watertight.

Peter Look here. (*Crosses to foot of bed*) I am not going to the stables. That's definite.

Marguerite No, I was thinking of Pansy.

A sharp rapping on the door outside and Mrs Spoker's voice is heard

Mrs Spoker (*off*) Silence in there, please!

Peter crosses right to fireplace

It is hight time everyone was in bed and asleep.

Peter All right. I know that.

Mrs Spoker (*off*) Then let me have no more of it. The old lady is not well. And in any case I cannot have a disturbance in my hotel. So kindly get into bed, without further noise.

Peter All right, all right.

Marguerite He'll be in bed in a minute.

Mrs Spoker (*off*) So I should hope.

A pause. Peter goes up to the door and listens, then returns to above bed

Peter Well, keep on hoping. That settles it. It was bad enough before. . . . Upstairs and downstairs in my old lady's bedridden chamber. And now every landing I go on to, I shall meet this horrible old thing in night attire—awful.

Marguerite Look here, Peter. (*She sits up a little higher in bed and speaks in a most practical voice*) There is only one thing to be done.

Peter What's that? (*At foot of bed*)

Marguerite You can take this pillow and get down on the floor with your blanket and go to sleep.

Peter (*hesitating*) What?

Marguerite (*taking second pillow and throwing it at foot of bed*) Go on— that'll settle it.

Peter Yes. It very likely will.

Marguerite What d'you mean?

Peter Well, do you think it's wise?

Marguerite You keep grousing because you've got nowhere to sleep. Go on. Sleep on the floor.

Peter Suppose anyone found out.

Marguerite The only people who will find out will find out because
we shall tell them. To any decent-minded person there's nothing
wrong in your sleeping on the floor of my room, is there?

Peter Yes, but where's the decent-minded person?

Marguerite My husband hasn't got a nasty mind. Has your wife
got a nasty mind?

Peter No, but she's got a nasty mother.

Marguerite Oh, all right. I was only trying to help. Go to the
stables if you like.

Both grab pillow at foot of bed. Peter gets pillow and walks away L.

Peter No, I daresay it's all right. Only you know what some people
are. If they heard I'd stayed in your room all night, they'd be on
us like bees on a queen or a drone or whatever it is bees get on to.

Marguerite Look here, Peter, *I* don't want you in my room in the
least bit, I'm only thinking of you. And if you stand there arguing
that old woman is sure to come back.

Peter You're right.

Marguerite Well, of course, I'm right.

Peter All right, then—I said all right, then.

Marguerite All right—All right.

Peter I'll risk it.

Marguerite Risk what?

Peter (*mumbling*) Sleeping on the floor of your room.

Marguerite Oh!

Peter (*with a survey of the floor*) After all, the floor is no bed of roses.
(*Drops pillow and blanket on floor and loosens collar and tie. Up* C. *to
door, stoops with his handkerchief at bottom of door* C., *draught blows it
out. Picks pillow and blanket up after handkerchief business*) There is an
absolute Arctic blast blowing in under this door!

Marguerite You can get well in the corner under the washing-
stand. You'll be all right there.

Peter (*crossing* L.—*testing with his hand for draught at washstand*) On
the contrary the wind is blowing straight into the washing-stand.

Marguerite Hurry up and don't footle about.

Peter (*throws blanket and pillow on floor* C., *takes coat off and carries it on
arm. Annoyed*) Well, dash it all, if I've got to sleep on the floor, you
might let me pick my own pitch. I can't lie on a floor all night in
the teeth of a gale. I shall die. (*Throws his collar into the washstand
basin, snatches it up quickly and shakes imaginary water off it. He then
puts collar on washing-stand, crosses to foot of bed*)

Marguerite You can lie with your feet under the bed, if you like.

Peter (*he continues to investigate for draughts*) That's very extraordinary.

Marguerite What is?
Peter There's a three-cornered blast.
Marguerite Go on, hurry up and get settled.
Peter It doesn't matter much where I go. I shall die. (c., *puts coat on*)
Marguerite Well, if you've never had anything worse happen to
you than have to spend a night on the floor of an inn——
Peter Yes, but what an inn! (*Tapping floor with knuckles*) And what
a floor! You're all right—here, above the draught. (*Crosses up* c.,
gazing at picture of the soul on wall) That'd be me. (*Pointing to
picture*)

Marguerite looks at picture and smiles

Bus. of wing flapping with elbows

Peter picks blanket, etc., from c., *crosses to washstand, puts them down, takes
coat off and puts it over chair*

You will find my body 'neath the shade of the old washing-stand.

*Wrapping himself round in the blanket, he gets down very awkwardly on the
floor, near leg of washing-stand, which he bumps with his head down stage.
Peter props pillow against leg of washing-stand down stage, and keeps press-
ing both sides of pillow, which makes it bulge at top corner, which he knocks
down. Repeat pillow bus. Peter kneels down and rests his head on the pillow
but his arms are in the way. He puts his right arm behind him, then left arm,
then both, but is unable to get comfortably settled. Peter has great difficulty in
getting under washing-stand*

*Marguerite has resumed her book. Peter wriggles a good deal. After a few
moments he exclaims in an altered tone of genuine misery*

Oh, how uncomfortable this is!
Marguerite Why don't you try lying the other way round?
Peter That's not a bad idea.

*Peter does so, putting pillow up stage, lies underneath washing-stand and
gets feet entangled with chair. His head is up stage*

I'm round.
Marguerite Is that better?
Peter Better than what?
Marguerite Oh, Peter, would you mind blowing out this candle?

Rain starts

Peter tries to blow out candle from under washstand twice

Peter I can't reach it.
Marguerite Well, just jump up and do it.

Peter (*struggling to his feet, bumps head, and catches his foot in chair. Crosses* R., *blanket on head*) I wish you'd think of things in their proper order.

He blows out the candle on mantelpiece, which he snuffs and burns his fingers, and attempts to put the lamp out, but Marguerite stops him

Marguerite No, I'll keep this one until I've finished reading.

Peter (*crossing*) Back to the old four-poster. Now remember, no more of this just jumping up business.

Peter kneels on the mat, slips and bumps his chin on floor

Marguerite Peter, do you mean to say your wife never thinks of things at night and sends you out of bed?

Peter Certainly not. And don't remind me of my wife. (*Lying down. He is on the floor again and settles himself*) Oh, how I love my wife! (*Brief pause*) Oh, I do love her, little darling. (*Loudly*) Blast this blanket. If I pull it down I get a draught, and if I pull it up it tickles my neck; oh, utterly blast and curse this nght!

Peter groans twice. He holds on to top of washstand, but his hand drops and his elbow knocks the floor

Oh, how I hate washing-stands!

Marguerite Oh, Peter, do keep quiet. I'm going to try and get some sleep now. Oh, Peter, I'm sorry I forgot. Would you mind opening the window?

Peter Open the window! Do you *want* me to die?

Marguerite We must have air.

Peter I've got some, thanks.

Marguerite If we don't have it open I shall have such a headache in the morning.

Peter I've got one now. (*Puts blanket over his head*)

Marguerite If you won't do it, I must try again myself.

Peter No, no, Marguerite, you musn't get out of bed. Where are you? (*Struggles to get out*) I'll do it. (*Puts coat on. He gets up again and goes to window*) A little walk will bring the blood back to my feet.

Peter releases blind, which flies up. He pulls it down again and releases it two or three times—enjoying it, looks round at Marguerite, smiling

Marguerite (*severely*) Open the window, can't you?

Peter (*trying*) No.

Marguerite There's a catch somewhere.

Peter Yes, I think there is.

Marguerite (*sitting up in bed*) That's right—that's right. Pull it down from the top.

Peter I can't pull down from the top.

Marguerite Then push it up from the bottom.

He pushes up window, which opens suddenly and almost falls out. Moves down L.

That's too wide, now. Won't it stay half-way open?

Peter (*tries to move window*) I can't move it at all now.

Marguerite Well, never mind, leave it—leave it.

Peter sits on chair to operate blind again; it flies up. He does blind bus. two or three times, then turns round and smiles at Marguerite

Leave that blind alone and get back to bed.

Peter Isn't it time to get up yet? (*Takes off coat and hangs it on chair L.*) Bed! I'm sick of that spot. (*Looking round room*) I'm going to find a fresh position.

Peter crosses to fireplace L.

Marguerite Why didn't you think of that place before? It's much warmer there.

Peter I can't argue at this time of night.

Peter crosses over to fireplace—throws down blanket and pillow and lies down, head near fireplace—feet up stage. Chimney smokes—he puts his head in coal scuttle—after the second draught he crawls towards trunk C.

Marguerite Peter, I believe the chimney is going to smoke.

Peter Watson, you surpass yourself.

Marguerite It's caused by that window. You'll have to lie somewhere else.

Peter I'm not going to lie under the window, I can tell you that.

Marguerite makes herself comfortable. She takes up her book again and starts to read. Peter settles himself against trunk, blanket over his head. Suddenly there comes the sound of Pansy howling outside. At first it passes unnoticed

Marguerite lowers her book and raises her head, listens. She starts to read again. Two dog howls

Marguerite Peter, it's Pansy. Can't you hear her?

Peter (*emphatically*) No!

Dog howl

Marguerite Peter, you know it's Pansy. Oh, please go down and fetch her, will you?

Peter No, thank you.

Marguerite I know if you were Claude you'd go down and get her in.

Peter If I were Claude I shouldn't have cramp in my spine.

Dog howl

Marguerite Oh, Peter, please!

Peter I can't move my right leg. It is numb-a. All my right side is more or less numb-a. I can't do that. (*Opens and shuts right hand*)

Dog howl

Marguerite Poor little girl!

Peter She can't be worse off than I am.

Marguerite Yes, but somehow it's much more pathetic in a dog.

Peter And here am I, a human being—— (*Desperately, getting up*)

Marguerite Peter, have you no regard for dumb animals?

Dog howls loudly

Peter (*indicating dog—throws clothing* D. C.) Yes, when they *are* dumb-a.

Marguerite Well, you can easily get to the stables. You said so yourself.

Dog howl

Peter (*calling to dog off*) Quiet! (*Crosses up* L. *puts coat on*)

Marguerite (*making herself comfortable*) Bring her in your arms and don't let her bark.

Peter crosses R. *and takes candle*

Dog howl

Peter (*he comes back* R.) If I find her, she'll never bark again.

Peter puts table centre on head, ties it under his chin, crosses up C. *to door and exits*

Pause. A dark landing outside is faintly illuminated by the light of his candle. Marguerite sits up in bed listening eagerly. Suddenly there comes from the passage the sound of a tin can being hurtled downstairs. Marguerite jumps out of bed, crosses to door, sees Mrs Spoker and gets back. Mrs Spoker, in night attire, with a dressing-gown peers into the room

Mrs Spoker Was that Mr Hickett?

Marguerite It sounded to me more like a can.

Mrs Spoker It was a can placed outside the door o' Number One. What is the meaning of this?

Marguerite My husband has gone to get the dog. She was howling.

Mrs Spoker (*coming into the room* L. C.) What is he going to do with the dog?

Marguerite Bring her in here, of course.

Mrs Spoker I won't allow it; I've said so once.

Marguerite She's not going to stay out there and howl all night.

Mrs Spoker I can't hear any noise.

Bang of a door from outside

Peter (*off* L.) Pansy, Pansy, come here, come here, come here!

Hens are heard cackling. Peter whistles for Pansy

Mrs Spoker (*turning, very sternly*) What's he up to now? I've never heard such a thing. (*Crosses to window. Sees blanket on floor at foot of bed*) And what, may I ask, may you be doing with my best blanket and pillows all over the floor?

Marguerite He was trying to make a bed there.

Mrs Spoker A bed?

Marguerite Yes, for the dog, you see.

Mrs Spoker Oh really? I'll soon settle this.

Exit C.

Peter is heard whistling dog. Hens cackling in the distance

Marguerite quickly puts her book on the table and gets out of bed. She puts on her slippers and hurries to the window. She puts her head out, but withdraws it again quickly. She calls through the window

Marguerite Peter! Peter!

Peter (*heard off* L.) Hallo!

Marguerite Come back! Mrs Spoker is on the war-path; come back.

Peter I don't know that I *can* come back. I'm all tied up in pig buckets.

Noise of buckets

Oh!

Marguerite Besides it's pouring with rain.

Peter (*very testily*) I know that.

Bucket noises

Marguerite Peter be careful with those buckets. The poor pigs won't get their food.

Marguerite watches Peter's movements through the window

Door slam

Pause

Marguerite returns to bed. Takes off her slippers and gets in. Mrs Spoker and Peter are heard in altercation outside the door of the room and the landing outside is again lit up

Mrs Spoker (*off*) Are you finished?
Peter (*entering* C.) Yes, I'm finished.
Mrs Spoker Where is the dog?
Peter Run away; and pray heaven it'll stay away.
Mrs Spoker You keep your prayers for yourself.
Peter That's just what I'm doing.

Peter enters, and he is very wet

Marguerite Peter, didn't you go after Pansy when she ran away?
Peter Of course I did. You've no idea what it's like out there on a night like this with rain like that.

Warning: light out

Marguerite But *imagine* what a wretched night she'll spend.
Peter That's one thing I can imagine.
Marguerite (*leaning forward and scrutinizing him*) But, Peter, you're wet.
Peter Of course I'm wet. You can't go dog-hunting in the rain without getting wet.
Marguerite You must take off those wet clothes at once.
Peter I'm not going to take off any clothes in here.
Marguerite You can't catch pneumonia.
Peter I can. (*Crosses* L.)
Marguerite Go on. You can't sleep in wet clothes. I'll put the light out if you're so modest. (*Puts out light on chair by bed*) There!

Light out

Peter You needn't have done that. I'm only going to take off my coat and shoes.

His figure can be dimly seen. Takes off coat and puts it on horse L.

Marguerite (*after a brief pause*) Got your coat off ?
Peter Not yet—yes.
Marguerite Hang it over a chair.
Peter (*stubs his foot suddenly*) Oh, my right toe.
Marguerite. Now your shoes. Got your shoes off ?
Peter No. It's very difficult to balance. I've only one foot on the ground.

Marguerite Well, take it off.

Peter overbalances and clutches at the nearest thing to hand. He falls and smashes the china jug from the washstand

Good heavens! What's happened?
Peter (*in a desperate voice*) Light the light! Light the light!

Marguerite strikes a match and lights the lamp. Peter is on his hands and knees, looking very scared

Marguerite What *have* you done now?
Peter I overbalanced and caught hold of the jug.
Marguerite It made a ghastly row.
Peter I think it only sounded loud.
Marguerite Is the jug broken?
Peter Yes, but the handle's all right.

Peter picks up the handle of the jug

Mrs Spoker and Gladys talking off

Marguerite Peter, she's coming. Stand over there. (*Indicates* L.) And pretend to be undressing.

Peter makes movement of taking off imaginary trousers

Mrs Spoker What is it, Gladys?
Gladys (*off*) It's cats.
Mrs Spoker Cats, rubbish!

Entering, leaving door open, followed by Gladys

And what are you up to now, may I ask?
Marguerite My husband was undressing and knocked over a jug.

Gladys in an overcoat over her nightdress and curl papers peers round the door—crosses to Peter

Peter I'll pay for your jug. Go away, Gladys.
Mrs Spoker (*crosses to front of Gladys*) Go you back, Gladys.

Exit Gladys

Unless you're in bed and asleep in five minutes——
Marguerite Yes, yes, he shall be . . . he's always like this.
Mrs Spoker Does he break a jug every time he undresses?
Marguerite I'll pay for it. Or rather he will.
Peter Oh, go away.

A moaning sound from outside. Mrs Spoker turns

Mrs Spoker Now you've gone and shook up Number One. I'll go and settle her, and when I come back I shall expect to find you in bed like a respectable gentleman.

She goes out, closing the door

Peter She's gone to settle her. It doesn't matter what happens to me now.

Marguerite Never mind, take those wet clothes off.

Peter No, I can't undress here.

Marguerite Well, go outside the door.

Peter goes out, taking a towel with him from U. L., and starts to undress outside

Peter (*opens door and looks in*) We're utterly compromised. (*Closes door—pause*)

Marguerite Compromised—nonsense! I tell you what does she matter?

Peter (*looking in*) It isn't only she. We've tied ourselves in knots all the evening. (*Closes door. Pause—opens door again*) We're husband and wife in the register book.

Marguerite I know, Peter, but we're all right in the book from which there is no rubbing out.

Peter (*peeping in again*) We're in the same room.

Marguerite. I am in the same room, but you seem to be doing a little travelling.

Peter You can laugh. You'd laugh while Rome fiddled.

Peter closes door

(*Peeping in again*) And we've been identified by that parson, Up Jenkins, or whatever his damn silly name is. (*Closes door*)

Marguerite Hurry up, I tell you—good gracious, what does it matter?

Mrs Spoker's voice heard off

Peter enters. He has draped himself with a towel, and carries his trousers over his arm. He hides on floor by trunk

Mrs Spoker again heard off

Mrs Spoker There's more noise in Number Two. Come along, Gladys, I'll soon settle this.

Mrs Spoker enters with Gladys, pushing door open

Mrs Spoker Where's your husband?

Very startled and coming indignantly towards him

And what are you doing down there?
Peter I'm looking for my collar stud.
Mrs Spoker Come up.

Mrs Spoker is very shocked when she sees Peter's attire

Marguerite Bring your trousers here, dear, and press them under
the mattress.
Gladys (*following Peter*) 'Ere, I'll take 'em for 'ee.
Peter Leave them alone. (*Crosses to bed, raising the mattress. He puts
trousers under mattress*) I want to press them in the creases.
Mrs Spoker Now Gladys, get you back to bed.
Gladys All ri'.

With a grin at Peter as she goes off C.

Mrs Spoker Has he got his nightshirt?
Peter Yes; and go away.
Mrs Spoker Directly I turn my back there's a row.
Peter There'll be a bigger one if you don't.
Mrs Spoker (*crosses up* C.) Why don't you look after him—— (*At
door*) I knew how to *manage* my late husband.
Peter No wonder he's late.
Mrs Spoker Oh!

Exit Mrs Spoker up C.

Peter That's one to me.

Loud knocking off door R.

Mrs Spoker (*off*) Who and what is that? (*Calls*) Gladys!
Gladys (*off*) There's someone at the door, Mrs Spoker.

Noise continues until Peter goes to door

Peter (*at door*) Stop that row! How do you expect a respectable
gentleman to sleep. (*Closes door and comes down* C.)
Marguerite Who was it, Peter?
Peter I don't know! Someone trying to get a drink or something.
(*Sits on trunk*)

Enter Mrs Bone and Major Bone

Mrs Bone (D. L. C. *to Major Bone*) There!

Peter jumps up. Crosses down R.

Look!

Major   Mrs Bone
(R. C.)   (D. L. C.)
Marguerite
Peter
(D. R.)

Peter This is very unexpected.

Mrs Bone (*crosses* L.) Not in the least.

Peter Oh well—now you are here, let me introduce you, Marguerite —Mrs Bone, my mother-in-law.

Mrs Bone turns her back on Marguerite

Major Bone, my father-in-ditto.

Major Bone (*affably*) How de do? (*Shaking hands with Marguerite*)

Mrs Bone (*to Major Bone*) Stop that.

Marguerite (*who remains totally unperturbed—to Mrs Bone*) Won't you sit down? I'm afraid the space is rather limited.

Mrs Bone (*to Marguerite*) So you are the woman?

Marguerite Yes. I am the woman and this is the man. (*Indicates Peter*) I admit his costume is rather effeminate at the moment.

Bone advances to bed and leans against the bed-rail, looking down at Marguerite

Mrs Bone I knew very well I should find *you* here.

Peter Let me explain.

Mrs Bone Explain! This explains itself. Here you are in this room with this scarlet woman——

Peter What colour? (*Crosses* L. *very indignant*) How dare you say a thing like that in a room like this!

Mrs Bone Barbara will be here in the morning, and I'll see you don't get away till then.

Peter But Barbara's at the Bunter's.

Mrs Bone Yes, that's what you *think*.

Peter Think?

Peter looks very concerned

Mrs Bone So you spend the night here with your alleged wife— she in bed and you in a towel.

Peter My trousers are there.

Mrs Bone Where?

They turn towards the bed. Bone blissfully unaware that he is under observation is looking with great interest at Marguerite

Marguerite Under the mattress, if you want them.

Major Bone Allow me. (*He comes eagerly to the bed, places hat on trunk and takes hold of mattress*)

Mrs Bone stops him

Mrs Bone No, you don't. This room shall stay as it is until Barbara arrives. That'll be evidence enough.

Marguerite Evidence of what?

Peter There isn't another room in the house. They are all completely occupied.

Marguerite Oh this is all very restless. (*Standing up on bed*)

Enter Mrs Spoker C.

Mrs Spoker Out you go, all of you.

Marguerite I cannot go out in the night, in the middle of the rain.

Major Bone Hear! Hear!

	Bone (R. C.)	Mrs Spoker (C.)	Mrs Bone (L. C.)	
Marguerite (D.R.)				Peter (D. L.)

Mrs Spoker (*to Major Bone, brushing him aside*) I don't know who you are—this is my hotel and out you go, all of you. (*To Marguerite*) You with your lies and deceit and sin.

Mrs Bone I quite agree.

Mrs Spoker (*brushing Mrs Bone aside*) And don't you interfere.

Peter is sitting on chair D. L. *enjoying the joke*

(*To Peter*) And as for you, out of my house you go.

Peter now looks helplessly at Mrs Bone

You——— (*Pause*) You sheik!

Peter looks very annoyed and indignant, repeats 'Sheik', crosses to step of door, strikes an attitude of injured dignity and goes out

As he goes Alfred appears in the doorway in nightshirt and lighted candlestick in hand, looking off R.

CURTAIN

ACT III

The Parlour

Morning

Peter, Bone, Marguerite and Mrs Bone all discovered asleep in various places. Marguerite and Mrs Bone on bench. Mrs Bone has Major Bone's overcoat over her. Major Bone on chair R. *of table, and Peter on the floor, resting his head against front leg of table* L. *All dressed as at end of Act II*

Enter down L. *Gladys with hot-water can. She is followed by Alfred*

Alfred Gladys!

Gladys What?

Alfred (*to Gladys*) Walking with a pig-lad won't never win success.

Gladys merely snorts and exits R.

Peter opens his eyes and in rising rubs his neck and shoulder, which are obviously stiff by lying in a draught. He crosses to bar

Peter Here Alfred!

Alfred Sur?

Peter Sh! Listen! Was that Gladys went through?

Alfred Aye, sur.

Peter Well, tell her to try and get into that bedroom somehow and get my trousers. They're in the bed.

Alfred On the bed?

Peter *In* the bed?

Alfred What, under the clothes?

Peter Yes. Under the mattress.

Alfred Under the mattress? How come they to have got corrt there, sur?

Peter They didn't get corrt. Tell Gladys. She knows. Oh, and Alfred?

Alfred Aye, sur.

Peter Get me a beer.

Alfred A beer, sur?

Major Bone (R. C., *opening his eyes*) What's that?

Peter Sh! (*To Alfred*) Two beers!

Alfred Aye, sur. Which first? The trousers or the beers?

Major Bone The beers.

Alfred Aye, sur.

Exit into bar

Peter (*crosses to* R. *above table, glances at Mrs Bone*) I say, Bone! (*Takes Bone by* R. *arm, crosses* L. C. *by front of table*)

Major Bone Yes, my boy?

Peter Where did mother put the key of that room?

Major Bone In the tail pocket of her skirt. (L. *of table*)

Peter I suppose you wouldn't care to try and get it?

Major Bone H'm! (*Looking at seat* R.) Pretty ticklish job.

Peter Oh, of course, if she's ticklish it's hopeless.

Major Bone Anyhow, don't let's risk waking her up until we've had the beers. There are one or two devilish awkward points about this affair, you know.

Peter There shouldn't be (*moving to* R. *end of table, front of it, looking at Marguerite*), because Mrs Hickett is even more virtuous than she is beautiful.

Marguerite (*opening her eyes quickly*) Don't be rude.

Major Bone Hallo! Good morning. (*Leaning on left end table facing* R.)

Marguerite 'Morning. You ought to know better than to make remarks about a lady when she is asleep. Because she never is.

Mrs Bone (*opening her eyes, speaking pointedly to Bone*) Never.

Peter (*crossing to Mrs Bone, to her*) Well, if you're awake, you'd better give me the key of the room.

Mrs Bone You will stay as you are till Barbara comes.

Peter crosses down L.

Marguerite (*shivering*) Boo! Well, I hope Barbara is better at catching trains than her husband, or there will be two bedridden ladies in this hotel.

Major Bone Quite right—this lady must have her clothes.

Peter Yes, and the same remark applies to this gentleman and his trousers.

Marguerite (*rises and crosses to above chair* R. C.) If this goes on, and the natives come in for their morning beer, what will they say to see me standing here like this?

Mrs Bone H'mph!

Marguerite H'mph, yes. That is just what they *will* say. And do you think I am going to stand here and be h'mphed at by Maiden Blotton?

Mrs Bone puts Bone's overcoat over back of bench and sits on bench

Major Bone (*to Peter*) I say, that reminds me. What about those two beers?

Peter That's all right. I'll go and have them.

Peter goes into bar

Major Bone That will be nice for me. (*To Mrs Bone*) Look here, Constance, I entirely agree with Mrs Hitchcock. It's a bit too thick.

Marguerite No, it's a bit too thin. (*Is above chair* R. C. *to Bone*) Do you know that pretty little picture 'September Morn'?

Major Bone Rather!

Marguerite The poor little girl with no clothes on, standing shivering in the cold pond?

Major Bone Yes. But why she wanted to go paddling dressed like that I'm blowed if I can say.

Marguerite Now that I know how cold she felt, *I* can't say either.

Major Bone And there was a stork——

Mrs Bone George!

Major Bone (*turning from Marguerite*) Where's Peter gone, I wonder? (*He is crossing to bar when——*)

Chauffeur enters at front door

Chauffeur (*up* C.) Begging your pardon, but 'ow much longer——? (*Seeing Marguerite*) Oh, my lord!

Marguerite There you are! There's the first! (*Crosses and sits* R. C.)

Major Bone It's all right. It's the gentleman who's driving our car.

Chauffeur Driving it? It's the gent. who wants to. I've bin sleeping in it. What's the game?

Mrs Bone Wait for further orders.

Chauffeur All very well. I——

Major Bone (*going to him* L. C.) Now don't argue—you come in here with me.

Chauffeur Yes, guv'nor, but listen now——

Bone and Chauffeur argue at back

Enter Peter and Mrs Spoker up L. *Peter close on her heels crosses* D. R.

Mrs Spoker I will not 'ave this person in my 'otel. Give him his trousers at once.

Marguerite rises and goes to Peter, R.

Mrs Bone He will wait here for his wife.

Mrs Spoker He can wait in the trousers. And that person dressed. I will not 'ave my parlour looking like a swimming bath.

Marguerite and Peter go up stage

Enter Alfred L. *with beers*

Mrs Bone (*going to* L. *of table*) I will not give up the key.
Mrs Spoker (R. *of table*) You will!
Mrs Bone I will not!
Mrs Spoker This is my 'otel——
Mrs Bone Hotel—humph!
Mrs Spoker And I keep my own keys.

Alfred places beer-mug in front of each of them

Mrs Bone I do not intend to give up the key. I depend on it for my
evidence.
Mrs Spoker I will not have it.
Marguerite I demand to get my clothes. (*Crosses* R. C.)
Mrs Spoker Yes, and I'll see that you do.
Chauffeur Look here, I can't wait.
Mrs Bone Don't you dare to speak to me!
Marguerite I'm as cold as ice.

Peter obtains his beer from table C. *Major Bone also obtains beer*

Mrs Spoker You wait till you get to the next world. (*Crosses* R.)
Chauffeur I've been here all night; I ain't going to stay here all
day.
Mrs Bone Most men try to get paid for doing nothing.
Chauffeur What I wants to know is, how much longer have I got
to wait?
Mrs Bone George! Take this blot of a man away.
Major Bone You come in here with me.

Takes Chauffeur into bar

I'll look after you.
Mrs Bone I must have my evidence.
Mrs Spoker (*crosses* L., *to Mrs Bone*) You've proof enough. I saw
'em myself, and there's the Visitors' Book.

Crosses to sideboard

(*Coming back with book*) Here it is.

Mrs Bone Give it to me—let me see it.

Mrs Spoker places Visitors' Book on table. The other three all collect over it

Peter Now, now, girls, please!
Mrs Bone (*reading an entry scornfully with sarcasm*) 'Mr and Mrs Love.
Room Number Two.'

Mrs Spoker That ain't them.

Marguerite That ain't us.

Mrs Bone (*reading*) 'Remarks—most comfortable.'

Peter That *certainly* isn't us! What have these Loves been used to?
(*Crosses* R.)

Mrs Spoker This is what applies to them. (*Pointing to register*) 'Mr
'Ickett, M.P., and Mrs 'Ickett. Room Number Two.'

Peter Remarks? Give me a page and a pen!

Marguerite I should put 'one bed and one board'. (*Sits* R. C.)

Peter And three blasts.

Mrs Bone Very well. (*Closing book*) This book will suffice. I'll take
charge of it till my daughter comes. You may take your key.
(*Hands key to Mrs Spoker*)

Marguerite Then I'm to go and dress?

Mrs Spoker You're to dress and go!

Marguerite crosses R.

(*Gives Marguerite key*) And when she's finished (*to Peter*) you can
get your trousers.

Peter What about breakfast?

Mrs Spoker You'll get no breakfast from me!

Peter Oh, come now—bed and breakfast.

Mrs Bone I shall require some breakfast. (*Up* L. C.)

Peter Certainly. (*To Marguerite*) Tea or coffee, Mrs Hickett?
(*To fireplace*)

Marguerite Strong coffee. (*To Mrs Spoker*)

Peter And I'll have two boiled eggs.

Marguerite Hard or soft? (R. C.)

Peter Medium.

Marguerite (*to Mrs Spoker*) You hear? Two strong coffees and four
sticky eggs!

Exit Marguerite R.

Mrs Spoker You won't get a bite out of me!

Peter I don't want one. I'm a vegetarian.

Exit Mrs Spoker D. L.

Mrs Bone (*going after Marguerite, at door* U. R.) I don't want to let
that woman out of my sight.

Exit Mrs Bone R.

Peter I can't say the same about you! (*Closes door* R.)

Major Bone looks out of bar, sees her go, and comes out, down L. C.

Peter (*crosses to Bone, below table*) I say, look here, Bone, old boy, I'm in an awful fix. Barbara will be here at any moment—be a sport and help me.

Major Bone All very well—but it's no easy matter. This lady friend of yours is foreign and very attractive, and the two together are generally looked upon as a foregone conclusion.

Peter Still, by the time Barbara comes, I shall be in my trousers. At least I hope so. I can't stand and make speeches in a towel. I'm not a Roman Senator.

Major Bone You needn't worry about your towel. If you are going to tell Barbara that you stayed here last night in that delightful creature's room only to keep away the mice, it won't make the slightest difference whether you are wearing a towel or a suit of chain armour.

Peter (*crosses* D. R.) But that's not the point. The point is—what am I going to tell her?

Major Bone Tell her the truth.

Peter Impossible. She wouldn't believe it. She oughtn't to doubt me. It isn't as if I were you!

Major Bone What d'you mean?

Peter I mean my record's pure.

Major Bone Well, isn't mine? I like that, when I'm trying to help you, you start abusing me! That's not the way to get assistance.

Peter I don't mean that. What am I to tell her? You ought to know. Besides, really you're an expert.

Major Bone (*pleased*) Do you really think so? That's very nice of you. I oughtn't to help you. It isn't playing the game, you know—but there you are. Well, I'm a man of the world, and you're a very decent boy, and so I don't see why you shouldn't have the benefit of my experience. Now I'll tell you. When Barbara arrives, when she comes in this door—I presume that's where she'll come in—you stand there looking bewildered and ill-used.

Peter That's easy.

Major Bone Now, the first thing she'll say will be, 'Peter! What is this I hear?'

Peter 'What is this I hear?'

Major Bone Yes, they always say that.

Peter Do they? I didn't know.

Major Bone Yes, you can lay odds on that. And you turn round and say, 'It's nothing, darling. Surely you know me better than that?'

Peter Better than what?

Major Bone Better than what?

Peter Better than what?

Major Bone What what? Oh, better than what? Why, better than what she has heard. Then *I'll* step into the breach——

Peter Out of the bar.

Major Bone Thank you very much—and say to her, 'Oh, believe me, Barbara, you're utterly wrong.' And you must tell her the tale.

Peter What tale?

Major Bone The tale of the old iron pot.

Peter Old iron pot?

Major Bone That's another way of saying 'Spin her the yarn'. This is a good one. Tell her that Hitchcock stayed here with his wife——

Peter Who?

Major Bone Hitchcock.

Peter *Hickett.*

Major Bone Hickett—is that the name? Good Lor'! I've been calling her Mrs Hitchcock. The husband stayed here with the wife and you went on elsewhere.

Peter By Jove, Bone, that's fine! Shall we try? You be Barbara!

Major Bone It's rather difficult—but I'll have a shot at it.

Peter crosses, Bone U. L. *to* C.

Peter (D. R.) Bewildered and——

Major Bone Ill-used.

Peter I'm ready. (*Strikes attitude*)

Major Bone knocks

What's that——?

Major Bone That's in case she knocks. (*Coming down* R. C.)

Peter Barbara, darling!

Major Bone Peter! What is *this* I *hear*?

Peter It's nothing, darling. Surely you know me better than that! (*Places hands on Bone's shoulders*)

Major Bone Good! (*Places hands on Peter's shoulders as he says this and they bob together*) Then she'll say, 'You've been false to me.' (*Throwing Peter off*)

Peter What? (*Poses with arms outspread*)

Major Bone That's good—hold that! Now I'll be me. (*Crosses* L. C. *to* L. *corner of table, his left hand supporting him*) Oh! Believe me, Barbara, you are utterly wrong! (*His hand slips from table and he overbalances slightly*) Then you go on with the tale.

Peter And you go back to the bar.

Major Bone Thanks very much. (L. C. *front of table*) You see, the husband stayed here with the wife, and you pushed on and stayed elsewhere.

Peter (R. C. *front of table*) By Jove, Bone, that's fine! Then there's the Visitors' Book. Mr and Mrs Hickett not in my handwriting—all cut and dried.

Major Bone 'Course—it can't go wrong.

Peter Then I can rely on you?

Major Bone Absolutely.

Peter Thank you, Bone, thank you——

They shake hands

Major Bone Don't thank me, my boy. I hope one of these days you'll be able to do as much for me.

Peter crosses up to door R.

Peter, they're wonderful things, wives.

Peter Oh, wonderful! I'm delighted you've got yours!

Exit Peter R.

Major Bone He's a very good boy, with a very promising future. (D. L. *of table*)

Enter Mrs Spoker. Major Bone is just going back into bar, gets in her way, they try to pass each other, but both move the same way

I'm afraid you'll have to excuse me, I'm not very good at the Schottische.

Exit Bone into bar

Sloley-Jones enters at front door

Sloley-J. Good morning, Mrs Spoker.

Mrs Spoker sees him and speaks indignantly

Mrs Spoker We don't want you here. (*Crosses* D. L.) I am not yet open to the public.

Sloley-J. Righto! Righto! I'm only just giving myself an early morning test. (*Crosses above table* C. *and takes off gloves*)

Mrs Spoker Quite enough trouble without you. (*Crosses* L. *with back to audience*)

Sloley-J. Trouble?

Mrs Spoker (*at bar door*) Alfred!

Alfred enters from bar

Alfred Aye, Mrs Spoker?

Mrs Spoker Come you here. I am going to make the tea. When those two persons come down from dressing, make sure they don't go without they pay.

Alfred Aye, Mrs Spoker.

Exit Mrs Spoker down L.

Sloley-J. What two persons? (*Crosses* L. C.) Surely she doesn't mean the Hicketts?

Alfred Aye, there's trouble. In and out of his bed all night 'e were. 'E lost his dog, he lost his trousers, he grubbled up his room and he burst his jug.

Sloley-J Lost his dog? How did he come to lose his dog?

Gladys enters R.

Alfred It happened loike this—the dog were in the stables—and it were howling so much that he thought——

He sees Gladys as she crosses L., *and without another word he follows her fascinated out down* L. *with a broad grin*

At the same moment Noony enters cautiously at front door, carrying Pansy

Noony Here! Mister! (*Coming down* L. C.) Oh, good day to 'e, parson. (*Taking off hat*)

Sloley-J. (*up* L.) Hallo, by Christopher! You've found the dog! (*Putting gloves in his left-hand pocket*)

Noony Be this the one that belong to the lady?

Sloley-J. Yes! Splendid! Give it to me.

Noony No, sur. Finding be delivering. (*Inside* U. L.)

Sloley-J. Well, then, you'd better stay in here with it.

Noony Be Mrs Spoker in?

Sloley-J. Yes, of course.

Noony Then I reckon I'll bide in the road! (*He turns as if to go out* U. C.)

Hickett, a middle-aged man, wearing lounge suit and overcoat and cap in his hand, enters front door U. C., *running*

Hickett Ah, there you are, my man! Excuse me, what dog's that?

Noony I found her down along.

Hickett Where did you get that dog? Let me see it.

Noony She belong in here—she belong in here.

Hickett I want to see its collar.

Noony (*coming down a little*) She belong in here.

Hickett examines Pansy and her collar. Then looks up, quite convinced

Hickett Yes, of course, I knew it—I'd recognize that dog anywhere. How the devil did it come here?

Sloley-J. Excuse me, sir; I can tell you all about the dog.

Noony She belong to a lady.

Hickett I know quite well who it belongs to.

Sloley-J. He's quite right, quite. It belongs to a man and his wife who are staying here for the night on their way to Lady Bunter's at Rushcombe.

Noony attempts to go

Hickett Lady Bunter's is where I'm going myself. This is Mrs Hickett's dog.

Sloley-J. That's right. Mr and Mrs Hickett had a breakdown in their car and had to stay here.

Hickett Mr and Mrs Hickett?

Sloley-J. Yes. They're here now. I know all about it.

Hickett But Mrs Hickett went by train to Rushcombe yesterday afternoon.

Sloley-J. You'll excuse me, but Mrs Hickett is still upstairs with her husband. (*Crosses* D. L.)

Hickett (*after a moment's bewildered thought, turning on Noony*) Here, my man, here's half-a crown for you, now give me that dog. (*Taking Pansy*)

Noony I thank you, sir, you can have her—I thank you. (*Takes the coin and creeps out up* c., *crossing in front of Hickett*)

Hickett (*crossing down* L. c. *to Jones, in more practical tones*) You're under some delusion, sir. Whatever has happened to Mrs Hickett, I can tell you on very good authority that her husband spent last night in Bristol on his way from London.

Sloley-J. Indeed he didn't, if you'll pardon me. He spent last night getting in and out of bed after this dog, poor fellow. From all accounts he and Mrs Hickett had a very rough time!

Hickett But——

Sloley-J. I saw them here myself last night.

Hickett Oh, then *you know* Mr Hickett?

Sloley-J. Yes, I knew his wife before. She introduced me to him. He's Hickett the M.P., you know. I was agreeably surprised—a very decent fellow. I'd always been told that the man was a bit of an ass!

Hickett Indeed! (*With meaning*) I think I'll wait here and see. (*Crossing* R.)

Sloley-J. Righto! You might be very useful to them. (*He moves up as though to go*)

Hickett By the way, as you go, you might be kind enough to put the dog in my car.

Sloley-J. In your car?

Hickett Yes, I'll see that Mrs Hickett gets it. It's a two seater. (*Crosses* U. L.)

Sloley-J. (*taking Pansy*) With pleasure. (*To Pansy*) Come along then, naughty to run away from kind mistress! (*Going*) Oh dear, oh dear, it spat on my chin!

Exit

Hickett stands spellbound up stage

Mrs Spoker enters down L. *and comes and puts tablecloth on table. When she speaks she barely notices him*

Hickett Oh, excuse me, please——

Mrs Spoker I am completely occupied.

She goes out again down L.

Major Bone puts his head out from bar

Major Bone Barman!

Hickett Oh, excuse me, sir——

Major Bone I beg your pardon.

Hickett I'm just looking for a couple——

Major Bone Yes, so am I, but I can't find the barman.

Exit into bar

Enter Mrs Bone and Peter R. *Peter is now fully clad. Mrs Bone still holds the Visitors' Book. During the next few lines Peter takes much interest in the proceedings without suspecting in the least who Hickett is*

Peter comes down first—R.

Hickett Oh, are you the manageress? (*Crosses* R. C.)

Peter laughs and crosses to fireplace D. R.

Mrs Bone Manageress! (*Coming down* R. C.)

Hickett Oh, I beg your pardon. I thought that looked like the register.

Mrs Bone So it is. Why?

Hickett Ah! May I see it, please?

Mrs Bone Certainly not!

Hickett But I wish to see it.

Mrs Bone Who are you?

Hickett I have every right to see it, madam.

Peter (*taking book from Mrs Bone and giving it to Hickett*) Certainly.
Give the gentleman the book. (*Crossing* L., *takes ink bottle from
dresser* L., *puts it on table* C.) Where are the pens, the ink and the
blotting-paper? (*Bus.*)
Hickett (*after examining book keenly, takes stock of Peter*) Did you stay
at this hotel last night?
Peter Yes—in and out.
Hickett Is this your name?
Peter (*up to above table—looks at book*) Yes, why shouldn't it be?
Hickett Because it's mine!

Mrs Bone is obviously pleased

Peter Oh, then you'd better have it.
Hickett Quite by chance I recognized my wife's dog and stopped
here. Will you explain?
Mrs Bone I can do that.
Peter No, no, I'll see Marguerite.
Hickett Marguerite!
Peter My wife—your wife—our wife——
Hickett Who the devil are you?
Peter I don't know now. I used to be a nice little fellow. I've
gone off.
Mrs Bone He spent the night in her room. (*Crosses* C.)
Hickett Is this true?
Peter Well, yes, in a way. (*Crosses* D. L.)
Hickett What the devil d'you mean, sir? (*Crosses to Peter*) How can
you spend the night in a lady's room in a way.
Peter Oh, you can—believe me.
Hickett What excuse have you got?
Peter The landlady wouldn't take us in unless we were married.
So we were married.
Hickett Married?
Peter Well, you know what I mean. We *said* we were.
Hickett Why wouldn't the landlady take you in unmarried?
Peter Because she's a sort of Prussian Baptist.
Hickett That's not good enough. (*Crosses* R.)

Peter follows Hickett R. *Mrs Bone follows* C.

Now look here, sir. I've always had the best reasons to regard my
wife as a sweet and innocent woman.

Enter Bone from the bar

Major Bone (*blundering in from bar, coming down* L. C.) Then believe
me—you're utterly wrong!

Peter (*crosses* L. C.) Pull yourself together! This is something entirely different!

Major Bone (*staring at Hickett*) Good lord! Have I dropped a brick?

Peter No. You've pushed over the whole building.

Major Bone Oh, I'm frightfully sorry! (*Returns to bar*)

Peter (*crosses* R.) What he really means is—if you think your wife is capable of doing anything wrong——

Hickett Wrong? My wife? I should be sorry for the person who dared say so!

Mrs Bone (*staggered*) You'd be sorry?

Hickett My wife is the most innocent woman in England.

Mrs Bone But I tell you I caught them red-handed.

Peter Oh! That is a false-*hood*.

Hickett (*to Peter*) Where is my wife now?

Peter Getting up.

Hickett How do *you* know?

Peter She said, 'I'm going to get up.' (*Crosses* U. C.)

Hickett (*impatiently, crosses up* R. C.) Now look here, sir. I'm going to learn the truth about this.

This line takes Hickett over R. C. *and—Marguerite opens the door and confronts him with a cry of surprise*

Marguerite Claude, darling!

Hickett (*in fervent anxiety*) Marguerite!

Marguerite How on earth did you get here?

Hickett My angel! What has been happening to you!

Peter Marguerite! I'm so glad you've arrived—do take him away and explain.

Marguerite Yes, darling. Come with me, and I'll make it all clear to you.

Hickett But the *fact remains*—— (*With emphasis*)

Marguerite No, no, it doesn't, dear.

Peter No, no, it doesn't, dear. (*To Mrs Bone*)

Hickett Well, I'll hear what you have to say.

Marguerite Well, come with me.

Hickett goes up with Marguerite and out at porch

Mrs Bone (C., *to Peter*) You needn't think you've scored. I'll bring proof.

Gladys enters L. *with broom and dustpan. Alfred follows her*

(*Turns to Gladys, to her*) Where is the landlady?

Gladys (*crossing—in front of Peter*) Gone to get some milk.

Mrs Bone Where from?
Gladys From the cauw.

Exit Gladys R.

Mrs Bone (*to Alfred, who is going to bar*) Here, you! Where is the cow?
Alfred Being milked.
Mrs Bone But *where's* the cow being milked?
Alfred (*at bar door*) Well, you knows where to milk a cow, don't 'ee?

Exit Alfred into bar

Peter R. C. *Mrs Bone looks round*

Marguerite and Hickett appear at porch

Mrs Bone (*going* L.) I'll find her. (*Glancing back at Marguerite*) His angel! Hoo!

Peter crosses up L. *round table, meets Marguerite*

Exit Mrs Bone down L.

Hickett Now look here, sir, don't interrupt.
Peter (R. C.) I'm delighted, Mr Hickett, to say you're an ideal husband.

Bone enters from bar

Marguerite It's easy to be an ideal husband to a wife like me!
Peter Is it? I didn't find it at all easy.
Hickett What's that? (*Crosses* R. C. *to Peter*)
Peter I didn't mean that. (*Falling back on Bone for support*)
Major Bone (L. C.) All right, I'm here. Leave this to me, my boy. I know what I'm going to say.
Peter Well, don't say it! (*He whispers to Bone*) This is Hickett!
Major Bone Oh, is this the husband?
Hickett Yes, it *is* the husband!
Major Bone Oh, that's very awkward.
Hickett (*to Marguerite*) As regards you, I'm prompted to believe what you tell me——

    Marguerite   Hickett   Peter   Bone

Marguerite Well, you always have so far.
Hickett Yes. (*Crosses to Peter* L. C., *pulls him round*) It's you.
Peter Who, me?
Hickett Now look here, sir, I want to trust my wife. I've always thought her above suspicion. That's been my greatest pride and joy.

Peter Many happy returns of the day!

Hickett (*to Peter with contempt*) But you tell me you couldn't sleep anywhere else.

Peter I tell you I couldn't sleep anywhere at all!

Hickett Oh, rot! That's past belief. I won't put up with it.

Peter Put up with it! I wish you'd had to put up with it. If that's the sort of night you spend with your wife, you ought to be grateful to me.

Hickett Grateful to you?

Peter Yes, for spending one for you.

Hickett Now look here! (*He shakes his fist in Peter's face*)

Major Bone gets between Peter and Hickett. Bone turns to Peter, who is holding up his right hand

Major Bone Put it down, put it down! Come, come, none of that! No fighting here. You listen to me for a moment. I am a man of the world, and I happen to be the father of this man's wife's daughter.

General movement. Marguerite and Hickett go up stage R., *and come down again. Peter crosses to dresser and rattles cups, then comes over to Bone, kneels on table and whispers in his ear*

Hickett (*to Peter*) Is this your father-in-law?

Peter I'm afraid it is.

Hickett Then you have a wife?

Peter Yes. I've got a little wife.

Marguerite She'll be here soon, perhaps she'll believe what you say.

Peter Yes. I shall say what she believes. And get her away quickly.

Hickett (*to Peter*) Oh, so I'm to sit and endorse lies? (*Crosses* L. C. *turning away angrily*)

Marguerite (*crosses to Hickett, to him*) Claude! Listen!

Hickett Quiet, please!

Marguerite But listen. His wife's mother still accuses me. He and I are still in the same bed——

Peter and Hickett look at Marguerite

Peter What?

Marguerite —boat.

Peter Yes, and if her mother gets hold of my wife first the boat will sink.

Major Bone Hear, hear!

Peter Quiet!

Hickett But you haven't finished with *me* yet. *I've* got to decide too.

Marguerite Let me do that for you, as usual.

Hickett Oh, leave me alone. I want to think. (*Goes up* L. *to* C.)

Peter Yes, let him think.

Marguerite But he thinks the worst.

Hickett (*quickly*) No, I haven't said that.

Marguerite Then what *do* you think? (*Crosses to Hickett*)

Peter He's trying to think what to think.

Hickett I know what I think of *you*.

He walks off, annoyed

Marguerite is following, Peter stops her, brings her down L. C.

Marguerite I want to speak to Claude.

Peter Let him get some fresh air. We've got Barbara fixed. (*To Bone*) Haven't we, Bone?

Major Bone Well, we *had* before he turned up.

Marguerite makes movement towards door, but Peter holds her back

Peter When Barbara comes she's sure to say—'What is this I hear?' and I'll say, 'It's nothing, darling. Surely you know me better than that!' Then Bone will breeze in from the bar——

Major Bone Thanks very much.

Peter And say, 'Believe me, Barbara, you're utterly wrong.'

Marguerite And so you think that is going to 'fix' Barbara?

Peter No. Then I shall explain.

Marguerite What are you going to say?

Peter Never mind that now. So long as you back me up when the time comes.

Car heard off

Major Bone Listen! (*Crosses up* R. C.) I think the time's come. Don't you hear?

Marguerite What?

Major Bone It sounds like Carbara in a bar. Barbara in a car. (*Crosses up stage and looks out of door* C.) Yes, it is!

Peter Go on, Bone old boy—you go back in the bar.

Major Bone Now don't forget. (*Up stage* L.) She'll say, 'Peter, what is this I hear?'—and you say——

Marguerite 'It's nothing, darling. Surely you know me better than that.'

Major Bone Good. 'Believe me, Barbara, you're utterly wrong——' Yes.

Bone goes into bar

Peter (*crosses* D. R.) One moment—my attitude—— (*Poses*) Bewildered and ill-used.

Marguerite No, no. Nonchalant.

Peter Oh, nonchalong? (*Poses—mutters*) 'What is this I hear?' 'It's nothing, darling. Surely you know me better than that!'

Enter Barbara C.

Barbara, darling!

Barbara Peter, what is this——?

Peter Well——? Go on—what is this you what?

Barbara Well, what is this I—find?

Peter (*muddled*) You don't hear anything? It's nothing, darling. Surely you don't know me as well as all that.

Marguerite L. *of table*

Barbara Peter! What's happened?

Peter Nothing, darling. Do I look as if anything has happened?

Barbara Think of what's happened to me!

Peter Yes, I know. All my carelessness—and Mrs Hickett's—Mrs Hickett, my wife.

Marguerite rises

Barbara Oh, indeed! (*Crosses* L. C.)

Marguerite Don't be alarmed. We're only so pleased you've come.

Peter Yes. Lucky I was back in time to meet you.

Barbara Back? Haven't you stayed here, then?

Peter No thanks, no fear. No, I'll tell you. Mrs Hickett and I met on the platform. She was going to the Bunters' too.

Marguerite (*crosses* L. C.) We talked, you see, and missed the train.

Peter (*to Marguerite aside*) Yes, all right, I'll tell you when I want you to recite. (*To Barbara*) So we took a car after you, the car exploded and we came here.

Barbara Yes, I heard that.

Peter Oh, you heard that—well now hear this: and we hadn't been here long when in came Mr Hickett. (*To Marguerite*) Didn't he?

Marguerite Certainly.

Peter He certainly did. He was going to the Bunters too.

Marguerite Yes, he heard about us——

Peter —and came in his two-seater. So he stayed here with Mrs Hickett, and I pushed on where—else—elsewhere.

Barbara To the Bunters'?

Peter No. To the next town.

Barbara Why didn't you stay here?

Marguerite There are only two rooms here.

Peter Yes. The Hicketts had Number Two—very nice room, I believe.

Barbara I see. But why didn't you stay in Number One?

Marguerite There's an old lady in bed there.

Barbara (*with a smile*) Oh!

Peter Yes, and she wanted to be alone—so I went on. Rang up the Bunters. Heard you weren't there, and came back here this morning.

Barbara Oh, Peter! Then I need never have had any doubt or anxiety. (*Embracing him*)

Bone enters from bar

Bone (*crosses* D. L.) Oh, believe me, Barbara; you're utterly wrong!

Peter (*crossing to him*) Well meant, but a bad spot.

Major Bone (*subsiding*) What? Have I done it again?

Barbara Father! Are you here?

Major Bone Yes. I think so. Yes, I'm here.

Barbara Is mother here?

Major Bone } (*together*) { No!
Peter   }   { Yes!

Then correcting themselves

Major Bone } (*together*) { Yes!
Peter   }   { No!

Barbara Peter, where is mother?

Peter Mother! (*To Bone*) You know mother, don't you? Mother's gone to see a little cow.

Barbara A little cow? Why?

Marguerite Oh yes, the most famous little cow. The champion cow of Somerset.

Peter A long distance cow.

Barbara Yes, tell me. (*Moves* L. *to Peter*) How did you get to the next town last night?

Peter What?

Marguerite He borrowed my husband's two-seater. (*Sits down* R. *of table*)

Major Bone Good, good! (*Moves up* L. *to* C., *behind table*)

Peter Yes, splendid little car. It's out there now, with tyres all round it.

Barbara I wish I'd known all this before. What was the name of this town?

Peter Which town?

Barbara The town you stayed at.

Peter What?

Marguerite Witchtown, wasn't it?

Peter Yes, I was just telling my wife, Mrs Hickett. Witchtown, darling. They used to burn witches there, you know.

Barbara Did you stay at an hotel?

Peter Yes—I stayed at the—local—hotel.

Barbara What was it called?

Peter No, no, you mean what name was it? It gives me more time to think. The—er—what? Hotel? An old English name. The —er—Cow and Litter.

Barbara The Cow and Litter! (*Laughs in ridicule*)

Bone looks up, anticipating trouble

Peter Yes. (*Laughs*)

Barbara Nonsense. Cows don't have litters!

Peter laughs

Major Bone Of course they don't. It's only a name. If it comes to that pigs don't have whistles!

Peter Anyhow, Barbara—you see everything's all right——

Hickett appears at back c.

Barbara Of course, I never wanted to doubt you, Peter, darling— only it was all so queer. And when I saw you from the train with Mrs Hickett——

Marguerite (*crosses* R. *to Barbara*) Well, now you have seen me again I hope you realize there was nothing the matter.

Bone moves R. *of table*

Barbara Yes, of course. Now that I know you stayed here with Mr Hickett.

Peter Yes. Hickett was here all right.

Bone R. C. *sees Hickett and makes violent gestures at Peter. Peter sees Bone, so does Barbara*

What's up?

Barbara What's the matter? Mr Hickett did stay here, didn't he?

Peter Yes, yes.

Marguerite Well, there is the book. You can see.

Barbara No, I don't want to see the book.

Peter Oh, yes, you'd better see the book. Yes, you'd better see the book. (*Seeing Bone again, looks round and sees Hickett. Gets confused and tries to change his plan of showing Barbara the book*) No, you'd better *not* see the book.

Hickett crosses D. L.

(*To Bone*) Nice fellow, Hickett, isn't he? You like him?

Major Bone Very.

Peter You like him very. What about three half-hearted cheers for him?

Peter
Major Bone } (*together, weakly*) Hooray, hooray, hooray!

Barbara All right, Peter, it's quite clear. He stayed here with you, and I quite believe it.

Hickett (*coming down* L.) Then believe me, you're utterly wrong.

Major Bone Well meant, sir, but a bad spot. Do you mind not butting in?

Marguerite (*seeing Hickett*) Claude! You are being stupid and interfering!

Barbara Who are you, please?

Hickett. I'm Mr Hickett. Are you this man's wife?

Barbara Yes, of course I am.

Hickett I don't ask you to mistrust him. I don't mistrust my wife. But I think you'd better hear the truth.

Barbara Oh! (*Tiny pause. Turning to Peter*) Then you haven't been telling me the truth?

Peter The truth, what's that? I thought you would like to hear something else.

Barbara Peter! You've been lying to me!

Peter Well, let me try again. I want to tell you the tale of the old copper pot.

Marguerite I hope you don't think *I've* done anything wrong.

Bone makes his way behind table to L. C.

Barbara The best thing I can do is to see mother.

Peter But Mrs Hickett will tell you herself——

Marguerite Of course I will.

Barbara I'd rather see mother.

Bone has moved U. L. C.

Peter You'd rather see mother than Mrs Hickett? You must be feverish.

Barbara goes U. L. C. *beside Bone*

Mrs Bone (*off*) George!

Mrs Bone enters R.

George!

Barbara comes down L. C.

Barbara—here you are! I should have been here to meet you. But, George—— (*To Bone*) I've been chased by a bull! (*Falls on Bone's shoulder*)

Hickett crosses behind Barbara and goes over R. *of Marguerite*

Peter (*takes Barbara's arm*) I told you she'd been to see a cow and the bull didn't like it.
Mrs Bone I suppose he's been trying to deceive you.
Barbara (*crosses* L.) Mother, did Peter stay here last night?
Mrs Bone Yes, he did. I came down with your father and found him in the same room as this woman.
Peter (*to Marguerite*) I wish that bull had caught her.
Mrs Bone It's no use disguising. He's been false to you.
Marguerite (*indignantly. Crosses to Higgett* C.) Now, do you think that can be true of *me*?
Hickett No. That I will not believe. (*Crosses up* R.)

Peter crosses R.

Marguerite turns up to Hickett again. He remains half-hearted and uncertain

Mrs Bone George, call that chauffeur!
Major Bone (*through bar door*) Hi! you. Finish that up and come out of there! (*Crosses* L.)
Mrs Bone (*to Barbara*) Come after us in *your* car to Bristol.

Enter Chauffeur from bar, staggering. Major Bone steadies him, gives him a gentle push, and he goes out through porch

Peter (*crosses* D. L. *to Barbara*) Barbara, what are you going to do?
Barbara (*crosses* D. L.) I'm going back to Bristol, after mother.
Mrs Bone Yes. Immediately. (*Crosses up towards* C. *To Bone*) George are you coming?
Major Bone Is it optional?
Mrs Bone No! Where's your hat?
Major Bone Here it is. (*Hat in bar. To Mrs Bone*) You go ahead and get in the car.
Mrs Bone Yes. I've something to say to you when we get in the car.
Major Bone Oh, then I'll ride on the top.

Exit Mrs Bone through porch, followed by Bone

Peter (*as Barbara turns to follow*) Barbara! Darling, listen to me!

Hickett, who has been standing R. *with Marguerite, who has given up trying to talk to him, now comes across and stops Barbara*

Barbara No!
Hickett One moment!

Marguerite moves L.

Gladys comes D. R. C. *with dustpan*

Marguerite There's Gladys. Ask her.
Hickett Did you see this lady and gentleman upstairs last night?
Gladys Yes, sur. I went into the room with Mrs Spoker. She was in a rare temper with 'em.
Hickett Why was she?
Gladys (*snorts*) The lady were in bed. But Mrs Spoker she couldn't get the gentleman to undress and go to bed too.
Marguerite There you are!
Peter Absolutely!
Marguerite Just what I told you!
Gladys He kept pottering about and wouldn't settle.
Peter That's right, Gladys. (*Crossing to her* R., *he shows her across* L.) What are you doing on Thursday?

Exit Gladys

Car noises—hoots and back-fires

Major and Mrs Bone cross back of stage in taxi

Hickett (*crosses* L.) What is that?
Peter It's the Bones rattling!
Hickett (*crossing* R. *to Marguerite*) I knew I could trust you.
Marguerite Wait a moment, I want to hear what Mrs Wykeham has got to say.
Barbara (*crosses* C.) All I've got to say is that you missed the train on purpose, you brought her here, you stayed in her room, and you told lies—no, I'm going after mother.
Hickett I'm quite satisfied.
Barbara Then you are easily satisfied. (*To Peter*) It's a preposterous story. (*Turns* U. C.)
Peter Barbara, listen, please.
Marguerite (*crossing* R.) Oh, let her go. What does it matter? The whole world will soon know now.
Hickett Marguerite——
Marguerite Oh, Claude, I may have to hurt you—but I can't help it. (*Going to Peter* L.)

Hickett R.

But when you love a man as I love Peter, what does anything matter?

Barbara comes down R. C.

I love you, Peter, and now that we missed that train and have
taken the plunge, we will go out into the great world together
and not worry what it thinks. Yes, yes, take me to Paris, Monte
Carlo, Nice, up the Nile and down the Zambesi!

Barbara comes down slowly

Peter Yes, we'll go to Hurst Part, Sandown and Goodwood.
Marguerite Together, mine, mine! (*Embraces Peter*)
Peter Yes, darling, let us go.
Barbara (*crossing* L. *to Marguerite*) Leave my husband alone!
Peter No! (*Embracing Marguerite*)
Barbara Oh! Peter! (*Sits on chair* L., *crying*)
Peter I can't keep it up, Barbara, darling. (*Crosses to her*)
Marguerite Don't worry, Claude, you haven't lost me yet. (*Crossing*
R.)

Enter Mrs Spoker

Hickett I never doubted you.
Peter I never doubted you. I was only teasing.
Marguerite Sweetheart!
Peter Darling!
Mrs Spoker What is this I hear?
Peter (*to Mrs Spoker, unconsciously*) It's nothing—darling——
(*Looks into Mrs Spoker's face*) Oh! (*Then kneels at Barbara's side*)

		Mrs Spoker
Hickett	Marguerite	Barbara
		Peter

CURTAIN

ROOKERY NOOK

A Farce in Three Acts

CHARACTERS

This play was produced on June 30th, 1926, at the Aldwych Theatre, London, with the following cast:

Gertrude Twine	Miss Ethel Coleridge
Mrs Leverett	Miss Mary Brough
Harold Twine	Mr J. Robertson Hare
Clive Popkiss	Mr Tom Walls
Gerald Popkiss	Mr Ralph Lynn
Rhoda Marley	Miss Winifred Shotter
Putz	Mr Griffith Humphreys
Admiral Juddy	Mr Gordon James
Poppy Dickey	Miss Ena Mason
Clara Popkiss	Miss Stella Bonheur
Mrs Possett	Miss Vera Gerald

The Action takes place in the lounge-hall of 'Rookery Nook', Chumpton-on-Sea, Somerset. It begins on a night in Summer

ACT I

The lounge-hall of 'Rookery Nook' is in darkness as it is late on a summer night. There is a trace of daylight left, and as the front door stands open facing the audience R. C. *of the back wall, the shrubbery across the drive can be faintly seen. As the Act progresses the moon rises. From the hall the staircase runs up* L. *and the balcony for landing in each case is seen. On this balcony is a door* L. *(and, if the balance and appearance of the set requires a second opening, that which leads to the back stairs which are not shown). The balcony runs off the set* R. *and* L. *On the* R. *there are two doors which lead to other bedrooms. On the ground floor are two doors on each side of the hall. These, as explained later, lead* R. *to drawing-room and study,* L. *to kitchen quarters and dining-room. The electric light switches operating the hall lights are just inside the door,* D. L. *The hall is well furnished with a very fine hall table slightly* R. *of* C., *a Chesterfield sofa and hall chairs. A parquet floor with rugs: in the back wall are large windows*

Gertrude Twine discovered C. *above table*

Gertrude Mrs Leverett! (*Raps on table*) Mrs Leverett! (*No answer. She is a woman in the thirties, a critical, suspicious type of seaside resident. She is in semi-evening dress with a wrap. Calls again*) Mrs Leverett!

Mrs Leverett (*heard off*) Oh, is that Mrs Twine? Very good; I'll come.

Gertrude C. *Mrs Leverett enters from down left. She is a stout person wearing a striking tartan blouse, tweed skirt and no hat; leaves door open through which a strong light shows*

Gertrude Hasn't he arrived? (*Moves to Mrs Leverett*)

Mrs Leverett (*querulously*) No, he has not, Mrs Twine, and look at the time. I may say I was engaged by the day and not by the night.

Gertrude (*freezingly*) All right, all right. 'Has he arrived?—*No.*' That's all I wanted. *No.*

Mrs Leverett (*getting rattled*) I suppose there is no question he *is* coming to-night?

Gertrude Of course he is. That's why you're waiting here.

Mrs Leverett Yes, but I should never have consented to wait had I known he was going to keep me here at improper hours. (*Cross* L., *switch on lights*)

Gertrude You must make allowances. In the ordinary way the whole party would have been here by this time.

Mrs Leverett H'm. I prefer to work for parties of regular habits.

Waves imaginary cat away into kitchen and closes door

This fires Gertrude. A breeze springs up

Gertrude My sister is a most considerate person. Was it *her* fault that my mother was taken ill at the last moment? (*Crosses* L. *of table to front*)

Mrs Leverett I'm not saying—(*crosses to Gertrude* L. C.)

Gertrude And couldn't be brought here?

Mrs Leverett I know, madam, but—I can't worry about their troubles.

Gertrude Don't talk like that of your betters, please.

Mrs Leverett I'm not talking like that of my betters.

Gertrude Yes, you are. (*Slight pause as they glare at each other*) My sister did the only possible thing—stayed and looked after my mother. (*Crosses to front of table*)

Mrs Leverett Madam! I am not making any complaint about your sister. But her husband was coming here alone——

Gertrude It isn't 'he *was* coming'. He *is* coming.

Mrs Leverett When?

Gertrude I only know he's coming to-night. (*This as if trying to drum home a thing for the twentieth time*)

Mrs Leverett Yes, but *when* to-night?

Gertrude Oh, how can I tell? (*Breaking off with a little 't'ck' of annoyance, cross* R. *in front of table*) When a man gets left alone with a car, there's always trouble. If the car doesn't go wrong, the man does.

Mrs Leverett (*much more patiently*) Well, excuse me (*cross* D. L. *and come back*), but can't you wait here for him, madam? Or can't Mr Twine?

Twine (*appearing at front door*) Yes. Hallo! What's that?

Twine is a short, feeble man of about forty in a dinner suit and straw hat

Gertrude Oh, there you are, Harold.

Twine (*coming down*) Yes, dear.

Gertrude Gerald hasn't arrived.

Twine No, dear.

Gertrude How did you know?

Twine I didn't, dear.

Gertrude Then why say 'no' like that?

Twine Like what, dear?

Gertrude Is Clive there?
Twine Yes, dear.
Gertrude Call him in.
Twine Yes, dear. (*Crosses to door—at door* R. C. *calling*) Clave! Clave!
Gertrude Where is he?
Twine (*calling*) Clave! Clave!
Gertrude Clive!
Twine Clave!
Clive (*appearing at front door*) All right; don't make an anthem of it.

Clive is a sport in the thirties. He wears a dinner suit

Twine crosses L. *to Mrs Leverett, and she tells him her troubles as Clive comes down* R. C. *to Gertrude*

Gertrude Come in. Come in.
Clive Oh, so this is the house you've got for them, is it? What a nice house! Nice, peaceful atmosphere for a change.
Gertrude What do you mean—for a change?
Clive For them. For Gerald and Clara. They're coming here, aren't they?
Gertrude I don't see why you should say they want a peaceful atmosphere for a *change*. They've only been married six weeks.
Clive I don't mean that.

<table>
<tr><td></td><td>*Gertrude*</td><td></td></tr>
<tr><td>*Clive*</td><td>C.</td><td>*Twine*</td></tr>
<tr><td>R. C.</td><td></td><td>L. C.</td></tr>
<tr><td></td><td></td><td>*Mrs Leverett*</td></tr>
<tr><td></td><td></td><td>L.</td></tr>
</table>

Gertrude Well, what *do* you mean?
Clive (*long-suffering, stifling his impatience*) They're on a holiday, aren't they?
Gertrude Well?
Clive Just like I'm on a holiday—(*cross to Gertrude*)—staying with *you*.
Gertrude Well?
Clive Yes—well, I say—what a nice house they're coming to. Lucky people.
Gertrude (*a little jealous*) Haven't you come to a nice house? Isn't mine nice?
Clive (*getting past his patience*) Oh, very. There can be two nice houses, can't there?
Gertrude (*who shines at female argument*) You don't suppose I'd have got them a house that *wasn't* nice (*turning away* L.), do you?
Clive (*turning, cross* D. R. *desperately, speaking to himself*) Oh, hell!

Twine crosses to Gertrude

Twine Dearest!

Gertrude What do *you* want?

Clive watches them, listening

Twine It isn't I that want anything.

Gertrude Well, who is it that wants what?

Twine (*apologetically*) Mrs—er—em——

Gertrude Yes. I know what she wants. She wants to go home.

Mrs Leverett Quite right.

Clive moves towards c.

Twine She was asking me what time I thought Gerald would arrive.

Gertrude (*very annoyed*) Well, gracious me, how can I tell? I've been asked that twenty times. Don't ask me again.

Twine (*very subdued*) He only had to come on from your mother's at Bath. Bath isn't far—a matter of two hours. He ought to have started——

Gertrude Started! He ought to have been here hours ago.

Twine goes up L.

Mrs Leverett Well, something's got to be done about it.

Clive (*sauntering back to Gertrude* c. *with malice aforethought*) I say, Gertrude——

(*Table*)			
		Twine	
Clive	*Gertrude*	L. C.	(*Settee*)
R. C.	C.		
		Mrs Leverett	
		L.	

(*Airily, crosses to Gertrude*) About what time do you suppose old Gerald will breeze along?

Gertrude Clive, you're trying to annoy me.

Clive (*with injured innocence*) Annoy you, Gertrude? I like that. I wouldn't do such a thing. I was going to suggest something.

Gertrude I shouldn't think *that* would be likely to help.

Clive Oh, all right. I was only going to suggest a suggestion. (*He crosses* L. C. *to Mrs Leverett*) P'r'aps *you* might like to hear it. It's really a good one.

Mrs Leverett I have no time to listen, sir. I must be *off*.

Clive Oh, don't be that.

Mrs Leverett If you knew in what a hurry I was to get home, sir, you'd offer to wait here yourself for the coming gentleman.

Clive You must be psychic.

Mrs Leverett (*obviously shocked*) I *beg* your pardon–I'm nothing of the kind.

Clive We've got the same idea. (*Turning to Gertrude*) There you are. We've fixed it. I'll stay here till Gerald comes, and Mrs Flannelfoot will waddle off home.

Gertrude (*considering this*) Oh—I see.

Mrs Leverett (*briskly*) If the gentleman is willing, that settles it. I'll get me hat. (*Goes off* D. L.)

Twine comes down L. C.

Gertrude Oh, well, if you're going to be left here alone, I hope you're to be trusted. You'll be responsible for the house, not only to Gerald, but also to the Mantle Hams.

Clive (*cross to Gertrude*) To the who?

Gertrude The Mantle Hams. The people this house belongs to.

Clive Oh, the Mantle Hams. That's a good one. But I fail to see what trouble I can get into here alone for a few minutes. (*Sits on table* C.) If you can think of any, I wish you'd let me know.

Gertrude (*decisively*) Someone's got to hang about here, so I suppose you'd better.

Clive Righto then. I'm very good at hanging about.

Twine (*tentatively*) Erm——

Clive (*looking at Twine curiously*) Yes?

Twine (*looking at Gertrude*) Erm——

Gertrude (*who has turned towards door, looking round again*) Well, what's the matter?

Clive Shh! Don't discourage him. I think Harold is going to lay an egg.

Gertrude Clive, don't be coarse.

Twine No, I only thought——

Gertrude You thought what?

Twine Wouldn't it be as well for me to stay as well?

Gertrude What?

Clive Now, old sportsman, sort yourself. (*Patting him gently*)

Twine (*precisely*) Shall I stay too?

Clive No.

Gertrude No.

Clive Carried.

Gertrude Why do you want to stay?

Twine I don't, dear.

Gertrude Then why say you did?

Twine I didn't mean I did. I meant if you'd rather I did, should I?

Clive The answer is a sponge cake.

Gertrude Oh, come home. (*Cross* U. R.)
Twine Yes, dear.

Clive trips him playfully as he crosses

   (*Apologizes*) I'm sorry.

Clive Oh, it's all right.

Gertrude turns back; Twine is following close on her heels: he drops down R.
and starts to nibble his straw hat

Gertrude (*to Clive*) Let me know directly Gerald arrives. I've got
   several things to see to at home, or I'd wait myself. Tell him I
   may be able to come over and see him later.
Clive That'll amuse him.
Gertrude What?
Clive Oh, nothing.
Gertrude (*is going*) Harold! Don't stand there nibbling your straw
   hat. I'm always telling you about that. Put it on your head.
Twine Yes, dear. (D. R.)

   The Twines depart up R.

Clive And those whom the gods love die young.

*He gives an elaborate gesture of pent-up fury. Then he turns and crosses to
the door* D. L., *which he opens*

   I say, you haven't gone——?

The noise of a cat is heard. He steps back quickly

   Oh, sorry.

*He steps out again into the hall. Mrs Leverett, now wearing a hat,
follows him*

Mrs Leverett Was that you, sir?
Clive Yes.

Mrs Leverett shoos cat away, and shuts door D. L.

   I'm afraid I trod on the cat. (*Cross* L. C.)
Mrs Leverett Then kindly do not do so.
Clive Ah, too late. I've done it now. (*Up* L. C.)
Mrs Leverett You know this gentleman, I take it?
Clive Who? Mr Popkiss? (*Behind table* C.)
Mrs Leverett Yes. The one that's expected.
Clive Oh, rather. He's my cousin. My name's Popkiss, too.
Mrs Leverett Oh, I see. Then you're also related to Mrs Twine?

Clive No, that I'm not. He's my cousin and he married Mrs Twine's sister; that's all.

Mrs Leverett Oh, is that all?

Clive Yes, quite enough. And Mrs Twine (*cross back of table to* R. *and looks at knick-knacks on the desk*) very, very kindly invited me to stay down here. And knowing my cousin was coming here, I like a fool fell for it.

Mrs Leverett (*cross* R. *to Clive*) Oh! Yes, I know Mrs Twine's house well enough—Frascati. A very nice house.

Clive Personally, I'd much rather be in this one (*Cross* D. R.)

Mrs Leverett (*betrayed from her hurry into the love of gossip, cross* R.) Yes? Well, this house—Rookery Nook—now, I reckon it's in the wrong part of Chumpton.

Clive Not for me.

Mrs Leverett I mean, this here Lighthouse Road don't lead anywhere.

Clive No, I've noticed that. (*Cross in front of table* C., *sits*) Not even to the lighthouse. But *all* this place is exceedingly quiet. There's nothing doing—you know what I mean—no amusement—no fun.

Mrs Leverett (*cross to table*) No. I'm glad to say Chumpton is a very respectable place—for the *most* part.

Clive In which direction lies the *least* part?

Mrs Leverett Though I suppose every place has its black mark. (*Cross to* L. *of table*) Well, I must really be getting home, sir.

Clive I say, where is the black mark here?

Mrs Leverett (*again lured into gossip, crosses to Clive, returning in a more confidential manner*) Well, sir, just what I was saying about this particular part of the place—one of these houses nearby here, for instance, has a most improper reputation.

Clive No?

Mrs Leverett Yes.

Clive (*with interest*) Really! Oh, go on. Where and what?

Mrs Leverett Meself I wonder Chumpton puts up with it. A foreigner living here, with a step-daughter. So-called. Huh!

Clive Oh? And—isn't she really his step-daughter?

Mrs Leverett (*decidedly*) No, sir.

Warning for car

Clive How do you know?

Mrs Leverett Well, Mrs Twine knows most things.

Clive You're quite right, she does.

Mrs Leverett And her cook told me that the story of the step-daughter was all sheer hullaballoo.

Clive Is that so?

Mrs Leverett Yes. Well, the very name of the house is enough. Malmaison Cottage. And you, sir, being a scholar, will know that that is French, and *means* 'a bad house'.

Clive I see, a sort of advertisement on the gate.

Mrs Leverett Yes. And now, sir, reely, I must hurry away. (*Cross* L.)

Clive What, again? All right. Off you trot.

Mrs Leverett (*cross* L. C.) Mind you, I don't actually know these persons. At least, I know them both by sight very well, but that's all. And that's enough, seeing he's a foreigner and she as good English as what I am.

Clive Yes. But she might still be his *step*-daughter.

Mrs Leverett Why, sir?

Clive Her being English wouldn't stop her being his step-daughter.

Mrs Leverett Oh! Then all I can say is it's a very slippery step. Now, sir, if you please. I cannot remain and let you talk to me any longer.

Clive Quite right. We must be careful, or Mrs Twine will be saying things about *us*. (*Pushes Mrs Leverett playfully*—L.—*goes up towards door* R. *At front door looking off* L. *hears a motor-horn and sees reflection of car lights through window, with sudden exclamation*) Hallo! Wait a minute; here is my cousin.

Mrs Leverett (*pausing*) At last.

Clive I'll go and help him.

Gerald is seen driving the car past the windows from L. *to* R.

Mrs Leverett (*cross* R., *going to door*) The garridge doors is open. (*Cross to* L. C.)

The car is heard to stop

Mrs Leverett comes C. *and stands facing door*

Gerald enters, a young, smiling, and cheerful man, in travelling outfit, and carrying a handbag and light overcoat. He wears a cap

Gerald (*taking his cap off*) Rookery Nook?

Mrs Leverett (*snappily*) Yes.

Gerald (*putting down bag*) Good. I'm coming here.

Mrs Leverett You've bin coming for some time.

Gerald A month. I was told I should be met by a daily woman. Are you it—the daily woman?

Mrs Leverett (*with a sniff*) H'm. I'm not so sure that I *am* now.

Gerald Well, perhaps you could find out. (*Puts bag on table*)

Mrs Leverett I am a working wife and mother, and there at home waiting for me is my five children and cetera, not to mention my husband and what not.

Gerald Oh, you've got five children and a what-not—I wonder you can find time to be a daily.

Mrs Leverett 'Owever, now you have come, I may as well show you the house and quit.

Gerald Where's the quit?

Mrs Leverett Quit. Go. I'll go.

Gerald Oh, go. You'll go. Good! Yes, thanks very much. I see. Quit—I thought you meant the quit was some sort of—well, I mean, quit—it might be anything.

Mrs Leverett Well, this is the main 'all.

Gerald Oh, that is the main hall, is it?

Mrs Leverett (*cross up* L.) This is the dining-room. (*Indicating off up* L.) I suppose you've had all the food you need to-night.

Gerald Yes, I had something on the way.

Mrs Leverett Yes, I should think you *did*. (*Indicating off* L.) The dining-room.

Gerald (*looking in*) Oh, a nice square room; thanks very much.

Clive enters R. C.

Clive I say, Gerald, you didn't leave me out there with the idea that I was going to wash the car and put it away for you, did you?

Gerald No. Have you unstrapped the trunks?

Clive Yes, I've done that.

Mrs Leverett crosses to study do⌐r D. R., *which she opens. Throughout this scene she hustles Gerald unwillingly from room to room*

Mrs Leverett The study! (*Impatiently*)

Clive crosses to back of table

Gerald (*turning to study*) The study? That's very nice. (*To Clive*) We might go and sit in there——

Mrs Leverett (*closing study door*) I can't sit anywhere.

Gerald Why, what have you done to yourself?

Mrs Leverett (*looking fiercely at Gerald and crossing up* R., *opening drawing-room door and immediately closing it again*) Mrs Mantle Ham's drawing-room.

Clive crosses to R. *front of table*

Gerald Oh! (*She closes door*) Very nice outside.

Mrs Leverett (*cross* L. *in front of settee, followed by Gerald; opens kitchen door* D. L.) The kitchen and so on. Those are my quarters. You don't want to see them, do you?

Gerald (*to Clive*) I don't think we want to see her quarters, do we?
No, we won't.

Mrs Leverett (*pointing up* R.) The stairs.

Gerald Oh, impossible!

Mrs Leverett The door there is the main bedroom. The bed is
made. The bathroom is next door. The other bedrooms is elsewhere.

Gerald (*to Clive*) I wonder who thought of that.

Mrs Leverett (*crosses to kitchen*) I must get back now hurried.
(*Crosses to Gerald*) Oh, here is the front-door key. I have the back.
I will come at eight-thirty in the morning. Earlier than that I
cannot be. And good night to you. (*Turns towards kitchen door*)

Gerald Yes; but, I say, hold on one moment.

Mrs Leverett What, sir? Quickly, please.

Gerald There were just one or two things I wanted to ask you.

Mrs Leverett What was it you wanted to know, please?

Gerald It's all right. Only I thought there were to be some other
girls here besides you. You know—maids.

Mrs Leverett Ah! (*Cross to Gerald*) But not yet, sir. Mrs Twine put
them off directly she heard you were coming alone.

Gerald Why? (*Mrs Leverett gives an elaborate shrug*) Oh, I see. (*To
Clive*) You hear that?

Mrs Leverett Good night then. And eight-thirty in the morning.
(*Cross* L. *at kitchen door*) Oh, and there is also a cat. It lives in the
kitchen. (*Coming back* L. C.)

Gerald It had better.

Mrs Leverett Kindly mind out for it. It's been trod on once to-
night already (*looks at Clive freezingly*) even in there.

She goes off D. L., *closing door*

Gerald Well, here we are. It was very nice of you to be over here to
meet me, old boy.

Clive You needn't flatter yourself. I only stayed over here away
from those blasted Twines.

Gerald (*laughs*) Yes, I wanted you there.

Clive Dash it, what have I ever done to you?

Gerald I wanted *you* there, so that I shouldn't have to go about
with Harold.

Clive Well, anyway, I'm very glad you've come.

Gerald Yes, and I'm very glad you're here. You can help me in
with my portmanteau. (*Cross* R. *back of table*)

Clive Oh, hell! is it heavy?

Gerald Yes, it is very. Come on, old boy. (*Going to door*)

Clive (*going reluctantly up* R. C.) All right. If I'd only known, I'd have had Twine over to do it.

They go out R. C. *together and can be heard getting the portmanteau off the car*

Gerald (*off*) Stand there. I'll give it a heave.

Clive All right. Go on then, You go first. You can be the one to go backwards.

They reappear carrying the portmanteau, Gerald walking backwards

Gerald (R. C., *looking up* L. *over his shoulder*) I suppose that's my room.

Clive I don't care. I'm not going to carry it upstairs.

Gerald Righto. Put it down.

They put it down up stage L. C.

Clive Too hot for that stuff.

Gerald Yes. You're quite right. We ought to have had Harold.

Clive I suppose you've got a bottle in it?

Gerald That's in that one. (*Indicating suitcase* R.)

Clive (*cross* R. *to suitcase on table*) Then why not say so? We need never have got the portmanteau.

He opens suitcase; pushes several miscellaneous contents out on to the floor, handkerchiefs, etc.

Gerald I say, Clive, careful, old boy.

Clive (*picking things up*) I'm sorry, but you had to unpack, didn't you?

Gerald (*taking whisky bottle from the suitcase*) There you are, old boy. (*Handing it to Clive*) Shall I get some glasses? (*Goes to kitchen*)

Clive Yes, I hate drinking out of the bottle!

Gerald I'll get some glasses. (*Opens door down* R. *and bus. driving imaginary cat away*) Go out—I mean—don't do that—stay in—Pss!

Clive What's up?

Gerald (*off*) Cat.

Clive Did you tread on it?

Gerald No. I missed it.

Clive Oh, pity. (*Puts bag back* R. *and comes back to table* C.) And see if that fellow left any soda.

Gerald What fellow?

Clive The owner of the house. You know—Brindle Stag or whatever his damn silly name is.

Gerald Yes. Oh, here's some water. I'd better bring that.

He returns, carrying two glasses and jug of water. Kicks backward to scare the cat and shuts the door with his foot

Get back there—shoo! I hate cats!

Clive That's better. (*Leaves Gerald to mix drinks at table and strolls over* L.) Ye gods, if you knew what it was like over at those two teetotal Twines'!

Gerald (*pouring whiskies, one strong, one weak*) Well, think of me, old boy. I've got Gertrude permanently as a sister-in-law. How different from dear little Clara? Queer thing that—two sisters so unlike.

Clive (*looking at the drinks*) Gerald, which of these is mine?

Gerald Just as you like. (*Looks carefully at drinks.*) Take that one. (*Pushes small one to Clive—turns to portmanteau*)

Clive changes tumblers. Gerald sees him. Gerald returns from portmanteau to re-change tumblers. Meanwhile these lines are spoken

Clive Righto. Shall I do this for you? (*With water jug*)
Gerald Yes, please.

Clive pours water in each glass and changes them again, taking the strong one

Clive Yes, poor little Twine. At times he must long for death— probably Gertrude's.

Gerald tastes drink, takes more whisky

What's the matter—too strong?

Gerald Not yet. I'm afraid Harold will never assault Gertrude. (*Crosses to* L. *front of table*)

Clive No. I might. (*Crosses to* R. *front of table*) Poor little Twine. The way she dosses him up, and makes him trot about after her, wearing his little straw hat and looking like a rabbit at a stoat's tea party!

Gerald Well, you'll have me and Clara here now. (*Crosses to portmanteau*)

Clive When's Clara coming? (*Crosses behind table*)

Gerald (*returning to his unpacking*) Oh, she'll bring the old woman along pretty soon. (*Places ties on table* C.)

Bus. Clive walks with Gerald each time backwards and forwards, getting in his way each time

Clive What's the matter with the old woman?

Gerald I don't know. (*Pushes Clive gently*) She didn't say much. (*Putting bottle encased in wood with screw top on table, also pyjamas and loofah on table* C. *front*)

Clive Didn't she? That sounds as if she were dying. (*Getting between Gerald and table*) Well, couldn't we wangle that I come and put up here with you? (*At portmanteau* L.)

Gerald I don't know, old boy. Rather impossible if you're staying with Gertrude. Clara might be able to get you over. (*Crossing to table with bath gown*)

Clive is standing in his way

Get out of the way, old boy. (*Pushing him*)

Clive Couldn't I stay here now—I mean—before Clara comes? (*Has picked up a tie and is toying with it*) How do you do these things?

Gerald takes it and pushes him gently away

I mean you do want me here, don't you?

Gerald Do I? (*Going to portmanteau*)

Clive If you only knew what I've suffered at the hands of those relations of yours.

Gerald It doesn't worry me. I'm not there.

Bus. Clive is now toying with a screw stopper on bottle

(*Taking it from him*) Don't do that, old boy; if you want to play with one of these, that's the place to get them. (*Pointing at name*) The name's at the bottom. (*Crosses to portmanteau and brings other things back*)

By this time Clive has picked up a bath gown

(*Taking it from him*) Don't mess that gown about, old boy, you'll get it all creased.

Clive It's a lovely colour.

Gerald Yes. All the more reason not to mess it about.

Clive Well, what am I to do?

Gerald You must find something else to do. This is my favourite garment. I'm very fond of that.

Clive I mean about getting away from Gertrude's. (*Crosses R. C. to R. front of table*)

Gerald You can't; that's all.

Clive (*strolling round R. of table to front*) No, I suppose not. After all, I suppose when you've been married six weeks you don't want other people knocking around all the time.

Gerald (*coming round L. of table to front, grins*) Very little of the time.

Clive How's it going? (*Sitting on table*)

Gerald Marriage? Oh, fine, old boy.

Clive A veil is drawn over the past, eh?

Gerald What do you mean?

Clive (*taking whisky*) Well, dash, it, we had a few bright adventures in our time, didn't we?

Gerald Oh, a veil. Yes, a very thick veil. (*Clive pours out whisky*) You'll help yourself, won't you?

Clive Yes, I will, old boy. Do you remember——

Gerald (*quickly*) No, I don't. And look here, I say, Clive—while you're staying in this place—I mean with the relations here and that sort of thing—don't go and get into trouble, will you? You know what I mean—with anything *local*.

Clive You needn't be afraid. There's nothing to be found in this place.

Gerald How do you know?

Clive I've been here a whole week and drawn a complete blank. There's nothing here at all.

Gerald Oh, that's a pity.

Clive Yes. Well, I suppose we shall have to play golf, that's all.

Gerald Don't give up hope. We thought we were going to play golf that time at Bognor, d'you remember?

Clive Oh yes. That was the time we met—Annie and Winnie.

Gerald Oh, Annie and Winnie. Yes. What a memory you've got! Annie was the stout one and Winnie was the pretty one.

Clive Yes.

Gerald You, you old devil, you pinched Winnie.

Clive Oh, I pinched old Annie too.

*Warning—distant door bang and short bark of dog—*O. P.

Gerald Well, as I say, old boy, none of that Annie and Winnie stuff this time.

Clive As I say you needn't worry, there's nothing here at all. Gertrude only lives in this place because here she's comparatively good-looking.

Gerald Of course, so far the only one I've seen is the daily one. And she looks like a non-swimmer in deep water.

Clive You've only got to look at this place. (*Cross* R. C.) Look at it now. Only just dark and you can hear the silence.

Gerald Yes. (*Cross to Clive*)

Bang

Dog and bang of door in distance

Clive What was that?

Gerald A dog, I think.

Clive Yes, but there was a sort of bang.

Gerald Oh, then perhaps somebody shot the dog.

Clive It sounded more like a door bang.

Gerald Somebody letting out the dog.

Clive Why should he bang the door like that?

Gerald He probably ought to have let the dog out sooner. (*Pause*) You can't see anything from there, can you?

Clive Well, you don't want to see a dog being let out. Now are you going to start clearing up this ghastly mess?

Gerald I haven't begun yet. I've more things in the car. (*Turns*)

Clive Well, you'd better hurry up or you'll have Gertrude round.

Gerald Why, she's not coming over, is she?

Clive You bet she is—she'll come along, nosing about like an old hen that's had her run dug up. (*Flapping his arms and scratching with his foot as a hen*)

Gerald. Well, go and tell her I haven't arrived.

Clive But, you silly old fat-head, I've only been left here till you did.

Gerald Oh, I see. Well, tell her I'm too tired.

Clive All right. I'll do my best, and then come back. Don't take that up to your bedroom. (*Indicating whisky. Turns towards door* R. C.)

Gerald If you're coming back, there won't be any to take.

Clive Well, I'll try and put the lid on Gertrude.

Gerald And Harold.

Clive If I get the lid on, he can sit on it.

Exit up R.

Gerald tidies the table and looks about for something in his portmanteau L. *and goes out* R. C.

The figure of Rhoda, a young and very pretty girl in pink silk pyjamas, passes window L., *just glancing in. She then comes to door* R., *pauses, looks round, crosses to* L. *in front of table, looks up to balcony* L., *then sees bath gown on table* C. *and sits on table drying her feet with the bath gown; she is facing half* L.

Gerald returns with a case and golf clubs; he puts them down R., *clubs* R. *of case; he sees her, then picks up bag and clubs, goes out again to make certain he's made no mistake about the house. He comes back, puts things down again, looking at her in a dazed way, shutting and opening his eyes. He then goes to the door* R. C., *calling helplessly*

Gerald Clive!

Rhoda (*as she turns and sees him*) Oh! Er—is this your house?

Gerald Yes, I think so.

Rhoda I mean, you've just got here, or something?

Gerald Yes, but haven't you, or something?

Rhoda Yes. My name's Rhoda Marley. I come from up the road. I live there with my step-father.

Gerald Oh, did you?—I mean, do you? Is he ill, or is your house on fire?

Rhoda No. It's nothing like that, but—shall I tell you?

Gerald (*getting closer*) Yes, please, I wish you would.

Rhoda Oh, thank you. Only—excuse me a moment.

She shifts her sitting position and extracts a loofah. She smiles half-bashfully

It was pricking me rather.

Gerald Oh, was it? It should only scratch. Hadn't you better sit on something softer?

Rhoda I sat up here to dry my feet. I had to come through some very long grass to get here.

Gerald Yes, I see—the ends of your——

Rhoda Pyjama trousers——

Gerald Pyjama trousers—oh yes, I couldn't remember the name.

Rhoda Yes, I know. They're very damp too. There's a heavy dew, you see.

Gerald Yes. I can see there is. (*Getting closer*) Still, it's supposed to be a sign of fine weather, isn't it?

Rhoda Yes. (*Embarrassed pause*) Well, I'd better tell you why I've come.

Gerald Do, will you, please?

Rhoda Well, it's rather a long story.

Gerald Oh, it can't be. I mean, here you are in pyjamas on my table

Rhoda slips off table

Oh, that's all right. But why? That's all—why?

Rhoda (*appealingly*) It's all quite harmless. But I'm in such trouble. Oh, please, do be kind to me.

Gerald (*softening*) Kind to you? I'd do anything. But that's just it. What do you want me to do?

Rhoda Well, first of all—could you lend me a dressing-gown?

Gerald Oh yes—(*doubtfully*)—a dressing-gown? Certainly. (*Cross up L., pulling dressing-gown from trunk and holding it up for her*) Here you are. This one's rather shot.

Rhoda (*notices pyjamas on table, getting into dressing-gown*) Thanks awfully. I'm afraid I've rather spoilt that bath wrap.

Gerald Oh, never mind about that rotten old thing. (*Throwing it down and kicking it*) Only that wasn't why you came here, to borrow a dressing-gown?

Rhoda No, I'll tell you everything. (*She shivers*)

Gerald You're cold. (*Nearly touches her*)

Rhoda No, it's all right. It's only that wet grass.

Gerald Here, drink this. (*Taking up whisky and changing it for the jug of water*)

Rhoda No, I don't want that.

Gerald Well, what else can I do?

Rhoda (*hesitating, rubbing one leg on the other*) I hardly like to ask. (*Smiling*)

Gerald Don't be afraid. What is it?

Rhoda (*taking a pair of his striped blue pyjama trousers from the table*) The ends of mine have got so awfully damp.

Gerald You—you want to put on those of mine? (*She nods*) But—are you going to be here long?

Rhoda Well, I'm afraid that depends on you.

Gerald Oh, does it? Well, then, you'd better put on those of mine.

Rhoda I'm honestly in great trouble. (*In a little outburst, getting a little closer to Gerald*) You do trust me, don't you?

Gerald Of course. (*Making shapes with hands*) Only can't you give me just a hint of what it's all about, before you put on my trousers?

Rhoda I shouldn't be a minute putting them on.

Gerald No, I don't take long putting them on—well, you'd better put them on.

Rhoda Yes—but—— (*Looking round at door on balcony* L.)

Gerald Oh yes. Here you are. (*Opening door* R. *and switching on light*) The study.

Rhoda Thanks awfully. I think you'd better shut the door.

Gerald Oh, I was—(*holding door open* D. R.)—I'm going to shut the door.

Rhoda No—I mean that front door.

Gerald Oh! Why?

Rhoda You'll understand when I tell you.

She goes into study

He shuts study door, crosses to table, takes cigarette case from his pocket and puts cigarette in his mouth deep in thought; he takes his match-box out of his pocket, strikes a match and lights cigarette; still gazing at door D. R., *he absent-mindedly throws cigarette away and puts the lighted match almost in his mouth. This brings him back to earth, he picks up his cigarette and starts to smoke; he looks thoughtfully straight in front and whistles quietly to himself*

From outside comes the sound of the dog barking. This is checked by a weird foreign command in the distance: 'Hoi—Na-na-na-na!' Gerald picks up bath gown and throws it on portmanteau L., *goes to door* R. C., *opens it. There is the sound of a blow*

Rhoda enters from the study on sound of whip—blue striped pyjamas—

trousers over her feet; she wears the dressing-gown. She stands just inside the hall, listens nervously

Then the voice again: 'Zo! Na-na!'—*whip again. Gerald closes the front door*

Gerald Are those noises anything to do with you?

Rhoda Yes (*cross to front of table nervously*); that's my step-father and his dog Conrad.

Gerald (*cross* c. *above table*) Oh, really! It doesn't sound too good, does it?

Rhoda (*nervously*) No, I'd better tell you everything. (*Sits on table* c.)

Gerald Oh, don't sit on that. (*Indicating settee* L.) This is softer.

Rhoda Thank you. (*Crosses to settee* L.)

Gerald That's all right.

Rhoda As I say (*sitting on back of settee*), that's my step-father; he's a German. His name is Putz.

Gerald Putz! (*Sitting on settee up stage*)

Rhoda Yes. P-u-t-z. I live with him and a housekeeper. Her name is Nutts—Mrs Nutts.

Gerald Putz and Nutts?

Rhoda Yes.

Gerald Is this quite true?

Rhoda Yes.

Gerald Oh! Well, go on.

Rhoda Well, first of all, I'll tell you what's happened to-night. That's easily told. My step-father has run me out.

Gerald What?

Rhoda That's his own expression for it. I annoyed him; so just after I'd gone to bed he came up and took me up in his arms and ran me out. (*She demonstrates this with a little sound,* 'Ph't!')

Gerald You mean to tell me he ran you out in your pyjamas—ph't?

Rhoda Yes, and slammed the door on me. He wouldn't let me stay in the house any longer.

Gerald He must be very hard to please.

Rhoda Yes, that's his way. He makes rules, and if I disobey them that's how he treats me. He did it once before. But he came and took me back then.

Gerald But what did you do to-night?

Rhoda Oh, nothing really. Simply a trifle. Only it was against his orders. He wouldn't have found out only Nutts split.

Gerald But what was this forbidden thing?

Rhoda I ate wurts.

Gerald You did what, in heaven's name?

Rhoda I ate wurts—wurtleberries—a local Somerset fruit—wurts.

Gerald You ate wurts and Nutts split? It sounds like a fruit salad. But you mean to say that when Nutts split to Putz he ran you out for eating wurts?

Rhoda Yes. He dislikes wurts.

Gerald Dislikes them! He must loathe the very sound of wurts! (*Goes up* c.)

Rhoda They leave a nasty stain on the face.

Gerald You ought to have put them in your mouth.

Rhoda Well, that is all it was. He found I'd disobeyed him and eaten the forbidden fruit. So he ran me out.

Gerald (*closing portmanteau*) Is he quite sane?

Rhoda Oh yes. But very Prussian and masterful.

Gerald But why do you stay with him?

Rhoda (*stepping off settee and cross to back of settee* D. L.) Because I promised my mother before she died that I'd stick to him.

Gerald Not a very easy promise to keep if he runs you out.

Rhoda No. I'm through with it now. When he recovers his temper he'll try and get me back. But I'm not *going* back this time.

Gerald Quite right. Don't you. I never heard of such a thing. Wurts. But—but where will you go to-night?

Rhoda (*softly, quite genuinely at a loss*) I don't know.

Gerald Don't you know anyone here you can go to?

Rhoda (*shaking her head*) None of the people here will have anything to do with *me*.

Gerald Why?

Rhoda I don't know them. Besides, one of them invented a scandalous story about me.

Gerald (*cross to above settee* L.) About *you*—a dear little innocent girl like you?

Rhoda Yes. A woman here started the rumour that I wasn't really his step-daughter, but—something else.

Gerald What woman said that? (*Moves towards Rhoda*)

Rhoda Oh, one of these seaside residential cats.

Gerald Was it Mrs Twine?

Rhoda Yes. How did you know?

Gerald By experience. Mrs Twine is my sister-in-law.

Rhoda Oh, I'm sorry. (*Apologizing*)

Gerald Oh, don't apologize. I'm delighted to hear nasty things about her. So Mrs *Twine* said that about you, did she? (*Crosses to front of settee*)

Rhoda Yes. The whole place believes it now.

Gerald Right. (*Crosses to* c.) If Mrs Twine said that, I'll do anything in the world to help you. There!

Rhoda (*crosses to Gerald with a little run*) You're very kind, but if it's going to mean any bother to you——

Gerald I don't care. Now this man Putz. You must go back there to-night, of course. But come here in the morning.

Rhoda (*nods, crossing to* L. C.) I'll do what you think right. I have been lucky to meet *you*. (*Moves close to Gerald*)

Gerald (*smiles, pleased*) Yes.

Rhoda But I'll only go back there for one reason, and that's because you ask me to.

Gerald Yes. It's very nice of you to say that about me.

Rhoda Perhaps he won't take me back now. (*Nervously*)

Gerald Oh, I'll soon see to that. I'll come over with you and talk to Mr Putz.

A loud rap at the front door up R.

Rhoda I think he's saved you the trouble. (*Crosses to behind settee*)

Gerald Wait there. I'll see. (*Cross to door* R. C., *calls*) Who is it? (*Very nervously, but trying to put on a bold front*)

Putz (*heard outside*) Open, please.

Rhoda Yes. That's him.

Gerald (*she crosses up* L.) Come in. The door's not locked.

The door is opened, but only slightly. Putz enters backwards, keeping his dog out. He is a finely-built German, wearing loose cloth trousers and a white alpaca coat like a dentist

Putz (*to the dog, as he enters* R. C.) No, no. Hoi! Stay out from heah!

He gets in, closes door, turns and, taking horn-rimmed glasses from his pocket, takes stock of Gerald. His manner is quarrelsome. He sees Rhoda and exclaims

Ah! Alzo!

Gerald Are you Mr Putz?

Putz You are who? (*Cross* D. R. *to Gerald*)

Gerald I've just been told——

Putz You are who? Speak it out.

Gerald How dare you run this girl out. Take her back at once.

Putz I do not care for you.

Gerald I don't care very much for you—take her back.

Putz (*advancing angrily, at which Gerald retires a little*) You are who to say of what I shall make?

Gerald I beg your pardon?

Putz You are who——?

Gerald Eh?

Putz You are who?

Gerald Don't bark at me like that. You ran her out in her pyjamas.
Putz Vell? (*Becoming still more threatening*)
Gerald Vell, I mean—I mean—you mustn't do things like that.
It's——
Putz (*advancing again, loudly*) It is *vot*?
Gerald (*stepping away*) Well, it's—it's very naughty.
Putz You—are—who? (*Slowly*)
Gerald Yes—I—am. But I don't see it comes into it at all.
Putz Speak!
Gerald Dash it, I'm speaking as quick as I can. Just because she ate
a few—wu——
Rhoda (*prompting him*) Wurts.
Gerald Wurts.
Putz It is not only that she eat die vurrt. It is that she disobey me to
eat die vurrt. (*Crosses door* R. C.)
Rhoda I've had enough of your orders. I'll come back to-night and
I'll leave to-morrow.
Putz Zo? You t'ink? Eh?
Rhoda Yes, I've kept my promise long enough. When I go, my
mother's money goes with me.
Putz (*furious*) Too much. You t'ink you can command me.
(*Advancing towards her*) Herr Gott! I show you——
Gerald (*stepping between them*) Stop that, you rude—rude Putz.
(*Takes a drink of whisky*)
Putz (*challenging him, quivering*) What you make?
Gerald I'll show you what I make. Now, you—please—step-
daughter——
Rhoda Yes?

Gerald still facing Putz. Putz walks up and down furiously

Gerald (*pointing to door on balcony* L.) That room up there—that's
your room. The bathroom's next door and the other bedrooms is
elsewhere. You'd better go up at once.
Rhoda Very well. (*To the stairs* L.)
Gerald If there's anything else you want, let me know.
Rhoda Thank you.

Exit up stairs L.

Putz turns his head to watch her enter the room, so does Gerald. She goes in

Gerald (*to Putz*) You hear that. Zo! And now I'll come to your
house and get some of her clothes.
Putz No.
Gerald Yes. (*Leaning his elbow on table for support*)

Putz Nein.

Gerald Ten.

Putz Finish.

Gerald Good!

Putz If you come to my house I will call my dog and have you run out.

Gerald If you go on like this I'll call the police and have you run in.

Putz Nah! (*Crosses* D. R.)

Gerald takes another drink

Gerald (*with an effort*) Now don't be a naughty boy. (*Going to door* R. C.) Come on.

Putz stays still R. *As Gerald opens door* R. C., *Putz makes a sudden ejaculation to the dog outside*

Putz Tzt! Putta-putta!

There is a sound of furious canine attack from outside. Gerald hastily closes the door again

Gerald I see. You have to be protected by a dog, do you?

Putz (*feeling his biceps*) No, no. Also Swedish drill—first certificate. (*He starts to do Swedish drill*) Ein, zwei, drei, vier—Frisch, from, frühlisch, frei.

Gerald I don't care about your fried fish. Give me her clothes or I'll keep her as she is.

Putz Das ist mir egal.

Gerald All right——

Putz Finish. I go.

Gerald In that room.

Putz Das ist mir schnuppe.

Gerald Half in her pyjamas and half in mine.

Putz Too much. Finish. (*Opening door*) Und if you follow, my dog shall run you out, biting strongly. (*He goes, slamming the door behind him, shouting at dog*)

Pause and bus. Gerald smells whisky as a tonic—cue for Rhoda—she opens bedroom door again

Gerald All right, he's gone; come down.

Rhoda What happened—was he very cross? (*She comes down* L. C. *a little nervous*)

Gerald I ran him out; I don't mind doing that sort of thing. Do you mean to say that man is content to leave you here all night alone with a stranger?

Rhoda That's just like him. (*Leaning on table* C.) Anything rather

than give way and say he was in the wrong. My poor mother used
to admire it.

Gerald Still, I don't suppose he ran your poor mother out in her
nighty all over the shop.

Rhoda No, she was very happy with him.

Gerald She wasn't, I suppose, cursed with this craving for wurts?

Rhoda She used to say he was what a man was really *meant* to be.

Gerald That depends who meant it.

Rhoda Yes—(*pause*)—I suppose so.

They both laugh with embarrassment

Well, what am I to do?

Gerald Well, I'm not quite sure. You see *we* know what's happened,
and we know it's true. But I ask you, would anyone else believe it?

Rhoda But where do you think I'd better go? (*Smiling*)

Gerald You'd better go to bed. I don't see where else you *can* go in
those.

Rhoda crosses L. *to stairway. She is very shy and looks round twice as she
crosses*

Wait a minute. What are we going to do if Mrs Twine comes back?

Rhoda Mrs Twine—she won't come here, will she?

Gerald She may; my cousin's coming back anyway—he's all right—
but she might come back too.

Rhoda Well, couldn't I lurk somewhere? (*Looks at door* D. L.)
What's in there?

Gerald The kitchen quarters. Perhaps you could lurk in there?

Rhoda (*opens kitchen door*) She wouldn't come in here, would she?
(*Goes in*)

Gerald No, I don't think so.

Rhoda (*off* L.) There are some back stairs here.

Gerald Well, there you are. If she goes in there you could nip up
the back stairs.

Rhoda (*returning*) Yes, that's quite safe.

A knock at front door. He turns. She speaks in a whisper

Is that your cousin?

Gerald No, he'd come straight in.

Rhoda There you are then. (*Turns* L.) Kitchen, and back stairs if
necessary. (*Gerald nods*)

Gerald You've only got one step-father, I suppose? (*She goes
quietly off* L., *closing kitchen door*)

Picks up bottle as protector; crosses to front door and calls

Who is it?

No reply is heard. He opens front door. It is Twine

Twine (*heartily*) Hallo! (*Entering*)
Gerald No.
Twine Welcome to Chumpton.
Gerald Who said so?
Twine Clave told us you were here.
Gerald Where *is* Clave? (*Edging towards* L. *in front of table* L.)
Twine Behind with Gertrude.
Gerald But I want to go to bed.
Twine (*cross* L. C. *following Gerald*) I'm sorry. Gertrude would come.
    She insisted.
Gerald Go and meet her and tell her I'm just going to bed. (*At foot
    of stairs*)
Twine Yes, but that's just it. She wants to come and see you——
Gerald See me going to bed?
Twine No. To see that you're all sort of——
Gerald Sort of what?
Twine Well, sort of O.K.
Gerald Then run quickly and meet her and tell her I am A1.
Twine (*stubbornly*) No, I don't——
Gerald Well, I do. (*Up the stairs a little*)
Gertrude (*off*) Come along, Clive!
Clive (*off*) All right.
Twine Here she *is*. (L. *of table* C.)
Gerald (*turning back into hall*) Curse!

Gertrude enters with Clive

*Before looking at Gerald, Gertrude surveys the disorder of the hall with
severity. Clive and Gerald interchange glances of protest and helplessness
respectively. Gertrude catches them at it*

Gertrude (*cross to above table* C.) Well, this is a nice time to arrive!
Gerald Oh, don't apologize.
Gertrude You seem to have made the place in a beautiful muddle.
Gerald Yes, that's right. I did that so that I could clear it up. (*At
    foot of stairs*)
Gertrude So this is what happens directly you get away from Clara.
    (*Cross* L. C. *to Gerald*)
Gerald What do you mean? (*Anxiously*)
Gertrude All this mess. (*Indicating the mess in the hall*) Is mother very
    seedy? Will she and Clara be coming soon?
Gerald I hope not.

Twine at back of stage, looking over L. *shoulder at Clive and Gertrude*

Gertrude What?

Gerald I hope mother's not very seedy.

Gertrude H'm! Which room are you going to? (*Looking up to balcony* L.) That double room?

Gerald Yes, that's the one Mrs Lightfoot said.

Twine up L. C. *Looking over* L. *shoulder with back to audience*

Clive	Gertrude	Gerald
R. C.	L. C.	D. L.

Gertrude I think that room had better be left. Clara may want to sleep with mother.

Gerald Well, I don't mind.

Gertrude I'd better just see. (*Going upstairs*)

Gerald Yes.

Gertrude Come up with me, please.

Gerald (*following*) But surely I can sleep in that room *to-night*?

Gertrude That would only give trouble, moving your things about. (*Opens door of bedroom*)

Gerald looks down at Clive, who is helping himself to another whisky R. C., *and they exchange looks of sympathetic affliction*

Now let me see. What other rooms are there?

She goes towards R., *Gerald following*

Twine Can I help at all, dear? (*Standing* C., *looking up at Gertrude*)

Gertrude (*going off at* R. *end of landing*) No—stay where you are.

Gerald (*leaning over banisters, to Twine*) You can move about a bit, you know.

She goes off R. *of landing, followed by Gerald*

Gertrude (*off*) Now this looks a good room. What's the matter with this?

Gerald (*off*) I don't know. I haven't been in there yet.

Twine sits L., *near kitchen door. Clive sits on table*

Clive (*with a sigh—after a slight pause*) Go on, boy, now's your chance. Have a nibble at your straw hat.

Twine (*who has turned his head towards kitchen door*) Hush a moment.

Clive What's the matter?

Twine I thought I heard something. (*Rising*)

Clive (*unexcited*) Heard—what?

Twine (*cross* L. *to door* D. L. *and listening, looking at Clive*) I thought I heard a sort of sound.

Clive Oh, don't be a fool, Harold.

Twine Oh, it's a cat.

Clive Don't you let that cat out here.

Twine Poor thing—it's mewing.

Clive Well, let it mew.

Twine Perhaps it's lost its milk.

Clive What do you mean, lost its milk?

Twine Poor pussy! (*Opening kitchen door*) Where are you? Come along. (*In practical tones*) It's all right, come out.

Rhoda (*voice off*) Thank goodness!

Twine falls back amazed. Clive leaps into a sitting attitude. Rhoda sails out into the doorway

I was getting cramp. (*She sees them, claps a hand to her mouth and hurries back again, closing the door*)

Twine stands back L. C., *opened-mouthed. Clive leaps to his feet and crosses* L. *There is a crash in the kitchen*

Clive Ye gods! Where did he find that?

Twine It's the girl from up the road.

Clive Oh! Then me for up the road.

Gertrude What was that noise?

Gertrude and Gerald heard up R. *Clive closes kitchen door, turns* C.

Clive Not a word. On your honour, Twine. Leave it to me.

Twine All right.

Gertrude and Gerald on balcony
                    Table
                                    Settee

Twine   *Clive*
   C.   D. L.

Gerald, as he enters up R. *and comes downstairs* L., *wildly alarmed*

Gerald Well, I don't know. Stay there and I'll see.

Gertrude appears and follows Gerald down. Clive turns to them blandly

Gertrude What was that noise?

Clive It's all right. It's Harold.

Gerald But that noise?

Clive That's right. Harold.

Gerald crosses to L. *in front of settee*

He went in the kitchen.

Gerald (*alarmed*) In the kitchen? Why?

Gertrude Did you make that noise, Harold? (*Coming down and crossing to* c.)

	Table		
Twine	*Gertrude*	*Gerald*	*Clive*
c.	L. c.	L.	D. L.

Clive Yes, he did.

Gerald (*to Clive*) But why did he go in the kitchen?

Clive Good job he did. Next time he wants to make a noise like that he'd better go in the garden.

Gertrude What was it? Why did you go in there, and what happened?

Gerald (*to Clive*) Leave this to me. (*Cross to* L. c.)

Gertrude (*to Twine*) Why did you go in the kitchen?

Clive I told him not to.

Gertrude I'm asking *him*. (*To Twine*) Why did you?

Twine I heard a mew.

Gertrude A what?

Twine A mew, dear. I heard mews.

Clive Don't be stupid. A mew is a sort of sea-gull.

Gerald And mews are stables.

Twine Well, then, a mi-ow. I heard a mi-ow.

Clive Oh, don't be a baby. He heard the cat.

Gertrude Did you hear the cat?

Twine Yes, dear.

Clive He went to let the cat out.

Gerald (*to Clive*) And *did* he let the cat out?

Clive (*quickly to Gerald*) Yes, a beauty.

Gerald I see. He ran up against something?

Clive He certainly did.

Gerald Oh, I'd better have a look. (*Opens kitchen door and goes in saying as he goes*) Look out!

Gertrude (*turning* L.) What do you mean—look out?

Clive gets in front of Gertrude; they bump

Gerald I mean, look out if you're coming here. There are saucepans all over the floor.

Clive intentionally obstructs Gertrude from going into the kitchen by standing in front of the doorway looking in

Clive (*to Gerald*) Is it all right?

Gerald Yes, old boy, its all right now.

Gertrude (*pushes past Clive*) Clear out of the way. What a nuisance you are, Harold!

Goes in. Clive cross C. *to* R. *of Twine*

Gerald returns and comes hastily down to the other two

Gerald You saw? (*Confidentially*)

Clive Yes, but not long enough.

Gerald And you saw? (*Nervously to Twine*)

Gerald takes Twine's left arm and Clive his right

Twine Yes.

Then the three cross R. C. *arm-in-arm*

Gerald Listen, quick! It's on the level. She was driven from home. She had to come here. But don't tell Gertrude.

Clive No, no.

Twine Oh, I say, but——

Gerald But nothing. As man to man—swear not to say a word.

Twine Oh, but it's awful.

Clive It isn't.

Gerald It isn't. Come round early to-morrow and I'll tell you all. Till then, swear!

Clive Go on. Swear, blast you!

Twine Oh!

Gerald You're always in the vocative. Swear!

Clive Hurry up! Swear!

Twine Oh, botheration!

Clive Not that kind of swear, you fool! Promise.

Twine Well, I daren't tell Gertrude that that girl's here.

Gerald Daren't? That's all right. That's a swear. And come round in the morning early.

Twine But the harm will be done by then.

Gerald Harm? There's no harm, I tell you.

Clive Of course not, you evil-minded little man.

Gertrude appearing at kitchen door D. L.

Gertrude Harold!

Clive and Gerald pretend to be having a joke with Twine

Gerald Harold's just told a beauty.

Twine Oh, what, dear?

Gertrude Are you going to leave me to pick all these things up?

Twine (*cross* L. *to her*) No, dear.

Gertrude I should hope not.

They go, leaving kitchen door open

Clive and Gerald cross C.

Clive (*to Gerald*) Now then, you naughty boy. Explain this windfall.
Gerald A perfectly innocent, sweet little girl driven from home.
Clive Go on.
Gerald True. You wait till you see her.
Clive I'm going to. But Gertrude'll see her now.
Gerald No, she won't. She's gone up the back stairs. But you must
help.
Clive With pleasure.

Voices heard off

Gerald She's got to stay here to-night. What shall I do? I can't
stay here alone with her.
Clive No, you oughtn't to.
Gerald I know. You ought to stay here too. Can't you manage it?
Clive I ought to.
Gerald You must if you can.
Clive Well, you ask Gertrude.
Gerald No, you ask her.
Clive It would seem better coming from you.
Gerald No, but you lie better than I do.
Clive Do I? All right. I'll have a pop.
Gertrude (*off*) Leave things alone.

Enter D. L.

Gerald Go on then. Now.

*Gertrude and Twine reappear from kitchen. She is still upbraiding Twine.
Close door*

Clive (*cross to Gertrude*) Oh, Gert——(*Stops to look back at Gerald, who
prods him*)

	Table		
Gerald	*Clive*	*Gertrude*	*Twine*
C.	C.	L. C.	L.

Gertrude (*coldly*) Gert?
Gerald (*aside to Clive*) That's a bad start, old boy.
Clive No. Gertrude. Er—we thought it wouldn't be a bad idea if I
stayed here, just for to-night, with Gerald.
Gertrude Why?
Clive (*to Gerald*) Why?

Gerald You know why, old boy. I told you.

Gertrude Well? Why?

Gerald (*cross to Gertrude*) You see—the daily woman isn't coming till eight-thirty; earlier than that she cannot be—and I oversleep—and he doesn't—do you?

Clive Yes.

Gerald Yes. And I want to be up early—because I want to have lunch before breakfast at seven—or half-past—well, a quarter to eight—and——

Gertrude What are you talking about?

Gerald Dinner. (*Crosses up* L. *of table to behind table* C.)

Clive (*cross to Gertrude*) No—simply—I'd like to stay with him.

Gertrude You're staying with me, aren't you?

Clive Oh yes.

Gertrude Very well then. Come along. I'm going now. (*Cross to door* R. C.) Harold!

Twine Yes, dear.

Clive All right then. You go ahead, you two—I'm just coming.

Gertrude (*to Clive*) You can catch us up. I'm not going to hang about.

Exit R. C.

Gerald (*seizing Twine as he is following*) Remember, Twine—you've sworn.

Twine Oh, misery me!

Gerald Haven't you?

Twine I'm not going to keep my mouth shut indefinitely.

Clive You've sworn, until to-morrow.

Twine Oh-h!

Gerald Haven't you?

Twine Very well. Yes.

Gertrude (*heard off*) Harold!

Clive Don't hang about. Go on.

Gerald Go on. Get out.

Twine exits up R. C., *leaving door open*

Door open

Clive Well, you made a nice show of asking Gertrude.

Gerald You said you'd ask her, and didn't.

Clive How could I, when you were standing there blathering a lot of tripe about early lunch—seven-thirty—eight-fifteen?

Gerald Well, don't blame me, and if you stay here long she may get suspicious and question Twine.

Clive He won't tell.

Gerald Don't give him the chance.

Clive Dash it, he's bound to get the chance. He sleeps with her.

Gerald Yes, poor devil!

Clive Gerald, just let's have another *look*.

Gerald All right—shut the door.

Clive shuts front door R. V. *Gerald calls upstairs*

Hi! Step!

Rhoda appears at L. *end of landing. She is anxious again and penitent*

Rhoda Is it all clear now?

Gerald Yes, she's gone.

Rhoda (*coming downstairs* L., *pointing to door*) I thought Mr Twine was with you.

Gerald Yes, but *Mrs* didn't see you.

Rhoda *Mr* did.

Gerald That's all right. Don't worry. This is my cousin I told you about. Clive Popkiss—same name as me. I'm Gerald Popkiss.

Clive How d'ye do?

Gerald Very likely he'll help us to-morrow.

Clive There's no very likely about it. He's going to.

Rhoda (*who has come half-way downstairs*) Thank you. You've been most awfully kind to me.

Clive Oh, you wait until to-morrow.

Gertrude (*voice heard outside*) Clive!

General scurry. Rhoda runs up to the landing, stands at back of balcony up L.

Clive and **Gerald** Look out! Quick! Gertrude! *etc.*

Gertrude opens front door. Rhoda is hidden from her by the floor of the landing jutting into the hall, under which Gertrude stands

Gerald What was that you said?

Clive (*cross* R., *referring to golf bag* R.) This is a nice top.

Gertrude (*to Clive*) Why have you shut this door again? Will you please come along at once? (*She turns indignantly and goes out again*)

Clive Oh, sorry, Gertrude. (*Going*) Well, I'll have to go, old boy. (*Looks up smiling at Rhoda*) Good night, old boy.

Gerald Good night, Clive, old boy.

Clive goes, leaving door open

Clive comes back to door, looks up at Rhoda, smiles

Clive Good night. (*To Gerald*) Good night, Gerald.

Gerald Good night, Clive, old boy.
Clive Good night.
Gertrude (*heard off*) Clive!
Clive Blast!!

Exits R. C., *closes door*

Gerald is staring straight in front

Rhoda exits into bedroom L.

SLOW CURTAIN

SECOND CURTAIN: *Gerald is seen with his pyjama coat; he picks up a pair of flannel trousers and sits on the sofa, preparatory to turning in*

CURTAIN

ACT II

The hall next morning. Bright sunshine is seen through the open doorway. The hall has been cleared and the portmanteau and unpacking have disappeared

Gerald and Clive in fresh, clean attire are talking things over. Clive at door R. C., *Gerald on settee* L. *up stage*

Gerald So that's the whole story of why she came here.

Clive 'M.

Gerald What do you think of it?

Clive (*with a grimace*) I believe it, of course. (*Cross to above table*)

Gerald But you don't think anyone else would?

Clive Oh, I don't know. The marines *might*.

Gerald I know it sounds unlikely. I told her so last night.

Clive It sounds a great deal worse this morning. (*Crosses to above table*)

Gerald Why? I haven't seen her since last night.

Clive I quite believe that too. But I wouldn't press that even on a marine.

Gerald You don't think Clara would accuse me?

Clive (*shrugs, crosses behind to table* L. C.) I don't know. You see, you've been married such a short time.

Gerald Yes. (*Smiling*) That's an advantage.

Clive Is it?

Gerald (*his face falling*) Isn't it?

Clive Well, you can't have broken her in much in six weeks. (*Sits on table,* L. *corner up stage*)

Gerald Oh no, old boy. I'm sure she'll trust me.

Clive Oh, good. I hope so, I'm sure.

Gerald I'm certain she will. Our first night apart. (*Rising, cross* D. L.) Good Lord!

Clive Well, that's all right then. You know her best.

Gerald Yes. Oh, Clara won't suspect me for a moment.

Clive Fine. There you are, then.

Gerald I mean, of course, if she doesn't hear anything about it.

Clive Oh, I thought you meant you'd tell her.

Gerald Tell her? Oh, why? If we get this girl away there'll be nothing to tell. (*Cross* R. C.)

Clive If Gertrude finds out—Clara will be told all right.

Gerald She'll be told all wrong. If there's a chance of that I must tell Clara first.

Clive Oh yes, old boy, I should tell her in any case. You know— airily, as if you had nothing on your conscience—I should say (*acting*) Ha! rather a funny thing happened the other night. A little girl drifted in here—pretty little thing she was—no, perhaps you hadn't better say that—driven from home.

Gerald You think that sounds as if you've nothing on your conscience?

Clive Well, it's difficult for me to say what a married man's conscience is like—me being single mine's rather elastic. (*Crosses* R. *to front of table*)

Gerald Much better get the girl some clothes and take her away.

Clive Yes. You're quite right. (*An afterthought*) What's the time?

Gerald (*looking at his watch*) Oh, about a quarter-past.

Clive A quarter-past eight?

Gerald Yes.

Clive (*jumping up*) Well, what about eight-thirty?

Gerald What?

Clive The daily woman, you fool.

Gerald Good Lord, yes. Eight-thirty. Earlier than that she cannot be. (*Looks over at kitchen and crosses* R. *to Clive*) What shall we do? She's got the back door key.

Clive Stop her getting to the back door, that's all.

Gerald What—you mean go and meet her?

Clive Yes, and tell her not to come.

Gerald (*crossing to door* R. C.) You come *with* me. You can tackle her better than I can.

Clive All right. You go to one gate, I'll go to the other. You never know which way she's coming; these fat women live in all directions.

They exit R. C. *Clive goes off* R. *Gerald is seen going off* L., *leaving door open*

Rhoda comes out of bedroom L. *and looks out of the window* C. *of balcony; she stretches her arms as she looks out*

Then the kitchen door is opened and in comes Mrs Leverett. Surprised to see the front door open, she crosses towards it and looks out. She has already removed her hat and left it in the kitchen. She stands beneath the canopy of the jutting landing. By standing where she is Mrs Leverett can see without being seen. Her expression becomes one of furious amazement as she hears Rhoda call

Rhoda (*comes to front of balcony and looks down into hall—calling softly*)
Mr Popkiss! Mr Popkiss!

*No reply. Rhoda turns and goes back into the bedroom, again closing the
door. Mrs Leverett comes forth from her hiding-place as though in a sort of
indignant trance. Then she rouses herself to action; hurries into the kitchen;
hurries out again, putting on her hat as she does so and, after taking another
look at the bedroom door, goes quickly away through the kitchen. Closes door*

    Voices are heard outside R. C. *The first person who appears is Twine, who
is in plus fours. He is speaking over his shoulder as he enters* R. C. *from* R.

Twine Well, now that I am here—(*anxiously*) come inside, please.
(*Cross to* R. *of table*)
Clive (*following*) Why? (*Cross door* R. C.)
Twine I don't want to be seen.
Clive Oh, I shouldn't worry. You look fairly all right.
Twine No, but I told Gertrude I'd go to the golf club. She asked
where you were. I said I didn't know.
Clive I see. And you came over here because of your last night's
swear?
Twine I felt it my duty to come here.
Clive And I don't believe you'd have come at all, if I hadn't caught
you dithering at the gate.
Twine You don't seem to realize. I told Gertrude I was going straight
up to the golf club. (*Turning away*) I've told her a *lie*.
Clive Oh, that's nothing. You'll do better than that.
Twine Oh, but, Clive——
Clive What?
Twine (*with emotion*) What is all this terrible affair? It must be
stopped. (*Close to Clive's face*)
Clive Quite right, old boy; we'll stop it between us. All boys
together.
Twine. No, no; I won't be mixed up in it. I've already *lied* to
Gertrude. I'm feeling very uncomfortable.
Clive What, already? You *wait*.

    Gerald returns breathlessly from running past windows. Enters R. C.
crosses to L., *looks in kitchen*

Gerald I've looked right down the road—there's no sign of that
daily woman.

        Clive   *Twine*
        R.   R. C.

Clive Well, if she comes, we'll get rid of her somehow. I was just
telling Harold—now *he's* here to help us, we'll get on better.

Gerald (*crossing to* R. *of table, taking Twine's hand*) Indeed, yes. Thank you, Harold.

Twine Oh——

Clive	Twine	Gerald
R.	R. C.	(*Front of table*)

Clive No, no—stop that!

Gerald Yes—from the start, Harold, that 'oh' business is out.

Twine I've lied to my wife.

Gerald You have? Stout fellow! A very good beginning.

Twine Oh, don't, please! This is not the time for funning.

Clive There you are. The very first comment he makes. Sound common sense. (*Slapping Twine on the back*)

Gerald Yes. Bravo, Harold!

Clive Now, first of all, you've got to believe, Harold, that that girl is a pure, nice, good, innocent little child.

Gerald Absolutély. I know it's hard for you to believe, Harold, because a man like you—a man of the world, who's knocked about with all sorts of wild women——

Clive Yes, of course—when a man like this sees a girl in your house, naturally he leaps to conclusions.

Gerald Leaps—why, he bounds!

Clive Yes, the old scoundrel—he's been knee-deep in daisies many a time.

Twine Oh——

Clive Ah!

Gerald Another 'oh' and we shall have to swear you about it.

Twine The girl's got a very queer reputation, anyhow.

Gerald Yes, and who queered it?

Clive Now, look here, Twine. Experience may have made you a cynic about women. (*Crosses down* R.) Possibly you may have been stung once too often. (*Coming back* R. C.) But, believe me, old boy, there can still be such a thing as a good girl.

Gerald Yes, Harold. Even in the same town as you.

Twine Then why should she be here—at night, in——

Clive In what?

Twine (*hesitating*) Well, wearing those things——

Gerald She was run out.

Twine What?

Clive She had trouble at home. You know what trouble at home is, don't you?

Twine Yes.

Clive Yes, none better.

Gerald You'd better see her for yourself and judge. (*Crosses* L. C.)

Twine Why, good *heavens*, is she still here?

Gerald Yes, of course she is—up in that bedroom. I'll introduce you. (*Turns to go upstairs* L.)

Twine (*cross in front of table to* L. C.) No, no, no. I'm going to golf. (*Edging towards* R. C. *door*)

Clive and **Gerald** (*who pause incredulously on stairs*) Golf!

Twine Yes. I'd rather go to golf.

Clive You'd rather golf than see this girl?

Twine Much.

Gerald You'd rather golf *much*? (*At top of stairs* L.)

Twine Yes. Not only that, I told Gertrude. Besides, I've got a match.

Clive But dash it, man, noblesse oblige.

Gerald Yes, and honi soit—you stay there. (*Goes to bedroom door up* L. *and knocks*)

Rhoda (*from inside bedroom*) Come in.

Gerald No, you come out.

Rhoda appears

Rhoda Good morning.

Gerald Good morning.

Rhoda (*to Clive*) Good morning.

Clive (*heartily*) Good morning.

Gerald goes down two or three stairs L. *Introduction*

Gerald Here we are. Mr Harold Twine—Miss Rhoda Something.

Rhoda Good morning. Rhoda Marley, my name is.

Clive (*to Twine*) Go on—How do you do?

Twine (*unable to resist*) How do you do?

Clive Good! Well, now that you've how do you done, just look at that girl.

Gerald (*beaming at Rhoda*) Yes.

Clive I mean, can you, Harold—can you possibly suspect?

Twine (*feebly*) N-n-no.

Gerald No. Come on, heartily, Harold. *No.*

Clive Perish the thought.

Twine Yes, certainly.

Clive Go on then. Let's hear it.

Twine Perish the thought.

Clive cross R.

Gerald brings Rhoda downstairs L. *to* L. C.

Gerald And you admit that Gertrude was and is wrong in saying things about her?

Twine I don't know. (*Cross* L. C.)
Gerald You *do* know, Harold.
Twine Oh dear, well—yes.
Gerald So now it is your duty to make amends.
Clive That's right. And to do what we tell you to help Miss Marley.
Twine I can't make any promise, but I'll tell you what I'll do. I'll tell Gertrude——
Gerald What!
Clive You blithering idiot!
Twine No, now Clave. (*To Clive*) Gerald, I'll tell Gertrude I think she's made a mistake.
Rhoda (*quickly—as Clive and Gerald protest*) Please, Mr Twine!
Twine What?
Rhoda I'd rather you didn't tell Mrs Twine I'm here.
Clive Of course he won't. Don't you worry.
Twine (*obstinately*) Then I'll take no part in it at all. And in any case I've got to go to golf now. (*Turns up* R.)

Gerald crosses back to table to Twine as he attempts to go; pushes him towards L. and goes to door. Twine crosses R. to Clive as he speaks line 'I've arranged to play with Admiral Juddy'. Gerald then comes down L. of Twine

Gerald Harold, if this is your attitude, you'll see the inside of no bunker to-day.
Twine But I must. I've arranged to play with Admiral Juddy.
Gerald (*crosses down* L. *of Twine*) But not yet.
Twine Yes, before nine. Because the course gets so congested at this time of year.
Clive Well, you can't; that's all.
Twine (*in a panic*) Oh, but I must. You don't know Admiral Juddy.
Clive No, and I don't want to.

All move down stage a little

Twine He's been years in China and he flies into rages and uses terrible expressions.
Gerald That won't matter. You won't be there to hear them.
Rhoda Oh please, Mr Popkiss.
Gerald Yes?
Clive Yes? (*They both turn to her, softening quickly*)
Rhoda I'm sure Mr Twine won't do or say anything to hurt me if I ask him nicely. Can't he go to his golf?
Twine Thank you. I won't say a word about you to anyone.
Gerald And if you can help, you will?

Twine Yes. Willingly.

Rhoda (*smiling sweetly at Twine*) That's right.

Noise of door latch in kitchen D. L.

Gerald (*crosses down* L. *front of table, listening, then speaking in a hoarse whisper*) Look out! Listen! (*At noise in kitchen—*)

    Twine   *Rhoda*

    O   O

        Clive   *Gerald*

        O   O

(*Then—*)

               Rhoda

               O

      Clive

      O

                  Gerald

  Twine   O

  O

The Others (*turning*) What?

Gerald (*as before*) The back door. (*Crosses* L. C.). It's the d.w.

Clive (*crosses to front of table* C.) Damn it, she's come after all.

Gerald What shall we do?

Clive (*to Rhoda and Gerald*) You go up in that room. (*Indicates bedroom on* L. *of balcony*)

Twine (R. C. *to Clive*) Who is it?

Clive The daily woman.

Twine (*turning towards front door*) Oh!

Clive catches at his arm as he attempts to go. The subsequent scene is played in quick subdued manner

Clive Don't go now, you fool. She may see you and tell Gertrude. Then Gertrude will know that you've lied to her.

Twine Oh, my gracious!

Clive You come up to that bedroom, too.

Gerald crosses to stairs and goes up. Rhoda follows. Twine is following behind, being hustled by Clive

Twine (*very scared*) What, to the bedroom? No——

Clive Yes. Shut up! (*Giving Twine a lift with his knee*) Now up you go, quick!

   Rhoda exits into bedroom

Twine Oh!

Clive Go in there. (*He turns*)

Clive and Gerald shove Twine into bedroom after Rhoda

(*Turns to Gerald*) Gerald, you wait for her at the top of the stairs, and when you hear her coming upstairs, stand in the doorway and sack her.

Gerald Good! You go in, old boy.

Clive exits into bedroom

Twine (*reappearing in doorway*) Look here, I say——

They bear him forcibly inside and close the bedroom door

After a moment Mrs Leverett comes very stealthily into the hall. She looks about her. Gertrude follows into the hall close on her heels

Mrs Leverett (L. C., *with her head thrown back. Whispering hoarsely*) If she's still here she's in the bedroom.

They both look up at bedroom L.

And also he too has gone back in there himself as well, what's more.

Gertrude (L. C., *whispering back*) It seems incredible. You honestly promise me you saw her yourself with your own eyes?

Mrs Leverett Yes, by the Testament I saw her with me hand on me heart.

Gertrude (*to herself, pensively*) H'm. Six weeks. Well, I shall know what to do if it's true. I shall go straight to Bath and get his wife.

Mrs Leverett She ought to be told.

Gertrude She will be told. She'll not only be told, she'll be brought here and shown.

Mrs Leverett. When will you go for her, madam?

Gertrude At once, if it's true.

Mrs Leverett Oh, it's true enough.

Gertrude (*looking up* L.) You'd better go up and knock and see what happens.

Mrs Leverett (*crosses to foot of stairs* L.) Yes.

Gertrude Don't appear to suspect anything.

Mrs Leverett No. (*Going upstairs*)

Gertrude I shall wait by the back door. (*Crosses to door* D. L.) You come out and tell me what happens.

Mrs Leverett Yes.

Gertrude Very likely you'll find there's no one in the room at all.

Mrs Leverett (*very certain*) Oh! (*Goes up two or three stairs*)

Gertrude If so, go along there to the room I told him to sleep in and see if he's there.

Mrs Leverett Yes.

Gertrude Go on then. You'd better not be wearing your hat. Give it to me.

Mrs Leverett hands it to her. Goes upstairs quietly and listens outside bedroom door. Then knocks. Immediately the bedroom door flies open. Mrs Leverett falls back a step or two, as Gerald stands in a commanding attitude in the doorway. Gertrude waits in a listening attitude at the foot of the stairs, just inside the kitchen door L.

Gerald (*loudly*) What! At *this* hour?

Mrs Leverett I beg your pardon?

Gerald *Not* granted.

Mrs Leverett Eh?

Gerald How dare you do this? You're very late and very late.

Gertrude exits D. L.

If you can't come here at all, don't come here at the proper time.

Mrs Leverett I don't understand your meaning.

Gerald Luckily for you. You—you dare to come here like this, hours afterwards, crawling upstairs like a balloon——

Mrs Leverett Balloon!

Gerald Yes, and me with no tea and early cot hold water—shave— you know—hot pot tea and shaving—go away with you—right away——

Mrs Leverett I'm not far be'ind me time. I have come here as promised. What more do you want me to do?

Gerald There's only one thing for you to do, and that is your old friend, the quit.

Gertrude exits into kitchen D. L.

Mrs Leverett Oh, indeed! Very well, then.

Gerald Yes, awfully well then.

Mrs Leverett You dont want me here?

Gerald Not a bit of you.

Mrs Leverett Oh, in that case——

Gerald Yes?

Mrs Leverett I say, in that case—I give you a week's notice.

Gerald (*taken aback*) A week?

Mrs Leverett (*turning to go downstairs*) Yes. A week from now.

Gerald Oh! (*Prompted evidently from the bedroom*) What? Wait a minute! Oh, yes, I know. Here! You're going to be weighed——

Mrs Leverett What?

Warning for door slam

Gerald Paid—you're going to be paid off now. How much?

Mrs Leverett H'm—you seem in a great hurry to——
Gerald Not a word. How much?
Mrs Leverett I'll take a pound——
Gerald (*over his shoulder*) She'll take a pound. (*Correcting the impression that he was addressing anyone else by grinning at Mrs Leverett, then correcting himself for grinning*) You'll take a pound.

Gerald turns to go into bedroom. Mrs Leverett attempts to go into bedroom, but Gerald stops her

Stay there!

She takes two steps back upstairs; he goes in and shuts door. Mrs Leverett nods to herself triumphantly and moves to bedroom door again

He reappears. Nearly bumping her with door

Take this and go. (*Hands her a pound note*)
Mrs Leverett I did not like the looks of you from the start.
Gerald And I don't like the look of you at the finish.
Mrs Leverett (*coming downstairs*) Very good then. I may say I'd 'ave *given* this *not* to work here.
Gerald Why didn't you say that before?

She goes out indignantly and shuts door D. L.

Short pause before door slam off L.

He runs down the stairs and listens. A door is heard to slam off L. *He crosses to* C. *and calls to Clive and Twine up* L.

(*Crosses* D. L. *to* C.) Come on; it's all right. She's gone.

Clive comes downstairs, followed by Rhoda and Twine

Clive I don't think you did that very well.
Gerald Well, she's gone anyhow.
Twine Yes, and I must go now, please. (*Crosses to* L. C.)
Gerald (*detaining him*) Is it all clear for Harold now?
Clive Yes, let him go.
Twine I must, please. Admiral Juddy——
Clive All right—go.
Twine Yes. (*Starting up* L. C.)

(All up stage)

Gerald	Twine	Clive	Rhoda
R. C.	L. C.	L. C.	L.

Oh—well, all right. (*Goes towards door* R. C.)
Gerald Stay there a moment—I'll see if it's all clear.

He opens the door. Gertrude is standing on the threshold

Not to-day, thank you (*Closes door again and turns breathlessly*) Gertrude!

Twine (*letting himself go, below his breath*) My God!

Stands by door R. C. *Clive steers Rhoda across* R. *and opens door* D. R., *pushing her in; he then bundles Twine in, closes door* D. R.

Gerald (*opening door* R. C.) Gertrude!—I beg your pardon, I thought it was the laundry.

Gertrude (*entering* R. C., *leaving door open—quite amiably*) I thought you didn't see who it was. Oh, good morning, Clive.

Clive Good morning, Gertrude.

Gertrude You must have found your way over here very early this morning.

Clive Yes, I thought poor old Gerald might want help.

Gerald Yes. (*Above table*)

Gertrude Why, hasn't Mrs Leverett arrived? (*Crosses* L. *of table*)

Gerald Oh, most.

Gertrude What?

Gerald Most attractive—er—attentive.

Gertrude And the room I chose for you was quite comfortable?

Gerald Oh, more.

Gertrude You slept well?

Gerald More—er—most—er—quite.

Gertrude Oh!

Clive, with a frown at Gerald, strolls up near study door

Well (*crosses to* L. *of table* C.), my reason for coming over so early was that I've had a card from Clara.

Gerald Oh, Clara! Yes, I remember. Oh yes, my wife—I mean—yes? Well, have you brought the postcard?

Gertrude No, I left it at home. Apparently, mother is still very seedy.

Gerald Really. That's very sad—and—terribly awful.

Gertrude So I'm afraid it will be quite out of the question for Clara to come on here to-day.

Gerald and Clive exchange glances

Gerald Oh!

Gertrude She asked me to come and break it to you.

Gerald Yes. (*Assumes very saddened expression*)

Gertrude And to make matters worse (*casually*), I'm afraid I've arranged to be away all day myself.

Clive What a pity!

Gertrude, tidying cushions on settee L., *takes a sly look at bedroom door on balcony* L.

Gerald Oh! (*Assumes even more sadness*)

Clive signals to him not to overdo it

Gertrude So you two must keep each other company and get on as best you can.
Gerald (*looking at Clive*) We'll do that.
Gertrude Harold will be free later.
Gerald Yes; he's gone up to the golf club.

Clive digs Gerald with his knee. Gerald's knees give way through the shock, and he has to hold on to the corner of the table. Gertrude is looking on, so he turns it off by doing a few gymnastics; stands balancing on the same place

Gertrude Why, have you seen him then?
Gerald Yes. (*Clive digs him*) No, he—he told me last night he was going early to play much golf—golf much—this morning—all the morning—early this morning.
Gertrude I see. And what will you do with yourselves?
Gerald Yes.
Gertrude Just take it easy. I should.
Clive I shall knit.
Gertrude You've got a nice long time in front of you, with nothing to worry about. Then I'll say good-bye (*crosses to door* R. C.) till this evening.
Gerald Thank you very much.
Gertrude What?
Gerald I beg your pardon.

Gertrude goes off R. C. *to* L.

Twine enters cautiously from study, and he, Clive and Gerald exchange confidential grimaces

Twine Has she gone?
Clive Yes.
Gerald Yes.

Juddy is heard off L. *talking to Gertrude*

Juddy (*off* L.) Day ter yah.
Gertrude (*off* L.) Good morning, Admiral Juddy.

Clive, Gerald, and Twine exclaim 'Juddy'! Clive and Gerald bundle

Twine back into the study. Clive closes the door as Juddy appears at door
R. C. *with Gertrude*

Gertrude (*at door* R. C.) Harold has gone on a long time.

*Admiral Juddy, a fierce and weather-beaten veteran with heavy eyebrows,
pounds on to the scene. He is heated and annoyed. He has a habit of relieving
his feelings in Chinese oaths below his breath*

Juddy He has not.
Gertrude What?
Juddy Not! (*Crosses to* L. *of table, glares at Gerald and curses in Chinese
below his breath*)

Gerald and Clive stand close together R.

Gertrude But he left the house over half an hour ago.
Clive I saw him go myself.

Clive and Gerald are R., *Gertrude* R. C., *Juddy* L. C.

Juddy I didn't say he didn't leave the house. I said he didn't go to
the b— to the b— to the golf club.

*He has a mannerism in the form of a little bob which he does here and repeats
later. Gerald and Clive stand arm in arm* R. *and imitate the bobbing of
Juddy*

Gerald (*to Clive*) It's all right. Stand firm. Hearts of oak.
Gertrude Where do you suppose he went?
Juddy I called at your house to see if he'd gone, and the maid told
me she'd seen him coming over here.
Gertrude (*incredulously*) Over here?
Juddy Yes, madam, over here.
Gerald (*to Clive*) Yo ho, the anchor's weighed!
Gertrude He didn't come here, did he? (*To Clive*)
Gerald Not in the least.
Juddy Well, she said he had. Said he's probably come to see you.
(*To Gerald*) You're the tenant here, aren't you—his cousin or
something?
Gerald Jack's the boy.
Gertrude He's waiting for you on the links. (*Going* R. C.) I'm going
back now. I'll speak to the maid.
Juddy Well, I hope you'll punish her. I'm sick of these servants—
gossiping and messing about instead of doing their work.
Gertrude I *know* Harold was going straight to the club; because
he *told* me so. So there. (*To Gerald*) Well, till this evening, Gerald.
Gerald Till—till——

Gertrude exits R. C.

Clive (*crosses to* R. *of table. To Juddy*) Well, sir, look here. I think the best thing will be for you to go to the golf club as quickly as possible——

Juddy I'm damned if I'm going to take orders from you, sir. (*Bobbing business*)

Gerald crosses R. C. *to Clive*

Clive (*imitating business*) No, please, don't misunderstand. I was going to suggest running you up there in my cousin's car.

Juddy Oh, I see.

Gerald protests

Clive (*to Gerald*) All right. We must get rid of the old blighter.

Juddy That's a different matter.

Clive Good, then that's a bet. I'll get the car.

Juddy Thank yah.

Clive ignores him

Gerald (*to Clive*) Clive, he said 'Thank yah'.

Clive exits off R. C. *hurriedly*

Juddy approaches Gerald, who flinches again

Juddy Now, sir, this fellow Twine—(*crosses to Gerald* R. C.)—he's an infernal nuisance.

Gerald Yes. Oh! he's very troublesome.

Juddy Timid little ass. (*His manner is very fierce*)

Gerald changes his ground again

Gerald (*as he moves away*) Yes. I hate that sort of thing.

Juddy (*going to him again*) He's the same at everything. Golf—bridge —now, bridge. Yesterday at the club he was my partner. I dealt and called a brace of shovels. No—no—no. Right. Two shovels it was. This feller here led something—I don't know—a small sparkler. Twine, if you please, lays down a hand stiff with blood-thumpers.

Gerald. Not really? Stiff?

Juddy Yes, stiff. And never a murmur! Don't you understand—he ought to have called!

Gerald Called! He ought to have screamed!

Juddy Of course. There it was, I lost six tricks. He hadn't a trump in his hand—where were they?

Gerald Up his sleeve.

Juddy Don't you play this game?

Clive in car starts from off R. *and pulls up outside door* R. C.

Juddy turns away up stage disgusted, swearing in Chinese

P'twee! Pong choo! (*To Gerald*) Day to yer. Blast yeh!

Clive (*stopping at window in car*) Come on, sir. The car's alongide.

Juddy Right away then. Don't keep me hanging about all day, *etc. etc.*

Exit, raging, door up R.

Juddy gets in car talking volubly, and while he is still standing the car starts, throwing him into seat, his hat flying off into the roadway as the car disappears off L.

Gerald closes door R. C. *and goes to study* D. R., *opens the door and brings Rhoda on by the hand; she crosses* L. C.

Gerald (*looking into study*) Twine, where are you? Come out from under that arm-chair. Old Jetty's gone.

Enter Twine D. R., *closes door, Gerald crosses* C. *in front of table.* *Twine* R. C.

Rhoda (*cross* C.) I've told Mr Twine all about it.

Gerald (*to Rhoda*) Right! (*Then to Twine*) Now the first thing to do is for one of us to go to her house and get her clothes from Putz.

Twine Yes, but who?

Gerald One of us. I'd like to go myself, only if I go I shall have to leave you alone with Rhoda. (*Twine smiles*) But of course Gertrude would very likely come back.

Twine Oh! (*Face falls*)

Gerald So that's agreed; he'll get them all right. (*To Rhoda*) He's a man of great strength of character; he carries a lot of weight.

Twine (*modestly*) Oh no.

Gerald Oh, you're a member of the Urban District Council.

Twine Yes.

Gerald And—(*to Rhoda*)—he's President of the Girls' Friendly Society.

Twine No, not *this* year.

Gerald Oh! Too friendly *last* year. (*Taking Twine to door* R. C.) Well, all you have to do is to see Putz, get clothes—come back.

Twine I'd rather not.

Gerald You'll find Putz an awfully nice chap.

Twine Shall I?

Gerald opens door R. C.

Gerald Oh, awful.

Exit Twine R. C.

Gerald closes door after him

Rhoda I expect you want to get me out of the way soon, don't you?
Gerald Yes. There's no great hurry. Mrs Twine's gone away for the day. (*To settee* L; *she sits up stage*)

Gerald sits on table facing her

Rhoda Well, I suppose—I don't know much about things, and I didn't realize at the time. But when I woke up here this morning, I thought it over and I saw what—what the world might think—isn't that the expression?
Gerald (*getting closer, crosses to settee, leans over back*) Don't worry about the silly old world. There's plenty of other places besides that.
Rhoda I suppose it's because human nature is so cruel that people always think the worst.
Gerald No, I think it's that the worst is the most likely.
Rhoda Whatever anybody thinks, you've been tremendously kind to me.

Warning for dog

Gerald Yes, haven't I? No, I mustn't say that. (*About to smooth her hair, but stops*)
Rhoda I say it anyhow; you've been wonderful.

He holds her hand for a moment and then lets it fall, then moves down stage behind settee

Rhoda (*in a more practical voice*) Well, the thing now is to get away.
Gerald Yes. My cousin's going to take you in the car. Where do you want to go?
Rhoda I've got friends in London. (*Moves down to Gerald on settee*)
Gerald (*crosses to top of settee*) Oh! Then you'd better go to London.
Rhoda The station will do.
Gerald Well, we'll see. First of all, what about some breakfast?
Rhoda Is there any?
Gerald Well, tea. There's surely tea.
Rhoda Shall I skirmish for tea?
Gerald Right you are.

Dog growl

Twine entering at door R. C. *breathlessly*

Twine Saved!

Gerald (*looking round at front door, then at Rhoda*) Here's another skirmish.

He opens front door. Conrad is heard in the distance. Twine, very heated and breathless, appears at front door

You've been very quick, Harold.

Twine Yes, I—(*out of breath*) I had to be—oh, my goodness——

Gerald Don't stand there sizzling. Tell me what happened. (*Brings chair down to table*)

Rhoda Did you see my step-father?

Twine (*coming in, mopping his brow*) I—I saw him.

Gerald Did you go to the house?

Twine I didn't get as far as the house.

Gerald Why not? Did you get stung by a butterfly or something?

Twine No, there was a dog.

Rhoda Oh! Was the dog *loose*?

Twine Yes, very.

Gerald But a dog—good Lord! What's a dog? Do you think I'm afraid of a dog?

Twine *You* may not be. (*Cross* D. R.)

Gerald I should think not. (*Crosses to door* R. C., *opens it*) *You* go back.

Rhoda Wait a moment. You say you saw my step-father?

Twine Yes, he came to the gate and—er—leant——

Gerald Lent what?

Twine Over.

Rhoda Did he seem more polite?

Twine No, he didn't.

Rhoda Oh! (*Very perturbed*)

Gerald What did he say?

Twine I told him what I wanted. He said something I didn't understand. Then he said something to the dog. I didn't understand that either.

Gerald But the dog did.

Twine Yes. (*Quickly*) It appeared to. (*Looks round at door* R. C. *furtively*)

Gerald (*to Rhoda*) You'll be here for breakfast.

Twine sits R. *of table*

Rhoda Yes. Skirmish for tea.

She exits D. L.

Gerald (*coming and sitting down beside Twine on sofa*) Well, I'm very glad you went over.

Twine Glad? (*Rising—Gerald puts him down*)
Gerald Yes. Now you can see the kind of man we're up against.
Twine Yes.
Gerald I've got a little scheme. The situation may yet be saved.
Twine By me? (*Trying to rise again*)
Gerald (*putting him down*) Yes. Don't keep popping up and down like that, old boy. You're already hot. Now this is my great idea. This girl must get some attire.
Twine It's all very well to say that——
Gerald Now don't interrupt. Gertrude has gone out for the day.
Twine Gertrude? No.

Twine is fidgeting with his trousers

Gerald Yes. She said so herself. Don't fiddle about with your knickers, old boy. We must concentrate. As I say, this girl must have something to wear.

Twine, inquiring look

And Gertrude has gone out for the day.
Twine Well?

Gerald taps his knee and speaks emphatically

Gerald As I say, the girl must have some female garments—well, Gertrude has plenty. And she has gone out for the day.

Twine slowly turns a horrified expression of inquiry towards Gerald. The latter pulls out a cigarette case

Have a cigarette old boy?
Twine No, thanks. D'you mean—?
Gerald Yes, by Jove! you're a marvel. I don't know anyone who would have seen it so quickly.
Twine (*rising*) You don't really seriously suggest that I should go and get some clothes of Gertrude's?
Gerald (*rising*) Well, old boy, you had your chance of getting Rhoda's own clothes from Putz. You come back sizzling with your stocking half mast and say we can't get them. Well, we must get some.

Twine fiddles about

Keep still—do. I've told you that before. Have you got woollies on? Now listen—if you get some things of Gertrude's——
Twine *That* I positively will not do.
Gerald (*incredulously*) You won't get them?

Twine Absolutely no.

Gerald You—in fact—you don't agree with my idea?

Twine No. Certainly not.

Gerald No. Well, well—it's a pity, but there you are. The best of friends must differ.

Clive enters R. C. *quietly and stands just inside door*

Twine I abso——

Gerald Now, old boy. No need to be pugnacious about it. I'm perfectly sure that I'm right, but you don't hear *me* saying I abso——

Twine Nothing will induce me.

Clive stands inside doorway R. C.

Gerald Quite. Quite.

Gerald looks at Clive

And mark you, you may be justified. I want to be quite fair. I say it's a good idea, you say no. Of course what one really wants in these cases is a third party—as referee.

Twine Nobody would persuade me.

Gerald Now, there you lose sympathy. For my part I'd agree to abide by a third party's decision. Of course we must find somebody entirely disinterested—you agree to that (*taking it for granted*)—yes. (*Look at Clive*) Now, who can we find? You don't know anyone, I suppose?

Twine stares vacantly

Twine No.

Gerald Old boy, I've got it.

Twine What?

Gerald Clive shall decide.

Twine *No.* (*Nervously*)

Gerald Oh, who better! He's neutral. We'll put it to him.

Twine Oh!

Gerald Now personally I think you'll win.

Twine smiles broadly. Clive slams door R.

Clive Hallo, boys!

Gerald Hallo, Clive!

Clive What's up?

Gerald Harold and I are just holding what might be called an extraordinary general meeting.

Clive Oh? (*Surprised*)

Gerald We're at a deadlock about a certain proposition and need an arbitrator, and we thought of you.

Clive Thank you very much, Harold—that's nice of you. What's the snag?

Gerald This. (*Pacifying Twine*) No, I'll put it fairly. We can't get a rig-out from Putz. But a rig-out for this girl we must have.

Clive There can't be any dispute about that.

Gerald No. Oh no. But Gertrude having gone for the day——

Clive Yes, I saw her go off in her car——

Gerald Yes, I was telling Harold about that. Well, one of us says 'Get a rig-out from Gertrude's wardrobe'. The other says 'No'. That's all.

Clive Oh, don't be a blithering idiot.

Gerald You think I'm wrong?

Clive Wrong? Of course you're wrong.

Twine is very pleased

Gerald (*to Twine*) It's all right—you've won.

Clive Here's a heaven-sent inspiration, and you turn it down. (*To Twine*) Congratulations, Harold.

Gerald crosses to settee, sits L.

Twine I beg your pardon?

Clive I think it's a fine idea of yours. I unhesitatingly vote for it.

Twine But I'm against it.

Clive Against it?

Gerald Yes, old boy, I don't want to boast, but I'm the one who said 'Do it'.

Clive It doesn't make any difference. My decision stands. It's the best idea of the whole morning, and, besides, Gertrude has got some very nice things.

Gerald Well, then, I think—the sooner the better. What?

Twine (*jumping up*) Listen, you fellows——

Clive No. *You* listen for a change. You've done nothing but yap, yap, yap all the morning. Just think what we've done for you. We hid you from Gertrude. We saved you when that Admiral came in here, breathing fire from his nostrils.

Clive and Gerald exchange looks

Twine Yes, I dare say. Thanks.

Clive We're not asking for gratitude. But something has got to be done quickly—poor old Gerald may get into trouble.

Gerald Yes. That's the most important point.

Clive And we must stand by him. We're in the same camp.

Gerald Yes. And we must have loyalty in the camp.
Clive Yes. And if necessary enforce it.
Twine (*nervously*) What?
Clive The alternative is surrender. Make a clean breast of it all to Gertrude——
Gerald And the Admiral——
Clive Tell Gertrude the girl was in that study while she was in the hall——
Gerald And you were in that study——
Clive With the girl——
Gerald Alone——
Clive For a long time. *Or*—keep Gertrude from finding out——
Gerald Ever——
Clive By getting the girl some clothes.

Pause. Twine stands miserably. Gerald speaks dramatically into his ear

Gerald So clothes——
Clive Or Gertrude——
Clive and **Gerald** Choose!

Twine only moans. Gerald and Clive lift Twine by the arms and seat him on the table. Gerald turns to Clive practically

Clive Carried.
Gerald Now, what will she want?
Clive We'd better ask Rhoda what she wants. Where is she?

Gerald turns to the kitchen door D. L. Twine attempts to go, but Clive holds him by the arm

Gerald (*speaking into kitchen*) How are you getting on?
Rhoda (*off L.*) Splendidly. I've found some tea.
Gerald We want you here a minute.
Rhoda Yes?

Gerald crosses L. Rhoda enters L., crosses to L. C.

Gerald Mr Twine is just going to get some clothes.
Clive Some of Mrs Twine's.
Rhoda Oh, but really——
Clive Well?
Rhoda It's very kind of Mr Twine to think of it—but I couldn't wear hers.
Twine No. You see?
Rhoda I mean they'd be too old for me.
Gerald Oh, but she's got some new ones.

Clive (*to Gerald*) No, you fool. (*Crossing to Rhoda*) It's simply to have an outfit here in case you can't get your own.

Rhoda Oh, I see.

Clive Yes. Now what will you want? Will you just tick off the items with Mr Twine?

Twine attempts to go—Clive holds him by the arm

Rhoda Well, it's very kind of Mr Twine——

Gerald Never mind that. Tick off the items.

Rhoda Well, just a frock and something to go under it.

Gerald (*severely to Twine*) Do you know what goes under it?

Clive All right. *I* know. I'll tell him. (*To Twine*) A bodice.

Gerald (*to Twine*) Has Gertrude got a bodice?

Twine (*resignedly*) Oh, I suppose so.

Clive You mustn't suppose.

Gerald No—you must know. You've been married for years. Get a bodice.

Twine All right. A bust one.

Gerald (*in horror*) Certainly not—a sound one.

Clive (*to Gerald*) That's all right.

Gerald Is it?

Clive Yes. Bust. You know. Be careful what you're saying!

Gerald Oh, sorry. Harold began it.

Clive Well, then, a frock and its underneath——

Rhoda And, I suppose, some shoes and stockings——

Clive (*to Twine*) Only with the stockings you'll want—(*trying to be tactful*)—to arrange for them to keep up.

Rhoda (*to Gerald*) And possibly a hat if he can manage it.

Gerald Oh, easily. (*To Twine*) Manage a hat. And choose the things that Gertrude won't miss. Put 'em all in a bag.

Twine (*with an air of one delivering an ultimatum*) When I've done this, I've finished with you.

Gerald Then do it quickly.

Clive You can take Gerald's car. Go on.

Gerald (*turns, crosses towards* R. C.) Steady on, old boy, it's my car.

Clive Yes, let him have the car.

Gerald All right. (*To Twine*) Hurry up then. Hop in the car. (*Taking Twine's arm and leading him to front door*) I'll see you off.

Twine (*trying to shake Gerald off*) Oh, let me go!

Gerald (*turning to Clive as he takes Twine out*) There you are. He *wants* to go.

Gerald goes out with Twine R. C.

Rhoda (*to Clive*) Oh, Mr Popkiss——

Clive Yes?

Rhoda Do you mind if I ask you something? I want your advice.

Clive Do you? Come on then. (*Cross to table* c.) Sit down here and tell me all about it. (*Sitting on table*)

Clive R. C. *Rhoda* L. C.

Rhoda It's only—I couldn't help coming here. But isn't it my duty now to give in and go home?

Clive Your duty—who to? Me?

Rhoda No. I meant to your cousin.

Clive Oh, old Gerald—but you needn't worry any more about *him*. You're not going to stay here anyhow. You're coming with me in the car, aren't you?

Rhoda Yes, if you—really—don't mind.

Clive If *I* don't mind. You needn't let that worry you. But you like to come with me, don't you?

Rhoda Yes.

Clive I'll take great care of you.

Rhoda I'm sure you will. I knew that directly I saw you.

Clive Did you? That's fine, because, you know, directly I saw *you* I knew something too. When you came out of that room last night on to the landing and smiled that little smile of yours—

She smiles

yes—that's the one—do you know what I knew then?

Rhoda No——

Clive (*seeing her embarrassment*) Well—I—er—never mind—we've plenty of time for that. Anyhow, you're glad you're coming with me in the car, aren't you?

Rhoda Yes, very. But I want to go to friends in London. Can you go all that way?

Clive Can I? You try and think of some friends in Scotland!

She smiles again

What a bit of luck that I'm here, isn't it? (*Taking her hand*)

Rhoda (*again embarrassed*) Yes.

Clive, hands bus.: Clive takes Rhoda's right hand in his left, palm to palm, and with his right hand lifts her fingers, letting them drop back

Clive I mean—of course, old Gerald would probably take you himself if I wasn't here. I say, isn't that funny? Do you see the way your fingers flop back, like a piano? He's married—and so on.

Rhoda Yes. I'm afraid I've done quite enough to compromise him already.

Clive Yes—I didn't mean that—but what I meant was—it would be wasted on him.

Rhoda Oh, I see. Then—*you're not* married?

Clive Me? No, I'm not married. Not—yet.

Rhoda Oh. Then you're going to be?

Clive What? Well, I—I didn't think so; but if—I—— (*Hums a few bars of a song*)

Gerald enters R. C., *comes down* R., *and Clive sees him*

Rhoda Oh, I think the kettle's boiling.

Gerald Oh, is it? Good! (*Makes no effort to go*)

Rhoda I'd better see to it.

Goes to kitchen

Clive Yes, I'll come with you. (*Going after her*)

Gerald No, stay here, old boy.

Clive Oh, but I haven't seen a kettle boil for years!

Gerald (*holding door* D. L.) This is no time for kettling. Quick now! What are we going to do? (*Cross* R. C.)

Clive She's coming with me.

Gerald In Gertrude's clothes? (R. C.)

Clive Yes. Why not?

Gerald This is desperate stuff.

Clive I know, but every minute's delay is dangerous.

Gerald But Gertrude's gone away.

Clive Other people will see her.

Gerald Who?

Clive Tradesmen, you fool. Milkmen—gardeners—probably the vicar.

Gerald Yes, all right, old boy. Don't be impulsive. It was I who said we must do something quickly.

Clive Well, do it.

Gerald But do you think she'll be all right in Gertrude's things?

Clive Of course she will. She'd look lovely in anything.

Gerald I don't mean that. You don't have to tell me that. I've known her a good deal longer than you have. I mean, oughtn't we to get her own if we can?

Clive And let Putz know that we're trying to smuggle her away?

Gerald What about an offensive on Putz? A combined offensive?

Clive No. Cut Putz clean out of it.

Putz appears silently R. C. *and walks slowly down* R., *unnoticed*

Unless, of course, we can *wangle* her things from Putz.

Gerald Ah! By diplomacy with Putz?

Clive Yes. But better ignore him completely.
Gerald Simply don't see him at all.
Clive No. Let sleeping dogs lie.

Putz is now down R. C.

Gerald Quite right, old boy. *You're* right. (*Turns and sees Putz, assumes a false heartiness in his embarrassment*) Hallo!
Putz (*with challenge*) Who shall go out from hereout in a motor? (*Pointing through window up* L.)
Gerald He heard what we were saying.
Putz Not only do I hear, I see him. Who shall go?
Gerald Oh, you mean, who went?
Putz Aller right. Who shall vent?
Clive (*crosses to Putz*) You think that your step-daughter's gone. Well, allow me to tell you she's going, and you needn't think you're going to stop her. So you'd better not come and try any of your bluff on us, you damn great stiff. (*To Gerald*) Introduce me, will you?
Putz Speak. (*To Clive*)
Clive Well, what d'you think I'm doing—singing?
Putz (*crosses* D. R., *addressing Gerald. Aggressively*) Who shall go presently already in the motor hereout? Also *that* I see and hear.
Gerald (*to Clive*) Diplomacy. Oh yes! Now look. Putty, old thing. (*Approaching Putz*)

Clive backs him up

Don't you worry about that car. That was just my brother-in-law —or, rather, not exactly my brother-in-law—because sisters and brothers have I none. But that man's father——
Putz Speak!
Gerald Yes; try not to say that, old boy. It's just one of those little things that irk.
Putz I know of you.

Gerald moves back

(*To Gerald*) My howskeeper she know all of it of you. Die vife of der little man is die enemy of Rhoda. Und she is die sister of your vife. And if your vife shall come, und Rhoda remain herein der whos, it make for you some hell of a business. *Fürchterlichkeit. Sturm und Drang.* (*Pronounced: Fear-ster-lick-kite—Fearfulness. 'Sturm und Drang'—Thunder and lightning*)
Gerald Speak. (*Turns to Clive*)

Clive crosses to Putz

Clive (*to Putz*) Now, you. Quick. One way or the other. Are you going to give us her clothes or not?

Putz I give.

Clive What?

Putz I give. I bring heah. Und I vait. Und she put on dis clode. Und she com back wit me to der hows.

Clive No damn fear.

Putz (*flaring up*) Zo. I also have no fear already. You shall try to send her from me, und, Herr Gott! I will make for you hot like hell.

Gerald But you ran her out.

Putz You t'ink you shall send her away also from hereout? Aller right. You shall try. Mit out die clode she cannot flee. Und I keep from her die closeys aller der time.

Clive (*to Gerald*) Oh, go on. Kick him out.

Gerald (*to Putz*) Allez—Goosen-tight!

Putz You t'ink you can fight it mit me, ja?

Gerald What? (*To Clive*) Tell him to go.

Clive (*cross* R. *to Putz*) Get out.

Putz (*folding his arms*) I go ven I vish.

Gerald What can we do to make him wish? (*Crosses behind table to* R. C.)

Twine enters heatedly, carrying a bag. He has a lady's hat in his hand and shoes sticking out of his pockets

Twine Now look here, you chaps. I've brought these things, but I've determined——

They signal to him violently to keep quiet

Clive Shut up, you idiot!

Putz (*turning on them, suddenly seizing the bag from Twine with an angry roar*) Zo! You t'ink to give her die clode. You shall not it.

Dialogue during struggle

Gerald Hold him, Harold.

Twine Don't! Don't!

Clive I've got him!

These lines are repeated until Putz is heard at door R. C. *('I win,' etc.)*

Putz snatches bag from Twine and moves L. C. *Twine catches Putz by the leg and they both fall; Gerald throws himself on the top, catching hold of Twine; then Clive comes round top of table to* L. *Putz wriggles out* L. *front with bag and crosses* L. *Clive intercepts Putz and tries to snatch the bag— they struggle. Putz hits Clive on the head with the bag. Clive sinks on to the settee dazed. Putz then crosses behind table to door* R. C. *and—with bag raised in his right hand—exclaims*

Putz (*at door up* R. C.) I win—Deutschland über Alles!

QUICK CURTAIN

SECOND CURTAIN: *Gerald is still holding Twine down* C, *but he is looking at Clive, who is just recovering from the knock on his head. Rhoda appearing at kitchen door* D. L. *with tray of tea, etc. Clive looks at her and smiles broadly*

ACT III

Door R. C., *closed*

The hall—about two and a half hours later

The curtain rises on angry voices. Clive discovered seated on stairs; Gerald
L. C.

Clive She didn't say it to you; she said it to me.

Gerald Liar! That's all. Liar!

Clive Are you calling me a liar?

Gerald I said to her, 'He'll help us', and she said 'Thank you' to me for asking you to help.

Clive You know as well as I do, I said, 'I'm going to help', and she, poor little soul, burst into a smile.

Gerald That was simply because she saw your face for the first time. I did the same.

Clive Ah, wait a minute. (*Crossing round back of settee to front*) Don't you begin on faces. The enemy's well in your country if you do.

Gerald (*crossing to* R. C. *front of table*) You're jealous because I found her first.

Clive (*crossing to* L. C. *front of table*) And you're as wild as hell because she likes me best.

Gerald Lies and muck!

Clive And I like her far better than you can.

Gerald And I like Harold better than I like you. Also Putz, Nutts, and Conrad.

Clive You tried to keep her a secret from me. When you knew I was coming you bunged her in the kitchen along with that humming cat.

Gerald That's another hideous lie. But I'd rather she met the cat than you.

Clive I saved the whole situation from the start.

Gerald What! Who started that drivelling idea for outing that woman?

Clive What woman?

Gerald The daily one—Mrs Thunderguts.

Clive That'll do. Over the only nice thing that happens in this place you butt in and down me, or try to, you blighter.

Gerald I butt in! I like that. I come in here and find you sitting on
the table holding her poor little hand and trying to sing.

Clive I sing a damn sight better than you do. I've heard you, thank
you. Like the last bit of the bath running out.

Gerald Anyhow, I don't want you to sing any more. I promised
her decent treatment.

Clive Yes, that's just it, and now you're sorry you promised her
anything.

Gerald Oh! The champion lie. That's yours.

Clive I'll take it. You'd send her back to Putz if I let you.

Gerald. Clive, be careful, I warn you. Don't rouse me too much.
I get like a lion.

Clive You were a damn fine lion when Putz came in this morning.

Gerald You made a bee-line for the door.

Clive I went to the door to try to cut Putz off; and what did you
do?—you sat on the floor and cut poor Harold off.

Gerald For all the use you've been you'd better clear out.

Clive I'm going to, and she's coming with me. (*Cross to* L. *of table*)
She told me herself she wanted me to take her.

Gerald I told her to tell you so, and you know it, you dog's-body.

Clive (*crossing to Gerald, threateningly*) You—you——

Rhoda has appeared above from bedroom

Rhoda (*shocked*) Oh!

Clive (*seeing Rhoda, starts to sing*)—Ukelele lady.

Rhoda If you're going to quarrel about me, I'd better go home.

Gerald (*To Rhoda*) We were only just wondering which of us was
most anxious to help you.

Rhoda You're both most anxious. That's been proved. (*Coming
down* L.)

Gerald I proved it first.

Clive I'm going on proving it a long time after you are.

Rhoda Well, I think I'd better go home. (*Cross front of settee to* L. C.)

Gerald No, no. That would be a pity.

Clive Pity! You're not going back there.

Rhoda Oh, I don't want to. I only meant for his sake.

Gerald There you are—for *my* sake.

Clive It's for your sake she's willing to go, and for my sake she
doesn't want to.

Rhoda moves away L.

Gerald Oh, do at least be fifty-fifty while she's here.

Clive Yes, all right, old boy. Sorry!

Gerald That's all right, old boy.

Rhoda (*crossing to Clive* R. C.) Only it seems hopeless. I can't really get to London without my own things.

Clive (*to Gerald*) Are you sure there are no more of Clara's things among your luggage?

Gerald Another pair of golf shoes and two more pairs of golf stockings—oh, and an umbrella!

Gerald looks away

Clive Oh! A string of beads and we're home. (*To Rhoda*) Anyway, couldn't you trick Putz somehow?

Gerald Me? No, old boy, I don't think so.

Clive I was talking to Rhoda.

Rhoda I wonder. Of course if I went over there dressed—I mean in any old dress——

Clive Well?

Rhoda I could say, 'Here I am—all ready to go to London,' then he might give in.

Gerald And hand over your own things?

Rhoda Yes. I know him. When he's winning he's a devil. But if he thought I'd beaten him, he might plead.

Gerald You hear that? Just any old frock and we could get all her things from pleading Putz.

Clive Yes. There's something in this. It's worth trying.

Gerald Yes. I said so, old boy.

Clive Well, we'll set about it. (*To Rhoda*) You'd better get back to that room. (*Indicating room up* L.) There's always a chance you may be seen.

Rhoda Yes. (*Going upstairs* L.) Any kind of frock would do, and I believe I could fool him.

Clives smiles at her as she goes into room up L. *on balcony*

Gerald (*to Rhoda*) Good girl. (*To Clive*) Isn't she?

Clive (*with smile disappearing*) All right. Don't start that again.

Gerald (*with a very tolerant smile*) Now don't start arguing.

Clive What? I wasn't arguing.

Gerald I didn't say you were. I said 'don't'.

Clive That's the same thing as saying I was.

Gerald Oh, is it?

Clive Yes, it is it.

Gerald Then I'm sorry.

Clive That's quite all right.

Gerald Not at all, old boy. Still, personally I don't think it is.

Clive You don't think it is what?

Gerald The same thing to say to a person 'don't' as to say 'you are'.

Clive What the hell are you talking about?

Gerald Well, old boy, you ought to know. You began it.

Clive Began what? (*Raising his voice*)

Gerald I said 'don't', and you said——

Clive Don't what?

Gerald I forget now. Oh yes, I remember. I said 'don't let's argue'.

Clive Well, anyhow, this frock—the shops will be open now.

Gerald But I've told you. No shops are open today.

Clive You went down before the shops were open, and that was why you found the shops were shut.

Gerald I keep telling you there are no shops open in the place today; it's a sort of local regatta.

Clive (*crosses to settee and sits*) I know you did.

Gerald The man who keeps the milliner's shop is in the town band.

Clive I don't care if he's in the fire brigade. Round him up.

Gerald I can't. He's in the band on the front, shaking his exhaust out of the butt end of a cornet.

Clive (*crossing to* L. C. *above table*) Well, there are other towns within reach—without regattas.

Gerald I never said there weren't.

Clive (*cross to Gerald*) No, but you never remembered there *were*.

Gerald Well, go and find one if you're so clever.

Clive I'm going to, and I'm going to take the car. (*Cross up* L., *Gerald* R. C.)

Gerald There you go again. My car. (*Crosses to* L. C. *front of table*)

Clive (R. C.) Well, hell's delight, it's for your sake.

Gerald You don't say 'May I take the car?' You say 'I'm going to take the car'. That's what gets my goat.

Clive Anyway, I bet you I get into a shop here.

Gerald I bet you. There! I've been and seen. The only things you can buy are flags and beer.

Clive Then why didn't you get some beer?

Gerald I did.

Clive You *would*.

Gerald Go on, Good-bye.

Clive, going R. C., *turns back and goes to kitchen door*

Clive Well, I hope you'll enjoy yourself. You'll have nice company.

Gerald (*with a smile*) Yes. Why are you going that way?

Juddy is seen through window R. C.

Clive Because old Admiral Bloodhead is coming up the drive.

Exit D. L. *to kitchen*

Gerald Oh, curse him! What does he want?

Knock at door R. C.

Come in.

Juddy enters as Clive goes

Juddy Hallo, yer young devil! (*Door* R. C.) I've heard about you. Where is she?

Gerald Where's who?

Juddy That girl. Come on. I'm not one of the people who abuse that girl. I like her. Like her looks. Always have.

Gerald Yes. I always have too.

Juddy Well, you needn't think I'm going to let her be kicked out of the house like this.

Gerald Oh, it's not a question of her being kicked out at all.

Juddy It is. I'm going to make the devil of a row about it.

Gerald But, Mr—Captain—she's not being kicked out.

Juddy She was kicked out by that swine, wasn't she?

Gerald Oh, by Putz. Quite right. Yes, old boy, old salt.

Juddy How long is she going to be here?

Gerald Well, the trouble is she's got no clothes.

Juddy Hasn't she? Oh! (*Cross* L.) I'd rather like to have a word with her. Where is she?

Gerald No, I'll tell you what. Have you a wife?

Juddy It doesn't matter if I've got fifty wives.

Gerald I refer to the one in this port.

Juddy Eh?

Gerald I mean what size is she?

Juddy Mind yer own business.

Gerald I was only thinking I might perhaps be allowed to look through her clothes.

Juddy What?

Gerald No, no. All right. On second thoughts I won't.

Juddy I didn't come here for you to insult my wife for me.

Gerald Didn't you? What did you come here for?

Juddy To take that girl away.

Gerald Where?

Juddy To my house.

Gerald *You'll* take her?

Juddy Certainly. I'll wait for her.

Gerald She's just waiting for a frock.

Juddy Oh, well, I'll go and arrange for her to come. You bring her over.

Gerald Ay, ay, sir. Very likely. Very quickly.

Juddy See yer do it then. (*Cross* R. C.) And show a leg. Bustle about.

Gerald Oh, show a leg and a bustle.

Juddy (*cross up* R. C.) And if yer don't I'll come back and fetch her myself. Day ter yer.

Exit, shutting door R. U.

Rhoda appears on balcony

Gerald Ah! Day ter yer.

Rhoda Well, what did he say?

Gerald Oh, a lot of nautical nonsense I didn't understand. I think the old rascal likes you rather.

Rhoda Yes, I think he does. (*Coming downstairs to behind settee* L.)

Gerald Why, do you know him?

Rhoda No, but when I've passed him in the road he's been looky. You know—(*bus.: looking coyly*)—like that.

Gerald Looky! If he's been looky like that it's off.

Rhoda What's off? (*Cross in front of settee to Gerald* L. C.)

Gerald There was an idea you might go there.

Rhoda Where? To Admiral Juddy's? (*At the bottom of the stairs*)

Gerald Yes, and Mrs Juddy's.

Rhoda And those horrible Juddy girls?

Gerald Good Lord! Has he got young?

Rhoda Oh, please. I couldn't. Those two Miss Juddies would make an awful scandal.

Gerald Well, you shan't go.

Rhoda sits on L. *of settee*

I don't want you to go at all—don't think that.

Rhoda No, I quite understand.

Gerald (*sitting on settee*) Our little friendship mustn't end here.

Rhoda Your kind of friendship never ends.

Gerald Oh, dear, dear, dear! No. Isn't that nice to think of?

Rhoda (*looking into Gerald's eyes*) And the same with your cousin.

Gerald As a matter of fact, I'm very glad he's taking you. He's an awfully simple, soft-hearted chap. He's very fond of canaries. Oh, well, I'll go and tell old Juddy and say you're not coming. (*Leads Rhoda across to stairs* L.) Will you be all right? (*Cross* R. *to door up* R.)

Rhoda Yes. I'll stay in the bedroom. But you don't think my step-father will call again, do you?

Gerald I hope not. You do like Clive, don't you?

Rhoda Yes, I think he's awfully nice.

Gerald Yes—(*pause*)—and I'm a nice little chap too.

Exits door R. C. *to* R. *Close door*

Rhoda up at window on balcony. Mrs Leverett puts a stealthy head through the kitchen door. She catches sight of Rhoda, who is waving to Gerald, who is going off round the drive. Rhoda calls to Gerald 'Goodbye'. Rhoda wheels round and they see each other. Mrs Leverett L. C.

Rhoda What are *you* doing here?

Mrs Leverett Same to you, (*at table* C.) only from last night onward.

Rhoda (*anxiously, coming down* L. *behind settee*) How do you know about that?

Mrs Leverett Oh! I've known about it from first thing this morning. And I'm not the only one that knows.

Rhoda No, in that case I don't suppose you are. (*Cross down stairs to* L.)

Mrs Leverett That'll do, miss. (*Turns to Rhoda*) Impertinence always goes with the other.

Rhoda (*hurrying down*) Come here, please. I want to speak to you.

Mrs Leverett (*moving to Rhoda, her temper rising*) You'll get spoke to all right before long; I'll promise you that.

Rhoda (*cross* L. C. *to Mrs Leverett*). But you weren't told to come back by Mr Popkiss.

Mrs Leverett Him! No. And he'll pop no more of his kisses after this.

Rhoda What d'you mean?

Mrs Leverett You wait and hear what his wife's got to say.

Rhoda (*very alarmed*) His wife?

Mrs Leverett Yes. Oh, you can't get away. *I* saw you, this morning. Out you comes on the landing—(*putting on voice. Cross* R.)— 'Mr Popkiss! Mr Popkiss!' Yes. And back he went to the room, what's more.

Rhoda Why didn't you speak?

Warning for knock

Mrs Leverett Oh, I *did* speak.

Rhoda (*horrified*) I can guess. You sneaked to Mrs Twine.

Mrs Leverett Don't you call it sneakin'. That's brazen—(*cross to Rhoda*)—that is—brazen. I know me dooty.

Rhoda I see. And Mrs Twine went off to get his wife.

Mrs Leverett (*with satisfaction*) And will shortly be back.

Rhoda (*greatly agitated*) Oh, good heavens!

Door knock

There is a sharp knock at the front door. Rhoda instinctively runs upstairs L.
She pauses by bedroom door

See who that is.

Mrs Leverett (*looking up at Rhoda*) You order such about as what
is yours to order.

*Rhoda is half hidden by standing close up to the wall. Mrs Leverett opens
front door*

*Poppy Dickey appears. She is a local maiden in a bright summer frock and
carrying a tray of small flags. She laughs a little laugh in two notes, rather
like the cry of the cuckoo*

Poppy (*seeing Mrs Leverett, she laughs*) Flags for the Lifeboat?

Mrs Leverett No, thank you. (*Cross* D. R.)

Poppy Oh, support our Lifeboat. (*Coming down to her*)

Mrs Leverett No thank you. My husband is on board.

Poppy What about the gentleman who's come here? Has he got
his little flag?

Mrs Leverett Out.

Poppy Well, what about the one who's staying with Mrs Twine?
They said *he* was here (*Laugh—cuckoo laugh*)

Mrs Leverett Oh, well, he's not here now, miss.

Poppy Oh, how too crushing of him! No little flags at all? Well,
good morning. P'r'aps I'll meet one of the gentlemen in the road.

Exits R. C., *and Mrs Leverett closes the door*

Mrs Leverett (*at door*) P'r'aps you will. (*Cross to* C. *behind table and
look towards door* R. C.) And it wouldn't be the first time you've
done that!

She returns to kitchen. Closes door

Rhoda immediately runs down to door R. C. *She opens it and runs a
few yards out in front drive*

Rhoda (*calling in a guarded voice*) I say! I say! Come here! (*Cross*
D. R. C.)

*Poppy reappears, looking extremely surprised and intrigued. Rhoda
beckons her in. Poppy enters wide-eyed. She crosses* D. R.

Poppy (*taking stock of her*) Well, it takes a good deal to surprise me.

Rhoda. I know you by sight. You live in Chumpton, don't you?

Poppy That's right. My name's Poppy Dickey. I've heard about
you too. But what's *this* little episode?

Rohda Oh, do be kind and help me.

Poppy But I'm selling flags for the Lifeboat. I'd love to know what *you're* doing!

Rhoda I simply *had* to come here. (*Close door* R. C.)

Poppy Why? Did you know these boys before?

Rhoda No. But I came in here last night.

Poppy What, and said, 'Oh, I simply had to come'—like that?

Rhoda. No. Well—I came here because—there was nothing else to do.

Poppy (*breezily*) Really? (*Cross to front of table*) That's what I call a good reason but a bad excuse.

Rhoda Listen, please. (*Glances at kitchen door, then speaks intensely*) I'm in great trouble.

Poppy I'm not surprised. I've asked for a bit of trouble myself before now, but I've never chased it quite as hard as this.

Rhoda Let me tell you. I had a row at home. So I came here.

Poppy Last night, this was?

Rhoda Yes.

Poppy And met these boys?

Rhoda Yes.

Poppy And you've stayed here?

Rhoda Yes, I've had to.

Poppy Like you are now?

Rhoda Yes, more or less.

Poppy All night and ever since?

Rhoda Yes.

Poppy Think of that! And me selling flags!

Rhoda But I do want help. (*Very distressed*)

Poppy You don't strike me as wanting much help.

Rhoda I do. Terribly. Oh, stay and help me! There may be trouble. That's why I want your help.

Poppy (*crosses to settee*) Well, I like that. If I didn't have a hand in the crime I don't see getting stung for the inquest. (*Sits on arm of settee down stage*)

Rhoda (*cross to settee, kneels*) Listen. Lend me that frock for ten minutes and I shall be saved.

Poppy Really? And what'll *I* be?

Rhoda Those two will be back directly. You wait in that bedroom and tell them.

Poppy (*rise*). Me wait in that bedroom with no frock on for the two boys?

Rhoda Yes. Oh, it would be wonderful if you would!

Poppy laughs

(*Imploringly—rising*) You'll do it?

Poppy Well, it's a bit out of the usual. But I can see you're in trouble.

Warning for knock at door

(*Hesitating*) Yes, but—(*cross to lower end of settee*)—you're sure these boys will enter into the spirit of the thing?

Rhoda Of course. They're darlings. (*Laughs*) You'll be doing *them* a good turn too.

Poppy Yes, but it's me I'm thinking of.

Rhoda Well, you too. Because, you see, you can sell them flags for the lifeboat.

Poppy (*with her cuckoo laugh*) Strikes me, I *am* the Lifeboat. (*She turns, goes upstairs, with Rhoda following. Halts half-way up*) But if I do this, you will bring back my frock?

Rhoda Yes, yes. I promise I will. Immediately.

Poppy Righto. (*Cross upstairs* L.) You needn't overdo it. I dare say *fairly* quickly will do.

A loud knock at the front door. Rhoda hustles Poppy into bedroom L.

Rhoda Look out. Come on. In here. Quick!

She gets Poppy into bedroom as Mrs Leverett enters from kitchen

Rhoda pretends to be looking out of bedroom

There's somebody at the front door.

Mrs Leverett You kindly keep your orders for such as is theirs to get. My name is not Nutts.

Rhoda goes into bedroom

Mrs Leverett goes and opens front door. Twine is waiting outside. He is startled to see Mrs Leverett, and much embarrassed

Twine Oh!

Steps inside

Mrs Leverett Well, sir?

Twine Well?

Mrs Leverett Well? (*Brief pause*) Well?

Twine I—I didn't expect to see *you*.

Mrs Leverett Why not?

Twine I didn't think you were here.

Mrs Leverett Why shouldn't I be here, sir?

Twine Oh! For no reason I know of.

During these lines Twine moves down R., *Mrs Leverett follows*

Mrs Leverett Then why didn't you expect to see me?

Twine I don't know exactly.

Mrs Leverett You knew I was working here, didn't you?

Twine Yes, dear.

Mrs Leverett What!

Twine I beg your pardon. I mean yes.

Mrs Leverett Well, then?

Twine Mr Popkiss told me you'd gone.

Mrs Leverett Oh! Then have *you* been here this morning?

Twine (*cross to* R. C.) Oh! No—I—I met him out.

Mrs Leverett Ah! just now when he went out? (*Cross to Twine* R. C.)

Twine (*gladly*) Yes.

Mrs Leverett (*with triumph*) Then if you met him just now, who did you come here expecting to see?

Twine Oh! I came—(*with an inspiration*)—about a bag I lost.

Mrs Leverett Where?

Twine Here.

Mrs Leverett When?

Twine Oh! No, I didn't lose it. (*Crosses to* C. *front of table*) He lost it. I want to know if it's come back.

Mrs Leverett Come back from where? (*Following Twine* C.)

Twine From wherever it went to.

Mrs Leverett You said it went here.

Twine Oh!

Mrs Leverett (*peering at him suspiciously*) Mr Twine!

Twine What?

Mrs Leverett Do you know anything?

Twine (*very nervously*) Know?

Mrs Leverett Yes—know.

Twine No.

Mrs Leverett No?

Twine Yes. No. Really. It's all right about the bag. Don't mention it. (*He turns tail and goes between table and Mrs Leverett*)

Exit R. C.

Mrs Leverett follows him into porch and stands staring after him and shaking her head suspiciously

Rhoda in Poppy Dickey's dress nips out of the bedroom—glances into the hall, then goes quickly down the stairs, having ascertained that Mrs Leverett is in the porch; exit door down L.

As Mrs Leverett returns to L. *of table, Twine again enters* R. C. *and comes down very stealthily to* R. *of table*

Mrs Leverett——

Mrs Leverett (*very startled*) Oh, well, what now, sir?
Twine (*moving towards her* c. *front of table*) You said something about
—did I know? Tell me, do you know something? (*Very close to
Mrs Leverett*)
Mrs Leverett Do I know what?
Twine Oh! I don't know—I'm sure I don't know.
Mrs Leverett Do I know what you don't know?
Twine (*gladly*) Yes.
Mrs Leverett Well, if you don't know what you know, how do I
know if I know it?
Twine (*turning* R. *towards door* R. C.) Oh, I think I'll get out. (*Turns*
R.) Oh dear!—(*in fear*)—here comes Mr Popkiss back.
Mrs Leverett Oh, does he! I've had enough of him today. I'm
going back to my kitchen.

Exit D. L.

Twine tries to sneak out D. L. *Gerald enters and stops him*

Gerald Hallo, Harold!
Twine Oh, blow!
Gerald What's the meaning of this?
Twine Of what?
Gerald Of this. This—this. You know what *this* means, don't you?
Twine Yes.
Gerald Well, what's the meaning of this?
Twine I don't know.
Gerald You told Admiral Thing!
Twine I had to.
Gerald You swore you wouldn't.
Twine I couldn't help it.
Gerald You broke a swear. That's one thing a gentleman never
breaks.
Twine I don't think anything will matter now. (*Look over* L.) That
woman's back in the kitchen.
Gerald What! Why not say so? (*Crossing to door* D. L. *quickly and
calling in*) Where are you? No, not you, cat. (*To imaginary cat*)
The other one.
Twine Isn't she there?
Gerald No. What's the meaning of this?
Twine (*annoyed*) Don't keep asking me *that*.
Gerald I didn't say *that*; I said *this*.
Twine I don't even know what you mean by *this*.
Gerald Come, come, Harold. That's what I was asking *you*.

Enter Clive R. C. *from* L., *running, with very small parcel, which he puts on the table*

Clive Here you are. I told you I'd get it.
Gerald A frock?
Clive Yes. And everything else.
Twine But what about Gertrude's bag?
Gerald Well, go and get it back from Putz.
Twine I won't.
Gerald You won't?
Clive But you gave it to Putz.
Gerald Well, get out of this, anyhow. We don't like your trousers or your face.
Twine Blow you both. (*Cross up* R.) I beg your pardon, but really you make me lose my temper.

Goes off R. C. *to* L.

Clive I'll take these things up to Rhoda.
Gerald No. *I* will. (*Taking parcel*) I shall only go as far as the door. (*Going upstairs*)
Twine (*Rushing back* R. C.) Quick! Look out! Something appalling.
Gerald (*halting on stairs*) Then don't bring it in here.
Clive What is it?
Twine Gertrude, Clara, and mother. And the daily woman at the gate.
Gerald Clara! (*He comes downstairs again and throws away parcel*)
Clive Treason. Somebody's done the dirty.
Gerald You swine of a Twine.
Twine No; it's Gertrude. But don't say I said so. Good-bye, you fellows. (*Hurries out through kitchen door* L.) Good-bye.

Exit

Gerald. Clive! What'll I do? What'll I say?
Clive Show her the girl.
Gerald But her mind's been poisoned by Gertrude.
Clive Show her the girl. That's enough for anyone.

Enter Clara R. C., *cross* D. R. C.

Gerald Clara! Darling!

Mrs Possett, Gertrude, and Mrs Leverett enter R. C. *from* L. *They go to settee*

Clara Oh, Gerald, if there were anything wrong, could you kiss me like that?

Gerald Of course I could, darling.

Clive Couldn't, you fool.

Gerald Couldn't, you fool. Couldn't, darling. (*Turns*) You needn't sit down all over the place. I want to speak to Clara.

Clive Yes, alone.

Gertrude Certainly not.

Clara Thank you, Gertrude. I prefer to speak to him alone. (*Cross* L. C.)

Gertrude Mrs Leverett, is that girl still here?

Mrs Leverett She is. In the bedroom.

Gertrude There.

Clara She *is* still here?

Mrs Possett. I feel sick.

Clive Oh, stop that. (*To Mrs Possett*) There's quite enough on hand without that.

Gertrude Mrs Leverett, take my mother to the drawing-room.

Gerald That'll be nice for the drawing-room.

Mrs Leverett (*helping Mrs Possett*) I didn't come here for that.

Clive No, but she *did*. Take her away.

Mrs Leverett I came here to say my say, and say my say I mean to do.

Exit with Mrs Possett R. *to drawing-room*

Clara (*to Gerald*) Now, perhaps you'll tell me why that girl's still here.

Clive Go on, the gong's gone.

Gerald (*cross to Clara*) Certainly. I'm very glad she is. (*To Clive*) Am I?

Clive Delighted!

Gerald There you are. I'm delighted. She came here last night— poor little soul—alone in pyjamas. In pyjamas alone. Driven from home. Driven by Putz.

Gertrude Rubbish! She's a notorious girl.

Clive She's the sweetest little girl I've ever seen.

Gerald She's certainly the sweetest *I've* ever seen—almost.

Clive I tell you she's above suspicion.

Gerald Yes. Like Potiphar's wife.

Clive She radiates purity and innocence.

Clara Well, I haven't accused. I'll see her and judge.

Clive Yes, go on. Call her out of that room.

Gerald (*boldly*) Quite right. (*Calls*) Little girl. Come out of that room.

They all look up at bedroom, with their backs to audience

Clive Now you shall see.

Poppy Dickey enters in cami-knickers from bedroom on balcony L.; crosses to the other end of the balcony, singing and dancing

Poppy 'Oh, sir, she's my baby—
        Yes, sir, she's my baby;
        Oh, sir, she's my baby now!'

She turns to look over front of balcony; as she does so she calls out, 'Flags for the Lifeboat!' *Realizing the situation, she gives a scream and rushes back into bedroom L. Gerald and Clive turn to each other, looking thunderstruck*

Gertrude What's the meaning of this?
Gerald Don't ask me.
Clara Is *that* the girl?
Gerald No, it isn't.
Clara Then who is it?
Gerald (*to Clive*) Who is it?
Clive I didn't put it there.
Gerald Some mistake, darling.
Clara Rubbish! You said 'Come out', and out she came.
Gerald Yes; but this wasn't the one we wanted to come out.
Gertrude That's another local girl—she's one of the Dickeys.
Gerald (*to Clive*) You hear that! She's one of the Dickeys.
Clive Yes, she looks it.

Poppy re-enters from bedroom wearing Rhoda's dressing-gown

Gertrude They've evidently been collecting all the fast girls of the place.
Poppy (*above*) Don't you start on me, Mrs Twine.
Gertrude (*crosses stairs*) Where's that girl from up the road? Is she there too?
Poppy I don't know anything about any girl from up any road.
Gerald (*to Clive*) What happened?
Clive Don't ask silly questions. I'm not a wizard.
Gerald Somebody is.
Gertrude Why did you come here?
Poppy I came selling flags, and I went upstairs to mend my frock. I caught it on the gatepost.
Gerald Is this friend or foe?
Clara It's all a pack of lies. I know that.

Gertrude goes upstairs

Gerald Oh, darling—not a whole pack.
Poppy (*to Gertrude*) Where are you going? That's *my* room.

They exit into bedroom up L.

Clara There you are. *Her* room.

Clive Yes, but the other bedrooms is elsewhere.

Gertrude (*off*) Just as I thought.

Poppy (*off*) Mind your own business.

Gertrude (*enters*) There's not a sign of a frock in that room.

Poppy enters from bedroom L. *on balcony*

Clara Then this is the one that was here all night.

Gerald No, darling. I keep telling you. A much better one than that. The other one radiates purity. Nothing like this Dickey thing at all.

Poppy Well, you're a nice one to try and help.

Gerald You think you're helping me?

Clive Of course she is. A jolly fine effort. Well tried, Miss Flags.

Poppy Thank you. I'm glad someone's got a glad hand.

Gertrude It's quite clear. You were to stay here and tell lies while the other little wretch escaped. Go into that room. I'll tell your mother.

Poppy You try. Mother's a sport, and she hates you like hell.

Exit into bedroom on balcony L.

Clara I see. There are two of them.

Gertrude crosses behind table

Gerald That's right.

Clara One each.

Gerald That's right. No, there aren't two. Well, yes, there are two —but—— (*To Clive*) Go on. Can't you say something?

Clara Why are there two?

Gerald (*to Clive*) Why are there two? That's you.

Clive Now get this, Clara. For some reason, about which we're a trifle hazy, there are two—namely, radiates purity and Flags for the Lifeboat.

Gertrude And one's as bad as the other.

Gerald No; she's worse.

Clive We've never set eyes on this Dickey thing—neither of us. I don't quite know why *I* haven't—

Gerald digs Clive, drawing his attention to the fact that Gertrude is eyeing him suspiciously

—but there it is.

Gertrude (*crosses to* R. C. *from behind table*) If it wasn't all some intrigue, why didn't you ask for my help last night?

Clive I'll tell you that. Because you're a jealous, green-eyed, backbiting woman.

Gerald Thank you, Clive.

Clive That's all right. She's got some more to come. (*Then to Gertrude*) You're very fond of calling other people liars—but what about you, with your vile scandals and venomous libels and dirty little tattling tea-parties?

Gertrude You'll gain nothing by rudeness.

Clive I don't care whether I gain or not. It's well overdue to you. (*Turns to Clara*) And, Clara, don't you accuse Gerald. The girl he's defending is the victim of a wicked scandal. So long as Gertrude can find some mud to fling she doesn't care a damn whether it sticks.

Gerald Quite right.

Gertrude You needn't lose your temper. Just because you arranged for the girl to be here last night and then weren't allowed to stay here yourself too.

Goes into drawing-room R.

Clive That woman's got a mind like a very ingenious sink.

Clara crosses R. C.

Gerald Clara darling. Don't go.

Clara Oh, I know it's true what she says. You're only trying to deceive me.

Gerald No, I'm trying not to.

Clara exits up R.

Clive Look here—we must play our trump card, that's all.

Gerald Have we got one?

Clive Yes, I'm going along to that house.

Gerald No, don't risk bringing Rhoda back. She's too pretty. She wouldn't go well. I know she wouldn't.

Clive No, no, I don't mean her. I'm going to get Putz.

Gerald Putz?

Clive Yes. I'm going to get a big boulder and fling it in the pit of Putz's stomach and run like hell with him after me.

Gerald Fine, Clive!—that's fine! That'll show Clara. Infuriate him. Don't throw stones, throw wurts.

Clive (*going*) All right. Oh, if you can, Gerald, have that cat handy——

Gerald Why?

Clive Because with any luck I'll bring Conrad too.

Clive goes hurriedly up R. C.

Gerald takes thought, then he picks up the parcel that Clive gave him with the dress, and makes for the stairs

There are sounds of dissension in the drawing-room and Clara returns. She speaks as she enters

Clara (*entering from* R. *and saying as she enters*) Quite enough to stand without that.

Gerald (*running down the stairs with the parcel behind him, hiding it from Clara*) What's the matter, darling?

Clara I wasn't speaking to you.

Gerald Oh! you sounded so cross, I thought you were.

Clara It's Gertrude. You can't even misbehave yourself without Gertrude finding it out.

Gerald No, I know I can't. Nobody can.

Clara Then you *did* misbehave yourself?

Gerald You don't believe that, do you?

Clara I hate to. But a girl coming in here with pyjamas on. (*Looking away*)

Gerald I know, dear. I didn't want her to have them on.

Clara What!

Gerald I mean I'd rather she'd been wearing a hat.

Clara Oh, be honest with me. I'm trying to be loyal and loving.

Gerald I know you are, darling, and I'm trying to explain it away—to explain, I mean—without the away.

Clara I don't think you need try to tell me any more.

Gerald Thank you, darling. (*Attempting to embrace her*)

Clara No. (*Pushing Gerald away gently*) You admit to keeping the girl here all night?

Gerald No, dear, letting her stay here all night. That's all the difference. Think of this poor little girl. She came here last night through the long and dewy grass. She was soused—I mean soaked.

Clara I don't care.

Gerald But you must care—the poor little soul, she was cold. Her poor little toes were rattling like dominoes. Her trousers were wet up to the knee, so what did I do? I gave her mine.

Clara Your trousers?

Gerald Yes, my spare bedwear pair. I couldn't turn her out again into the dark and dewy night.

Clara Why not?

Gerald Why, I didn't want mine wet as well.

Clara Why did she leave home?

Gerald Why, think of her home-life with only this man and Mrs Nutts. A great, big brute of a step-father stepping all over the place. A bully of a man cracking a whip, cracking her and cracking Nutts. Oh, think of it—a poor little child in distress, a life in peril. I said I must save her. Clara would wish it, so I saved her till this morning.

Clara It sounds a very unlikely story.

Gerald Yes, that is what I told Clive.

Gertrude entering from drawing-room

Gerald crosses L. *of table to* C.

Gertrude. Clara, I must see you about a room for mother.

Clive comes hurrying back R. C. *Crosses* L. C. *to Gerald.*

Clive One moment. Look out! (*To Clara*) There's someone here I want you to see.

Gerald (*to Clive*) Putz?

Clive Yes.

Gerald Is he all right?

Clive (*with a nod*) Livid with fury. (*To Clara*) Now, listen, Clara. You've got to be told about this man—the step-father.

Gertrude He's not her step-father at all.

Clive You shall judge that when you see him.

Gerald Yes, and once you've seen him you won't want to see her.

Clive No. You'd help to save any girl from a devil like that.

Gerald He's a monster—a fiend in human shape.

Clive A violent, savage swine.

Gerald Without respect for God or man. You wait and see!

Putz appears in the doorway; he knocks loudly, a double rap

(*Seeing Putz*) This is the man.

Clara crosses D. L.

Yes, come in.

Putz comes down R. C.

And say your worst.

Putz (*cross behind table, speaking very gently*) Zee worst? Ah, nein— I want to say you something nice. It is now aller right.

Gerald It doesn't look all right to me.

Clive (*cross* R. *to Putz*) No, certainly not. Look here! If you can't misbehave yourself properly you'd better get out of this.

Gertrude (*to Putz*) Will you kindly say what happened last night?

Putz (*crosses* D. R.) They try to take her from me. Aller der night she stay away from me. But I forgive her. Und I forgive you, my dear frent, absolute. (*Cross* C. *in front of table to Gerald*)

Clive (*to Putz*) You liar! (*To Gerald*) This is no good. (*Behind table* R.C.)

Gerald No. Go on. Infuriate him—wurts!

Clive (*cross to Putz, who is* R. C. *in front of table*) If you don't send her straight back here I'll come and fetch her. Come on. You come with me now.

Putz Wait, please, I wish for peace. (*Goes up to chair*)

Clara Is this the fiend in human shape?

Gerald He's the wrong shape to-day.

Putz (*coming down* R. C.) Look, please. The trunk and the hud.

Gertrude (*seizing hat*) What's the meaning of this outrage?

Clive (*cross* L. C. *in front of table*) Clara! You mustn't believe this lying German humbug.

Clara I believe my own eyes and ears!

Gerald Yes, but you can't believe his nose and mouth.

Clara He's the quietest man I've ever seen.

Gerald Don't go, Clara!

Clara No. One hour apart from me and back you go.

Gerald Back where?

Clara Back to your old life with Clive.

Rhoda

O   *Putz*   *Clive*   *Gerald*   *Clara*

        O   O   O   O

Gerald It's Bognor again.

Enter Rhoda, cross down R.

Clive Look out! Here she is!

Rhoda is in her own clothes—outdoor costume

Clara Is this the girl?

Gerald Yes. But don't be misled. She doesn't look nearly so nice in pyjamas.

Clara She certainly doesn't look what Gertrude says.

Rhoda I'm not. But your husband's been tremendously kind to me all the same.

Gerald Oh, not tremendously—just kind.

Enter Mrs Leverett R.

Mrs Leverett Well, I've finished this job.

Clive (*to Gerald*) Hold on. I see a ray. (*Cross to* R. Mrs Leverett) You,

Mrs Flanagan—that was a deliberate untruth you told me last night!

Mrs Leverett Me? How dare you! and what do you mean?

Clive (*pointing to Putz*) You told me this little girl and this man Putz were living in sin.

Putz (*changing his manner quickly*) Was is das? (*Fiercely*) What you make?

Gerald crosses up L. *of table to* R. C.

Gerald That's an awful thing to say.

Putz Who shall say of her?

Clive (*bringing Mrs Leverett forward*) Come on. Ask *her*.

Putz (*cross* R. *furiously to Mrs Leverett*) You are who?

Mrs Leverett I only said I'd always heard. (*Cross to other side of Putz* L.)

Putz You are who to say of her and Rhoda——

Mrs Leverett Mrs Twine told me——

Gerald (*pushes Mrs Twine forward to Putz*—L. *of Putz*) This is Mrs Twine.

Gertrude Gerald, how dare you?

Putz (*wheeling on Gertrude*) Herr Gott! you shall say of my step-daughter that she is not *so* gut. *Allerferdampter—Schwein—verfluchter Cammail!*

During this speech he forces Mrs Twine and Mrs Leverett over and backwards L. *Gerald and Clive follow behind Putz to* L. C.

Putz turns back and clears his way between Clive and Gerald. Finally, he picks up the bag of clothes and flings it to the ground, and with a final roar of anger——

Exits R. C.

Kreuz! Himmel!! Donnerwetter!!!

Pronounced: Croyts, Himmell, Donner-vetter.
        (*Cross, Heaven, Thunder-weather.*)

At Putz's outburst Clara has instinctively gone to Gerald for protection and Rhoda to Clive

First Curtain

Second Curtain: *Rhoda is in Clive's arms and Clara in Gerald's. Unseen, Clive and Gerald, who are standing back to back, shake hands, Clive's* L. *hand and Gerald's* R., *with their eyes still on Rhoda and Clara*

Curtain

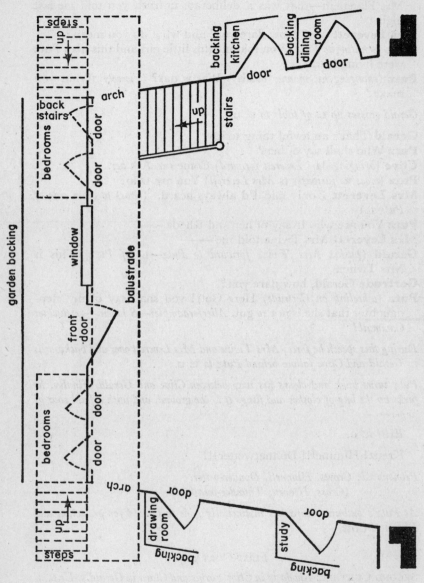

Stage Plan

THARK

A Farce in Three Acts

CHARACTERS

The play was produced on July 4th, 1927, at the Aldwych Theatre, London, with the following cast:

Hook	J. Robertson Hare
Warner	Ann Furrell
Cherry Buck	Ena Mason
Lionel Frush	Kenneth Kove
Mrs Frush	Mary Brough
Sir Hector Benbow, Bart., M.F.H.	Tom Walls
Ronald Gamble	Ralph Lynn
Lady Benbow	Ethel Coleridge
Kitty Stratton	Winifred Shotter
Jones	Gordon James
Whittle	Hastings Lynn

ACT I
  Sir Hector Benbow's library in his flat in Mayfair. An autumn evening

ACT II
  The same. Next morning

ACT III
  Scene I   The dining-room at Thark. A week later, after dinner
  Scene II   Ronny's room at Thark. 3 o'clock the following morning

ACT I

The library of Sir Hector Benbow's flat in Mayfair, on an October evening. The room is described as the library, but really it is the large room in the flat which is apportioned to the husband, as contrasted with the wife's drawing-room. It is the room of a man of ample means, out-of-door and sporting tastes, rather than indoor and bookish; and really more at home in the country than in the West End. It is a sumptuous room with oak-panelling, a fine ceiling and with an ample degree of comfort in its furniture. A door in the C. background leads from the passage, the front door of the flat being just outside this room, which is the first room one comes to in the flat, as it were. The front door is not necessarily seen outside. There is another door in the R. wall, also an opening up L. The windows are up in the R. C. corner in a bow, and the fireplace down L., with a fire burning. The furniture is Japanese blue and gold lacquer upholstered grey. There is a settee R. A round table up R. C. A small armchair L. of table, another down L., four other chairs, one L. of cabinet, one R. front of cabinet, one down R. below door, one R. of centre door. An electric chandelier hanging from ceiling C., also four two-light brackets, one up R. on wall, one on back wall and two on L. wall. A standard lamp up R. above settee. What pictures—and such decorations—there are, relate almost entirely to sporting tastes, whether hunting, shooting or the turf. There may be relics of big-game shooting expeditions. There is a table up L. of door. On this is a telephone. Between the door and the window up R. C. there are two foxes' brushes hanging and a huntsman's horn underneath

Hook, a middle-aged and rather careworn manservant, with a manner which is the result of years of bullying, discovered talking on the telephone, when the curtain rises. He is R. of writing-table

Hook (*on 'phone*) Yes? . . . (*More keenly*) Yes. It's me speaking . . . (*Surprised*) Is that you, mother? . . . 'Ere, what are you doing, telephoning to me 'ere? . . . Had to? Why? . . . *What?* You mean it's *happened?* It's all over? . . . Well, what is it? . . . A girl? . . . Oh, jest a girl? I mean, that's *all?* . . . (*Relieved*) Ah! 'Ow's Florrie—keepin' *up?* . . . She is—all right, I'll come round as quick as I can. The boss isn't in, but I told 'im it was on the cards. I'll leave word.

During the last few words Warner, a smart maidservant, has put her head in from the opening up L. As Hook hangs up the receiver she comes down excitedly

Warner Oh, Mr Hook, has it happened?

Hook (*agitated*) All right, all right. (*Cross to table* R., *picks up letters and moves* D. C.) Now, don't you worry me. I've got to get along there.

Warner (*moves to Hook*) A little girl, is it? Dear little thing! Oh, Mr Hook, aren't you *proud* of it?

Hook I haven't seen it yet. Now look here (*cross down to Warner*), if the master returns before I do, just attend to this.

Warner Me? What?

Hook (*picks up telegram from table* C.) There's a telegram for him— see?

Warner notes it

It came this morning and (*cross to table*) there's his letters—that's all. Oh! no, there's another thing. (*Cross* D. C.)

Warner What?

Hook He's expecting a lady to call in. She hasn't yet. But if she does, she's to be asked to come back. He's taking her out to dinner.

Warner (*coming down*) What lady?

Warning door bell

Hook He didn't say.

Warner Well, but how am I to know? What sort of a lady? Is it business or pleasure?

Hook Is that for you to ask? Simply if a lady calls by appointment, you say, 'Oh, it will give Sir 'Ector much pleasure if you will dine with him, calling here at seven-fifteen.'

Warner All right. (*Moves* L.)

Hook. That's all. (*Puts telegram on desk up* L.) Now I'll get along.

Bell heard outside. He is agitated

Oh, Lawd! There's someone there now.

Warner I'll see to it, if you like.

Hook (*going up* C.) No, no. If I'm here, I'd better.

Warner Oh, very good then.

Warner goes off L.

Hook goes out at C., *leaving door open*

Cherry's voice is heard off just afterwards

Cherry (*off* R.) Sir Hector Benbow in?

Hook (*off*) Not yet, madam.

Cherry (*off*) Oh, dear! He told me to call.

Hook (*off, cross* D. L.) *Ah!* Then will you kindly step this way, please, madam?

He reappears followed by Cherry Buck. She is about twenty-five, smart and confident

Cherry I thought he'd be here. (C.)

Hook You were the lady Sir 'Ector was expecting? (*Cross* L. C.)

Cherry (*cross* D. C.) Well, Sir Hector said something about—what about a little dinner?

Hook That's quite correct, madam. It will give Sir 'Ector much pleasure if you will dine with him, calling here at seven-fifteen.

Cherry Oh, strong! When will he be in though?

Hook is restless and is trying to get away

Hook (*coming down* C.) I hardly know, madam. He went to the races this morning with his nephew and hasn't got back yet. Lady Benbow is away from 'ome, you know.

Cherry I didn't know, but I guessed. What nephew is this, then?

Hook (*trying to go*) Oh, there is only one, madam. Mr Gamble— Mr Ronald Gamble.

Cherry Oh! Is that the Mr Ronald Gamble who's engaged to Miss Stratton?

Warning door bell

Hook Yes, yes. That's quite right, madam.

Cherry Yes. I saw her picture in the *Mirror*.

Hook Yes. But she's also out of town. In fact, she's with Lady Benbow. (*Moves away a little*)

Cherry I see. (*Watching Hook's movements*) Are you anxious to get away or something?

Hook Well, yes, please. I want to get 'ome. I've—er—had news, from 'ome, you see. (*Coming down a little*)

Cherry Not bad news, I hope?

Hook Well, I dunno. Half and 'alf, I suppose. The fact is, madam I've just had a baby!

Cherry (*with a short shrill laugh*) Sounds as if you ought never to have *left* home. Well, I'll trot away and get dressed. (*Moving up stage*)

Hook. Very good, madam.

Door bell rings

Oh, dear!

Cherry Is that Sir Hector?

Hook No, madam, it can't be—er—he's got his key with him. I'll
see. (*Cross* L., *calls to Warner*) Warner, attend to the door.
Cherry Well, p'r'aps I'd better not be seen around in here.
Hook Well, madam, that's hardly for me to say. But I shall be going
down by the servants' stairs, if—you'd care to be shown the way.
Cherry Oh, strong! That is, if someone's coming in. Shall I come
with you now?
Hook. Just half a jiffy, while I get my 'at.

He goes out up L.

Cherry looks door c. *and listens, opening door a little. Mrs Frush's voice is
heard. Then her son's*

Mrs Frush Oh, but it's by appointment.
Lionel Well, never mind, mother——

Cherry moves D.L.

Warner If you'd come in, please, I'll see.

Warner shows Lionel on and—exits c.

*Warner immediately opens door and shows in Lionel, but does not herself
enter. Lionel is a boy of twenty or so—very feeble but affable and with a
keen eye for the ladies. He eyes the Maid as he comes down* R., *then seeing
Cherry he bows half inquiringly.*

Lionel (*little laugh*) Oh, I beg pardon. (*To Cherry*)
Cherry (*also slightly self-consciously*) That's quite all right, thanks.
Lionel. I didn't know there was anyone here. I came to see Sir
Hector.
Cherry Yes. So did I, as a matter of fact.
Lionel Oh, perhaps I'd better call later.
Cherry I'm just going. (*To* c.)
Lionel Don't go on my account.

Cherry laughs softly. He laughs in response. Brief pause

Nice evening.
Cherry (*nodding*) Not bad for London.
Lionel I'm a stranger to London. I've just taken a place in the
country.
Cherry Lucky you. I do love the country.
Lionel London's all right for a change, but I get awfully lonely,
when I'm alone.
Cherry I never go out with strangers.
Lionel My word! I wish I could find somebody like you who
does! (*Cross* R. c.)

Hook reappears L. *carrying a coat and a bowler hat. He does not notice Lionel*

Hook (*to Cherry*) If you're ready, madam?
Cherry (*airily*) Oh—no hurry.

Lionel coughs. Hook turns away and faces Lionel

Lionel Oh, are you the butler? (*Looking him up and down*)
Hook Yes, sir.
Lionel I'm Mr Frush. I called to see Sir Hector. Did the maid tell you?
Hook No, sir. I haven't seen the maid. Sir 'Ector shouldn't be long, sir.
Cherry (*to Lionel, indicating Hook*) He wants to get off home.
Lionel Oh, righto! I'll wait here, if I may.
Hook Certainly, sir. (*To Cherry*) It's this way, madam.
Cherry (*to Hook*) Thanks.

He shows Cherry way out L. *She, as she goes, nods to Lionel*

(*To Lionel, smilingly*) Good evening.

Lionel (*smiling, following her to exit up* L.) Good evening.

Cherry and Hook go off

Immediately afterwards Warner re-enters at door C.

Warner Oh, excuse me, sir—was that the butler, sir?
Lionel Yes, It's all right. I've seen him. I'm going to wait.
Warner Oh, very good, sir. (*Cross* D. R.)
Lionel (*going up to doorway*) Mother! Mother!
Mrs Frush (*off* L.) All right. I'm just having a look round.

Entering C. *from* L.

(*To Warner*) Isn't there anyone at home?

Mrs Frush is an elderly dame of middle-class, a new-rich caricature, a woman who has lost her natural homeliness under the influence of money and ambition. She is a shade over-dressed, but not grotesquely so

Warner I'm afraid not, madam.

Warner R. C., *Mrs Frush* C., *Lionel* L.

Mrs Frush Well, I may tell you I've come all the way from Norfolk to keep this appointment. (*Takes out a letter from her handbag*) Here's the letter if you don't believe me.
Warner Certainly I believe you, madam.

Lionel (*always on tenterhooks when his mother is about*) Of course she does. Hush, mother!

Mrs Frush (*with vigour*) Hush yourself! (*Takes letter from bag. Reads:*) 'Please call here on your arrival from Norfolk and I will make an appointment with you.' There!

Warner (*brightening up*) Oh, well, I see. Then I was to say that if the lady Sir Hector expected called in, would she please dine with him, calling back here at seven-fifteen?

Mrs Frush Ah, that's better. Yes, with pleasure.

Lionel (*cross to Mrs Frush*) Well, there you are then.

Mrs Frush Yes, that's very nice. But what about you, though? I don't think I mentioned you were coming?

Lionel Oh, that's all right. You dine alone with him. If you can be trusted.

Mrs Frush (*with lorgnettes*) What d'you mean, Lionel?

Lionel (*to Warner*) Well, I mean, perhaps—if I might just have a word with my mother alone?

Warner I beg pardon, sir.

Exit up L.

Lionel (*after seeing her go*) Now, look here, mother dear—you must be more careful what you do and say here.

Mrs Frush (*moves* D. R.) I don't care. I'm as good as he is even if he is a Bart.

Lionel (*cross to Mrs Frush*) Do, please, be tactful. I mean—for instance, you ought to have come straight in here just now, instead of nosing about in the hall.

Mrs Frush Nonsense! I like to see how such people furnish. And, Lionel—(*moves up to him*)—you need never have bought an umbrella-stand. They don't have one here. They've got one of them 'igh Chinese vaises.

Lionel Well, don't comment on things. Anyhow, they're not vaises —they're varses.

Mrs Frush To those as likes to call them varses they're varses. And to such as prefer to call them vaises they're vaises.

Lionel Well, whatever you do, don't start complaining about Thark to-night.

Mrs Frush Why not? That's why we're here. He sold us the place and it's non-inhabitable.

Lionel But leave all that till to-morrow. Besides, it wasn't Sir Hector's house. It was Miss Stratton's house. He was acting for her, that's all.

Mrs Frush I don't care. I'm here to complain, and complain I'll see I do. If you buy a house that size you expect to find it all right.

Lionel I always told you the house was much too big.

Mrs Frush But it isn't too big! You can't find a house too big for me. But all *right* it is *not*, and he knows it. (*Turning away*)

Lionel Well, don't discuss it to-night. You can't accept a man's invitation to dinner and accuse him of sharp practice while you're eating it.

Warning door bang

Mrs Frush Oh, I suppose that's some of your usual college 'how-to-behave' talk. Still, never mind. I'm not going to refuse his dinner. Come on, I must go and get into my best evening.

Lionel No, you go on. (*Cross* D. L.) And I'll wait and make a business appointment—

Mrs Frush is going up C.

for to-morrow. (*As Mrs Frush is going up*) One moment, mother. You must let the maid show you out.

Mrs Frush All right, all right! I know.

As Warner appears up L.

Show me out, please.

Warner crosses up C.

Mrs Frush goes off C.

After a moment Warner opens door C.

Lionel I'm waiting a little while longer. I'm Mr Frush.

Warner (*vaguely*) Oh—yes, sir? (C.)

Lionel *We* bought Thark.

Warning door bang.

Warner I beg your pardon, sir?

Lionel I say—(*moves to her*)—*we* bought *Thark*. The house in Norfolk, that belonged to Miss Stratton.

Warner Oh, yes, sir.

Lionel And, of course Sir Hector's her guardian and does all that sort of thing for her so—that's what it is.

Warner Yes, sir.

Lionel (*rather nervously*) I suppose it's all right my waiting here? I mean—it won't upset Sir Hector? I know he gets rather easily —upset. (*Gives a little nervous laugh*)

Warner (*with the housemaid's slow wriggle of embarrassment*) Well, it's not for me to say, sir——

Lionel Still, I think we'll risk that, shall we?

Door bang

The voice of Sir Hector Benbow heard off in a loud summons. Lionel crosses
D. L.

Benbow (*off*) HOOK!
Warner (*turning quickly*) Excuse me, sir! (C.)

Benbow appears in the doorway. Lionel is L. *Benbow is a middle-aged very-
well-turned-out man of the Master of Hounds type. He is dressed for racing
with field glasses, etc. There is a good deal of ginger in his character. He has
grey military moustaches and grey hair*

Benbow (*as he enters*) Hook! (*To Warner*) Where's Hook? Where's
Hook? (*He hands her his coat, hat, stick and race glasses*)
Warner If you please, sir, he had to go home.
Benbow Why?

She dithers in silence

Why?
Warner (*in subdued tones*) Oh, sir—he had a domestic event.
Benbow Oh, yes, of course! (*Who has now seen Lionel, who smiles
uncomfortably*) Hallo! Oh, yes—I forgot about you.
Warner There's a telegram, sir, and also——
Benbow (*to Warner*) All right, girl. You can go—needn't wait.

Warner goes out L.

(*Then to Lionel*) Yes, your mother wrote to me. What is it? Any-
thing about Thark?
Lionel Yes, I'm afraid it is.
Benbow 'Smatter?
Lionel I beg pardon?
Benbow (*loudly*) Stand up!—'Smatter?
Lionel Oh—well—(*crosses to Sir Hector*)—it's rather a difficult
subject to embark on.
Benbow Well, don't—(*glasses on*)—embark on it now. I've got to
dress for dinner.
Lionel Yes, yes, I know. My mother's coming along.
Benbow Yes, confound it, I forgot about her, too. (*Crosses to table,
picks up letter*) But I think we'll deal with Thark to-morrow. See
you in the morning. Good-night to yer.
Lionel That's exactly what I wanted.
Benbow Well, you've got what you wanted, and I'll see yah in the
morning. Good-night to yer.
Lionel Oh, good-night, sir. (*Pausing as he goes*) Only, don't let my
mother start telling you her troubles.

Benbow It's no good trying to stop a woman talking when once she gets started. We mustn't let her begin, that's all.

Lionel Good! As long as you won't let her begin.

Benbow Well, I'll do my best not to, and I'll see you in the morning. (*Waving him away.*) Good-night to yer.

Lionel But, sir, but how do I get down?

Benbow (*edging him up* C.) You can go down the stairs or take the lift . . .

Lionel disappears.

Benbow closes the door, returns, places letters on table C.

Or fall over the banisters and break your bloody neck. (*He turns to the writing-table and picks up a letter. As he tears it open—*)

Hook enters at door C.

Hook (*out of breath*) Oh, I was just—on my way home, Sir 'Ector——

Benbow Yes——

Hook And I saw your car—so I thought I'd best come back—in case you wanted me, sir.

Benbow Why, what's the trouble at home consist of?

Hook It's a girl, sir. Thank you very much.

Benbow A girl—eh? Clever boy! Oh, that reminds me. Has one called here to see me?

Hook Yes, sir. The lady says she'll be pleased to dine, calling here at seven-fifteen.

Benbow Good. What's the time now?

Hook Gone half-past six, sir.

Benbow Then put my bath on.

Hook Yes, sir. (*Crosses* L.)

Benbow And Hook——

Hook Sir! (*Stopping*)

Benbow Fetch me some cigarettes.

Hook Yes, sir. (*Crosses* R.)

Benbow And Hook!

Hook Sir!

Benbow Get me a whisky and soda.

Hook (*going*) Yes, sir. (*Crosses up* L.)

Benbow Stand still when I'm talking to you, can't you? Mr Ronny's in the car down below. He can take it on to his place and send it straight back here. Go and tell him.

Hook moves again up stage, fidgeting about

(*Halting him*) Now!

Hook (*halting rigidly*) Sorry, sir.
Benbow Get me the whisky first.
Hook (*remaining stationary*) Yes, sir.
Benbow Well, go on!

Hook vanishes L.

Don't stand there like a small-sized lamp-post with no light on top!

He follows Hook up stage and sees telegram on desk. He picks it up and opens it. He consults telegram—singing to himself—gives an exclamation of surprised dismay and again goes to door and calls:

HOOK!
Hook (*off* L.) Sir!
Benbow Her ladyship's coming home to-night. Did *you* know that?
Hook No, sir.
Benbow Well, she is. Arriving Paddington six-thirty.

Hook reappearing with a drink on a tray

Hook Very good, sir. (*Follows Benbow about with the whisky at a respectful distance*)
Benbow Very good be damned! (*Crosses* D.R.) It's very bad! She'll be here by seven-fifteen.
Hook Oh, before that, sir.
Benbow She'll be here *at* seven-fifteen, I tell you, that's the point. And that lady's coming here to be taken out to dinner.
Hook Can't she be put off, sir?
Benbow Well, if you're so clever, ring her up and put her off.
Hook Yes, sir. (*In a tone of polite inquiry*) I'm afraid I don't know the lady's name, sir.
Benbow No, and neither do I, you damn fool, that's just the trouble.

A short perplexed pause, and he picks up hunting horn which is hanging on wall L. *of window, goes to window up stage* R. C. *and sounds it. He then calls:*

Hi! Ronny! Come up here! (*Turns to Hook*) Did he hear?
Hook I don't know, sir.
Benbow Go and find out then. Don't stand there holding that damned thing. (*Waving him off*) Go on, go on, go on!

Hook places drink tray on table C.

Hook (*hurrying off up* C.) Yes, sir.

Hook goes hurriedly C., *leaving door open*

Benbow calls through the opening C.

Benbow Hi! you—girl—whatever your name is!—Warnah! Her ladyship is coming home tonight. Did you know that? Well, she is. You'd better light the fire in her room. (*Crosses down* L.) And you'll want another one in the drawing-room. What the hell am I going to do? I don't know!

He goes off stage L.

The library is empty for a moment

Ronald Gamble strolls in C. *He is a man of thirty or so, and like his uncle is very well dressed for his race-meeting. Seeing a whisky and soda on the table he has imaginary conversation as though trying to refuse it pushing his head forward with his left hand and takes the drink with his right. He drinks the whisky and soda. Just as he has finished it, Benbow re-enters* L.

Hey! That's my drink!

Ronny (*handing him the empty glass*) Oh, sorry! Where's mine?

Benbow Ah——

Benbow goes to door L. *and Ronny marches three steps with him, halting just behind him in the doorway. They both raise their voices together*

Benbow and **Ronny** HOOK!

Hook (*heard off*) Sir!

Benbow Bring the whisky in here.

Ronny (*handing Benbow empty glass*) I'll only have one if *you're* going to have another.

Benbow Thank you, I enjoyed that one immensely. Don't you run away with the idea that I called you up here to drink.

Ronny Then what did you call me up for?

Benbow I've had some very awkward news, my boy. Your aunt's coming back home to-night.

Ronny What? And Kitty?

Benbow No. Just your aunt—that's enough, ain't it?

Ronny I say, why is auntie coming home? Has she heard something about you?

Benbow What d'yer mean? There is nothing to hear about me.

Ronny I know. That's why I asked in that surprised way——

Hook enters with tray with drinks. He substitutes this for the other tray on table C., *shuts door* C., *and crosses* L., *behind Benbow and Ronny*

Benbow There's nothing to hear, I tell you. (*Hands glass to Ronny*)

Ronny I know—that's just what I say. And very glad I am of it.

Benbow Glad of what?

Ronny Glad that she heard nothing—because she can't have, because there's nothing to hear. (*Hands glass to Benbow*)

Benbow I can think of nothing that could have brought her home.

Ronny Well, naturally *I* can think of nothing.

Hook (*coming down* L. *of Benbow*) Excuse me, Sir 'Ector.

Benbow puts glass on tray

Ronny (*to Hook*) Why, can *you* think of something?

Hook (*to Benbow, ignoring Ronny*) After 'er ladyship's arrived, would it be convenient if I popped round home, sir?

Benbow Hell do you mean?—popped!

Hook (*with an embarrassed smile*) I feel I must do my duty to my wife, sir.

Benbow Oh—you appear to have done that. Go on, then.

Exit Hook up L.

Ronny I say, uncle, what's the matter with Hook?

Benbow He's got a little girl.

Ronny Oh, really, I thought he said he was going to see his wife. (*Crosses to table* C., *pause—bus.: pouring drinks*) But now auntie's coming home, Kitty will be left all alone in Bath.

Benbow That's all right, she's old enough to look after herself. (*He crosses to fireplace, looks at telegram*)

Ronny I know, and that's just when girls begin to get looked after. You know, uncle, Bath's a very dangerous place. (*Gets drink*) Full of Beaux —you know—Beau Somethings.

Benbow Not now. Only old people with gout.

Ronny Oh, I see, bow legs.

Benbow (*crosses to Ronny*) They only go there to drink water.

Ronny (*takes a drink to Benbow*) Oh, really? I'm surprised you've ever heard of the place. Well, good luck, uncle! (*Drinks*)

Benbow Thank yer—but I don't think there's much good luck coming my way to-night.

Ronny Why not?

Benbow Yer aunt'll be here in five minutes. Is *that* good luck?

Ronny Oh, well—*fairly* good luck. (*Raising glass, drinking*)

Benbow Now listen, Ronny. At seven-fifteen a lady who thinks she's being taken out to dinner by me—will arrive here for that purpose.

Ronny Who is she?

Benbow That's the trouble. I don't know.

Ronny You don't know? What do you mean? Have you won her in a raffle, or something?

Benbow Now listen, my boy. I want you to help me.

Ronny looks suspiciously

No, no, it's all right. Now there are one or two things I'm a pretty good judge of. I'm a pretty good judge of a horse——

Ronny Good Lord! You're not going to have dinner with a horse, are you?

Benbow (*ignoring this*) You can't tell me anything about a terrier——

Ronny I wasn't going to.

Benbow I know a good glass o' port as soon as I *smell* it.

Ronny That's very funny! That's just how I know the terrier.

Benbow And I've never had occasion to mistrust my judgment of a pair of ankles. Now listen. (*He crosses* L., *puts his glass on mantelpiece, and sits on club fender*)

Ronny Ankles—I will listen. (*Brings chair down* L. *and sits, after putting glass on mantelpiece*)

Benbow I was walking down South Molton Street yesterday morning. You know those women's shops there—little places with nothing in the window except a hat on one peg and frock on another, and a damned stuffed cat in the corner, and that's all.

Ronny A cat now! Why do you keep on being zoological! What exactly is your trouble, uncle? Tell me.

Benbow I'm telling you, ain't I?

Ronny As I interrupted, sorry; yes?

Benbow As I passed by there was something else in the window.

Ronny Not one of the girls who work in the shop?

Benbow Why not?

Ronny Well, you said you passed by.

Benbow I didn't hurry by. I just strolled by—anyway, there she was —fiddling about—you know—arranging something.

Ronny Yes. I expect she's arranged it very well.

Benbow She was a good looker, my boy.

Ronny Yes. I bet you were, too.

Benbow I had a good look at her through the glass——

Ronny Through the glass?

Benbow Well, there was glass in the window, wasn't there?

Ronny Oh, I'm sorry, I thought you meant you brought out a telescope.

Benbow I stood and looked at her through the glass. And when she went out of the window, I slipped into the shop, gave her my card, and said, 'You come and have some dinner with me to-morrow night, my girl.' She began the usual way—*you* know how they do—'Oh, I never go out with strangers.' (*Laughing*) They always begin like that——

Ronny (*laughing*) Oh, rather! (*Checking himself*) Do they?

Benbow (*hastily*) Well, anyway, this one did. Then along comes

the old woman who runs the place—you know, one of those old
prize pouters——

Ronny (*alarmed for himself*) And you had to ask her as well? No,
thank you. I'm not taking that on. (*Rising and crosses* c.)

Benbow crosses c. *to Ronny*

Benbow No! Don't be silly! Point is, I only had time to say to the
girl, 'Call at my address and say whether you're coming.'

Ronny And has she called?

Benbow She has.

Ronny And is she coming?

Benbow She is. (*Looking at telegram*) At seven-fifteen. That's why I
called you up, my boy.

Ronny *What's* why?

Benbow Now then, don't be dense. I can't have girls coming here
to be taken out to dinner with your aunt looking on.

Ronny Oh, I see. You want me to take auntie out to dinner to keep
her out of the way.

Benbow That's a good idea, I never thought of that! But no—I
think on the whole the little girl from the shop had better be
your friend. It'll be safer.

Ronny Safer for who?

Warning door bell

Benbow Well, ain't you pleased? You will be when you see her.
Only we don't want her coming up here, so I'll tell the hall-
porter to keep her down below. (*Looks to opening* l. *and calls:*)
HOOK!

Ronny I say, uncle, what about Kitty? She gets so frightfully
jealous.

Benbow (*scornfully*) That's all right. She can't possibly find out.
Where's that Hook?

Bell

As Hook appears l. *the bell is heard off. Hook is in a nervous state. They
put glasses on the table* c.

Hook Oh, sir, it's her ladyship.

Benbow Well, why should *you* worry? (*Crosses to Ronny* r.) Now
look here. You'll have to see the hall-porter about keeping her
down below. I leave it all to you.

Ronny Right you are, uncle. I don't mind doing you a good turn.

Benbow You're not doing yourself a bad one. You wait and see.
Well, what do you want? (*To Hook*) Well, move, can't you?
You know how to open a door!

Hook disappears C.

Now look here, you'll have to see the little girl, and tell her it'll have to be another time instead.

Ronny You mean, as well.

Benbow That's right—another time as well, instead

Ronny You another time as well, instead of *me*, as well as me this time. . .

Hook (*off stage*) Good evening, my lady.

Lady Benbow (*off*) Good evening, Hook.

Benbow (*listening*) Look out! Shut up!

Ronny I'll tell her——

Hook opens door C.

Lady Benbow appears from C.

Hook exits C.

Lady Benbow Oh, here you are! (*Crosses* D. C.)

Lady Benbow is a fashionable, shrewd and rather sarcastic lady—a nice character. She wears a becoming travelling costume. Benbow and Ronny welcome her in a self-conscious and effusive manner

Benbow Oh, welcome home—home, my love. Glad to see you (*Kisses her*)

Ronny We both are. How are you, auntie dear? What a good thing you've come back!

Benbow gives Ronny a look, then at Lady Benbow

Lady Benbow But why, Ronny?

Ronny I mean—he's missed you so much. Uncle's missed you frightfully. Why, only the other day out shooting he said to me, 'Ronny, I've missed her.'

Lady Benbow Oh, then I can understand you're both pleased to see me back.

Benbow Well, of course we are, my love. (*To Ronny*) Hall-porter, my boy.

Ronny What? Hall-porter?—Oh, yes. (*Smiles self-consciously at Lady Benbow and goes up* C.)

Lady Benbow (*crosses* L., *sits on club fender*) What do you want to see the hall-porter about? Some guilty secret?

Benbow crosses to table C., *takes drink*

Ronny Oh no, auntie. Knowing you were coming home, I ordered a few flowers to be sent in for you and I thought I'd go and see whether they'd arrived.

Lady Benbow Flowers?

Ronny (*making shapes with his hands*) Yes, you know, large at the top and peter off to nothing. They smell like nothing on earth.

Lady Benbow Oh, Ronny! (*Pleased*) How nice of you. What made you think of that?

Ronny Oh, don't know, auntie, I can generally think of something. (*Passes this faux pas off as best he can*)

Exits C. *with an expressive look at Sir Hector*

Benbow (*hastily changing the subject*) Well, what brings you home, my love? (*Crosses to Lady Benbow*)

Lady Benbow Kitty, of course!

Benbow Kitty? What! Is Kitty here, too?

Lady Benbow She insisted on coming to town—

Benbow looks anxiously towards door C., *he is thinking of Ronny*

to see you about this trouble at Thark.

Benbow Well, that's my trouble, not Kitty's.

Lady Benbow I know. She's never even seen the Frushes. But they wrote to her. They seem to think they've been swindled or something.

Benbow (*incredulously*) Oh, do they? Where's Kitty now?

Lady Benbow I brought on her boxes. She went on to Ronny's rooms. Thought he'd be there. She'll be here in a minute.

Benbow Now what the devil did you want to bring Kitty back here for?

Lady Benbow Well—why not?

Benbow What?

Lady Benbow *Why not?*

Benbow What? . . . Oh, well, it doesn't matter a damn. (*Sits by her* L.) Have you had a nice time, my love?

Lady Benbow Very! I said we should probably go back there again.

Benbow Oh, good! Splendid!—When?

Lady Benbow And how have you been getting on?

Benbow Oh—I don't think there's much I can tell you about myself.

Lady Benbow No, I can quite believe that.

Benbow What?

Lady Benbow Well, we'd better dress and dine out somewhere.

Benbow Quite right. Quickly! (*Rising and helping Lady Benbow up*) You must be hungry. We'll aim for dinner at seven.

Lady Benbow It's close on seven now.

Benbow Is it? My God! (*Takes watch out*) Then we must hurry.

Lady Benbow My dear, I'm not in the least hungry.

Benbow No?—well I am, and you ought to be. Come on, get a move on!

Lady Benbow Hector, what's the matter with you?

Benbow I don't know, but I've got a nasty faint feeling coming all over me.

They both exeunt L. *as—*

Hook enters hurriedly c. *He wears his great-coat and carries his bowler. Benbow hustles Lady Benbow out and Hook just fails to catch him. He turns. Ronny re-enters* c. *He is just about to take a drink, but puts it down quickly as Hook speaks*

Hook (*as Benbow goes*) Sir Hector—Sir Hector—— (*Then turning to Ronny*) Oh, Mr Ronald!

Ronny What's the matter now?

Hook I haven't told the master yet, sir, but I'm afraid there's been and awful mess-up.

Ronny Mess-up? What are you talking about, Hook?

Hook I mean about the lady who's coming here to dinner, sir.

Ronny Well, that's all right. I'm dealing with her, aren't I?

Hook Yes, sir; but Warner's gone and told another one to come.

Ronny looks straight into Hook's eyes

Ronny Instead?

Hook No, sir—as well!

Ronny What, *two* of them? Good Lord! Tell me about it.

Hook (*groaning*) It's all through this trouble of mine at home. Warner saw one I *didn't* see and told her, as well as the one I *did* see and told.

Ronny Yes, that's quite clear. (*Earnestly*) But who is this other one—Warner's pick? Who is she?

Hook The lady who's bought Thark, sir.

Ronny Oh, well. There needn't be any secret about her, surely?

Hook Not that I know of, sir.

Warning bell

Ronny I daresay I can manage somehow. Oh, Hook, are you going out?

Hook I was, sir. Just to see the wife.

Ronny Ah! That's very nice. Well, as you go, if you find a shop open, buy a few flowers, will you? (*Hands Hook a ten-shilling note*)

Hook Oh, thank you very much indeed, sir.

Ronny And bring them back here.

Door bell rings

Look out! There's someone here already.

Hook I'll take my coat off. Would you mind just helping me?

Hook pauses in doorway C *to divest himself of his coat. In his hurry he gets tied up and Ronny trying to help him only makes matters worse*

Benbow enters L. *very apprehensively in his shirt-sleeves and slippers*

Benbow Look out! Did you see the hall-porter?

Ronny (*struggling with Hook*) Of course I did.

Hook is still trying to get his coat off

Benbow (*furiously*) Hook! Will you stop that Houdini business and go and answer the door?

Ronny helps Hook to struggle out of his coat and—

Hook goes off closing door C.

Ronny (*holding the coat and hat*) Look here, there's been a muddle up. (*Crosses* D.R.)

Benbow I know, my boy. I'm awfully sorry. I didn't know she was in town.

Ronny and Benbow work down R.

Ronny You must have known. You asked her to dinner.

Mrs Benbow entering suddenly L.

Lady Benbow Asked who to dinner?

They look at each other hesitating

Before they can answer Kitty Stratton hurries in C. *She is a young and pretty girl dressed for travelling, rather put out at the moment*

Kitty (*as she enters*) A nice sort of way to be treated!

Ronny (*then completely taken aback, hands coat to Benbow and unconsciously puts hat on, crosses to Kitty, and realizing mistake hands it to Benbow, who is very annoyed*) Kitty! Hallo! Good Lord! Good-bye! Why didn't you come yesterday?

Kitty Why yesterday?

Ronny (*to Benbow*) Why yesterday? (*To Kitty*) Well, because it would have been a day sooner. I'd have seen more of you. But, darling, I'm delighted to see even this much of you.

Kitty Yes; what was the idea in trying to stop me from coming up?

                        Ronny
                        R.C.
Benbow   *Kitty*
R. C.   L. C.
                                              Lady Benbow
                                              L.

Lady Benbow What do you mean?

Kitty Well, the hall-porter said he'd had orders from Ronny.

Benbow (*to Ronny*) That's right. Muck it up!

Ronny That's quite right, darling. I said to the hall-porter—I simply said: 'Now look here, hall-porter'—I know his name, he had it on his hat—'don't let the lady come up to the flat.' I didn't mean you, darling. I meant the lady.

Lady Benbow What lady?

Ronny Uncle's lady!

Benbow Now then, don't be a B.F.! (*To Ronny*)

Ronny It's all right. You see, uncle has a lady coming here to dine this evening.

Benbow trying to control himself performs contortions at Ronny

Lady Benbow What for?

Ronny For to eat. And when you see her you won't blame him.

Benbow (*Trying to stop Ronny*) Oh yes, she will!

Lights check

Ronny Oh, no, she won't—oh, you won't. When you see who it really is.

Lady Benbow Why, who is it?

Ronny (*triumphantly*) It's the lady who's bought Thark.

Benbow opens his eyes wide, realizing it is a way out

Lady Benbow Oh, is that who it is?

Benbow drops coat and hat on settee R.

Ronny Not only who it is, auntie—but who it was—and who it's going to be. . . (*Looks at Benbow*) We hope!

Kitty embraces Ronny with relief

Benbow (*to Lady Benbow*) Yes, quite right. You know, you're very suspicious, Maud. Soon as I saw her I said: 'Come to dinner' instinctively.

Ronny As any complete gentleman would. But knowing you were coming home, uncle said to me: 'Ronny, you take it on—

Benbow and Ronny exchange looks

you take her to dinner,' because he wants to be alone with you for
once—

Lady Benbow looks

not for once, just alone with you for once again. That's twice.

*He fusses her, putting her coat straight and finishes up by pulling the end of a
waistcoat she is wearing*

Kitty Oh, but that's splendid! Ronny, I'll come and dine with you
as well!

Ronny Yes——

Benbow signals him not to

Oh, will you?—Oh!—— (*Crosses to* R. *of Kitty*) Oh, no, you
won't.

Kitty Oh, but why not?

Ronny (*to Benbow*) Why not? Have you got anything for that?
Because I haven't. (*Crosses to settee, sits*)

Benbow (*crosses to Kitty*) Now look here, Kitty, I won't have you
see this woman.

Kitty But I've come all the way to town to see her. She wrote and
asked me to.

Warning lights

Benbow I don't care. You're not going to see her before I do.
Whatever her troubles are, they're for me to deal with, not you.

Kitty (*submissively*) Oh, very well, then. No need to make a scene
about it. I'll dine with *you*. (*To Lady Benbow*) (*She crosses to Lady
Benbow*, L., *sits*)

Ronny (*rising, crossing. To Benbow*) Oh, I've been thinking.

Benbow Careful!

Ronny Now that it's the lady from Thark——

Enter Warner C., *switches on lights, draws curtains, takes tray from table*

Benbow Now?

Ronny Now that the lady from Thark *is*——

Benbow What are you trying to say?

Ronny Wouldn't it be better for all of us—I mean for all of me—
to dine with Kitty and for you to take on Mrs Thark?

Benbow (*to Ronny*) Now don't spoil it, you fool!

Lady Benbow (*rising to Warner who is going up* L.) Warner, a lady's
calling. Tell the hall-porter she's to be shown straight up.

Warner Yes, my lady.

Exit L.

Lady Benbow Hector—Hector!
Benbow Yes, my love?
Lady Benbow Come and get dressed.
Benbow I will. I love dressing. I'll be there, don't you worry.
Lady Benbow (to Kitty) You'd better go and dress too, dear.
Kitty All right. In a minute.

Lady Benbow goes towards door L. Kitty follows, has a word with Lady Benbow and crosses to back of stage to behind table c. She takes her hat off and takes her small mirror from bag and arranges her hair. Benbow manages to get a word in with Ronny

Ronny Look here, there's some mistake—there are two.
Lady Benbow (coming down c.) What are you whispering about?
Ronny Hello, auntie, there you are again! No, I wasn't whispering —I was just telling uncle about a little chorus.
Lady Benbow Oh, I don't think you can tell your uncle anything about the chorus!
Ronny Oh, yes—the chorus of a song. It goes like this—(To Benbow) The words: (Sings to Benbow)

> This girl is not the only girl,
>   Not the only girl for you;
> There's another one—coming afterwards—
>   You've gone and made a date with two!
> (Pointedly)   —You!—

Benbow Yes, that's what I should call a very pretty ditty, but what the hell are you getting at?
Lady Benbow Hector! (Pulling him by the arm up L.)—Come and get dressed. You said you were starving.
Ronny (crossing to Benbow, holding him by the other arm) But there's another verse.
Lady Benbow Oh, hurry up!
Ronny (still trying to detain him) It's about two birds.
Benbow Yes, I've got to go and moult. I'll see you later.

Benbow goes out R. with Lady Benbow

Kitty (coming to Ronny) I say, Ronny—Ronny, this is a shame. Ronny, I was looking forward so much to being with you this evening.
Ronny And you know, darling, how much I want to be with *you*. If I'd known you were coming, wild horses wouldn't have dragged me from you. Unless, of course, there'd been a lot of them.
Kitty I'm sure of it, Ronny, so don't worry any more about it.
Ronny *I won't* worry.

Kitty What?

Ronny I mean I won't *not* worry. But, darling, will you believe me
when I tell you that—all the time I am with her this evening at
dinner—every bite I take I shall wish it were you!

Kitty Well, I'm quite happy as long as I know that you really love
me.

Ronny Really love you! Darling, don't say that. Of course I do.
Why, if anyone came up to me—it wouldn't matter how big he
was—(*Bus.: gestures a very small man, then quickly changes to tall one*)
—and said, 'Ronny'—or Ronald, if he didn't know me very
well—'you don't love her!'—I—I—I wouldn't believe him—
honestly!

Kitty No—and if it was a lady who said so, you wouldn't believe
her either, would you?

Ronny Lady? No lady would ever talk to me!

Kitty protests

Kitty darling, you don't know how I hate the idea of dining with
this female to-night—she's practically a robber—

Kitty looks surprised

she's robbing *me* of the happiness of being with you. (*Crosses to chair*
R.C.) Kitty darling, I want to be with you.

Kitty is kneeling on the chair by the side of the table C. *Ronny holds her*
hands

Kitty No, never mind, it's all been fixed now. Besides, I want Mrs
Frush to be treated nicely.

Ronny Of course, darling. She bought the house.

Kitty Yes. But you get rid of her as soon as you can and meet me
for supper.

Ronny And lunch to-morrow.

Benbow, a stage more undressed in a dressing-gown, looks in fiercely L. *He*
is lathering his face; as he enters he catches Ronny's eye and indicates with
lathering brush the door. Ronny does not get it, and he absent-mindedly rubs
Kitty's chin as with a lathering brush

Benbow Why aren't you downstairs in the hall?

Ronny (*rising, crosses to* C.) Oh, yes. Quite right; I forgot.

Kitty Why should he go to the hall?

Benbow Because there's a—there's a little parcel coming for me.
Go on, go on!

(He grimaces at Ronny and exits L.)

Throughout the next scene Ronny is trying to get away

Kitty (*rising, crosses to Ronny*) Ronny, why can't the parcel be sent up here?

Ronny Well, darling, it's hardly a little parcel, you see. It's more of a large bundle. (*Runs to go to door* c.)

Kitty Yes, Ronny. What's the hurry?

Ronny Well, darling, I mustn't keep the parcel waiting.

Kitty (*crosses up stage*) Well, one moment, Ronny. We *will* meet for supper?

Ronny (*bringing her down stage*) Meet for supper, darling! Of course we will, darling! (*Returning*) Oh, supper with you—in some shady—night-club—with nothing between us but the table and knives and forks, of course—and flowers on the table, and waiters —waiters on the floor; with you by my side—by my front—good-bye! (*Kisses her. Crosses up stage*) Till that—(*Trying to go*) (*At door he misses the handle of the door, absent-mindedly picks up tall brass vase and puts it down again*)

Kitty (*holding him up again*) But, Ronny, where are we going to meet? And when?

Ronny (*bringing her back again*) Meet—and when? Lucky you called me back again. Meet—and when? Leave it entirely to me. As soon as I'm free, I'll 'phone you.

Warning bell—door

Kitty Yes, but where shall I be?

Ronny Darling, I don't care where you go. Wherever you are, I'll 'phone you. Darling, you do trust me, don't you?

Kitty Of course, Ronny.

Ronny Well, kiss me. (*Kissing her*)

Door bell—the bell is heard off

Good Lord! (*Rather in a panic, crosses up* L.)

Kitty There's Mrs Frush.

Ronny Yes, or——

Kitty Or what?

Ronny Or not.

Kitty What do you mean 'or not'?

Ronny Well, if it isn't her, it's not.

Kitty Who's not?

Ronny (*abstractedly, listening*) What not?

Benbow appears R. *He is in another stage of dressing and purple with anxiety. He has managed to get into his dress shirt and trousers and is fastening his collar*

Benbow Look out—there you are, you fool! Too late!

Kitty and Benbow look at each other

Go and meet her in the doorway. (*Twice*)
Ronny What?
Benbow Go and meet her in the doorway.
Kitty But Mrs Frush can come in here, can't she?
Benbow No. She can't. I don't want you to see her.

He moves Kitty over R.

Ronny goes to door C., *opens it and voices are heard outside*

Warner (*off*) I know, madam, but there's some mistake.
Cherry (*off*) There can't be! I was told at a quarter past seven.

Kitty and Benbow both over at R. C.

Ronny She's being brought in here anyway.
Benbow Blast! (*Pushing Kitty off* R.) Then, Kitty, you go in the
drawing-room.
Kitty But why shouldn't I meet her?
Benbow Because I say not. Go on.

Sends Kitty off R., *shuts door*

Get rid of her quickly, boy!
Ronny Supposing it's the other?
Benbow Hell d'yer mean—the other?

Kitty reappears R.

Kitty I really fail to see why I shouldn't meet this lady.
Benbow No, yer don't!

Pushes her off R., *crosses up* L.

Ronny (*as Benbow goes up* L.) She may not be the right one.
Benbow Not the right one be damned!—Did you ever know me
pick a wrong 'un?

Exit L.

Warner enters C.

Warner The lady, sir. (*With an anxious glance she goes, closing the
door*)

Exit

Ronny crosses and sits on club fender, L.

Cherry is boldly dressed for the occasion, with an evening cloak over her dress. She has her left white suède glove on and carries her other glove and her evening bag. She greets Ronny, then sees her mistake

Cherry Hallo! Oh, my mistake! Wrong one!
Ronny (D. L. *intensely and confidentially*) Are you Mrs Frush?
Cherry Me? No. My name's Cherry Buck.
Ronny Stuffed cat!
Cherry I've called to see Sir Hector . . . You're his nephew, I s'pose?
Ronny (*indicating door* C.) Yes. That's right. *Quick!* Come outside—come on!
Cherry What?
Ronny Come *out* with me. (*Opening door up* C., *trying to entice her out*)
Cherry Oh, but I'm going out to dine with your uncle.
Ronny No, you can't. He can't. You must come out and dine with me.
Cherry Oh, but perhaps I don't want to! (*Becoming rather coy*)
Ronny Well, you needn't come far. Just come outside. Come on. Come to dinner.

Goes out through door C *and coyly beckons her to come out*

Cherry (*moving down* R.) I never go out with strangers.
Ronny I know that's a very good idea of yours, but you must not be seen here.
Cherry But I was asked here!
Ronny Oh, but you can't stay here.
Cherry Who says so?
Ronny I'm sorry—I say so.
Cherry Really? Well, if you don't like the look of me, others do.
Ronny I do. Very much. That's just the trouble. You look wonderful. (*Very extravagantly*) Oh, you're marvellous! Oh, do please come with me out on to the staircase!
Cherry You *fresh thing*!
Ronny I *must* see you.
Cherry Well, here I am. You can *see* me, can't you?
Ronny Not properly. I want to see you elsewhere.
Cherry I *beg* your pardon!
Ronny I want you to let me see you outside. Don't you understand? I want to see you without. (*Crosses up to opening* L., *looks off, returns to Cherry*)
Cherry Huh! I daresay you do.
Lady Benbow (*off* C.) Are you ready, Hector?
Ronny Too late! Somebody coming. Stay there. Look here—be a

sport for my sake and uncle's, will you? You're Mrs Frush—
you've taken Thark.

Cherry I should love to know what *you've* taken.

*Ronny is trying to explain to Cherry by making shapes near the floor with his
hands*

> *Lady Benbow enters L. in evening dress and an evening cloak. She is very
> surprised at the appearance of Cherry. She comes down to the left of Ronny
> —he catches sight of her and starts to limp up to the table, holding his knee
> as if in pain—he pours some whisky out on to his hand and rubs his knee,
> looking as though in agony at Lady Benbow. He then moves down stage and
> explains to Lady Benbow by pantomiming a swing as if playing golf*

Ronny I've been playing golf and I've got golfer's knee. (*Then
pulling himself together*) Oh, allow me, auntie—this is Mrs Frush—
er–my aunt, Lady Benbow.

Cherry (*to Ronny*) Lady Benbow——

Ronny (*bus.:*—) Yes. The wife of——

Lady Benbow Oh, how do you do?

Cherry (*taken aback at finding Lady Benbow at home*) How do *you* do?

Ronny Do what?

Lady Benbow I understand my husband was taking you out to
dinner?

Cherry	*Ronny*	*Lady Benbow*
o	o	o

Cherry (*uncertain what to say, looking at Ronny*) Well—I——

Ronny Oh, yes, he was—but not now. I'm taking her instead.

Lady Benbow. I'm afraid he put you off because of me. I'm sure he
would have loved to have taken *you* out. You have met my
husband, haven't you?

Cherry Well, I—I——

Ronny (*quickly, seeing Cherry hesitate as before*) Oh, rather—yes—
she's met your husband and she goes on further to say—I mean
if she hadn't met uncle she'd never have taken Thark. Would
you, you rascal? (*Slapping her playfully*)

Cherry resents this.

Lady Benbow I'm so sorry to hear you don't like Thark.

Cherry (*exchanges looks with Ronny, who signals her to take care*) No,
I'm afraid I don't—but I suppose it's *got* to be taken.

Lady Benbow Doesn't it agree with you?

Cherry Well, the doctor seemed to think it was the best thing. But
—it's not very pleasant.

Ronny You see, auntie, that's the Norfolk air. (*To Lady Benbow*) You'll be all right. You're doing very well. Now—(*Taking Cherry up stage*) Come to dinner.

Lady Benbow There's no particular hurry.

Ronny Oh, isn't there?

Lady Benbow No, she'd like to see your uncle.

Ronny No, she wouldn't.

Lady Benbow Yes, she would. Go and see if he's dressed. (*Takes cloak off, puts it on chair* L.)

Ronny (*starting to go, but stops*) No, he isn't. I know he isn't dressed, because he was in here just now and he was undressed then. (*to Cherry*) Wasn't he?

Cherry gives Ronny an angry look

Enter Kitty R.

Lady Benbow Kitty! What are you doing in there?

Kitty Oh, I stayed in there so as not to meet Mrs Frush.

Lady Benbow Oh, nonsense! Come in. (*Bringing Kitty to Cherry*) This *is* Mrs Frush—Miss Stratton, my husband's ward.

Kitty (*obviously surprised at Cherry's appearance*) Oh! I'm sorry. Good evening.

Cherry Pleased to meet you.

Ronny bus.: keeping them apart.

Ronny She's delighted. (*Crosses to Kitty*)

Benbow enters up L. *and takes in the situation*

Kitty Yes. I've been told not to talk to you about Thark.

Cherry (*losing her control.*) Thank God for that!

Lady Benbow (*as Benbow is about to sneak off again*) Hector!

Benbow (*coming down, plausibly*) Yes, my love.

Lady Benbow Come in. Here's Mrs Frush.

Warning door bell

Benbow (*trying to evade it*) Oh! When?—(*Then seeing Cherry*) Oh, Mrs Frush—yes—How d'you do? (*With a sickly smile*)

Ronny Yes, here she is. Good old Mrs Frush. Dear old thing! (*Slapping her playfully on back*)

Kitty	Ronny	Cherry	Benbow
D. R.	R.	C.	*Up* L. C.

Lady Benbow

D. L.

Cherry looks at Benbow and makes a little face

Cherry (*overcome by her position and showing sudden resentment*) Now look here! Whatever you people are up to, I don't see why I should be made a fool of.
Ronny (*quickly, amid the general consternation*) Spanish! Now, now! Whatever your troubles are at Thark, you mustn't begin fighting here.
Cherry Then take me to dinner.

Door bell rings

Makes another little face at Benbow. Turns to say good-bye to Kitty and sees her looking very disdainfully. Cherry is looking at Benbow with anger

Ronny (*appeals to Kitty, who ignores him*) Kitty!

Ronny does wing-flapping bus.: as he crosses up c.

Warner, still looking very scared, opens the door c.

Ronny	Warner	Cherry		
Up R. C.	Up C.	Up L. C.		
	Kitty			Benbow
	R. C.			L.
				Lady Benbow
				D. L.

As Warner opens door—Mrs Frush, wonderfully got up for the occasion, advances into the room

Warner disappears

Mrs Frush at door c.*—to Ronny*

Mrs Frush (*to Ronny*) I hope I'm not too late. How d'ye do? (*Then crosses to Benbow*)

Cherry has a word with Ronny and crosses to R. C.

How d'ye do? (*Then to Lady Benbow, who is watching Benbow and Ronny* D. L.) How d'ye do? (*She pauses, then notices Kitty over* R. *She crosses to her and says:*) Miss Stratton, I think? How d'ye do?

Mrs. Frush	Ronny	Cherry	Benbow	Lady
R. C.	C.	L. C.	L.	Benbow
Kitty				D. C.
R.				

Kitty How d'you do? (*Looks over at Lady Benbow, surprised*) Who is this lady?
Mrs Frush Why—I'm expected. I'm Mrs Frush!

Kitty crosses to Ronny and says:

Kitty (*to Ronny*) You beast! (*Then crosses to Lady Benbow*)

Another slight pause—Lady Benbow watches the shrunken figure of Benbow—Cherry turns her head away

Ronny (*anxiously to Benbow*) D'you hear what I am? Well, can't you say something?

Benbow I could, but, my God, you'd be sorry if I started!

First Curtain

Second Curtain:

Ronny turns away from him to discover—

Hook, who has just come back L. *with a bunch of flowers—offering him the flowers*

Ronny takes the flowers absent-mindedly, whilst arguing with Benbow, looks at them, and pushes them back into Hook's arms

Curtain

ACT II

The same room next morning

Bright daylight

Warner, in a neat print costume, is putting final touches to the morning's work on the room

Hook arranging papers on table R. C.

Hook You're talking nonsense, Warner, that's what you're talking.
Warner No. I'm not.
Hook Yes, you are. How do you know Miss Kitty's thrown him over?
Warner If she hasn't, why is she going back to Bath?
Hook Well, it's very 'ard. Because it wasn't his fault.
Warner (*crosses up* C.) If you ask me, what really put the lid on it was you walking in with a bunch of flowers. (*Opens door up* C.)
Hook That'll do. You attend to your business.

Warner exits centre, goes left

Almost immediately Ronny hurries in C. *from* R. *with a troubled, inquiring air. He puts hat on table* C.

Ronny Good morning, Warner. I'm glad you're here. You've got to help me, you two. (*To Hook, who shows signs of quitting*) You, too.

Warner re-enters C. *closing door*

Warner Oh, Mr Ronny, anything we can do for you, we'll do gladly.

Hook	Ronny	Warner
R.	C.	L.

Ronny That's fine! (*To Hook*) And you? Gladly too?
Hook I don't see I can do much, sir.
Ronny Not so gladly.
Hook But, Mr Ronald, my first duty is to remember my place.
Ronny Your first duty is to remember a place I'm going to tell you in South Molton Street.
Hook (*startled*) What, sir?

Ronny Don't say 'what' unless you didn't hear. Did you hear?

Hook Yes, sir. . .

Ronny Yes, then don't say 'what'. Waste of time. I want you to jump in a taxi and bring back Miss Cherry Buck.

Hook Oh, I wouldn't do this if I were you, sir.

Ronny I'm not going to. You are. You see, Miss Warner . . . Miss Kitty won't listen to me. So I'm getting Miss Buck to come and explain.

Warner Miss Kitty's going back to Bath this morning, sir.

Ronny What! Good Lord! (*To Hook*) There! You see? . . . You must hurry. The address is 13A South Molton Street—bring her back at once. Here's your taxi fare. (*Hands Hook money and pushes him away*)

Hook (*as he takes the money*) Oh, I don't like doing this, sir.

Ronny (*pushing him to the door* C.) Not at all. It's only fair that I should pay for the taxi.

Hook unwillingly exits C.

(*Crosses to Warner*) Now, Warner. Where are they all?

Warner Still in their rooms, sir. They've breakfasted there.

Ronny Oh, I see.

Warner Sir Hector's now in his bath.

Ronny Oh, is that what it is? I thought it was a gramophone.

Warner And Mrs Frush and her son are calling here early, sir.

Ronny I don't like the mother, and I've never met the son. I don't care. Now I'm going to pop out and get a few flowers . . . (*Crosses up* C.) . . . for Miss Kitty, and I'll give them to her with a few words. (*Hands his hat as imaginary bouquet to Warner, with emotion*) I've brought you these flowers because I love you.

Warner looks down coyly

Not you, Warner, what are you thinking about? Give them back. (*Snatching his hat away again*)

Benbow's voice is heard off

Benbow (*off up* C.) Hook!

Ronny (*as Warner takes a step up* L.) No. (*Going up towards door* L.) Don't go to him.

Warner But, I think he's still in his bath.

Ronny Well—let him get out of it by himself.

Ronny hurries out C.

Warner stands irresolute for a moment. Then Benbow is heard again. Warner looks scared. Makes up her mind to go out, but has only just got to the door when—

Benbow enters L. *in bath gown, drying his ears*

Benbow Here, you!

Warner returns

Where's Hook?

Warner I—think he's gone out, sir.

Benbow Why? He hasn't had another baby, has he?

Warner No, sir . . . I—I don't think so.

Benbow Where's he gone?

Warner wriggles her shoulders apprehensively

Ah, stop that. We don't want any of that Salome business. Where's Hook?

Warner (*crosses* D. C.) He took a message for Mr Ronny, sir.

Benbow Where to?

Warner Oh! (*Moves down stage centre nervously*)

Benbow Now then, come on my girl. I'm not going to eat you.

Warner The message was to a lady, sir.

Benbow What, at this time in the morning? What lady?

Warner The lady who was here last night, sir.

Benbow (*impatiently*) Last night the house was stiff with ladies. Which one?

Warner Miss Buck, sir.

Benbow Well, then say so. What was it about?

As Warner hesitates

Warning door bell

Now then, come on my girl—I'm not going to be angry with you.

Warner He sent Hook to bring Miss Buck here, sir.

Benbow (*flaring up*) Wha-at! Here? Now? Is he mad?

Warner No, sir. I think he only wants Miss Buck to tell the truth.

Benbow The truth? My God, I'll see she doesn't tell the truth about *me*.

Warner He only wants Miss Buck to say he wasn't the guilty party, sir.

Benbow Well, isn't that the same thing as telling the truth about me?

Warner I don't know, sir.

Door bell is heard off

Benbow (*goes up to opening* L.) Bell! That can't be her already.

Warner I'll see, sir.

Exit up c., *disappears for a moment*

Benbow moves up L. *anxiously*

Warner returns

No, sir, it's Mr Frush.

Benbow Oh, it don't matter about him, he can wait. You can ask him in here and tell him to wait. Pop on your hat and go and stop Miss Buck from coming. (*Softening a little*) And you don't know anything about me. Mind you don't.

Warner (*stiffening rather*) Yes, I will, sir.

Benbow (*gently*) No, no; I didn't mean you'd better not for your own sake, that's all right—I meant—don't know anything about me if you're asked.

Warner Oh—yes, sir.

Benbow That's right. Not that I've done anything wrong, mind you.

Warner No, sir . . . I'm sure I don't think that.

Benbow No, I don't suppose you do. Because you're a very good girl. I know I speak rather sharply to you at times, but you're a good girl . . . (*Holding her chin*) I suppose. Are you a good girl?

Warner Yes, sir.

Benbow (*severely*) Then don't waste my time. Pop on your hat.

Benbow goes out L. *drying his ear*

Warner exits c.

Warner (*at* c. *doorway—crosses* R.) Will you step this way, sir?

Lionel (*as he enters, crosses* L.) Thanks. Topping morning, isn't it?

Warner Yes, sir. (*Anxious to get away*)

Lionel Do *you* get much time *off* ?

Warner No, sir. Excuse me, I must hurry away.

Exit c.

Lionel (*turns* R. *as she goes*) Oh, sorry.

He completes his turn as—

Kitty enters up L. *in a pretty morning frock*

Kitty Oh—did you want to see Sir Hector?

Lionel Yes—I'm Lionel Frush, you know.

Kitty Oh, I'm Kitty Stratton. How do you do? (*Shakes his hand*)

He is impressed

Lionel How do you do?

Kitty Is your mother here?

Lionel (*rather coldly*) Not yet. She's coming. Are you going to be in town for long?

Kitty (*cross* D. R.) No, I'm going away again.
Lionel (*crosses* R.) Oh! Pity—I—I find it awfully lonely here alone.
I don't know another girl. I swear I don't.
Kitty We must try and find you a little girl friend.

Ronny enters C. *with flowers, puts them on table* C.

Lionel (L.) I don't want another girl. I want *you*.
Kitty (*laughing frankly*) Oh, thank you very much. You don't waste
much time, do you?
Ronny (*after watching with distaste, coming down*) Hallo!

Lionel turns and shakes hands instinctively

How are you? Not at all. Good-bye. (*Takes him up* L. *Taking his
hand and placing it on arm of chair* L.) Just hook on to that a minute.
(*Crosses to Kitty*) Who and what?
Kitty (*with disdain, to Ronny coldly*) This is Mr Lionel Frush. (*She
moves away*)
Ronny Oh—that's Lionel Frush, is it? The son of the larger Frush.
(*Looking at Lionel*) Seems very attractive.
Kitty Oh, yes, yes, quite charming.
Ronny Yes. He's got a flashing eye. Sort of Ben-Hur type. More
Hur than Ben.
Kitty Quite.
Ronny (*still going after her*) Oh, you think so? I thought so too, the
moment I saw him. Yes. Quite. (*Turns to Lionel*) Good morning.

Lionel offers his hand to shake

Oh, you can keep that, that's yours. Isn't she charming?

Kitty moves up to table C. *looking at papers*

Lionel Quite.
Ronny Oh, you little chatterbox! She's so easy to talk to.
Lionel Oh, rather. We get on awfully well together.
Ronny Oh, do we really? (*Forcing him over the chair*) You like talking
to her?
Lionel She's so topping and friendly. Do you know I could talk to
her for hours and hours.
Ronny Yes, will you make it seconds and seconds.
Kitty Are you going to be in town for long?
Lionel Well, my mother's going back at once. But I shall be here
for some time.
Ronny Oh, that's fine. I hope we shall see—nothing of you.
Lionel I'm waiting for a car. It'll be about a week.

Ronny Oh, nonsense, my dear fellow, don't be absurd. (*Going up stage, calling out of window:*) Hi! Taxi! Taxi!

Lionel But it's a new car.

Kitty You're going to drive it to Thark?

Lionel Yes. That was the idea.

Ronny (*leading him over* c.) And a very good idea, too.

Lionel (*breaking away and crossing to Kitty*) Well, perhaps I'd better see you later.

Kitty (*cross* D. R.) Oh, but I thought you were waiting for your mother.

Lionel Oh yes, of course, but I think I'd like to go and buy a few flowers.

Ronny (*with challenge*) Who for?

Lionel (*suddenly getting into a fury*) I suppose I can buy flowers if I want to, can't I? If I'm so disposed . . .

Ronny (*moving away, feigning fear, then going back*) Did that come out of you? You'll be indisposed, if it did.

Lionel drops his stick and stoops to pick it up

Don't bend down like that, you look like a prawn. Go away.

He hustles Lionel out c. *and closes the door*

He picks up brass vase, right of door, places it in front of door c. *and strikes an attitude leaning on vase. Picks up flowers from table* c. *He holds them behind him in his* L. *hand; as he crosses to Kitty she turns and is about to cross* L. *Ronny stops her by moving towards her with his right hand raised, he then brings his* L. *hand from behind him and in a grand manner offers Kitty the empty paper (the flowers having dropped on the floor behind him). He looks down, and seeing what has happened, he quickly picks them up and puts them in the paper holder and again offers them. He then recites*

Kitty darling, I bring you these few fresh fragrant flowers because I love you. (*Rustling the paper they are wrapped in*)
Look, look, look, look!
Each one has a separate meaning. (*Taking one bloom*)
This one means devotion—(*Taking another*)
This one means emotion—(*Then pushing aside another*)
This one means—love and laughter. (*Laughing audibly*)
I won't tell you what that one means.

Kitty What about those flowers last night? You didn't buy those for me? (*Ignores flowers*)

Ronny puts flowers on table c.

Ronny (*crosses to Kitty*) We hadn't quarrelled then—don't be angry about last night. I know I did wrong.

Kitty (*keenly*) Oh, did you?

Ronny No, nothing wrong actually. But it wasn't my fault.

Kitty I see. You tried to? (*Turning to him*)

Ronny No, Kitty, listen. I was entrapped—and just as I was walking out, you walked in.

Kitty It's no good making excuses. Ronny, I'm terribly upset.

Ronny bus. goes to chair and mantelpiece

Ronny I know—I'm always upsetting someone or something. I upset a basin this morning. That's a terrible thing to do. Nothing's worse than a basin when it's upset. It either breaks into small pieces or else it runs round the room on the bias.

Kitty No, Ronny, no, you've hurt me very much. (*Crosses to settee— sits* R.)

Ronny (*crossing to her*) I'm sorry, Kitty darling—Kitty—Kitty——

She ignores him

Kitty—it's Ronny speaking. Will you forgive me? I ask you in so many words—(*counting them mentally*)—four words. Darling, I think of you by day as well as night; late last night when I was going home I was saying to myself: 'Kitty—Kitty—Kitty—Kitty —Kitty—Kitty, Kitty, Kitty . . .' and when I got to my gate there were fourteen cats behind me. (*Then sincerely*) Kitty, there's no one in the world means anything to me but you. (*Sitting holding her hand*)

Hook in a state of nervous enthusiasm, opens the door c. *quickly and ushers in Cherry in a neat morning costume with fur coat*

(*To Cherry*) What do you want?

Cherry (c.) Well, you sent for me.

Ronny (*blankly, looks at Kitty*) Did I?

Hook (*in self defence*) Yes, sir. (D. L. C.)

Ronny (*rising to Hook*) I wasn't talking to you.

Hook moves L.

Cherry He said you couldn't get along without me.

Kitty is furious

Hook That's right, sir, as per your instructions.

	Ronny	*Cherry*
	R. C.	L. C.
Kitty		*Hook*
R.		L.

Warning for door slam

Ronny (*to Hook, in a surprised voice*) Don't be audible. (*To Kitty*) And do you know why I couldn't get along without her?
Kitty (*rising*) Yes. I may be very young, but I'm old enough to know that.

She goes out L., *crossing between Cherry and Hook*

Ronny is about to follow her when Hook gets in his way

Ronny (*to Kitty as she disappears*) Not quite, Kitty. (*Cross to Hook*) What do you want?
Hook Your change from the taxi, sir. (*Has it in* L. *hand*)
Ronny (*taking it*) Well, you can't have it. (*Cross to* L., *looks*) Kitty, Kitty! Kit . . . ty!

Door slams off L.

She's slammed the door in my face—(*Then back to Cherry*) Just as I got everything straightened up you came in and bent it.
Cherry Well, I never!
Ronny I sent for you so that you could tell her——
Cherry (*interrupting*) All right—I had quite enough of that in the taxi.
Ronny (*to Hook*) Why, what have you been doing in the taxi? (*Walks round him and repeats:*) What have you been doing in the taxi?
Cherry He kept yapping at me all the way telling me what to do as if I were some baby.
Ronny (*severely at Hook*) Hook! So you think this lady is some baby?

Hook looks helpless

You've ruined everything. How dare you? You—you butler! There's no one can help me now. Except uncle. Hook, tell him I've something to show him.
Hook Thank you, sir.

Hook exits L.

Cherry Fancy her being so jealous of me.
Ronny (*going on innocently*) Oh, but—you know what young girls are. You just cast your mind back—to the days when you were young——
Cherry Well! I've never been so insulted for *years*. (*Going up*) I'm going back to the shop.
Ronny (*all over* R.) No, no—you can't do that. (*Holding her by the arms*)

Cherry sees Kitty L.

I want you to tell Kitty the truth. I want you here. I do really—I
want you.

He puts his hands on her shoulders. Kitty enters L. *She hears the last words.
Ronny pretends to be dusting Cherry's coat. He turns to Kitty embarrassed*

Hallo! What am I doing? I'll tell you. No. She'll tell you.
(*Breaking away from Kitty*)
Cherry Very well, then.
Kitty Yes, I expect you've got the story quite ready by now.
Ronny Yes. It goes like this. Two mornings ago . . .
Cherry Am I going to tell her, or you?
Ronny Oh, sorry.
Cherry (*to Kitty*) Two mornings ago I was in the shop where I
work—in the window——
Ronny She doesn't always work in the window. (*Catching Cherry's
eye*) Oh, sorry . . .
Kitty I won't listen to a lot of lies. (*Cross* D. L.)
Cherry Well, while I was there, along came a gentleman.
Kitty What gentleman?

Benbow enters L. *dressed. He speaks as he enters*

Benbow Look here, Ronny, what d'you want to send . . . (*Seeing
Cherry*) Good lor'! She's here!

Cherry	Ronny	Benbow	Kitty
R.	*Up* R. C.	*Up* L. C.	L.

Ronny (*to Kitty*) This gentleman. (*To Benbow*)
Benbow Why is this little girl here again?
Ronny To tell Kitty the truth about you.
Benbow Yes, that's just what I expected. (*To Ronny*) You go and
mess up the whole business, and then you blame it on to me.
Ronny (*taking Benbow aside*) It's up to you, as a sporting man, to
clear me.
Benbow But I can't tell this to a young girl. She's my ward. She
respects me.
Ronny (*soothingly*) No, she doesn't.
Benbow Besides, she'll tell your aunt.
Ronny No, she won't.
Benbow You don't think she would?
Ronny No.

Kitty crosses to Benbow

Benbow (*to Kitty*) Well—we—Kitty, I hesitate to tell you this——

Ronny Then I will. Two mornings ago this girl was in her shop window when uncle was coming down the street—(*Imitating Benbow's walk broadly and twirling an imaginary moustache*)

Benbow (*annoyed*) Now—that'll do, that'll do, that'll do, that'll do. That's quite enough of your version. Thank you. I'll tell my own tale. (*Pushing Ronny aside*) Now, Kitty, this is roughly— pretty roughly, I admit—what occurred. I was on my way to see old Dobbie— (*To Ronny*) You know old Dobbie—?

Ronny Yes—young Dobbie's old father.

Benbow Yes, old Davy Dobbie! Why, he was Master o' Hounds before me. Finer fellow never breathed.

Ronny Never mind about his breath. Go on with the story.

Benbow Will you shut up and not interrupt? Well, as I say, I was on my way to old Dobbie's flat—he's a great friend of mine. By Gad, that feller can shift port. Oh, a hell of a sportsman—married his cook. You ought to see him on a horse. He's got a wonderful seat—(*to Ronny*)—hasn't he?

Ronny Oh, enormous, but get on with the story.

Benbow Well, as I say, I was on my way to Dobbie's—I was going —past the shops, when I noticed someone——

Lady Benbow appears up L.

Benbow perceives Lady Benbow and pauses

Ronny Yes? And who was it?

Benbow I noticed someone—(*watching the door*)—and who was it?

Lady Benbow comes down L. C.

Who was it? Why, old Dobbie. (*Sees Lady Benbow*) Oh, good morning, my love. Nice morning

Ronny Oh, a beauty.

Benbow gives Ronny a look and moves up C.

Lady Benbow Why is this lady here again?

Kitty (*excitedly*) To try and put me off the scent.

Kitty sits D. L.

Cherry That's all rats, what she's saying. Sorry, but really it is.

Lady Benbow Yes. Will you sit down, please?

Cherry brings chair up from down R., sits R.

Ronny Oh, good morning, auntie.

Lady Benbow Sit down.

Ronny brings chair from L. of table and sits in front of it C. Benbow is up

stage c., *studying a picture which is hanging on the back wall. He is obviously trying to dodge the situation*

Hector!

Benbow pretends not to hear

Hector!

Benbow (*turning round unconcerned*) Yes, my love?
Lady Benbow You sit down, too.
Benbow Oh——
Lady Benbow (*she turns to Cherry*) Now, to begin with——
Benbow (*as he brings chair from back of table* c., *to Ronny on his* l.) This is going to be awkward.

They are all sitting obediently, after interchanging glances

Lady Benbow Whom did you really come here last night to see?
Ronny (*to Benbow*) Stand up.
Benbow (*Rising*) Really, Maud darling, I don't wish you to be lugged into this business.

Cherry	Ronny	Benbow	
R.	R. C.	R. C.	
		Lady Benbow	Kitty
		L.	D. L.

Lady Benbow ignoring Benbow. Benbow looks at Ronny in despair—sits

Lady Benbow (*to Cherry*) Who did ask you out to dinner?
Cherry You really want to know?
Lady Benbow Yes, of course I do.

Anxiety of Benbow and Ronny

Cherry All right then, Mr Hook.

Relief of Benbow and Ronny. Benbow sits back and crosses his legs right over left. Ronny follows suit

Kitty (*scornfully*) Oh, rubbish!
Ronny All right then, ask Hook. (*To Benbow*) Can we rely on Hook?
Benbow Yes. (*Definitely*)

Ronny rises, crosses c. *Lady Benbow protests*

Lady Benbow (*intervening*) No, Ronny! I won't have Hook brought in here to give your uncle away.
Benbow Give me away! My gad, he'd better not. Besides, I'm absolutely blameless.
Ronny Me, too. I'll prove it to you now and then—here and now.

Hook! (*Crosses up* L., *calls off* L.) Hook! Yes, you too, Warner! Come here. Come in here. (*Crosses to his chair*)

Hook and Warner follow him, standing up stage L. *looking sheepish*

(*To Warner and Hook*) Closer, closer.

They move down

Halt! (*Placing his foot on chair* L. C.) Now then, Hook, I understand that you are of American origin, are you not?

Hook Yes, sir.

Ronny Don't say, 'Yes, sir'—say, 'Yeah, bo.' Are you of American origin?

Hook Yes, bo-sir.

Ronny Right, then I know I'll get the truth. I believe that. Now then—(*Indicating Cherry Buck*) Did this lady come here last night to see me?

Hook (*looking at Lady Benbow, then to Benbow*) Er—no, sir, I hardly think that.

Ronny There you are—hardly. That's rather indefinite. Did she come here to see your master, Sir Hector?

Hook What, sir? (*Looks at Benbow*) Oh, good Lord, no!

Ronny Then I put it to you—(*pointing at Hook with* L. *hand*)—she must have come to see you. (*Putting his* R. *hand in his pocket, rattles his money suggestively*) You acknowledge that?

Hook Oh, no, sir.

Benbow (*to Hook*) Oh, yes, sir.

Ronny Why can't you tell the truth like everyone else? (*Indicating Benbow*)

Lady Benbow That'll do, Ronny. I won't have the servants questioned.

Warner and Hook move to go, but Ronny stops them by saying:

Ronny One moment. In fairness to me. Warner! Now then, Warner, your name's Warner, isn't it?

Warner Yes, sir.

Ronny I warn you, Warner, I want you to tell the truth, the whole truth, or something like the truth. You are a maid in the establishment of Benbow, are you not? (*Then looking from Sir Hector to Lady Benbow*) You are a maid of some sort or another—kitchen maid look after the kitchens—parlour maid look after the parlours—chamber-maid to look after the other things. It was you who asked Mrs Frush?

Warner Yes, sir. I didn't know Mr Hook had too.

Benbow He didn't ask her. He asked *her*. (*Pointing to Cherry*) Didn't you?

Hook No, sir, I didn't!

Benbow What?

Hook Yes, sir, I did.

Ronny You see, auntie, it's all perfectly clear.

Kitty (*jumping up*) Well, I don't care. You dined with her.

Cherry (*jumping up*) Well, why the devil shouldn't he?

Ronny Oh, hush, not in this department. (*Sits*)

Lady Benbow (*rising. To Hook and Warner*) Leave the room at once.

Hook Thank you, my lady.

They turn inwards—exeunt L.

Lady Benbow (*to Benbow*) Hector!

Benbow Yes, my love.

Lady Benbow You knew she wasn't Mrs Frush?

Benbow Yes, but I didn't want to give Ronny away.

Ronny Oh!—you—you wicked uncle.

Cherry (*to Benbow*) Give him away? Did you think I wasn't respectable?

Benbow Well, I—I never had the chance to find out.

Ronny moves and Kitty faces him

Kitty Well, I don't care. (*To Ronny*) And you can go and lunch with her. I'm going to Bath.

She goes out L. *in a temper*

Ronny is following, Lady Benbow stops him

Ronny (*rising*) Oh, Kitty, don't bath. She shan't blame me like this. (*Brokenly*)

Lady Benbow Leave her alone.

Ronny But if you only knew what happened.

Lady Benbow Of course I know what happened. D'you think I was married yesterday?

Exit L.

Benbow (*rising, to Ronny*) Now then, look here, Ronny, I won't have you telling Kitty things about my character.

Ronny (*at the door* L.) It wouldn't matter. Sooner or later she's bound to learn the disgusting side of life. (*Broken-heartedly*)

Exit L.

Benbow (*cross down* L. C.) Well, I'm awfully sorry about all this, my dear.

Cherry (*cross* L. *to him*) So I should hope.

Benbow (*putting his hand in his breast pocket*) If there's any little compensation that I can make by way of—what shall we say— half a dozen pairs of silk stockings——

Cherry No, thanks. Take a girl's character away and then offer her presents, is that it?

Benbow No, it's generally the other way about. I mean—quite the contrary.

Cherry Well then, we'd better say good-bye.

Benbow What, not good-bye for ever?

Cherry We'd better not meet again.

Benbow Oh, good Lord, why not? You needn't be frightened——

Lady Benbow (*heard off* L.) Hector!!

Benbow Curse! (*Taking Cherry up stage*) All right then, my dear. Under the circumstances, if you really wish it, what more can I say? Good-bye for ever. But don't you worry. I'll be able to see you again next week—they're going away again.

Exit Benbow L.

As Cherry turns up R. C. *Lionel Frush enters with box of flowers* C., *closes door*

Lionel (*seeing Cherry with interest*) Oh, good morning. I saw you here last night, of course.

Cherry Oh, yes. (*Moves up a little*) Excuse me, I must go.

Lionel Oh, you're always just going out when I come in. (*Cross* D. L.) I say—(*offering her box of flowers*)—just a moment. Would you care for these flowers?

Cherry But you didn't get them for me.

Lionel I've no one else to give them to. You have them. (*Gives her flowers*)

Cherry Well, that's very kind, I'm sure.

Lionel That's all right. Where are you going to lunch?

Cherry (*definitely*) Oh, really I mustn't. (*Fiddling with ribbon on box*) What time?

Lionel One o'clock—at the Berkeley.

Cherry I don't think I ought to.

Lionel I say, do. (*Moves to her*) I'm terribly on my own. I don't know another girl. I swear I don't. Or I wouldn't ask you.

Cherry You funny boy.

Lionel You will meet me, won't you?

Cherry (*pausing—taking stock of him*) Now look here. You seem a nice boy, and I'm looking for a bit of real friendship myself. Will you come out on the level?

Lionel Yes, rather.

Cherry All right then. I'll meet you just outside the Berkeley at one o'clock. 'Bye.

Lionel Good-bye. (*He runs up* c. *in time to open door for her*)

Bell warning

> *She goes out* c.

He stands and raises his eyebrows.

> *Kitty enters* L., *crossing* R. *with Ronny following her. She speaks to him in a petulant tone as they enter*

Kitty Oh, don't follow me all over the flat.

Ronny I'd follow you all over the sticks. (*Sees Lionel*) Is that the same one? Good Lor'! Are you still here? I didn't think you'd keep.

Pause—Bell—Door bell

Lionel (*to Kitty*) That'll be my mother, I expect.

Kitty Oh, well, now we are going to talk about Thark.

Ronny (*to Kitty*) Not you.

Kitty Why not?

Ronny Uncle said that *he* was going to talk to Mrs Frush.

Kitty Oh! Then I'll talk to *Mr* Frush. (*Turning her back*)

Lionel (*to Ronny*) Yes, if you don't mind, it's awfully private.

Ronny Yes, and whether you mind or not, you're privately awful.

> *Hook enters* c.

Hook Mrs Frush.

> *Mrs Frush enters. She is in quite an affable mood at the start*

Mrs Frush Oh, you've got there, Lionel. (*To Kitty*) Good morning.

Kitty Good morning.

> *Kitty and Lionel sit* R. C.

Mrs Frush (*to Ronny*) Nice day! (*Crosses* L.)

Ronny Who for? (*Cross* L. *to Mrs Frush*)

> *Hook exits* c. *closing door*

Mrs Frush I'm afraid I should have been here sooner.

Ronny Oh, don't be afraid of that.

Lionel

R. C.

Kitty   *Ronny*   *Mrs Frush*

R.   L. C.   L. C.

Mrs Frush The traffic always seems worse when you've got a bit behind. (*Moves* D. L.)

Ronny (*scrutinizing her figure*) Yes——

Benbow enters L.

Benbow (*coming down* L. C.) Good morning!

Mrs Frush *Good* morning.

Benbow Oh! There he is! (*To Lionel*) Good morning to you.

Lionel (*rising*) Good morning, sir.

Ronny (*to Lionel*) Sit down, you'll smash.

Lionel sits

(*Then to Benbow*) Good morning, uncle.

Benbow (*to Ronny*) You get out. You're not wanted.

Ronny No. Only when you want helping out of trouble. I suppose you don't anticipate getting into trouble with *that*!

He indicates Mrs Frush, who hears and gives a little exclamation

(*He crosses to her*) What's the matter? Has something happened to you?

Mrs Frush No, it has not.

Kitty and Lionel are sitting R. C.

Ronny Oh, I thought I heard you give way.

Ronny crosses to Lionel and Kitty and tries to join in their conversation—then turns to Benbow

Benbow (*to Ronny*) Will you get out when you're told?

Ronny All right! I'm going. (*Crosses* L. C.)—And remember, I'll never call you 'Uncle' again. (*Crosses up* L.—*at door.*) Good-bye, mother's brother.

Exits L.

Benbow (*to Mrs Frush*) Sit down, madam. (*Indicates chair* D. L.— *she sits next to him*)

Mrs Frush Thank you.

Benbow (*sitting* L.) Now, madam, come on, put your hounds in. Let's hear something.

Mrs Frush Have you ever been to Thark?

Benbow I've seen some very good photos of it.

Kitty I've been there. (*Crosses to* L. C.)

Lionel follows

It belonged to my family. Well, to *me*.

Benbow And I sold it for you. (*To Mrs Frush*) And you bought it. We all know that. Now, what's wrong with Thark?

Mrs Frush I'm going to speak my mind.

Lionel Careful, mother.

Mrs Frush Careful yourself! (*To Benbow*) Oh, I know you've been very polite and gave me a nice dinner and all that, but it shall not make me shrink!

Benbow No, I didn't expect it would.

Kitty Well, what's wrong with Thark, anyway?

Mrs Frush (*to Benbow*) You know well enough without being told.

Benbow It's a magnificent house, madam! It would do for a Dook.

Mrs Frush It would do for anyone.

Benbow Why? Come on, let's have it. Why?

Mrs Frush I'll tell you why. (*Dramatically, dropping her voice*) 'Aunted!

Benbow (*blinking densely*) Oughtn't it? (*Looks vaguely at Lionel and Kitty—then to Mrs Frush*) Oughtn't it to *what*?

Lionel (*cross to Benbow*) Well, sir, my mother thinks, sir, that Thark is haunted.

Mrs Frush I don't *think*.

Benbow Haunted? Preposterous!

Mrs Frush It's unliveable in.

Benbow Haunted, my—(*mildly*)—foot! You don't like the place, and you're trying to repudiate the deal.

Kitty (*to Benbow*) Well, of course—there always *was* some sort of a *legend* about Thark.

Benbow Legend! Bunkum! And what *d'you* want to say so for?

Kitty Well, it's only honest to say so.

Benbow I don't say don't be honest, I say don't be silly. Legend— my hat! What is the trouble—have you investigated?

Kitty moves away R. C.

Lionel (*crosses to Benbow*) Well, sir, how would *you* care to go down and investigate something funny that goes on in one of the bedrooms?

Benbow I mightn't mind. Whose bedroom is it? It's probably rats.

Mrs Frush It is not rats. There's more goes on there than was caused by any rat *you* ever saw.

Benbow Oh, thanks for the compliment!

Mrs Frush The butler went to have a look one night, and he came back trembling in every pore.

Benbow frowns at her

Benbow (*to Mrs Frush*) I know what your trouble is. When you've had a couple, you fancy things.

Mrs Frush Well, I don't fancy ghosts. (*Rising boldly*) So what are you going to do about it?

Benbow Ah! (*Rising*) Here we have it, this is what I've been waiting for. You're going to ask me to cancel the sale.

Mrs Frush I don't ask you to—I tell you to.

Benbow Oh, thank you, I am not going to try and sell that house again. I had enough trouble to get rid of it once.

Lionel Yes, sir, quite, sir; but——

Benbow Down, sir! No, madam. Certainly not. Business is business.

Lionel

L. C.

Kitty   Benbow

L. C.   L.

Mrs Frush

L.

Lionel (*to Mrs Frush*) I *told* you what it would be.

Kitty (*to Mrs Frush*) Don't be afraid. I'll see you're *properly* treated.

Mrs Frush Thank you. (*To Benbow*) There speaks at least a lady.

Benbow (*to Kitty*) I wish you'd mind your own business, my child.

Kitty It looks as if I shall have to. (*Crosses R.*)

Lionel (*cross to Benbow*) Don't be offended by my mother.

Benbow Go to hell! Get out of it!

Lionel cross R. C.

Mrs Frush It's all very well for *you*—(*Cross to Lionel*) you stay gadding about here in London, waiting for your motor, while I have to go back to Thark and sleep there alone for six nights with a butler and a bogey.

She exits C. followed by Lionel

Kitty turns with animation to Benbow, who is chuckling

Kitty (*crosses L. C.*) You're not treating that old woman properly.

Benbow (*cross R.*) Oh, nonsense! I've treated her all right. She understands it.

Kitty It's my house—or was. And it's quite true. It was always supposed to be haunted. (*Cross L. C. following Benbow*)

Benbow (*sharply*) Haunted! Tripe!

Kitty I don't care. If you won't go, I'll jolly well go myself.

Benbow What? Go to Thark?

Kitty Yes. I'll write to Mrs Frush and arrange to go down there next week. If you won't look into it, I will.

Hook enters L.

Benbow Now then, don't talk to me like that.

Benbow turns up R., *picks up morning paper from table*

Hook (*up* L. C. *to Kitty*) Excuse me, miss. Warner's done your packing for Bath. Would you see whether she's put in all you require?

Kitty Yes, I'll go in a minute. Oh, Hook, your wife was my Aunt Mary's parlourmaid at Thark, wasn't she?

Benbow up R. C. *listens unseen by Hook*

Hook (*apprehensively*) Yes, miss.

Kitty Did she ever say anything about Thark being haunted?

Hook Oh—(*with dread*)—frequent, miss.

Kitty exchanges looks with Benbow

I should be very sorry to go near the house myself.

Kitty Thank you.

Hook Thank you, miss.

Benbow Get out!

Hook goes out L.

Hook Yes, sir.

Kitty And you mean to say you never heard?

Benbow (D. R.) Never! And I don't want to now. It's a great mistake to encourage people like these Frushes.

Ronny (*entering* L.) Quite right, sir. I'm very glad to hear you say so.

Benbow (*ignoring Ronny*) If you go to Thark, further advances will only be made.

Ronny Advances? (*To Kitty*) You're not going to Thark?

Kitty Yes, I am.

Benbow What for? To be taken around at nights by young Frush and made to listen to a lot of rats?

Ronny I won't have you go ratting with young Frush.

Kitty (*to Benbow*) I tell you I am going.

Benbow (*roused*) Very well. Go, and you can manage your own affairs. (*Going up* L.)

Kitty I must go. It's only fair and friendly.

Benbow Friendly? What the devil do you want to be friendly with an old woman like that for? By gad! she looks like a female froth-blower.

Exit L.

Ronny Kitty! you're trying to make me jealous. Yes, you are—of this nasty new friend of yours—this Leopold Thark, that nasty little fellow with Chippendale shoulders and Adam's legs.

Kitty He wouldn't go about with Cherry Buck, anyhow.

Ronny Nor would I, Kitty, on purpose. She was thrust upon me when I wasn't thinking. I couldn't be unkind or rude to her, could I?

Kitty (*with meaning*) *No.*

Ronny (*not noticing her tone*) No, of course not. Kitty, let's be friends —you know I'm a friendly little chap.

Kitty (*pointedly*) *Yes, you are.*

Ronny Don't say it like that—say, yes, you are; not *yes, you are.* You're fond of me, aren't you?

Kitty Oh, yes. In a way.

Ronny (*trying to embrace her*) Well, how far away?

Kitty (*turning to him—they embrace*) Well, Ronny, you do promise not to see this girl again?

Ronny Well, what about you and this boy—this nasty little filleted sheik?

Kitty Don't be so absurd. I've only met him for five minutes.

Ronny Well, that's long enough, isn't it?

Kitty I don't want to see him, but I can't help if if I go to Thark.

Ronny You're not going to Thark.

Hook enters L. *and drops down by Ronny's* L.

Kitty You don't understand. There's something at Thark that's got to be done. Your uncle won't do it, so I must.

Ronny But what is it? (*To Hook*) What is it?

Hook Excuse me, miss—it's nearly time you went——

Ronny No, it isn't. Don't come and say things like that when I'm getting on so well. I had both her hands in mine before you came in, and now I haven't got one. I shan't tip you now. I wasn't going to anyway. (*Goes up to table* C.—*takes up paper and puts it on chair in front of table* C.)

Hook Warner wants to show you what she's packed, miss.

Kitty (*cross in front of Ronny and Hook*) Oh, very well. I'll go and see.

Ronny I say, Kitty, don't be long. I want to talk to you.

She goes out L.

Hook starts to go up L. *and stops*

Hook May I just say, Mr Ronald, I'm sorry, sir, about that slight 'itch this morning?

Ronny What hitch?

Hook Bringing the lady in at the wrong time, sir.

Ronny Oh, that! Yes. Oh, very bad that—oh, it's terrible—that *was* terrible! I don't know what's the matter with you. You're a mass of hitches. I suppose it must be this baby. You'd better not have any more.

Hook Very good, sir.

Ronny (*relenting, patting his shoulder*) All right, Hook. You can if you like.

Hook (*smiling*) Thank you, sir.

Hook goes out L. *as—*

Lady Benbow enters busily L. *followed by Benbow. She is dressed for travelling*

Lady Benbow (*to Ronny, who is at the table* C. *looking at a paper*) Where's Kitty?

Ronny She's just gone out there——

Benbow It's no use trying to stop her, the headstrong little devil. (*Cross to table* C.)

Ronny resents this

Lady Benbow (*to Ronny*) I won't have her go to Thark and do this business.

Benbow takes paper from table C., *cross down* L., *sits*

Ronny (*with sudden determination*) Look here, if Kitty wants anything done, it shall be done. *I'll* do it.

Lady Benbow Very well, then—you'd better. But it won't be a pleasant——

Ronny I'd do the nastiest job in the world to please her. I'll even examine the drains for her sake.

Benbow It isn't the drains, you ass! (*Cross* L., *sits*)

Ronny I don't care what it is. (*Cross to Benbow*) I'll do it. (*With less defiance*) What is it?

Kitty returns L., *crosses* R. C.

Kitty

L. C.

Lady Benbow		*Ronny*
R.		L. C.

Benbow

L.

Lady Benbow (D. R. *to Kitty*) Oh, Kitty, is this true that Hector tells me, that you're going to Thark?

Kitty Yes.

Lady Benbow Then I shall come with you. And so will he.

Kitty Oh, you needn't—either of you.

Lady Benbow My dear, do you think I'd let you go and tackle a job like that alone?

Ronny listens with increasing interest

Kitty Well, somebody's got to do it.

Benbow Well, Ronny says *he* will. So there you are.

Kitty (*joyfully*) Oh, Ronny! Will you? Really?

Ronny Yes, dear, of course.

Kitty Oh, how brave of you!

Ronny What?

Kitty (*holding his arm*) How splendid of you!

Ronny Oh, darling, it's all right, it's nothing. (*To Benbow*) Is it?

Benbow No. Of course it isn't.

Kitty Oh, isn't it? Well, I'm very proud of him—and I shall be very pleased if he comes out of it safely.

Hook enters C.

Hook The car is here, my lady.

Lady Benbow (*busily*) Oh, Kitty, I'm not nearly ready, are you?

Kitty Not quite, but there's heaps of time.

They exeunt L.

Hook at door C., *Benbow is* R. *with his paper*

Benbow Hook!

Hook Sir? (*Closes door, comes down to Benbow*)

Benbow You'd better arrange with your wife. I shall be going out of town in a few days, and I shall want you to come with me.

Hook Very good, sir. Excuse me, sir. Might I inquire—where shall we be going?

Benbow Thark!

Hook (*in an involuntary exclamation*) Thark! (*Turning to Ronny, aghast*) Oh, my God!

Exit C.

Ronny (*after watching him off, cross* L. *to Benbow, his knees shaking*) I say, uncle, what's all this about won't be safe, worse than drains, and Hook's looks?

Benbow Why, what's the matter? You're not frightened, are you?

Ronny (*trying to be brave*) Frightened, no! I'm not frightened, but it sounded strange for the moment.

Benbow Well, you know a lot of women—you know what they are—they're all scaremongers.

Ronny Yes. They do get excited.

Benbow Yes—you buck up. Don't you worry.

Ronny crosses R., *picks up the 'Tatler' and sits, crossing his legs*

Ronny I shan't worry. I've got nothing to worry about.
Benbow (*still unconcerned, looking at his paper*) No, of course not.
Personally, I don't think anything will happen to you at all.

Ronny looks across at Benbow suspiciously

CURTAIN

PICTURE: CURTAIN

Benbow L. *is looking over his glasses at Ronny, who is sitting over* R. *looking
very uncertain, with a sickly smile*

ACT III

Scene i

The dining-room at Thark, after dinner on a night a week later; it is a fine old room. There is a door to the hall c. back, another door down r. Fireplace d. l. Windows up l. in back wall. Staircase shown up l. leading to the bedrooms in the left wing. There is another entrance at the back of stairs left which leads to the front door, which is not shown. Three massive columns each side of the room, and Venetian lamps in miniature showing an amber light are dotted about—one each side of the stairs and one on the landing up l.—there are two large candelabra on the dining-table, which is set on the oblique down l. c. The candles are burning and casting shadows, giving the room a sombre and eerie effect. The furniture is all antique. There is a monk's stool on lower landing of stairs, an oak cabinet above door r., three armchairs, tapestried, one at the foot of the middle column r., the other two at the foot of the back columns. A three-seat cane settle set above opening r. An oak cabinet up stage r. There are two leather-backed armchairs at dining-table, one on r. and the other at the back. Curtains excepting one left of door up c. There is a bell-pull right, just below opening r.

Ronny and Benbow are sitting alone over their port and dessert at dining-table r. c. Benbow back of table, Ronny r. They are wearing dinner jackets. Benbow has dined well and is quite pleased with things in general, enjoying a cigar, but Ronny is doing his best to disguise extreme dislike for the business on hand. It is a wild night, and at the opening of the act and at frequent intervals the wind can be heard

Wind is heard loudly as curtain rises

Benbow (*sitting behind table near Ronny—as the storm is heard outside*) Wind's up.

Ronny (*sitting r. of table—with challenge*) What's that?

Benbow All right—I was only referring to the elements. (*Pause*) I think it's working up for a nasty night.

Ronny What do you mean—'working up' for one? It's one now, isn't it?

Benbow Well, I don't care. I'm not sorry we came. The old woman put up a very good dinner.

Ronny Yes, the lamb was particularly good. I didn't care for the butler. He eyes me eating.

Benbow M'yes. Perhaps he didn't like the idea of your sleeping in the haunted room.

Ronny He's got a fat lot to worry about, hasn't he?

Benbow Yes, he's like Pickwick's fat boy, he likes to make his own flesh creep.

Ronny Besides, the room isn't haunted. Ridiculous.

Benbow Well, of course not.

Ronny Then why did you say it was?

Benbow I didn't.

Ronny Yes, you did. You said just now, 'the haunted room'.

Benbow You seem very sensitive about it.

Ronny You needn't think I'm afraid.

Benbow Nothing to be afraid of.

Ronny I shouldn't be afraid if there was, I don't suppose.

Benbow No, of course not. Ghosts—bunkum. Have you ever met anyone who's seen a ghost?

Warning for wind

Ronny No; but I've never met anyone who hasn't met someone who *has*.

Benbow Go on. (*Passing decanter*) Have some more port. You'd better have plenty.

Ronny (*with challenge again*) Why?

Benbow Oh—because it's surprisingly good port, that's all.

Ronny Oh, in that case I will. (*He is obviously very nervy and shakes as he helps himself, rattling the glass with the decanter*)

Benbow It's no good your trying to tell me. You're scared of this place.

Ronny You said yourself just now there's nothing to be scared of.

Benbow I say so, yes.

Ronny And so do I.

Wind is heard only

I ought to know.

Warning for lightning

I dressed in the room.

Benbow Yes, and almost before you started you had yer head stuck out of the door shouting Hook! I believe you'd lost yer nerve.

Ronny Nothing of the kind. I'd lost my braces.

Wind (loud). Door bang. Lightning. Distant thunder.

The wind suddenly gains force. An outer door is heard to bang, followed by flashes of lightning, which light up the room and catch Jones's face as he enters C. Distant thunder is heard, lasting till Jones is down stage.

Jones is Mrs Frush's butler, a very sinister-looking man, who walks with a measured, gliding step, slightly on his toes. He carries a little silver tray with a letter on it. He fixes Ronny with his eye as he comes down stage, keeping dead centre, and stands on his R. Ronny is keenly aware of this

What are you looking at me like that for? What's the joke?

Jones (*fixing him with his eye, crosses to Ronny*) It's no joke, sir.

Ronny What isn't?

Jones (*looking straight in front*) This night's work.

Benbow Why, nothing's happened to you, and you've been alone in the house.

Jones No one is ever alone in this house, sir.

Benbow Oh, I heard that none of the other servants would sleep here, and that all the maids went home at night.

Jones (*to Benbow*) Yes, sir. (*To Ronny*) And maybe it's lucky for them they do.

Benbow Is this feller trying to be personal?

Ronny (*to Jones*) Now look here. You've been alone in this room at night—you know what I mean—this—my little room? (*Indicates room up L.*)

Jones (*eyeing him and nodding*) Yes, sir. (*Suddenly*) And don't you! (*Forcibly*) Don't you!

Ronny Why shouldn't I, if—if I'm keen on it? (*Drinks*)

Jones It isn't only that room, sir. (*Looking L.*) It's all down that wing. It's there. It's there. (*Looking straight in front*)

Ronny Yes, I know it's there all right, but what is it that is there?

Jones (*slowly*) Maybe *you'll* know, sir, better even than I.

Benbow Well, he won't know much if he don't.

Jones (*looking straight ahead*) It may not give him time to learn much, sir. (*Turns R.*)

Ronny Hi, you! Yes, but—here—— (*He comes back*) What's your name again?

Jones My name, sir? Well, here in this house they only call me Jones—that's all.

Warning for thunder

Benbow Oh, is it? Well, you wait till I've been here a bit longer.

Ronny They *call* you Jones? I see. A sort of pet name?

Jones Mrs Frush wouldn't call me by my real name. So she called me Jones. (*Straight in front*)

Ronny Why, what is your real name, Jones?

Jones My real name, sir?

Ronny Yes.
Jones Death.

Ronny is about to crack a nut. He does so involuntarily as Jones speaks

Ronny (*to Benbow*) Death!

As Ronny speaks, lightning flashes fiercely into the room, followed immediately by heavy thunder, which goes on for some seconds

It is obviously getting on their nerves. Ronny is particularly nervy, twitching and twisting the nut crackers round and round. Benbow shows more annoyance than fear; he tests his cigar with his fingers, then smells it, trying to appear unconcerned. After the thunder has died away he carries on with the conversation

Benbow Ah, well, that's nothing; I don't care a damn. I used to know a chap named Death. Major Death, he was in the Blues.
Ronny I'm not a bit surprised.

Benbow lights cigar

Jones (*to Ronny*) If you really mean to sleep in that room, sir, would you care for me to come along to you there to-night?
Ronny No thanks, Death! It's quite all right.
Jones Oh, very well, as you please, sir. (*Turns* L. *a little*)
Benbow I say, what is it you've got there? Is that something for me?
Jones No, sir. (*Looking at Ronny apprehensively*) It's only the last post.

Wind strong

   Exit up R.

Ronny Nice quiet sort of fellow, isn't he? Makes one feel so restful. The last post!
Benbow Yes, that reminds me. (*Cross in front*)

Wind drops to nothing

   (*Cross in front of table* L. C.) (*Taking a letter from his pocket*) I was going to ask you about *this*.
Ronny What is it?
Benbow I thought I hadn't seen much of you lately.
Ronny No, I haven't been about much.
Benbow This is from Cherry Buck.
Ronny What? That's not my affair.
Benbow Oh! Isn't it? We'll see. Listen to this. (*Reads*) 'Thanks for the invitation.'
Ronny Invitation? (*Rises*)
Benbow (*airily*) Oh, that's nothing. I didn't mean to read that.

That's another part of the letter altogether. I thought it only fair
to ask her out again.

Ronny (*excitedly*) What? Good Heavens! When I've lugged you
out of trouble once——

Benbow Never mind about that, listen to this. (*Reads*) 'The truth
is I'm cutting that stuff right out. I've met the boy who is really it.'

Ronny You don't think I'm the boy who is it—do you?

Benbow No. Well, what about this then—'You can console yourself
by knowing it was through you I met him. Happy days.—Cherry
Buck.'

Ronny Well, who has she met through you?

Benbow Only you.

Ronny Me?

Benbow Have you been seeing her again?

Ronny (*hesitating up* R.) Well, I—I just met her by accident.

Benbow Oh, then let me tell you I consider it rotten bad form—in a
chap who's just going to be married. (*Pouring out port*) Why can't
yer wait?

Ronny (*coming down*) But I tell you I just met her in the street.

Benbow Did you stop and talk?

Ronny Certainly not. I just halted and spoke a few words.

Kitty enters up R.

Benbow (*offering letter to Ronny, who crosses* D. R.) Well, there you are.
You can read it yourself.

As Ronny takes the letter, Kitty enters up R. *in a pretty evening dress. Benbow
turns aside with a nonchalant air. Ronny holds the letter out of sight in his
left hand*

Benbow cross D. L. *and sits*

Kitty (*to Ronny*) Hello! Have you had a letter too?

Ronny No, darling. Something of uncle's. A business thing. (*He
holds it in his hand while talking*)

Kitty Well, Mrs Frush has just heard from her son. He's coming
back.

Ronny I don't care. Do you care, Kitty?

Kitty (*to Benbow*) But Hecky's got his room.

Ronny Well, that's fine, he can have my room. (*Moves front of table*
L. *to Benbow*)

Mrs Frush and Lady Benbow enter up R. *Both are in evening dress. Mrs
Frush carries a letter*

Mrs Frush (*as she enters*) Well, I must see what had best be done.

Lady Benbow (*looks at Benbow, who has crossed to* L.) My husband won't mind. He's not very particular where he sleeps.

Benbow (*sitting*—D. L.) Oh, isn't he, thank yah.

Wind softly

Ronny (*crosses back of table—to Mrs Frush*) Does your son know that I'm here?

Mrs Frush No, he doesn't know anyone's here. You can see what he says. (*She hands the letter to Ronny*)

Benbow I suppose you didn't expect him home? That's why you put me in his room, eh?

Mrs Frush Yes. You see, we haven't furnished many of the bedrooms.

Ronny has now both letters in his hand. Still retaining both letters, Ronny turns aside and talks to Kitty

> Lady Benbow   Mrs Frush
>   R.   R.
>
>   Ronny   Kitty
>   C.   L. C.
>
>   Benbow
>   L.

Benbow (*rising*) Well, if he wants his room, where am I to go? What other rooms have you got?

Mrs Frush Well, the only other bedroom we've got furnished is the room in the East Wing (*Dropping her voice significantly*) next door—to his.

Wind loud

Indicates Ronny, who has gone up with Kitty and is still talking to her eagerly aside

Lady Benbow I won't have him sleep there.

Ronny You won't get him to sleep there either.

Benbow Oh, I'm not afraid. I'll show you. I'll tell Hook to move my things into the room next door to you. (*He goes up to door* C.)

Kitty crosses front of table to fireplace L.

Mrs Frush Allow me, I'll give the orders proper.

She crosses up R., *pulls bell-pull which is hanging on the wall just below extreme* R.

Benbow goes up to door C.

Lady Benbow When is your son coming? What does he say in his letter?

Mrs Frush goes down to Kitty

Mrs Frush (*indicating Ronny*) He's got it.
Benbow (*at door* C. *calling*) Hook!

Mrs Frush crosses back of table to Kitty R., *and sits*

Lady Benbow (*going to Ronny, who hands her Cherry Buck's letter.*) Let me have a look at that.
Ronny (*distracted from his talk to Kitty*) Certainly, auntie, you have it.

Benbow comes down from door

Lady Benbow stands L. C. *and looks at the letter. Her expression changes. Ronny sees Lady Benbow's expression. He glances at the letter in his hand— he realizes that she has got Cherry's letter*

Leaving Mrs Frush with Kitty, he comes across L. *and as Benbow comes down, Ronny attracts his attention to the appalling mistake he has made. Horrified dumb-show takes place. Lady Benbow, looking up, catches them at it, and they assume their respective forms of innocent carelessness. Finally Lady Benbow tears the letter into small pieces, and puts them on a plate on the table* L. C. *corner. Benbow looks at Ronny furiously*

Kitty Darling—(*With respect for Mrs Frush*) Why have you torn up Mrs Frush's letter?
Ronny (*quickly*) No, that's not it. This is it. You needn't worry about that. *You* needn't. (*Looks towards Benbow*)
Mrs Frush (*rising*) Well, let us return to the drawing-room. The atmosphere there is more vivacious.

Jones is seen coming down C. *from the distance*

Kitty (*still a little puzzled about the letter*) Are you coming, Ronny?
Ronny In two two's, darling. Less. One two.
Mrs Frush Well, come along all of you, and we'll have a nice rubber of Poker.

Exit R.

Kitty follows

Ronny signs to Benbow, turns to Lady Benbow

*Jones stands just above Lady Benbow—*R.

Ronny Look here, auntie—(*Seeing Jones*) What do you want?
Jones This bell rang. Did you ring it, sir?

Ronny (*back of table*) No, I did not.
Jones (*mysteriously*) Queer!
Lady Benbow Mrs Frush rang. She is in the drawing-room.
Jones Oh, thank you, my lady. (*To Benbow*) Still, it were *this* bell
that rang. (*To Ronny*) Queer, very queer.

Ronny glances up towards left wing

Jones exits R.

*Hook enters, comes down and stands looking at him. Jones stops, looks at
him and exits* R.

Ronny (*after looking at Benbow, to Lady Benbow*) Look here, auntie,
about that letter. (*He breaks off again*)

Hook has entered C. *standing* C. R. *of Lady Benbow*

(*To Hook*) Well, what do *you* want? Can't I be allowed to speak at
all? First of all—(*imitating Jones's voice*)—'Queer, very queer,' and
now you. Go away—(*Cross to Hook waving him back, then turns to
Lady Benbow*) That letter didn't refer to me. So don't tell Kitty!
Kitty (*reappearing* R.) Don't tell Kitty what?
Ronny (*assuming a very light-hearted manner*) Ah-h! You mustn't be
told that one. Oh, that was a beauty—(*To Benbow*) Wasn't it,
uncle?
Benbow Yes, a little too near the knuckle for my liking.
Ronny On the knuckle. That was one of auntie's best. You rascal.

Goes off with Kitty up R.

Benbow You just trot along to the drawing-room, my love, I'll
give Hook orders about moving my things into this other room.
Lady Benbow Hook, just wait outside a moment.
Hook Yes, my lady.

Exit C.

Benbow realizes he's for it, tries to appear unconcerned

Lady Benbow Well, Hector?
Benbow (*heavily*) Oh, I know you think the worst. But let me tell
you I wrote to that little girl to come and see me about a frock I'd
ordered for you, and she must have misunderstood what I wanted
her for.
Lady Benbow I think that extremely unlikely. Besides, she said in
her letter that she's cutting that stuff right out.
Benbow Yes, that's what I say—she's cutting out the stuff for the
frock.

Lady Benbow Oh, *no*, Hector.
Benbow (*lamely*) No?
Lady Benbow (*firmly*) No.
Benbow Nothing doing?
Lady Benbow Nothing at all.

Warning for crash

Benbow Well, all I can say is, it's a great pity. Still, I had to say something. You can't stand there like a damn fool when you've been bowled out.
Lady Benbow (*rising very suspicously*) Who does she mean in this letter that she's met through you? It can't be Ronny.
Benbow (*crosses to Lady Benbow*) Why not?
Lady Benbow Well, is it likely? Ronny thinks of no one but Kitty, otherwise he wouldn't be down here sleeping in that room.
Benbow (*crossing to table*) Why—you're not frightened, are you?
Lady Benbow Yes, I am. This house gives me the creeps. Doesn't it you?
Benbow (*cross to table, pours out a glass of port*) No, I don't let it.
Lady Benbow I wish we'd never come here.

A tray crash heard off up C. *She runs and clasps him—both are very startled*

My goodness, what's that? (*Falls in Benbow's arms for protection*)

Hook appears. He comes down centre agitated and in a hurry

Hook I beg your pardon, my lady, I just knocked over a brass tray in the 'all.
Benbow Well, you stop knocking things about or I'll knock you about. (*He kisses Lady Benbow's hand affectionately*)
Hook I'm very sorry, my lady. (*Down* C.)
Lady Benbow Never mind, I think we're all a little bit jumpy to-night.

Exits R. *into drawing-room* R.

Wind rises

Benbow Hook—(*Rather confidentially*)
Hook Yes, Sir 'Ector.
Benbow You know this room they call the haunted room? (*Picking up glass of port*)
Hook I've heard, sir.
Benbow Yes. Well, there's a room next door to it. I want you to go up there. (*Drinks a little port*)
Hook Me, sir?

Benbow Yes. I hope you'll find it all right. If you don't, you can come back and let me know. (*Drinks half the glass of port*)

Hook Oh, but you—you don't wish me to sleep there, sir?

Benbow Oh, I don't; that's the last thing I wish. I'm going to sleep there myself. I want you to move my things there.

Hook Oh, very good, sir.

Ronny returns up R., *comes down* R.

Hook moves up C.

Ronny (*eagerly to Benbow*) I say, uncle, did you tell auntie that wasn't me—in that letter?

Benbow Yes, I did. (*Cross to Ronny*) What the hell did you want to give it to her for?

Ronny I didn't give it to her at all; she grabbed it from me.

Benbow Grabbed it!—rot! (*Turning away*) What next will you say? (*To Hook, who is still standing centre*) Well, go on, move, can't you?

Wind gently

Hook (*going up* L.) Oh, you—ah—wish me to go now, sir?

Benbow I'm telling you now, ain't I?

Hook (*dithering*) Yes, sir; I—ah—I'm not quite sure of the way. I suppose I shall find it all right.

Ronny (*crosses up to Hook, who is on the stairs*) Yes, and while you're up there, go and look in my room next door. You stay up there for a long time. Then if something happens to *you*, I shan't have to go up there at all.

Hook Oh! (*Turns miserably towards stairs* L.)

Benbow (*in a sharp, altered tone*) Hook!

Hook (*halting*) Sir?

Benbow (*as before*) What are you frightened of?

Hook (*up three stairs*) I'm not frightened, sir. Just slightly uncomfortable.

Benbow Why?

Hook It's this butler, sir. I don't take to the man.

Ronny No, I don't take to him either.

Hook I think he's morbid.

Ronny I think he's putrid. But I say, Hook, you haven't heard sounds or anything coming from my room, have you?

Hook No, sir—I haven't listened yet.

Ronny Well, go and listen now (*Cross* D. L.)

Jones enters C. *and comes down* C.

Wind heard loudly

Hook Oh, yes, sir.
Benbow And, Hook.

Ronny crosses D. L.

Wind goes down a bit

Warning for bell

Hook (*halting*) Sir?
Benbow In young Mr Frush's room you'll find a duck gun and some ammunition.

Wind softly

Take 'em along with you.
Hook Oh, no, thank you, sir.
Benbow You do as you're damn well told. I want the gun beside my bed.
Hook Oh, I beg pardon, sir. Certainly. (*Turns again*)

Ronny crosses to front of table L. C.

As Hook is going, Jones moves to him

Jones (*to Hook*) I'll come with you up there.
Hook No, no, I'd rather go alone.

Bell

Bell heard off. They all come to attention—Hook is up the stairs. Jones moves down stage a few steps

Jones What was that?
Benbow (*rudely to Jones*) Hell, what did you think it was?—A cornet?
Jones No one here rang, sir. (*Pointing* R.) And it weren't that bell. I know the sound.
Ronny (D. L. *uneasily*) Queer? (*Looks at Benbow*) Very queer.
Jones (*with an exclamation that makes Ronny jump*) Ah! The front door bell. Young Mr Frush, maybe.
Ronny (*with relief.*) Oh. Not queer. (*To Benbow*)
Jones (*going—to Hook*) You go on up. I'll come after you with the sheets.
Hook Don't you come after me with no sheets. I won't have it.

Exits up the stairs hurriedly

Jones exits behind stairs L.

Benbow Well, I think we'd better join the ladies.

Ronny No, uncle, I want to talk to Kitty. D'you mind telling her I'm here?

Benbow Yes, I'll tell her. (*Crossing to Ronny*) Well, you'll be all right now, my boy, with me next door to you, with a duck gun.

Ronny Personally I don't think this trouble is caused by ducks.

They both drink

Benbow Nothing had better trouble me. You don't walk in your sleep, do you?

Ronny I don't know. If one's asleep, how does one know if one's walking?

Benbow Well, don't walk into me, that's all. Or I'll walk into you. Like a feller I knew—old Dasher Pink. His kid's governess used to walk in her sleep. Nice-looking girl she was, too.

Ronny Well, I don't care.

Benbow No, but old Dasher did. She walked into *his* bedroom one night. He thought *she* was a ghost. He must have been a bit tight at the time, I should think.

Ronny Why, what did he do?

Benbow Nothing. He thought she was a ghost.

He goes off R.

Ronny is about to take some port

Jones appears L. *followed by Whittle, who comes down* R. C.

Jones (*indicating Ronny*) Ah! Here's the very gentleman you want.

Whittle is a man in the thirties, voluble and pushing; he wears a leather coat and carries a cap. Whittle comes quickly down to Ronny. He shows signs of a journey. Jones stands up stage C.

Whittle (*to Jones*) Thank you. (*Then to Ronny—offering his hand*) How are you, sir, by Jove?

Ronny (*shaking hands*) Oh, I'm pretty well, great Scott! Who are you?

Whittle My name's Whittle.

Ronny Why? (*Signals to Jones to go*)

Jones looks furtively up L. *and exits up* C.

Whittle I've come from Norwich. I heard about this. Just at the right time. What a bit of luck!

Ronny (*feebly*) Luck? Who for?

Whittle For me. I say, can I be in this?

Ronny In what?

Whittle Why in this stunt. In that room. Can I be in *that*?

Ronny (*keenly interested, taking his arm*) You want to be in that room?
Whittle Rather, if I may.
Ronny To-night?
Whittle You bet. I'm awfully keen.
Ronny (*pleased*) Come inside.
Whittle Thanks. (*Crosses to table, helps himself to port*) You see, sir, I'm a reporter.
Ronny (*indicating port*) That's fine, then report.
Whittle (*helping himself to another port*) I'm a free lance.
Ronny Good! Make yourself at home. Have plenty of port—a couple of oranges—etc.
Whittle Oh, thanks most awfully, I say.
Ronny Not in the least. You mean you want to sleep in that room to-night, instead of me?
Whittle No, no, sir, I don't want to do *you* out of it.
Ronny That's all right, don't you worry about that, sir. *I* shan't.
Whittle (*in confidence*) What I really want is—when you go to bed— I want to come and sit and watch.

Ronny slides up and down the carpet, self-consciously

Ronny Well, I'm afraid I don't think I look very nice in bed. But—

Kitty enters from R.

I'll do what I can.

Kitty has moved over to Ronny. She touches his arm: he turns to her startled: he is obviously very nervy

Whittle That's fine.
Kitty (*coming down R. C.*) You wanted me, Ronny?
Ronny A gentleman from Norwich, darling. You've heard of Norwich?
Kitty Yes.
Ronny Well, this is the gentleman. He's a long way from home, he can't get home, nowhere near home—can you—no—and it's very late and Norwich is shut. He's very wet and my room's very dry. I thought it was a good idea to put him in my room and air him.
Kitty (*to Whittle*) Are you a friend of Mrs Frush's?
Whittle Thanks very much. I'd like to meet her.
Ronny You shall meet her, sir. You couldn't miss her.

Benbow enters up R. speaking as he does so.

Benbow I'll see who it is. (*Confronting Whittle*) Who is it?

Whittle (*cross to Benbow*) Good evening, sir. You're Mr Frush, I fancy.

Benbow Oh, thank yer. I don't very much fancy that myself.

Ronny Oh, uncle, this is Mr Lance of Norwich.

Benbow (*suspiciously*) Eh?

Ronny He's looking for rooms, and I find I'm not very tired so thought he might have my room.

Whittle I'm very keen to make a report——

Benbow Oh, I see, you're a newspaper man, are you?

Whittle Yes, sir.

Benbow Well, I'll make a report at you with a duck gun, if you don't get out.

Whittle I'd give anything to be allowed to stay.

Benbow (*losing his temper*) Get out, I tell you!

Whittle Oh, sir. The chance of a lifetime!

Ronny Let the gentleman chance his lifetime.

Benbow Get out, I say. And don't you dare to mention a word of this in your pestilent papers.

Walking him off up L.

Whittle It's a wonderful opportunity thrown away.

Ronny Yes, don't throw it away, sir, please.

Whittle Sir, I won't mention any names.

Benbow No. Well, I'll mention one or two in a minute, if you don't get out. (*Following him up stage*) Get out, you saucy monkey, coming into other people's houses without being invited.

He goes off L. *behind stairs*

Benbow goes D. R. C. *very angry*

And you're making quite big enough fool of yerself without putting it in the papers.

Kitty (*indignantly*) He isn't.

Benbow Yes, he is. And so are you.

Ronny (*firing up*) Well, do the job yourself. (*Cross to Benbow*) I'm doing it for Kitty, not you.

Benbow Yes. (*Going up to door* R.) If she's stupid enough to credit such stuff. Crass bunkum. It's wrong. Worse. It's next door to immoral.

Exit up R.

Ronny (*calling off up* R.) Yes, I've heard you're sleeping next door.

Kitty goes after them, watching from up R.

Jones enters, crosses L. *putting tray on table. Whittle peers in again, then, making sure he isn't seen, he creeps off in the direction of the East Wing up the stairs.*

Jones starts to put things on his tray. Ronny and Kitty cross down to ʀ.

Listen, Kitty.

Kitty is annoyed at Ronny's rudeness to Benbow

You have heard what he said. (*He sees Jones*) What do you want?
Jones (*behind table*) You don't mind if I clear, sir?

Wind softly

Ronny No. I *want* you to clear.
Kitty Ronny, if you don't like this business, don't do it, will you?
Ronny (*eyeing Jones, who is messing about at the table*) But you want it done.
Kitty Yes, darling, I thought you were keen to do it. You never said you minded till now.
Ronny I know, but—as night approaches—

Jones makes a strange groaning noise—'Ah!' and looks at Ronny

—and people come and look at you with the evil eye——
Kitty My dear, if you can't face it, I wouldn't dream of letting you. We'll tell them. (*Turns to go*)
Ronny (*stopping her*) Oh, no. You're disappointed in me, I'll do it.

Jones hisses and exists ᴄ., *having cleared table except plate on corner with torn letter on it and fruit-dish, cigar-box and ash-tray centre*

Kitty cross to table watching Jones off

Kitty Oh, that man's so weird.
Ronny I know, dear, but don't worry about him. He probably used to be in the syphon business.
Kitty I'd do it myself like a shot if they'd let me.
Ronny I know you would, darling—you're a brave little girl.
Kitty After all, if anything happened you could make some loud noise.

She has picked up a piece of the letter from the plate and is toying with it

I mean, as a signal. *I* know. Take the gong.
Ronny The gong?
Kitty The dinner-gong. Then if anything happens, you can beat it.
Ronny I shall probably beat it in any case.

Kitty has picked up a piece of the torn letter—she looks at it absently. Ronny turns and sees a shadow on the wall R., *this scares him a bit until he, after a few arm movements, sees that it's his own reflection—he turns to Kitty*

Kitty (*reading*) Cherry? (*Looking down at plate*) Ronny, what was this letter?

Ronny Oh, something of uncle's. Why?

Kitty (*examining the scrap*) Cherry!

Ronny moves away R.

That's that odious girl.

Ronny Yes. Horrible! Uncle's been writing to her.

Kitty (*crosses to Ronny*) Ronny!

Ronny What? You don't think I've been seeing her again?

Kitty I should hope not. You promised me you wouldn't.

Ronny I know I did. That's why I haven't.

Kitty (*rather sharply*) Oh, is *that* the only reason?

Ronny Darling, don't I always do what I promise? Aren't I sleeping in that—haunted room alone—with nothing to beat but a gong— just because you want me to?

Hook heard off from balcony up L. *screaming*

(*Turns quickly*) Good Lord, what's that?

Hook hurries on. He is yelling and in a dire state of funk. He is seen to run past on the balcony round the stairs and down to Ronny and Kitty

Hook Oh, Heaven! Oh, sir.

Kitty What's happened?

Ronny What? What? Speak, can't you?

Hook Hardly, sir.

Ronny Well, make signs or something.

Benbow, Lady Benbow and Mrs Frush enter R. C. *Jones enters up* C.

Benbow down L. C. *Mrs Frush down* R. *Lady Benbow down* L. C. *left of Benbow, Jones down* L.

Benbow What's the matter? What's up? What's happened? (*Cross* D. L. C.) What's he done? What is it?

Kitty (*indicating Hook*) It's him. He's just come downstairs.

Ronny Why did you fall downstairs? Come on.

Hook Oh, sir, it's happened to me.

Jones (*standing* L. *of table*) Ah! (*In a terrifying tone*)

This startles the others, making them all lose their balance. Mrs Frush, who is on the right, gets the full force of the bump

Mrs Frush (*terrified*) Ah!

		Hook		
	Kitty	c.	*Benbow*	
Ronny	R. C.		L. C.	*Lady Benbow*
R. C.				L. C.
Mrs Frush				*Jones*
R.				L. *of table*

Close together in semicircle

Ronny (*to Mrs Frush*) Quiet, please. *What's* happened?

Hook (*addressing Benbow*) I was in your room, sir—I'd just done your bed, and that——

Ronny And that? And what?

Hook And that, sir——

Ronny And *what*?

Benbow Stop that that-ing. Go on. And what else?

Hook Well, your bed and so on, sir.

Benbow Stop that, I say. What occurred?

Ronny Come on, let's have it?

Mrs Frush (*to Ronny*) Don't flurry him. It isn't easy to say what you've seen when all you know is you've seen something you don't know what it is.

Benbow Will you let the man speak?

Kitty Go on, Hook!

Hook Suddenly the door opened——

Ronny And then?

A brief moment's pause—all listening intently

Hook It shut again.

Kitty Who opened it?

Hook I don't know. Before I could look it was shut.

Mrs Frush That's right. The doors *do* open and shut.

Lady Benbow Well, so I suppose.

Mrs Frush (*quickly*) But automatic.

Ronny No one could have opened it. We were all down here.

Benbow Go on, will you? Well, what did you do?

Hook For the moment I stood as if rooted.

Benbow Why?

Ronny (*to Benbow*) Be reasonable. This is enough to root anyone.

Hook Then I looked out, sir, and saw—nothing exactly I can tell of. Something——

Benbow Nothing—something.

Hook Something—as it were a figure—flit.

Jones Ahh! . . .

They all look at Jones in anger and fury. Mrs Frush and Ronny bump back to back

Benbow (*to Jones*) Will you shut up there?

Hook It was worse than what it sounds.

Ronny (*to Kitty*) It doesn't *sound* any too good to me.

Benbow Go on! What did you do? Did you follow it?

Hook Oh, it disappeared somewhere—(*looks at Ronny*)—by the 'aunted room, sir.

Ronny grips Mrs Frush's throat unknowingly, making her shout 'Oh!' as he nearly chokes her

Benbow Never mind that. Did you follow it?

Hook No, I did not, sir. I 'urried down here, sir.

Mrs Frush (*to Benbow*) There, one of your own party has had a taste of it. What more d'you want?

Ronny (*cross to Benbow*) I don't think we want any more, do we?

Kitty and Mrs Frush cross to steps R.

Benbow Nonsense! (*to Hook*) Go on! You go back and have another look, Hook.

Hook Oh, sir!

Lady Benbow No, Hector. (*to Hook*) You can go to your own room, Hook.

Hook Thank you, my lady. (*Goes with alacrity* C.)

Jones follows him to the door and watches him off, then listens to the conversation at door up C.

Lady Benbow (*to Sir Hector*) And, Hector, you don't sleep alone in that room to-night.

Benbow Why not? (*Pointing to Ronny, who is standing with Kitty* R. C.) My room's all right—it's his room that's haunted.

Ronny And jolly glad you are of it.

Benbow What? You don't suppose I'm afraid of a draught blowing a door open, do you? (*Cross to Ronny*) I know what you'd like. You'd like me to sleep in the room instead of you.

Ronny Not in the least.

Benbow (*readily*) Oh! That's all right, then. (*Turns aside again*)

Ronny (*on second thoughts*) All the same—I dare you to.

Benbow That's about all the daring you're capable of. (*Turning away*)

Ronny (*with a satirical laugh, in an undertone*) Funk.

Benbow (*cross to him*) Don't you call me a funk while all the time you're doing your best to back out of it.

Ronny And all the time you're doing your best not to back into it.

Kitty Look here! Ronny's is a double bed. (*To Benbow*) Why don't you sleep there, too?

Lady Benbow Now *that* I wouldn't mind.

Ronny (*to her*) Thanks, she didn't mean you.

Mrs Frush There's safety in numbers.

Warning for thunder

Ronny I refuse to have numbers. (*To Mrs Frush*) You stay in your own room.

Kitty (*to Benbow*) Come on. You're so scornful and fearless. Will you sleep there with him?

Benbow (*goaded*) Yes, I don't care. (*To Ronny—to Lady Benbow*) And I bet you I sleep like a top.

Ronny Yes, a humming-top.

Benbow All right then, that's a bet.

Ronny We sleep together.

Jones, who has been listening at the stairs, comes down

Benbow We'll split the bed.

Ronny And sleep on the floor. (*Sees Jones, who has come down centre and stands just above Ronny and Benbow.*) Death!

Jones What time would you like your call?

Wind, lightning and thunder

QUICK CURTAIN

SCENE 2

Ronny's room at Thark. There is only one door, which is in the back wall
R. C. *Windows to the ground in the* L. *wall. Curtains hang over them. A fireplace* R. *with a fire, the glow of which lights up the bed. Dressing-table up in*
L. C. *corner. A chair near the fire* D.R. *A smaller chair near the door* L. C. *The bed runs down the centre. It is a large double bed of Jacobean type, with a canopy, but no foot-rail. By the side of the bed* L. *a small table against which is leaning the duck gun. By the* R. *side of the bed another small table on which is the gong and the gong-stick. On the table* L. *stands a decanter, also glasses and a syphon. There is a chest of drawers up* L. *above fireplace—on this are some dress clothes—those that Ronny has taken off—his dressing-gown, a silk one, is dangling over the foot of the bed. Benbow's clothes are on a chair up* L.

corner. His dressing-gown—a velvet one—is lying on a cabinet down L. *His slippers are just by bed* L. *side. It is not a dismal room, and there are some pictures, including one of the ancestral type, which hangs on the wall* R. *It is a portrait of considerable size, with a massive frame. Four electric light brackets—one* R., *one* L., *two back wall*

The room, however, is in darkness when the curtain rises. Only the light given by the fire flickers feebly. A clock in the distance strikes three. Another, not quite so distant, strikes immediately afterwards. Then a stable clock, heard off L., *strikes with a light, cracked note. Silence follows*

A light shows in the passage behind, as the door is silently and slowly opened. The figure of Lionel Frush can be seen, lighted by the illumination in the background. He is wearing a leather motor coat over his ordinary clothes. He peers into the room. Then the figure of Cherry joins him and peers in too

Lionel (*in a hoarse whisper*) They're *both* here.
Cherry (*also sotto voce*) Well, where am *I* to go?
Lionel I don't know. Mother left that note, but she didn't say who was sleeping where. You'd better try the little room next door.

They disappear. The door is closed with a slight click, and—

Ronny's voice is heard from the bed

Ronny What's that? (*He reaches out for switches on* R. *post of bed and turns on light*)

Lights on

Both are in pyjamas. Ronny creeps from the bed, puts slippers on and listens. Benbow wakes up. Ronny does not notice him. Ronny makes as if to open the door, then thinks better of it. Benbow quietly helps himself to whisky. Benbow's syphon is one of those which make a loud, hissing noise. This startles Ronny, who is still at the door listening

(*Swinging round*) I wish you wouldn't do that.
Benbow I wish you'd stay in bed, and not keep fiddling about the room all night. I haven't slept a wink.
Ronny If you don't know you've been asleep, you're the only one who doesn't.
Benbow What d'yer mean?
Ronny Why, you've been giving a nasal organ recital.

Ronny slips his slippers off R. *of bed*

Benbow Well, that's no reason for you to keep hopping in and out of bed. You made me dream I was trying to mate canaries.
Ronny Uncle, the door opened, and then shut again.
Benbow Get back into bed!

As Ronny gets back, he looks furtively at the door

Door opened! You're worse than Hook. My God, I'd rather sleep with Hook.

Ronny I'd rather sleep between Hook and Death.

Benbow Lie down. Put the light out. (*Reaches out to put down his tumbler—lies down*)

Ronny turns to switch the lights off; he notices the door opening and starts to waken Benbow terror-stricken

As Benbow is about to protest, the door opens slowly. Lionel appears, but is not seen by Benbow or Ronny, as they sit side by side and watch it. It shuts slowly. Ronny throws his arms round Benbow's neck, his nerve giving way. Benbow shouts and throws him off

Ronny It's your turn.

Benbow (*getting out of bed and taking up the gun*) By gad! I'll teach someone to play monkey tricks with me. (*Comes down, round the bed, towards the door*)

Ronny climbs out quickly R. *to intercept him*

Ronny Hi! Hi! (*Struggling with him, trying to get the gun from him*)

Benbow Let go of it.

Ronny Don't shoot in here. Shoot out of the window.

Benbow What the hell's the good of shooting out of the window at something at the door?

Ronny puts his hand over the muzzle of the gun—Benbow knocks it away

Now—you open that door when I give the word.

Ronny What word?

Benbow It doesn't matter a damn what word.

Ronny (*trying to gain time*) Yes, it does.

Benbow Open the door.

Ronny I won't.

Benbow (*rushing forward*) I'll open the door myself.

Ronny (*obtaining the gun*) All right. I'll hold the revolver.

Benbow (*throwing open the door*) Hands up!

The light is on outside, but no one is there. Ronny puts his hands up—he is still holding the gun

That's very odd.

Benbow leaves the door slightly ajar

Ronny I told you. We're up against the supernatural.

Benbow You go and have a look in the passage.

Ronny Why?

Benbow To see if there's anything there.

Ronny (*advances very cautiously, then turns back*) If there was something there, what would you do?

Benbow I'd hunt it.

Ronny Well, I wouldn't. So you go!

Benbow Go on. Have some guts. I'll foller.

Ronny (*holds gun as a walking-stick and limps up to door—speaking through doorway*) Be very careful, will you, please. I'm coming. (*Opens door*)

As he takes a step, Lionel appears—Ronny steps back, startled

Benbow steps back towards bed

Ronny points gun at Lionel, who has both hands up

Lionel (*cheerfully, dropping his hands at his sides*) Hallo!

Ronny, looking at Lionel, unconsciously points gun at Benbow's stomach

Benbow Hi! Hi! Hi! Mind what you're doing with that thing. (*Points to his stomach in horror*) D'ye see what you're doing, pointing it right there. (*Indicating stomach*)

Ronny points gun into fireplace

(*With sarcasm, to Lionel*) How are you? What do you want?

Lionel Oh, well, I'm sorry! I didn't mean to disturb you.

Benbow Go on out of it. (*Returning* L. *and pouring another whisky*) I like your idea of not disturbing people—jackassing about with their doors in the middle of the night.

Lionel Oh, yes, I've only just blown in!

Ronny Well, blow out again! (*Pointing to Benbow, who is standing with his back to the audience, head thrown back, finishing his drink*) Can't you see he's trying to get to sleep?

Lionel Yes, but I never got my car till late.

Ronny Go away now. Your own room's unoccupied. (*Indicating Benbow*) He unoccupied it on purpose.

Lionel (*well* D. R.) Oh! But what about the room next door?

Ronny I don't know anything about that.

Lionel There are somebody's things there.

Benbow (*getting back into bed*) Yes, they're mine. You leave 'em alone.

He attempts to climb into bed, but as he puts his foot on the bed it slips off, making him overbalance and fall flat face downwards on the bed

(*Very annoyed—to Lionel*) Get out of it! (*Climbs into bed*)

Lionel Oh, right ho! There's no one sleeping there. That's fine. Well, good-night. I hope you won't be disturbed at all.

Goes out up R., *closing door*

Benbow Well, what d'you think of that?

Ronny puts gun at foot of bed L.

(*Getting back into bed*). There's impertinence, if you like.

Ronny Yes. Lucky I didn't shoot. I nearly shot. (*Shoes off*)

Benbow Well, there's that ghost for you anyway.

Benbow is in the centre of the bed, with very little room left for Ronny, who kneels on his own side, measuring the amount of room Benbow has taken. Benbow is very comfortable, and is obviously nursing a hot water bottle under the clothes. Ronny gets in and there is a lot of shuffling for position—each trying desperately to get even a chance to lie comfortable, both are elbowing each other

Benbow Keep your own side.

Ronny (*trying to make room for himself*) I'll keep it when I get it.

Benbow (*as Ronny takes a handful of bedclothes*) Now.

He pulls clothes furiously, there is a struggle for bedclothes. Ronny at last gives in

Ronny You're awful in bed. From the very start you pinched both the hot water bottles.

Benbow (*taking most of the bedclothes and settling himself*) What does a young man like you want with a hot water bottle?

Ronny What does an old man like you want with two?

Benbow I like one on my stomach as well.

Ronny (*sitting up, trying to get some clothes*) Am I to have nothing on my stomach? Look at me! Not one piece of blanket have I got.

Warning light out

Ronny shuffling in bed

Benbow Keep still, will you? (*Heaves, pushing Ronny nearly out of bed*)

Ronny's leg shoots out of bed, which saves him from falling out completely— he rests his elbow on the table right of bed

Ronny Look out! You nearly pushed my elbow into my gong!

Benbow Oh, my God, what a night! (*As he turns over, facing Ronny's back*) Go on, put the light out. I want to drop off.

Ronny I am dropping off.

Light out

(*Very fed up*) Take your knees out of my back—they're like rock-cakes.

A short silence. Suddenly there is a sharp rapping on the window D. L.

(*Sitting up*) Uncle!

Warning lights up

Benbow (*well under bedclothes*) What's the matter now?
Ronny Something rapping at the window.
Benbow What's rapping?
Ronny Spirit rapping.

Window rapping is heard again

Benbow Spirit rapping be damned. Put the light up! It's that infernal boy again.

Lights up

Ronny (*turning on the lights*) How can he get outside the window?
Benbow There's a balcony runs all down the wing.

Knocking repeated

Well, don't sit there.

Ronny lies down again

Go on.
Ronny Me?
Benbow Yes. It's your turn.
Ronny Oh, is it?

Ronny, very unwillingly, gets out of bed. He wastes time with his slippers, and then advances towards window. As he does so, the rapping is repeated, and he makes a dive for the bed. Benbow, sitting up in bed, keeps him out

Benbow Go on! Pull the curtains aside and have a look.
Ronny (*pulling the curtain gingerly and peering*) Great Scott!
Benbow What?
Ronny It's a woman!
Benbow (*excitedly*) Open the window—quick! (*Scrambles from bed, puts his slippers on.*)

Wind is heard rising

Ronny opens the window

Cherry rushes in. She is obviously very cold. She is clad in pyjamas

Cherry (*clinging to Ronny*) Oh, help me!
Benbow Good Lord! It's Cherry Buck!
Cherry Oh, I've been frightened stiff!

Wind drops

Benbow How on earth did you come here, my child?
Cherry I came with Lionel. We've got engaged. I told you in my letter.
Ronny There you are! Lionel Frush!
Benbow I don't care! (*To Cherry*) Well, what happened?
Cherry He put me in the room next door here, and there's someone there.
Ronny Good Lord! Human or otherwise?
Cherry I went in there and undressed—and just as I was getting into bed, I saw the curtain of the cupboard move. Then I saw a foot.
Ronny How long? A foot? What shape?
Cherry Well, a shoe.
Benbow Well, that's nothing. Hook put my shoe there.
Cherry But it moved. Oh, I was scared. I daren't go past it to the door. So I got out on the balcony.
Benbow Who the blazes can this be, I wonder?
Ronny (*to Benbow*) It's your turn.
Benbow I don't care. Who's afraid?
Ronny No one's at all afraid, but it's your turn.
Benbow Whoever's found a way in here had better find a way out again. (*Going L. takes gun, crosses L. to window*)
Cherry You'll have to go by the balcony. I locked the door on the inside.
Benbow (*going to window*) I'll soon settle somebody's hash. (*Putting on dressing-gown*)
Ronny (*nervous at being left with Cherry, crosses to Benbow as he is going out*) I say, uncle, hadn't I better come as well?
Benbow (*pausing at window*) No, you stay here with her.
Ronny Oh, but I don't want to stay in here with her alone.
Benbow You don't? Here, you take the gun!

Ronny pushes him out

Ronny (*to Cherry*) Look here—this is rather awkward. You go over there by the fire—I'm going to bed.

Taking his slippers off and climbing into bed from L. he drops slippers on floor R. of bed

Cherry It's jolly cold. (*Crosses R. to fireplace, warming her hands*)

Ronny Yes, that's why I'm getting into bed.
Cherry I'll bet you're not as cold as I am.
Ronny Oh, yes, I am; you've got more on than I have.
Cherry I haven't. Look at me!
Ronny No, thanks. I'd rather not.

Benbow enters hurriedly through door. Ronny seeing door open, screams with nerves

Oh, no, no, no! Oh, no!
Benbow It's all right. There's no one there. And the door was open.
Cherry Well, there you are. There *was* someone there.
Ronny There isn't now. So you can go back.
Benbow (*to Cherry*) No, you stay here. Someone's up to mischief. I'm going to round him up.
Ronny Well, don't make a row about it.
Benbow Row! If I catch him, I'll make a hell of a row about it.

Exit, closing door

Ronny I hope he doesn't catch him.
Cherry I hope he does. I want to get into bed.
Ronny Well, you can't get into it here.
Cherry I could if you got out. I don't see why you shouldn't.
Ronny You'd better try and find out why, because I'm not going to.
Cherry (*coming to bed* R.) Oh, be a sport. I'm absolutely freezing.
Ronny (*sitting up alarmed*) Go away. You're too close.
Cherry All right, then. I'll jolly well make you get out.

Makes as though to get into the bed—Ronny gives a cry and prevents her

Ronny Stop that, you forward girl.

In his hurry he bashes into the table R. *The gong falls, making a resounding crash—he jumps out of bed—Cherry runs down* R.

(*Picking up the gong*) Now see what you've done.
Cherry I didn't do it.
Ronny That was the signal. We've roused the whole house. (*Replacing the gong on stand*)
Cherry It's all right. Lock the door.
Ronny Yes. (*At door*) No, there's no key.
Cherry On the outside.
Ronny Oh! Yes. (*Opens door, listens*) No, too late. (*Shuts door hastily*) Someone's coming. (*Turning to her*) Get back on that balcony.
Cherry I won't.
Ronny You must.
Kitty's Voice (*off*) Ronny!

Cherry runs towards window

Ronny Go on. (*Picking up dressing-gown*)
Cherry Your dressing-gown.
Ronny (*handing it*) Take it. Go on. Quick!

Enter Kitty

Kitty What is it?
Ronny Nothing, darling.

Ronny is helping Cherry on with dressing-gown, standing behind her, and half embraces her as Kitty runs on down stage

Kitty (*seeing Cherry*) What?
Ronny I don't want you.
Kitty You here?
Ronny It's all right. She was *just* going.
Kitty So you've got to bring her even down here?
Ronny No; she came after me—after I did. I didn't know she was here.
Kitty Didn't know she was here? When I find you holding her in your arms.
Ronny Directly she came there, I beat the gong for *you*. (*To Cherry*) That's true, isn't it?
Cherry Well, *you* knocked it over, I didn't.
Ronny Don't spoil it.

Lionel enters quickly—he is in pyjamas

Lionel What are you doing? She's my girl.
Ronny (*taking his dressing-gown off Cherry*) Oh, well, give me my dressing-gown.
Lionel (*crossing to Cherry and putting his own dressing-gown on her shoulders—to Ronny*) I didn't bring her up here for you.
Ronny Very well then, take her away and bring her up properly.
Cherry Oh, Lionel, I had to come in here, I was frightened out of that room.
Lionel Never mind, my darling. You shall have mine.
Cherry (*to Ronny as they cross* R.) You're a fine gentleman to protect a girl, aren't you?
Lionel (*taking her off* R. *turns to Ronny and speaks very sternly*) Don't you touch her again, or, my word, I'll touch you! (*To Cherry*) Come on, darling.

Exit Lionel with Cherry, shutting door up R. C.

Ronny There's a bully for you. (*Shot*)

Kitty Did that girl come here with Lionel Frush?
Ronny Of course she did, Kitty. And don't you keep accusing me
of things. You stop it. Or you'll never find yourself alone with me
in a bedroom again.
Kitty I don't care. I don't want to. (*Going to door*)
Ronny The girl came through that window—(*Indicating window
D. L.*)—and I——

Turns to find Kitty going out

(*Following her*) Kitty, but you must listen.

*During the following lines, Whittle enters from balcony. Tries to get through
room, finds way barred by Kitty and Ronny in doorway, and sneaks under bed
from* L. *side. He is limping badly and obviously in pain*

Kitty (*off stage* R.) She was here with you. That's enough.
Ronny (*at door looking off* R.) It isn't enough. You heard the reason.

Whittle enters

Kitty But who could have frightened her?
Ronny Uncle's going to find out. Come back here. I'm not going to
talk to you in the draught.

Whittle is now under bed. Kitty and Ronny come down C.

Kitty Well, Ronny, any girl would have suspected who saw what I
saw.
Ronny Why—what did you see?

Benbow enters from balcony L., *leaves window open*

Wind is heard and curtains blow

Benbow Where's he gone? I believe I winged him. I know I've
winged him. I'll get him.

Exit up R., *shutting door*

Ronny closes window L. *Wind drops*

Ronny (*on his dignity*) There you are, you saw what happened—now
what have you got to say?—I'll give you a hearing.
Kitty Well, I see now. I was wrong. Ronny.
Ronny I should think you *were* wrong. Making all this fuss over one
single girl in my bedroom. Remember I'm spending the night in
this awful room—I'm liable to see quite enough strange things
without you coming in. (*Pause*)

Kitty Oh, but listen, Ronny!

Ronny No—*you* do the listening. I'm the master here. I can't help my room having a girl in it, can I? Any more than that bed can help having uncle in it.

Kitty Yes, I know I was wrong to be angry.

Ronny You were very wrong—(*Cross* R.)—a girl in my bedroom—that's nothing. (*Puts his hand towards fire*) Besides, she was quite decently clad.

Kitty I'm very sorry.

Ronny So was I—so am I. I should hate to think I was going to have a suspicious little wife for a wife.

Kitty (*crossing to Ronny*) Oh, but you're not.

Ronny Oh, I am. At least we'll see. I've a jolly good mind not to have a wife at all.

Kitty Ronny!

Ronny Don't think I can't do without one. I've done without one before now—up to now.

Kitty Oh, Ronny—you will marry me, won't you?

Ronny Only if you're not jealous when you see me looking at another girl. That's always the trouble with wives—they accuse their poor innocent husbands even before they've had time to *do* anything.

Kitty Oh, please, don't go on at me, Ronny. You make me feel ashamed. (*Almost crying*)

Ronny (*not looking at her*) I'm telling you now because I might forget in the morning. (*Looks and sees that Kitty is crying; he at once relents, he rests her head on his shoulder*) Now don't cry, I can't stand anyone crying. We Gambles never could. I'm sorry. When we're married and go about together—sometimes—don't inquire too deeply what I'm doing or you may be ashamed again. Remember, I look on girls in a very peculiar way. Come on now, stop crying, dry your eyes. Haven't you got a hanky? Never mind, here's one.

Kitty is crying—Ronny dries her eyes on his handkerchief and places it at her nose

Come on, blow—blow that little bit of putty.

Kitty Well, I'll try to understand, I promise you.

Ronny That's right. (*Cross* L.) Just look on me as a very attractive man who can't help himself——

Benbow enters through door

Benbow Missed him—confound it, I missed him. (*Throws gun on bed —to Kitty*) Hi! And what are you doing here?—wandering about the house in the middle of the night, looking like a stick of Brighton rock. You go back to your bedroom.

Kitty Ronny, kiss me and forgive me.

Ronny Yes. But don't let it occur again.

Benbow No. It had better not.

Ronny kisses Kitty

And stop that! Quite enough time for that at decent hours.

Ronny Good-night, darling—(*Kisses her*)—till decent hours.

Kitty Good-night, Ronny. (*To Benbow*) Good-night, Hecky.

Benbow Good-night, you little monkey. (*He kisses her and slaps her playfully as she goes*)

Exit Kitty c., *closing door*

Benbow crosses L., *peeps through window* D. L., *holding the curtains apart a little. Ronny sees Benbow taking his dressing-gown off—at once slips his own off and his slippers and gets into the centre of the bed before Benbow sees him. Benbow turns towards the bed and sees Ronny, who is looking quite comfortable and unconcerned; he gives a little grunt, takes the gun from the bed and puts it by the table close to the bed*

Benbow (*pouring out whisky at table* R.) Are you going to have one just to rock you off? You'd better.

Ronny All right, then. A good stiff one. My nerves are shredded and tattered.

Benbow (*after handing Ronny a drink*) Let me tell you something. *I'm* not going to be disturbed any more to-night if you are.

Ronny I've got a sort of feeling I shall be.

Wind is heard and distant thunder

There's that confounded storm coming back.

Benbow (*getting into bed*) That only goes to show yer that all this talk of haunted places is absolute tosh.

Benbow again falls face on the bed

Everything that's happened in this house to-night has been accounted for. (*Drinks*)

Ronny Oh, has it?

Wind is heard rising and falling till the end of the act

Benbow Yes, it has.

Ronny Then who was it frightened Cherry Buck?

Benbow Why, that tick of a newspaper man.

Ronny Good Lord! Did *he* stay here?

Benbow Not quite long enough. But I think I dusted his trousers for him, all the same.

Ronny Oh, I thought Cherry Buck had seen the ghost.

Thunder louder and wind

Benbow Seen the ghost? Nobody's ever seen a ghost—or smelt a ghost—or heard a ghost.

Wind rising and falling

Whittle starts to come from under the foot of the bed; his head and shoulders appear, but the pain of his leg makes him groan and he gets back

What was that? Was that you?

Warning light on

Ronny Somebody moaned.

Benbow Oh, nonsense, only the wind.

Ronny Well—I don't know the cause of their suffering. But somebody moaned.

Benbow Go on. Drink that up—(*lies down*)—put the light out.

Light out

I want to get my beauty sleep.

Ronny You certainly do.

During the next few lines Whittle is seen dimly to come from under the bed and exit through window L.

Benbow Now then, keep your elbow down.

Ronny You lift yours even in your sleep.

Benbow Ah, well, good-night to yer.

Ronny And a filthy night to yer.

By this time Whittle is at the window; as he pulls the curtains aside the lightning flashes through, lighting up his face—he disappears through the window, leaving them open; the wind is howling furiously, blowing the curtains across the room—an enormous clap of thunder is heard, blankets and quilt are blown nearly off the bed

Ronny puts the light up and Benbow gets his gun and is pointing it towards the window—at that moment the force of the storm blows the brass candlesticks from the mantelpiece R., *also the huge picture falls from above the fireplace—*

which makes Benbow turn quickly and point the gun that way. Ronny jumps out of bed and starts to beat the gong as the

CURTAIN FALLS. (FIRST CURTAIN.)

TABLEAUX CURTAIN

Mrs Frush, Lady Benbow and Kitty rush into the room followed by Jones and Hook, who stand at the door—a huge branch of tree has fallen through the window—they are all scared. Ronny is still hitting the gong while Benbow is on the bed pointing the gun round the room from the window to the door

PLUNDER

A Farce in Three Acts

CHARACTERS

The play was first produced on June 26th, 1928, at the Aldwych Theatre, London, with the following cast:

Oswald Veal	Mr J. Roberston Hare
Prudence Malone	Miss Ena Mason
Mrs Hewlett	Miss Mary Brough
Simon Veal	Mr Gordon James
Freddy Malone	Mr Tom Walls
Mabel	Miss Ann Furrell
Joan Hewlett	Miss Winifred Shotter
D'Arcy Tuck	Mr Ralph Lynn
Sir George Chudleigh	Mr Archibald Batty
Lady Chudleigh	Miss Nancy Nielson
Harry Kenward	Mr John Charlton
Ruth Bennett	Miss Enid Maby
William	Mr Robert Adam
Buckley	Mr Fred Morgan
Mrs Orlock	Miss Ethel Coleridge
Chief Constable Grierson	Mr Philip Carlton
Chief Detective Inspector Sibley	Mr Herbert Waring
Police Constable Davis	Mr Alfred Watson
Detective Sergeant Marchant	Mr Arthur Williams
Detective Sergeant Bryant	Mr Fred Cavell

The cast of the revival in January 1976 at the National Theatre was:

Oswald Veal	Trevor Ray
Prudence Malone	Diana Quick
Mrs Hewlett	Dandy Nichols
Simon Veal	Paul Dawkins
Freddy Malone	Frank Finlay
Mabel	Catherine Harding
Joan Hewlett	Polly Adams
D'Arcy Tuck	Dinsdale Landen
Sir George Chudleigh	Michael Beint
Lady Chudleigh	Brenda Kaye
Harry Kenward	Michael Keating
Ruth Bennett	Carol Frazer
William	Desmond Adams
Buckley	Michael Stroud

Mrs Orlock	Barbara Keogh
Chief Constable Grierson	Daniel Thorndike
Chief Detective Inspector Sibley	Derek Newark
Police Constable Davis	Patrick Monckton
Detective Sergeant Marchant	Glyn Grain
Detective Sergeant Bryant	Andrew Hilton
Plain Clothes Detective	Peter Rocca
Cook	Rose Power
Maids	Jeananne Crowley
	Brenda Blethyn
	Nora Connolly
	Rynagh O'Grady

Director	Michael Blakemoor
Designer	Michael Annals
Lighting	Leonard Tucker
Staff Director	Sebastian Graham-Jones
Production Manager	Marshall Goodhew
Stage Manager	John Rothenberg
Deputy Stage Manager	Elizabeth Markham
Assistant Stage Manager	Angela Bissett
Assistant Stage Manager	Ernest Hall
Assistant Stage Manager	Jeremy Gadd

ACT I
The Library at Marvin Court, near Horsham (afternoon)

ACT II
Scene 1   Hall of Freddy Malone's House, The Gables,
          Walton Heath
Scene 2   A room at The Gables
Scene 3   Same as Scene 1

ACT III
Scene 1   Chief Constable Grierson's Office at Scotland Yard
Scene 2   Hall at The Gables

ACT I

Marvin Court, near Horsham, The Library

A February afternoon

A well-furnished library. Door from the hall L. *of back wall. Another door leading off* L. *French windows up* R. *These are practical French windows used as an entrance to the garden.* L. C. *a fireplace with a fire burning and a club fender. Some pictures, but not modern ones. Bookshelves with some uniform editions and a bust or two. A writing-table near centre with a swing chair. An armchair close at hand to the* R. *of writing-table* L. C. *The furniture is all good stuff and in good order, but belongs to a former generation*

Prudence is sitting on the club fender. She is holding her hands to the fire, but her attention is really given to Oswald, who is standing indecisively over by the windows. Prudence is well dressed in excellent taste, in a country outdoor costume and hat

Oswald is thirty-five or so. He wears a rather emphatic country outfit. He suggests what he is—a modest clerk promoted in the social scale and having rather a struggle to maintain the dignity of the position. He is essentially an underling. He glances round, then away, his lips moving nervously

Prudence takes a glance at him, then away and smiles. Then with an effort he rounds on her; advances centre and grips a chair

Oswald (*pacing up and down, crosses to Prudence*) I love you.

Prudence gives a quick nervous laugh

   Oh, I say; don't laugh at me.
Prudence I'm not. It's only nervousness.
Oswald You must have know I was going to say something.
Prudence Oh, but don't think I encouraged you, Mr Veal.
Oswald Please, please don't call me Mr Veal.
Prudence Well—Ozzy.
Oswald Oh, please, not Ozzy either. That's mother's dreadful name for me.
Prudence All right—Oswald then.
Oswald I don't mind your calling me Wal. May I call you Pru?

Prudence You seem frightfully fussy about what we're going to call each other. I mean—there's something to be done before that.

Oswald (*offering to embrace her*) You mean—this!

Prudence No, no. (*He pauses, taken aback*) Oh, I hope I haven't been too responsive. I like you and all that.

Oswald You mean—you won't marry me?

Prudence I don't know. That's what I mean, I don't know.

Oswald I suppose the fact is, when you first met me and Mother out at Monte Carlo, you thought we were better class people than what we really are.

Prudence Oh, rot! Of course I didn't.

Oswald I made no secret of it, did I? I mean about Mother being old Mr Hewlett's 'ousekeeper before he married 'er.

Prudence If I were in love with a man it wouldn't matter to me what his mother was. You must let me think it over.

Oswald Oh—how long for?

Prudence I don't know. But I'll begin right away.

She smiles at him and playfully tugs the lapels of his coat and exits

Mrs Hewlett puts her head in through the other doorway up L. C.

Mrs Hewlett (*coming down* C. *to Oswald*) Well?

Oswald Indefinite. She wants to think it over.

Mrs Hewlett Oh—you and your love-making. I don't know where you get your passions.

Oswald Well, Mother, it's all been too hurried, I think.

Mrs Hewlett We can't have you spooning all over the house now. There'll be trouble enough for us without that. You know Joan Hewlett's arriving here today from New Zealand.

Oswald That's why I wanted to bring Pru to a head.

Mrs Hewlett Why?

Oswald Because when Miss Hewlett arrives there's bound to be a row.

Mrs Hewlett Yes. She must have heard somehow that her grandfather had died. But she doesn't know that he married me before doing so.

Oswald How do you know she doesn't know?

Mrs Hewlett Because if she'd known she'd have addressed her telegram (*moving away*) to me as Mrs Hewlett and not as Mrs Veal.

Oswald Well, don't get rattled, Mother. (*Following her*)

Mrs Hewlett (*turning on him*) Who's rattled? I'm ready for her.

Oswald But she'll come here thinking all the place belongs to her.

Mrs Hewlett Then she'll very soon go away knowing it doesn't.

Oswald Look out! Here's Uncle Simon.

Simon Veal appears at French windows and enters

Simon What time's this girl coming?

Mrs Hewlett She didn't mention. She just said, 'Arriving this afternoon with a friend.'

Simon 'Oos the friend? (*Throws his hat on settee*)

Mrs Hewlett Oh, goodness knows who she is.

Simon (*to Oswald*) Well, your Prudence Malone and her brother stand to hear a pretty story when she *does* arrive.

Oswald They know Mother was Mrs Hewlett's housekeeper before he married her.

Simon Before she married him (*Look from Mrs Hewlett*) you mean. What about all the girl's letters you kept from the old man? And his to her that you never posted? She'll have something to say about *that*.

Mrs Hewlett I shall answer her quite straightforward. I shall tell her he got them all and made no reply.

Simon (*crosses to Mrs Hewlett*) And this is what she'll say. He was old and sick and silly, and you got 'old of him and married him—and *that's* the truth.

Mrs Hewlett You're a nice one to turn saint. Here was the chance waiting to be picked up. So I picked it.

Simon Oh, I'm not blaming you, Margery.

Mrs Hewlett I should hope not. You haven't done yourself a bad turn out of it.

Simon Maybe. But if Miss Malone and her brother hear the story a fine chance Ozzy will stand.

Oswald Why are you so against me marrying Pru?

Simon You can marry 'oo you like when I've got my share of this property.

Oswald It's Mother's money to do with as she likes.

Simon Oh no it's not. It's hers to do with as *I* like. I may want more than I'm getting now. (*He crosses towards door* R.)

Mrs Hewlett and Oswald exchange a helpless glance. After a pause Simon turns to Oswald

And I'll have none of your smart young women and their clever brothers wanting to know why I get it. (*Moves towards windows*)

Mrs Hewlett Don't aggravate him, Ozzy.

Simon (*turning*) You do my bidding. You know what I could tell if I choose. (*Takes another step towards windows*)

Mrs Hewlett Hush, Simon. That's never to be spoken of.

Simon (*turning to have a last word*) Well, if it's not to be spoken of it's got to be paid for. Don't you forget it.

He goes out

Oswald This makes it very awkward now I've asked Pru. She may come back and say yes.

Mrs Hewlett Don't let him frighten you. If he started telling secrets they'd recoil on him as much as on us.

Oswald I don't know. He can always threaten.

Mrs Hewlett That's all he can do.

Oswald Well, look here, Mother. Get the Malones and tell them Miss Hewlett is coming. It may save unpleasantness.

Mrs Hewlett All right. all right. I know what's best to be done. Go and get the Malones.

Oswald (*going up* L. *open door*) All right, I think it's safer, and we ought to play for safety. Oh, here's Pru, now, coming downstairs. (*Speaking off*) I say, come in here to Mother, will you? (*Stands up* C.)

Prudence enters

Prudence Has Oswald been telling you things?

Mrs Hewlett Yes, dear. And I've no doubt you mean to make him happy. Look at him. Isn't he a dear boy?

Prudence I wonder.

Mrs Hewlett I'm sure your brother would be delighted. (*To Oswald*) Go and get him.

Oswald I don't know where he is.

Mrs Hewlett (*pointing through French windows*) Well, use your eyes. There he is on the lawn. Practising hits with his golf-stick. (*Sits*)

Prudence (*crosses to French windows, calling*) I'll get him. Freddy!

Freddy (*heard off*) Hallo?

Prudence Here! (*Returning, leaving French windows open*) It won't matter what *he* says, you know.

Oswald I expect he'll say you ought to find someone better.

Mrs Hewlett (*severely to Oswald*) Don't keep picking holes in yourself.

Freddy Malone enters at French windows. He is in the thirties, very calm and polished. He carries a mashie

Freddy Picking holes in yourself, Ozzy? What's the matter with you?

Prudence Well, Oswald's—(*To Oswald*) You tell him.

Oswald No, no—please—you.

Mrs Hewlett *I'll* tell him. (*To Freddy*) He's popped it.

Freddy What! He's picking holes in himself and he's popped it?

Prudence He's asked me to marry him.

Freddy (*to Oswald*) You've asked *her*—to marry *you*? (*Prods him with golf club*)

Oswald Well, I—I shouldn't ask her to marry anyone else should I?

Freddy (*making a pass at Oswald with the mashie*) I would if I were you.

Prudence But, Freddy, I haven't said yes. And I haven't said no. I don't know *yet* what to say.

Freddy Well, it isn't for me to say, is it? (*To Oswald*) It's a jolly good job for you it isn't.

Makes another pass at him with the mashie—Oswald ducks

Oswald Yes, I say—don't keep dong that, please. D'you mind?

Freddy Well, you must be patient, Ozzy. You know what girls are.

Oswald No, I don't. I haven't mixed with them much.

Freddy Oh, nonsense! You can find out a thing like that without mixing. You must give Pru time to think. (*To Mrs Hewlett*) You always took a bit of time to think, didn't you?

Mrs Hewlett Well, in my days it was thought ladylike to get the flutters.

Freddy (*to Oswald*) Oh, was it, well then you leave Pru to me. I'll try and find out what's really behind the flutters.

Oswald All right, thanks.

Freddy That's it. Then you trot off.

He takes Oswald to door

Oswald I may have come out with it a bit previous; but my intentions——

Freddy (*following Oswald*) Go on, hop it. I know all about that.

Oswald goes out

Mrs Hewlett (*to Freddy*) Mind you, I'm not surprised. I always had a very big inkling.

Freddy Yes, I thought you looked as if you had. Well, I'll talk it over with Pru.

Mrs Hewlett Ah! But there's something I want to tell you.

Freddy Come on then, tell us.

Mrs Hewlett There's a girl calling here this afternoon.

Freddy A girl? Oh, but your news is good.

Mrs Hewlett Well, two of them. She's bringing a friend. I don't know who the friend is, but the girl's Joan Hewlett.

Freddy Joan Hewlett? Who's she?

Mrs Hewlett You won't have heard of her. She's my late husband's grand-daughter.

Freddy Oh? So Mr Hewlett had a grand-daughter, had he?

Mrs Hewlett Yes, but she's no claim to any of this. He left it all to me.

Freddy But does she pretend she has any claim?

Mrs Hewlett She can't. And serve her right. (*With feeling*) She left her grandfather. His only relative she was. And she deserted him and went abroad.

Prudence How very short-sighted of her.

Mrs Hewlett It was wicked of her. If I hadn't been here to look after the poor gentleman, I don't know what he'd have done.

Freddy No, indeed. Even as it was he died.

Mrs Hewlett Yes, but me being here with him he died 'appy.

Freddy I suppose he was tickled to death.

Prudence But why's this girl coming back?

Mrs Hewlett Oh, to try and make a scene about it, I suppose. But if she tries to argue the matter with me, she'll get a rude shock.

Freddy I should think there might be a bit of rudeness all round.

Mrs Hewlett If it comes to a rudeness match I'm afraid of no one.

She goes out

Freddy closes the door after her

The manners of both entirely change. They become absolutely practical and rather like a business man and his secretary

Prudence Is that all right?

Freddy Well, I didn't expect him to propose just yet. Don't you go and accept him. She'd pop it in the papers.

Prudence No need to accept him. He'll keep.

Freddy Then it's easy. But that's the danger. It's too easy. Now's the time we've got to go very, very carefully.

Prudence It's all right so far. None of your friends know we're staying here.

Freddy My God, they mustn't!

Prudence If Arthur Mills knew he'd be rabid.

Freddy Never mind about his being rabid. He'd be inquisitive—that's the point.

Prudence Yes. Of course no sane girl would turn down Arthur and dally with Ozzy.

Freddy Exactly. So what are we up to? That's what they'd ask. And the answer is something odd. Well, my strong suit is never to be up to anything odd.

Prudence I know that. But you're going to invite these people to your house.

Freddy I shall be jolly careful who they meet—don't you worry. This is the whole point. We *must* associate with them for a few weeks longer. And nobody that matters must find out.

Prudence If anyone did find out—you'd have to drop it.

Freddy By gad. I'd take a big risk before I dropped this. It's much too good to drop.

Prudence Well, can't you get through with it quickly?

Freddy I'm going to. (*Crosses up stage, rings*) I'll spring this invitation to Walton right away. You must keep Ozzy well in the strings.

Prudence Oh, I've got him like that. (*Under the thumb*) He's sloppy with it.

Mabel, the maid, opens door

Freddy (*raising his voice*) Yes, but it's double the horse-power of your two-seater.

Mabel enters as he speaks

Mabel Did you ring, sir?

Freddy Oh, Mabel, I want to speak to Mrs Hewlett, and young Mr Veal. Here, please.

Mabel Yes, sir.

She goes out

Freddy I think you'd better be taking it a little to heart, you know.

Prudence Shall I cry? I can easily cry if you like.

Freddy No. I think just a little nose business with the handkerchief.

Prudence I know. (*Prepares to be a bit upset*)

Freddy That's it. There's not much I can teach you in that line.

Prudence (*smiling with reserve, like a secretary being praised*) Thank you.

Mrs Hewlett (*heard off* L.) Well then, you shouldn't have.

Freddy (*raising his voice again*) Now, don't go and upset yourself. They'll understand.

Mrs Hewlett and Oswald enter

(*To Oswald*) You'll understand, won't you? You'd understand anything.

Oswald Yes, but what?

Freddy Pru's a bit distressed and uncertain.

Oswald Well, I hope—I may hope?

Freddy That's right. That's a good idea. You hope. (*To Mrs Hewlett*) Now look here. We're leaving here tomorrow. But suppose you two come to us in a few days' time?

Mrs Hewlett To stay with you?

Freddy Yes. At Walton. Pru will know her mind better by that time.

Prudence Freddy, don't forget we've asked the Chudleighs and Lady Kilkenny on the tenth.
Freddy I know, why not? There's plenty of room.
Mrs Hewlett Lady Kilkenny! I should like to meet *her*.
Freddy Yes. Smart woman. Oh, and she'll meet a smart woman too, if you're looking your best.
Mrs Hewlett (*delighted*) Oh, come off it. I can hold my own all right.
Freddy I'll bet you can. You'll be a regular little handful.
Prudence Well, Freddy—if they come on the tenth—
Freddy The tenth? Right! (*Crosses to Oswald*) That's a fixture. (*To Oswald*) Cheer up. You're as good as home.

Mabel enters

Mrs Hewlett (*to Mabel*) What's the matter with *you*?
Mabel Miss Hewlett,'m. She's just driven up in a car.
Freddy (*picking up the mashie*) Oh, perhaps we'd better leave you. Come on, Pru. (*Handing Oswald the mashie*) Here, do something with that.

Freddy goes off with Prudence

Mrs Hewlett Very well. Show her in here.

As Mabel turns

But Mabel! Mind what I told you. Don't you answer any questions.
Mabel No'm. (*Going*) It isn't a lady with her, it's a gentleman.

Goes off

Oswald (*crosses to Mrs Hewlett*) A gentleman! Then p'raps she's heard of the marriage. It may be her solicitor.
Mrs Hewlett (*showing signs of excitement*) Well, who cares? I'm going up to get myself together. And my proofs and that.
Oswald She'd better not see me. She'd want to know who I was.
Mrs Hewlett No, and don't let her see Simon either. If he comes in here, you must come and get him out again.
Oswald All right, I will.
Mrs Hewlett I must get up to my bedroom. Me marriage lines are in my ottoman.

Bustles off

Oswald looks across R. *hears Joan, then quickly puts down the mashie and —follows her off*

Joan's voice is heard off

Joan Oh, I've left my bag in the car!

Mabel, looking rather uncomfortable, shows in Joan Hewlett. Joan, who wears a becoming motor-coat and hat, is elated at seeing Marvin again, regarding it as her own property

Oh, it all looks just the same.

Mabel Yes, Miss Joan.

Joan But where's Mrs Veal?

Mabel I don't know, Miss Joan.

Joan I thought she was here. You'd better find her.

Mabel Yes, Miss Joan. She said, if you'd wait here——

Joan (*not unkindly*) Well, good gracious me, I shall wait where I like. I want to show Mr Tuck all over the house. He's the gentleman I'm engaged to, Mabel.

Mabel Really! Oh—I hadn't heard, Miss.

Joan No, I only met him on the boat coming home; well, go and find Mrs Veal.

Mabel (*after a second's hesitation*) Yes, Miss Joan.

Mabel hesitates as though to speak and goes out

Joan is going up to door when her eye falls on the mashie. She picks it up and frowns puzzled. Then she puts it down and opens door and calls

Joan (*calling through door*) D'Arcy! Come in here. This is the library.

D'Arcy Tuck comes in, parks her bag. He is in every-day London clothes, with a motor-coat and carrying a cap. He is looking around him eagerly at the house

D'Arcy So it is.

Joan Well, are you pleased with the place?

D'Arcy Can this be possible? It all belongs to you.

Joan Of course. And it's going to belong to you, too.

D'Arcy I love to hear you say that. But, Joan, remember, I loved you before I ever knew you had this house and property and money. I suppose there's some money, isn't there?

Joan Oh, yes. I don't know how much yet, but there's bound to be heaps.

D'Arcy Yes, there's got to be. I mean with a place this size it stands to reason. But I love you quite apart from this.

Joan This is nothing. This is only the library.

D'Arcy I don't care. I should love you just as much in any other of the rooms—drawing-room, dining-room, bathroom—I'm the same all over the house.

Joan Well, the place is all mine now for my very own. For ours, darling—together.

D'Arcy For ours, darling, together. Isn't that wonderful! All this lovely house, this delightful library, these nice books—look at this one. (*Pulls out a book and reads title*) 'Thoughts before sleeping' —can it be really true?

Joan Of course. My dear old grandfather always said it was for me. And now he's gone.

D'Arcy RIP. One of the best, I suppose?

Joan As soon as we get back to town, we'll find his lawyers and see exactly all about the money and stuff.

D'Arcy Yes. We'll take it out of their hands.

Joan Only I had to bring you here directly we landed to show you the house.

D'Arcy Yes. Let's go on seeing it.

Joan Wait a minute. I want to see Mrs Veal. I'm going to give her notice.

D'Arcy Why?

Joan I'm very annoyed with her. It was only quite by chance I heard about my grandfather dying. She might have let me know.

D'Arcy Yes.

Joan Besides, we shan't want a housekeeper now.

D'Arcy No, we'll do our own housekeeping now. I'll keep you when we're married, and you'll keep me—well—figuratively speaking. Never mind about Mrs Veal. Let's talk of jollier things—love and furniture.

Joan Oh, darling! Be quick and marry me.

D'Arcy Darling, I'm quick already—and I will.

D'Arcy kisses her

As they embrace Simon looks in through the French windows. He stands looking in. Joan suddenly moves away, neither of them see Simon

Joan (*in a changed tone*) But you know, D'Arcy, all the same— (*Looking over her shoulder*) there's——

D'Arcy What's the matter, darling?

Joan I don't know. There's something rather queer——

D'Arcy What d'you mean?

Joan Well, that maid—Mabel. I know her well enough. But she seemed sort of scared of me.

D'Arcy P'raps she's expecting the sack too.

Joan And Mrs Veal—(*Looking round the room*) why isn't she here? Why all this sort of silence and mystery?

D'Arcy Oh, my darling, if there's anything mysterious about we'll soon find it out.

Simon opens the windows and enters, causing them both to start violently. Joan catches hold of D'Arcy. Simon gives them a grim bow and comes down

Joan Who is it?

D'Arcy Don't you know?

Joan No. Ask him.

D'Arcy (*to Simon*) Who is it?

Simon Ah, then you don't know yet. You'll find out before long.

Joan What are you doing here, please? D'Arcy, make him say.

D'Arcy It's all right, darling. I think someone's let the house to Dracula.

Joan (*to Simon*) I'm Miss Hewlett, the owner of this house.

Simon Oh, are you?

D'Arcy (*to Joan*) I'll do it. (*More boldly, to Simon*) Why do you walk in here like this and—and why?

Simon I just came in because I laid a pipe down here somewhere.

D'Arcy (*crossing to Joan*) It's all right. It's only the gasfitter.

Oswald makes a nervous appearance at the windows, trying to attract Simon

Oswald (*clipping his fingers at Simon*) Wh't! Wh't!

He sees Joan looking at him and attempts to go

Joan Look! Somebody else.

D'Arcy (*going up to Oswald*) Here! Come in here, will you? Now— whoever you are—who are you?

Oswald I'm very, very sorry. I want to see my uncle.

D'Arcy I don't care if you want to see your aunt. This is Miss Hewlett's house; and this is Miss Hewlett. How dare you come and want to see your uncle in the library?

Oswald (*to Simon*) I say. Do come out. (*Standing close to Simon*)

Simon Why isn't she here?

Oswald She went upstairs.

Joan Who did?

D'Arcy (*to Oswald*) Listen, will you? Miss Hewlett arrives here and finds the place full of odd-looking people.

Oswald Yes, but please don't be put out.

D'Arcy I'm very put out. You may not think you're odd-looking, but you are.

Oswald You ought to have seen my mother.

D'Arcy Never mind who's to blame.

Joan Oh, I think I see. Your mother is Mrs Veal?

Simon Ha! She's not.

Oswald Yes, yes, yes. She is. At least—yes.

DArcy Well, good Lord! Aren't you sure about it?

Joan If you're Mrs Veal's relations, why not say so?

Oswald (*to Simon*) Oh, go and tell her to come down.

Simon I'll tell her. (*Cross in front of Joan and D'Arcy, turn at door to Oswald*) Don't you get talking.

Oswald No, no. I'll come with you. (*Is about to cross in front of Joan and D'Arcy but on second thoughts goes behind them*) I'm really sorry.

Exit

Joan Did you ever know such nerve? Fancy keeping those people here. That settles it. She goes at once.

D'Arcy She's afraid to see you. Don't worry, darling, I'll fix all this. (*He goes to door and opens it, then stands back in amazement*) Good Lord!

Joan What is it?

D'Arcy (*very surprised—through doorway*) Freddy!

Freddy D'Arcy Tuck!

Enters

But you're in Australia.

D'Arcy Am I? I've just got back today. This is Miss Hewlett. We met on the boat. (*to Joan*) A friend of mine, darling—Freddy Malone. We were at school together.

Freddy (*with approval, to Joan. Shaking hands*) How d'you do?

D'Arcy (*parting them*) Yes, very. But what on earth are you doing here?

Freddy Oh, I'm just staying here!

Joan But who with?

Freddy With my sister.

Joan Your sister doesn't live here?

Freddy No. I mean we're visiting.

D'Arcy *You*? Visiting these people?

Freddy Yes. Why not?

D'Arcy You don't mean to tell me that you're staying with this thing? (*Indicates where Oswald stood*)

Freddy What thing?

D'Arcy Well, it's gone now, but it *was* here. (*Indicates Oswald's exit*) The thing that went round behind. An awful sort of thing, like an egg.

Freddy Certainly. We ran across him and his mother the other day out at Monte Carlo.

Joan At Monte Carlo, Mrs Veal?

Freddy The old lady, Mrs Hewlett.

Joan What do you mean?
D'Arcy Don't be an ass, old boy, Mrs Veal.
Freddy (*puzzled*) No, Mrs Hewlett.

At this moment Mrs Hewlett enters. She has documents in either hand

Mrs Hewlett Yes, I'm here.
Joan (*to her, with indignation*) Now look here, Mrs Veal——
Mrs Hewlett Mrs Hewlett. (*Holds up paper in left hand*) My marriage certificate. (*Holds up document in right hand*) Your grandfather's will.

A pause

Joan and D'Arcy stare at her

Joan (*cross to Mrs Hewlett*) Are you trying to play some joke on me?
Mrs Hewlett (*handing her the paper*) That'll show you. (*Indicating D'Arcy*) Who's this?
D'Arcy (*going right up to her, with hostility*) My name, I may tell you, is D'Arcy Tuck.
Mrs Hewlett Well, keep it to yourself.
D'Arcy I'm not going to. I'm going to give it to *her*. So I'm in this and you look out. There's been some dirty work here. (*To Joan inquiringly*) Hasn't there?
Joan (*handing back paper*) My grandfather married you?
Mrs Hewlett (*loftily—taking it*) He did.
Joan He must have been mad.
D'Arcy He must have been blind.
Freddy Look here; I don't want to butt in on this. I'll see you later.
D'Arcy No. You'd better stay and hear the kind of woman you're paying visits to.
Mrs Hewlett *He* knows I'm all right, anyhow. Don't you?
Freddy I know the marriage was all quite in order. I've also heard about the will.
Mrs Hewlett (*to Joan*) Yes, you can see the will, too.
Joan I don't want to see it.
D'Arcy Nor do I. (*To Freddy*) What does it say?
Freddy Don't ask *me*. She'll tell you.
Mrs Hewlett Yes, I will tell you. It leaves me everything absolutely.
Joan (*quickly*) Give it to me. (*Takes the will and looks at it*)

D'Arcy glances at it over her shoulder

D'Arcy (*to Freddy*) Everything to her?
Mrs Hewlett Absolutely. For life and after.
D'Arcy (*looking up from will—to Freddy*) The house—the—the money?——

Freddy Everything he'd got, I understand.

Joan It's all some intrigue. He was out of his mind.

Mrs Hewlett The will was witnessed by his doctor.

Joan So this was your plot. Directly you got me abroad.

Mrs Hewlett (*boldly*) You left him. Did he want you to go? You went gadding off to your friends. He never forgave you that.

Joan Oh, that was your version? (*Crosses to her*) That's how you worked it?

D'Arcy I shall take action.

Mrs Hewlett (*fiercely*) Then get out of my house and take it.

Freddy Now, now. (*To D'Arcy*) It's no good trying to kick up the dust. You've got no dust to kick.

D'Arcy Mind your own business.

Freddy I'm afraid you've got to face the facts.

Joan He's quite right, D'Arcy. Yes, I see it now. I never knew you were so wicked. Or so clever.

Mrs Hewlett Don't you speak like that. He was grateful for all I did for him.

D'Arcy You did for him, yes. When did he die? Next morning?

Freddy Steady, D'Arcy. I hear he was happy to die.

D'Arcy What are *you* doing here, anyway?

Freddy Oh, very well. Perhaps I'd better retire.

Mrs Hewlett (*to Freddy, as he goes*) I'm sure I can trust *you* not to harbour any improper thoughts about me.

Freddy That, at least, is a certainty.

He goes into the garden

Joan (*to Mrs Hewlett*) Well, I'm not going to wrangle with you—

Mrs Hewlett You'd better not try.

D'Arcy watches Freddy off

Joan I know now why I never heard from him. I can guess all you did. (*Crosses to Mrs Hewlett*) You're a vile and sordid old woman!

D'Arcy (*crosses to Mrs Hewlett*) And now me——

Mrs Hewlett I want nothing from you.

D'Arcy But you're going to get it—nothing.

Mrs Hewlett (*to Joan*) And as for you, miss, it's always the cornered cat that spits.

D'Arcy (*crosses to Mrs Hewlett*) Stop that! How dare you tell my fiancée dirty proverbs?

Joan There are some things of mine here, anyhow. In my own room.

Mrs Hewlett Your former room, you mean. Oh, you can go and get them if you wish. (*Turns away, ignoring them*)

Joan (*to D'Arcy*) Come with me.

D'Arcy Oh, but we can't take this like this.
Joan We must if we've got to. I've finished with her.
D'Arcy Well, I haven't.
Joan It's terrible, but there it is. It's all proved. I've nothing for you at all.
D'Arcy Darling, I told you before all this happened. The money means nothing at all to me. It's just you.
Joan That's wonderful of you.
D'Arcy Yes, dear. All the same, this ought to be looked into.
Joan Well, I'll leave it all to you.

Exit

D'Arcy (*after seeing Joan off returns—assuming a very business-like manner to Mrs Hewlett*) Now I'm going thoroughly into this. Take a seat.
Mrs Hewlett Thank you. I take my own seat when I choose.
D'Arcy Yes, and where you choose. But I want to raise some questions.
Mrs Hewlett You're quite ad lib.
D'Arcy Firstly, how did you get the old man to marry you?
Mrs Hewlett What d'you mean—'the old man'? Do you refer to my late husband?
D'Arcy Well, if he was your husband, he was your old man, wasn't he? How did you get him?
Mrs Hewlett He turned to me because he was in need of someone to lean on.
D'Arcy And you leant back on him. And there he was . . . flattened out.
Mrs Hewlett I married him to nurse him. To nurse him proper.
D'Arcy Ridiculous! You don't have to be married to be a nurse. If a nurse nurses me is she improper?
Mrs Hewlett I shouldn't be surprised.
D'Arcy Now, it's no good quarrelling. Let me put it in a nice, friendly way. You married this poor imbecile old man and got his money. Never mind how. I want to keep this all quite pleasant. So never mind what lies or dirty work you used.
Mrs Hewlett Well, his grand-daughter's got you, anyhow. That ought to make up for a lot.
D'Arcy Yes. And she wanted to show me this house of hers. She'd been looking forward to that for a long, long time. Ever since we met on this voyage—the whole boat.
Mrs Hewlett I expect it's a bit of a disappointment for *you*.
D'Arcy Not for *me* at all. *I* don't care whether it's hers or yours—not a scrap. Except, of course, I'd much rather it was hers.

Mrs Hewlett She was always nasty to me. Now she can pay for it.
D'Arcy Oh rats! That girl couldn't be nasty to a worm. Well, when she was quite young she may have cut a worm or two in half—we all do that. But not now.
Mrs Hewlett She always said nasty things behind my back.
D'Arcy (*turning to her*) That's because there was very little room in the front.

Joan re-enters. She is more overcome

Joan Some of my things are locked up. I want the keys.
Mrs Hewlett I'll hand them to you. The sooner I've finished with you the better. (*To D'Arcy*) And with you, I'd finished before I began.
D'Arcy (*attempts to follow*) What!

She goes out

Joan Don't argue with her. I wouldn't take a thing from her now even if I could.

Follows Mrs Hewlett out in anger

D'Arcy I would. I'd take anything. I'd take her clothes when she was bathing. (*Shouting, at door*) And sell them to a man who makes circus tents! (*Goes to French windows and calls*) Freddy! Here!

Freddy re-enters from garden

Freddy Oh, you're alone? I say, D'Arcy, congratulations. What a charming little girl!
D'Arcy Don't you speak to me. Not a syllable. Hardly a word. You knew about it all. Did you? Speak up!
Freddy I never heard of that girl till just now.
D'Arcy What are you doing here, anyway? Staying here with these—vile Veals?
Freddy I don't require you to regulate my social activities.
D'Arcy But a fellow in your position.
Freddy I like to mix it a bit on the quiet.
D'Arcy You who go about rubbing shoulders with duchesses. Look whose shoulders you're rubbing now!
Freddy These are democratic days. Look at young Pevensey. His mother-in-law was a professional remover of the guts of fish.
D'Arcy An honest one, anyhow. She didn't remove other people's fishes' guts. Do you believe my little girl's story?
Freddy Yes. Oh, yes.
D'Arcy Well then. That's enough for you. You'll cut these robbers clean out.

Oswald enters rather timidly

Won't you?

Freddy Of course, old boy, of course, there's nothing for you to be concerned about.

Oswald Oh, excuse me.

Freddy What do you want?

Oswald Oh—ah—nothing in particular.

Freddy I see. Just dropped in to be matey.

D'Arcy Well, drop out.

Oswald Steady, I say, please. This is more my house than what it is yours, so half time with that. (*To Freddy*) It's only Mother asked me to look in here and—ah—cast an eye.

D'Arcy Then look out again or you'll cast a tooth.

Freddy Cast an eye? What at?

Oswald Mother thought you might be getting some wrong ideas.

D'Arcy He's got the right one. He's through with you.

Oswald What! (*to Freddy, anxiously*) That's not true is it?

Freddy I'll see you later. Run along now, there's a good fellow.

Oswald Oh, but—me and Pru? It's O.K. surely?

D'Arcy Pru! (*to Freddy*) Isn't that your sister?

Freddy (*ignoring D'Arcy to Oswald*) Here, I'll come and see your mother myself.

D'Arcy Freddy! Your sister and *this*?

Oswald (*boldly, to D'Arcy*) 'Ere, half time with that, too.

Freddy Don't bicker, Ozzy. Come with me.

D'Arcy I'll come, too.

Freddy No, thank you. (*Bundling Oswald to door*) Go and tell your mother she needn't worry.

Oswald Oh, good egg! Then it *is* all right about me and Pru?

Freddy Get out!

Oswald All right, all right. Sorry, thank you. I beg pardon.

He goes out

D'Arcy Freddy! What the devil are you up to? You'd never let your sister marry that rat?

Freddy D'you know my sister?

D'Arcy No. And if those are her tastes I don't want to.

Freddy I didn't pick him for her. Sisters are very peculiar things.

D'Arcy Yours must be. Why, good Lord, she's engaged to Arthur Mills.

Freddy Is that your concern?

D'Arcy I saw Arthur Mills this morning, and some others at the club. They said you were in Paris.

Freddy They just guessed that. Very likely guess, too.

D'Arcy Rats! You're ashamed of being here. And no wonder—
What's the idea—about your sister and this whelk?

Freddy Nothing. It's only a passing fancy in him.

D'Arcy Well, it's passed. Because you're through with this old
woman now. And your sister with her son.

Freddy Of course. I've told you so.

D'Arcy Good! And *I'll* tell the old woman so. That's *something* I
can get back at her.

Freddy (*as D'Arcy goes towards door*) Here! *I'll* do that.

D'Arcy (*calling through door*) Woman!

Freddy Stop it! I'll tell her myself.

D'Arcy No, let me, old boy. I want to be unpleasant to her. (*Calls*)
Woman! (*Picking up mashie*)

Freddy I tell you I'll manage my own affairs.

D'Arcy Oh, don't be a kill-joy.

Mrs Hewlett enters

Mrs Hewlett Who are you calling 'woman'? I'm not a 'woman'.

D'Arcy (*with mashie*) I don't want to inquire into that at all. I want
to warn you, that's all. I'm going to get my own back on you.
(*Flourishing the mashie*)

Freddy Put that down.

Mrs Hewlett Pooh! I'm not afraid of him.

Freddy (*takes mashie*) No, but it's my best mashie.

Mrs Hewlett (*to D'Arcy*) And what do you think you can do?

D'Arcy I don't know and I shan't tell you. But I'll do it. I'll take
any means. Fair or foul.

Mrs Hewlett Ah! Here we have the disappointed fortune-hunter.

D'Arcy What!

Freddy She jabbed you one in the jaw that time.

D'Arcy It's a lie. It's worse. It isn't even true. Now I'll make things
even nastier for you.

Mrs Hewlett (*to Freddy*) I wonder that any friend of yours can be
so ungentlemanly.

D'Arcy Well, *he's* finished with you now. And his sister—with your
nasty son, Nozzle or something.

Mrs Hewlett Rubbish!

D'Arcy Is it rubbish? (*to Freddy*) Go on. Tell her so yourself.

Freddy I tell *you*—I won't have you butting in.

D'Arcy (*reacting*) Oh! You're going back on it, are you?

Freddy I will not be dictated by you, that's all.

Mrs Hewlett I should hope not. (*To Freddy*) Thank you. Now I'm
going to see what that young woman's taking away.

D'Arcy You leave her alone.

Mrs Hewlett One thing I don't mind her taking away is *you*.

She goes off

D'Arcy (*angrily; to Freddy*) Skunk!

Freddy Oh, you're not worth getting annoyed over.

D'Arcy Aren't I? I'll tell the world about this. Talk of young Pevensey and his fish. His name will be Eau-de-Cologne compared with yours.

Freddy And have everyone say what she said—

D'Arcy What?

Freddy The disappointed fortune-hunter.

D'Arcy You know as well as I do that's a lie.

Freddy Then why make it out to be true? Only fools advertise their failures.

D'Arcy Well, Arthur Mills shall hear about this. I'll tell him. I'll tell them all.

Freddy (*very strongly, holding him by the wrist*) You'll tell nobody. Stop your damned interference. D'you hear?

D'Arcy I'm going to know the truth. What are you doing here with these people?

Freddy Well, listen. You're out to do that old woman down. Aren't you?

D'Arcy Well, haven't you been listening? Of course I am.

Freddy So am I, you fool.

D'Arcy *You* are? In what way?

Freddy I can see I shall have to take a hell of a risk with you. I'm going to let you into something.

D'Arcy Let me into something?

Freddy Hold on. We'll have this in writing. (*Sits at table and prepares to write*)

D'Arcy Why? Who are you going to write to?

Freddy I'll put it in your own words. 'We agree to get level with Mrs Hewlett by any means, fair or foul. Freddy Malone.' (*Handing pen to D'Arcy*) Go on. 'D'Arcy Tuck.' You sign it too.

D'Arcy Good Lord! But even so, why write it? I don't like writing things. It's a bit of a risk.

Freddy It's nothing to the risk I'm taking with you. Go on.

D'Arcy (*puzzled, hesitating*) All right. Still—I—don't think I'm very keen on—on this pen. (*Signs*) There you are. (*About to blot it*)

Freddy (*quickly*) Don't blot it.

Freddy pockets paper

D'Arcy But why should *you* take it?

Freddy To stop your silly tongue.

Crosses to window, closes it, comes back

I've got to take a big chance with you. Either that or lose a very good thing.

D'Arcy What thing?

Freddy What I'm going to tell you will be a bit of a shock. You'll find it difficult to believe. D'you remember at school we had an oath? There was an old stinks master with a beard—Allah we called him.

D'Arcy Yes. We used to swear by the beard of Allah.

Freddy Yes, and it held. You and I have been all over the world since then and broken every commandment in turn. But did you ever break that oath—by the beard of Allah?

D'Arcy No. No one ever broke that. It was sacred.

Freddy Right. You're going to swear it now.

D'Arcy Swear what?

Freddy That what I'm about to tell you you'll never repeat.

D'Arcy Good Lord! Is it as bad as that?

Freddy It's vital. Come on. Asleep or awake—sober or tight—you'll never tell a soul. Swear that.

D'Arcy I swear by the beard of Allah.

Freddy Sit down.

D'Arcy sits

Freddy sits on his right

Now I'll tell you what I'm here for.

D'Arcy Well? What are you here for?

Freddy Plunder.

D'Arcy Plunder? What do you mean?

Freddy That's what I do. That's how I live. That's my profession.

D'Arcy Do you mean you're a cr . . .

Freddy gestures with his hand to stop him

Freddy Only one other man knows it and he's a foreigner in Marseilles. And one woman. My accomplice. Passes as my sister.

D'Arcy She's *not* your sister. Why do you say she is?

Freddy Purely for business purposes.

D'Arcy But you! Your friends! The people you know!

Freddy Yes, rather. All the topnotchers. I'm Freddy to them all, aren't I? Quite a lad. Yachtsman—big game shot, anything you like. Oh yes—I do it on very high-class lines.

D'Arcy But what is it—that you do?

Freddy Steal.

D'Arcy What?

Freddy Steal.

D'Arcy Steal? But, good Lord, man, why?

Freddy I like it.

D'Arcy You like it?

Freddy I love it.

D'Arcy I don't believe it. (*Feels for his watch-chain—he can't find it for a second and gets a shock*) What! Wait a minute! (*Finds it*) No, I don't believe you.

Freddy Don't worry. I'm not that sort of thief.

D'Arcy What do you thieve?

Freddy Jewels, for choice, from big houses.

D'Arcy What? A house-lifter!

Freddy That's why I'm here. Hers are worth a packet.

D'Arcy You're going to take them?

Freddy I am. All of them. She hasn't got them all here. Some are in the bank.

D'Arcy You're not going to break into the bank?

Freddy No. She's coming to stay at my house. She'll have them all with her then. I've seen to that.

D'Arcy But if you were caught?

Freddy I'm not. I make that one of my strictest rules.

D'Arcy This all is a lie. Society crooks are only in books.

Freddy rings

Freddy Oh, very well.

D'Arcy What are you doing?

Freddy If there's time, I'll prove it to you.

D'Arcy How long—do you pretend—you've been like this?

Freddy Always. D'you remember that half-mile challenge cup that got lifted at school? That was me.

D'Arcy Good Lord! And I *won* it.

Freddy One of my earliest recollections is my father catching me cheating at cards. He caught me taking an ace from my shirt.

D'Arcy Good Lord! Then he ought to have lifted your shirt and flogged it.

Freddy He did. And after the flogging he showed me how to pull out the ace without being caught.

D'Arcy Appalling! (*Pause*) How do you pull out the ace?

Freddy I'd show you, only I don't happen to have an ace in my shirt at the moment.

To Mabel, who enters

Find Miss Malone and ask her to come here, will you?

Mabel Yes, sir.

Goes out

D'Arcy Tell me this. Where did you run across this old woman?

Freddy A few days ago at Monte Carlo. She'd come in for this money and she was flashing the jewels all over her stomach.

D'Arcy (*bitterly*) Our money—Joan's and mine—and our jewels.

Freddy Yes, old boy, but her stomach. I couldn't take them then. I'd just pulled off another job and the police were on a false scent so I let them stay there.

D'Arcy Oh, so that's why you're friends with them? That's why your sister's encouraging this—this growth?

Freddy That's it. And they're coming to stay with us on the tenth. And so's the jewellery.

Prudence enters

Prudence You want me, Freddy?

Freddy Yes. This is D'Arcy Tuck.

Prudence Oh, really. How do you do? I've heard a little bit about you. (*Offering her hand*)

D'Arcy (*taking it nervously*) And I've just heard a great chunk about you.

Freddy Don't let this worry you. I've just told him about us.

Prudence You've *told*? Him!

Freddy Only just now I was saying to you I'd face a big danger for this. Well, he's the big danger.

D'Arcy Yes. I can be a bit of a thunder-cloud.

Prudence (*to Freddy*) It's madness. What on earth's come over you?

Freddy He'll be all right. Treat him as a friend.

Prudence (*to D'Arcy*) Well, what do you think of it?

D'Arcy I don't know. I've never met a crook girl before.

Prudence I'll bet you have. (*To Freddy*) Why have you done this? He doesn't look dangerous.

Freddy I had to, that's all. You can trust me, can't you?

Prudence Of course. You know that.

Freddy Then you can trust him, too. (*To Prudence*) Run along now. I'll tell you all about it later on.

Prudence (*to Freddy, before she goes*) You've got him—? (*she clenches her fist*) You're sure?

Freddy Leave it to me.

She exits

(*To D'Arcy*) There you are.

D'Arcy Yes, but look here—Freddy—or should I say, Malone?

Freddy What?

D'Arcy Look here! You've planned to pinch this stuff and I've just realized it's my little girl's. Its hers by rights.

Freddy I'm not going to take it by rights.

D'Arcy (*excitedly*) You can't take that jewellery. Listen, you thief, you can't as a decent man!

Freddy What do you suggest I should do? Pinch the stuff and make her a present of it?

D'Arcy That would be the only really honest thing to do. How much is it worth?

Freddy Roughly round about forty thousand pounds.

D'Arcy Forty thousand! Look here! Suppose it's sold?

Freddy Oh, it's going to be sold. That's where the gentleman at Marseilles comes in.

D'Arcy Well, if Joan got it back that way—in money—coming from me. I could say it was part of a marriage settlement. What d'you think of that?

Freddy Something rather unrefined.

D'Arcy But its hers. Can't you be a sportsman?

Freddy (*with challenge*) Who isn't a sportsman?

D'Arcy Well, I'm sorry, but I think you—rather aren't.

Freddy Right. Now then. You shall be in this with me. We'll go fifty-fifty in the risk and fifty-fifty in the plunder.

D'Arcy Me? Steal? I couldn't pinch a dog's dinner!

Freddy Well, *I* wouldn't pinch *that*.

D'Arcy I mean I couldn't even if the dog were chained up. No thanks, I don't think I care to be in it.

Freddy I see. So much for your 'any means, fair or foul'?

D'Arcy And I meant it. At least, in spirit.

Freddy Oh! A man of spirit! Very well. I've made you a sporting offer. I don't want you.

D'Arcy (*after a pause, going to Freddy, wavering*) Freddy!

Freddy M'm?

D'Arcy Regarding this risk—is there much of it?

Freddy A hundred to one on success, but if *you* came into it—*ten* to one.

D'Arcy Ten to one. What's fifty-fifty of that? All right. You think I'm afraid. I don't think I am. I'll (*with determination*) very likely do it.

Joan re-enters. She is now very red-eyed and overcome

Joan We'd better get back to town.

D'Arcy All right, darling.

Joan All right! It's all wrong. (*Nearly weeping*)

Freddy All right, indeed! She's had the biggest shock of her life. (*To Joan*) I can't say how sorry I am for you.

Joan (*with spirit*) Well, if these people are your friends I'm sorry for you!

D'Arcy Good! A very apt retort.

Joan Come on. (*Turns up stage*)

D'Arcy goes up stage with her

I'll see if they've put my things in the car.

She goes off

Freddy Well, are you coming to me on the tenth?

D'Arcy Well—I should have to tell Joan, you know.

Freddy You'll tell nobody. Tell her you're going somewhere else.

D'Arcy Tell her lies?

Freddy Only one. Besides, you've got to begin sometime.

D'Arcy No. I've vowed a vow I'll never deceive her. I simply couldn't do it. You've no idea how cute she is. If it means lying to her it's off. Do the job yourself.

Freddy Oh, I can see there's only one way of trusting you and that's to incriminate you.

D'Arcy You needn't be afraid. I won't say a word about *you*.

Freddy I'll see you don't. (*Producing paper*) What about this? If I'm caught this'll fix you anyway.

D'Arcy Oh, so you're going to hold that over me?

Freddy draws it away as D'Arcy snatches at it

Freddy I don't go to work that way. But I'm going to use this to compel you to keep silent.

D'Arcy How?

Freddy Like this. (*He tears the paper up and puts the pieces in the fire*) That's the sort of feller you're dealing with.

D'Arcy Thanks, Freddy, But I won't take any further part in it.

Freddy All right, then. Don't blame me if I stick to the proceeds.

Joan returns. Mrs Hewlett follows as though chasing her. Joan is crying

Joan Come on, D'Arcy, hurry up.

Mrs Hewlett Yes, you've been here quite long enough. A short visit, though, compared with what you expected.

Joan Take me away quickly. Don't speak to her again.

Mrs Hewlett He can't say anything that'll hurt me. It's only spite. Spite does me no harm.

Joan D'Arcy!

She hurries out in tears

Mrs Hewlett (*pursuing her and shouting*) Came here in fine feather, didn't you? (*To D'Arcy*) Well, it's moulted!

She follows Joan off slamming door

D'Arcy (*closing door and turning, very worked up*) Did you hear that? I'll ruin that woman. I'll spoil her. Yes, and every bit of jewellery she's got I'll pinch. Are you in this? I make you a sporting offer. Fifty-fifty.

Freddy Once and for all. Am I boss?

D'Arcy Yes, anything you like.

Freddy You'll do what I tell you, when I tell you and how I tell you?

D'Arcy Anything! After the way she's treated Joan.

Freddy Right! That's final, you come to me on the tenth.

D'Arcy Any number you like. Tenth, eleventh, twelfth.

Freddy No, the tenth is the date I've fixed for the job.

D'Arcy I've a good mind to start the job now. (*He picks up a silver cigarette box*)

Freddy Put that down.

D'Arcy Why? Is it yours?

Freddy No. It's hers.

D'Arcy Hers, right! Then here goes.

He opens the box, takes out two cigarettes and hurries to the door

That shows you.

Goes out

CURTAIN

ACT II

SCENE I

The Hall of Freddy Malone's house at Walton Heath. A Roulette party is in progress.

Prudence is acting as Bank. Freddy is standing over her, and near him D'Arcy. Round the table are seated Mrs Hewlett, Oswald and four other guests, Sir George and Lady Chudleigh, Harry Kenward and Ruth Bennett. As the curtain rises the roulette is spinning. D'Arcy takes Freddy by the arm and speaks confidentially

Freddy Don't spin it so hard, Pru, we'll have to wait all night for the damn thing to stop.

Lady Chudleigh I don't mind. I think it's the most exciting part of the game.

Oswald (*to Mrs Hewlett*) Haven't you put on more than you meant?

Mrs Hewett Don't you interfere with me; you bet your own bets.

Harry (*to Sir George*) Can you give me eight half-crowns for a quid?

Prudence Twenty-six. Black.

Sir George hands Harry the money.

Freddy moves over to D'Arcy who is signing to him

D'Arcy Is this going on all night?

Freddy Don't keep fussing.

Harry Whose is that ten bob?

Mrs Hewlett Mine.

Ruth My lucky number, too.

D'Arcy But when do we start?

General buzz of conversation

Sir George (*rising*) I'm through, Freddy. Golf tomorrow.

D'Arcy Are you going to bed?

Sir George Yes.

D'Arcy Good.

Freddy Well, one more spin, then we'll all go to bed. No limit this time. Look out, Pru. Come on. I'll take the bank. No black or red—numbers only.

Prudence has risen; Freddy takes her place

Mrs Hewlett I'm going to have a plunge.
D'Arcy Oh, why not wait till the morning.

They all laugh

Prudence Last hand, Ozzy. Are you going to back your fancy?
Oswald Yes, thanks.
Prudence Well, what are you going to do?
D'Arcy He's going to sit it out.
Sir George Can I have a fiver on?
Freddy Yes, a pony if you like.
Lady Chudleigh Lend me ten bob, George.
Freddy Come on. Have you all done?
Harry Yes.   }
Mrs Hewlett I'm ready. } *(Together)*
Prudence Hurry up, Ozzy. }
Freddy Right. Well, here she goes. *(Spins)* Fricassée de Mouton!
D'Arcy *(to Mrs Hewlett)* How much have you lost, I hope?
Mrs Hewlett I've got something to say about finding you here.
Prudence *(earnestly looking at roulette wheel running)* Go on! Go on!
—don't stop! don't stop!!
Lady Chudleigh George, let's see.
Sir George You'll see soon enough—there goes my fiver!
Freddy Zero! That clears the board.
Oswald I wish I'd known.
Mrs Hewlett *(to Oswald)* What does Zero mean?
D'Arcy *(butting in, to Mrs Hewlett)* To you, nothing.
Freddy Fancy me doing that again. I hate taking your money this
way.
Sir George That settles it. I'm off to bed. What time's that four-
some in the morning?

Lady Chudleigh follows her husband

Freddy *(to Sir George)* We leave here at nine.

*The party breaks up. Mrs Hewlett stands apart with Oswald. The others
prepare to go upstairs*

Ruth *(to Sir George)* Well, you've got to be my partner, Sir George.
Sir George Rather!
Lady Chudleigh *(to Freddy)* Goodnight, Freddy.
Freddy Goodnight, Kathleen. We're together, remember.
Lady Chudleigh Are we?
Freddy Yes. But not till the morning, I fear.
Lady Chudleigh Oh, shame.
Ruth *(at top of stairs)* Goodnight, Mr Tuck.

D'Arcy I hope you'll have a very nice dream.
Harry Goodnight, Freddy.
Freddy Goodnight, everyone.

Lady Chudleigh and Ruth, followed by Sir George and Harry, go upstairs, talking as they go.

Mrs Hewlett (*coming to Freddy*) Now, Mr Malone—you know I had no wish to meet Mr Tuck, after what happened the other day.
Freddy He wants to make up for what happened the other day. (*To D'Arcy*) Don't you?
Oswald It's well meant, Mother.
Mrs Hewlett Yes, and I know well enough it's well meant who towards.
Prudence Oh, I think he's behaved very nicely to you all the evening.
D'Arcy Absolutely. Didn't I pass you the mustard at dinner? Even before you asked for it?
Mrs Hewlett Yes. With the fish.
D'Arcy I don't complain about meeting *you*.
Oswald I don't either. Not about meeting *you*.
D'Arcy Well, I should hope not.
Oswald That's quite right—I say, I don't.
Freddy (*severely, to Mrs Hewlett*) Will you stop quarrelling in my house?
Mrs Hewlett But I am not going to melt.
Freddy I hope not. If you started to melt, naturally I should keep well out of it. (*Crosses away from her to Oswald*) Where's your Uncle Simon?
Oswald He's in the library.
Mrs Hewlett Well, I'm going to bed.
Freddy I hope you'll have a very good night.
D'Arcy Goodnight, fair damsel.
Mrs Hewlett Oh, really? You'll have to go a long way to get round me.

She goes upstairs

D'Arcy Yes, you're quite right. I'd have to run round.
Oswald (*to Prudence*) I say. Can I have a word with you alone?
Prudence Where?
Oswald In the drawing-room. I haven't seen you alone all night.
Freddy You can't expect to see her alone all night just yet.
Prudence Oh, Freddy! (*Laughs*) Very well, Ozzy, but it can't be for long. I promised to see your mother before she gets into bed.
D'Arcy Yes. Better before than after.

Prudence Oh, Mr Tuck, I'm surprised at you.

Prudence and Oswald go into drawing-room

Freddy Now look here. What do you want to row with the old woman for? It only makes for danger.

D'Arcy Danger? All very well for you. You're an expert. I found it hard enough to get here at all. I had to lie to Joan.

Freddy Yes. By the way—what did you tell her?

D'Arcy I told her I was going to sleep at my solicitor's in Yorkshire.

Freddy That's a pretty feeble effort. What do you want with a solicitor in Yorkshire; And who the hell wants to sleep with a solicitor in any case?

D'Arcy It's all right. She trusts me, the little darling. She knows I wouldn't tell her a lie. But when are we going to do the deed?

Freddy Tonight, of course. Pru is going to the old dame's room to see to a few details and report.

D'Arcy But why do it at night?

Freddy Because she wears a lot of the best stuff all *day*. You don't suppose I'm going to hold her down on a couch while you go all over her neck and chest?

D'Arcy I hope not. I dislike mountaineering. It would be much safer in the daytime—

Enter the Footman, with a syphon, followed by the Butler

(*Noticing Footman*) Wouldn't it?

Footman (*puzzled*) Sir?

D'Arcy What have you got there? Oh, one of those things! Yes, I know them. (*Tests syphon*) No, thanks.

Footman puts syphon on table and exits

Freddy Anything you want, Buckley?

Buckley Yes, sir. Mrs Orlock from the Lodge is here, sir. She's been waiting to see you for a long time.

Freddy What about?

Buckley You know, sir, Orlock went to Beckhampton for you this evening.

Freddy Well?

Buckley He sent a message, sir, to say he can't get back till the morning.

Freddy Well, why worry me about it?

Buckley I don't know, sir; but the woman seems very put out.

Freddy Oh, I'll see her in a minute.

Buckley Yes, sir. (*Turns to go*)

D'Arcy (*up at the windows*) Wait a moment. Here's a car. He's probably come back.

Freddy (*to Buckley*) Go and see who it is.

Buckley Yes, sir. (*Goes up to front door*)

D'Arcy comes down to Freddy

D'Arcy (*to Freddy*) You may find this awkward.

Freddy What d'you mean?

D'Arcy It may be someone for you.

Freddy Why should it be someone for me?

Buckley opens door. Joan's voice is heard off

D'Arcy Well, you never know.

Joan (*outside*) It's all right. You needn't wait.

D'Arcy It's someone for me.

Freddy Blast!

Joan enters and sees D'Arcy

Joan Hallo, darling!

D'Arcy (*embarrassed*) Oh—I—don't think so.

Joan (*to Freddy*) Good evening.

Freddy Good evening. (*Offering his hand*) All right, Buckley.

Buckley closes front door and goes off

D'Arcy But darling—why have you come here and because of what?

Joan I called at your rooms tonight—just in case you got back.

D'Arcy Tomorrow, dear—

Joan And I saw a letter your man had re-addressed to you here.

D'Arcy What an ass that man is. I changed my mind at the last moment. I was absolutely in the Yorkshire train when I changed it.

Freddy But why mustn't he come to my house?

Joan Because you're trying to keep in with the Veals. And *she's* here, too.

D'Arcy Is *she* here?

Joan Yes. I telephoned to Marvin Court and found that out. Oh, I guessed what you were up to.

D'Arcy Guessed! But you ought to have warned me you could guess like that.

Joan I won't have it. You shan't be nice to that woman.

D'Arcy Oh, but I wasn't going to be very nice.

Freddy (*to Joan*) I see. You don't agree to letting us try to get the right side of her.

Joan No. I hired a car and came straight down to stop it. I wouldn't accept a penny from her.

D'Arcy But she's not likely to give you one.

Joan That's all right then, and now you'd better take me back in your car.

Freddy Oh, nonsense! You're not going home tonight.

Joan But I can't stay here.

D'Arcy No, we don't want her—(*Looks at Freddy*)—to stay here against her will, do we?

Freddy (*with a quick frown at D'Arcy, which the latter accepts with a resigned agreement*) I'll get you fixed up right away. (*Turns towards door*)

Joan But I haven't any things for the night.

Freddy My sister will see to that.

Joan But *Mrs Veal's* here.

Freddy You needn't see her. You can pop off in the morning before she's up. She's a late sleeper. I don't suppose she begins to unglue till about lunch.

He goes off in to the drawing-room

Joan I never meant to stay here.

D'Arcy Well, darling, you shouldn't have come so late.

Joan I don't care. I'm not going to have you making advances to that woman. Come on; let's get the car and go back.

D'Arcy I can't do that. I must remain.

Joan Why?

D'Arcy I've sworn to Freddy I'd do this.

Joan What?

D'Arcy Why this—remaining.

Joan That doesn't matter. You came to see Mrs Veal. You're not going to see any more of her. Are you?

D'Arcy Very little, I hope.

Joan Why did you do this? Does the money mean so much to you?

D'Arcy You know it doesn't. But it's yours. She wronged you, and I vowed I'd get it back by hook or—that other thing.

Joan You silly old thing. I know you were trying to help me. But never do this sort of thing again. Will you? Even for me?

D'Arcy Not likely.

Freddy enters from drawing-room with Prudence

Freddy (*as he enters*) Here she is. Come on—(*Speaking to Oswald in drawing-room*) Not you. You stay there. (*Shuts door*) Here you are —my sister.

Joan How d'you do. I'm sorry if I've caused you any trouble.

Prudence Not in the least. I've a room for you and everything you want.

D'Arcy She can have my room.

Freddy (*crosses to D'Arcy behind Prudence*) I'll see to this. I'm sure you must be very hungry after your journey—take Miss Hewlett to the dining-room and give her something to eat. (*Confidentially*)

D'Arcy Oh! Come on and eat.

Joan But I had a very good dinner.

D'Arcy Well, I *didn't*.

Goes off with Joan

Prudence Why do you want her here?

Freddy I don't. But if she goes, D'Arcy'll go. I must keep him here.

Prudence You'd be a lot safer without him.

Freddy Not when it's over. If he's going to be partly guilty, he's going to be entirely quiet.

Prudence That's true. You're going to tell the old woman that the girl's here?

Freddy Most certainly. You tell her.

Prudence All right. What room had the girl better have? We're full up.

Freddy (*going up*) That's easy. I'll send Simon Veal to the Lodge. (*Rings bell*) You go in there too. I think D'Arcy's safer under observation. I'll come along in a minute.

Buckley enters

Is Mrs Orlock still there?

Buckley Yes, sir.

Freddy I want her.

Buckley Yes, sir.

Prudence And Buckley—tell Brown to look out some pyjamas and dressing-gown, and put them in Mr Simon Veal's bedroom.

Goes off into dining-room

Freddy It's all right, Buckley, Mr Veal's going to the Lodge.

Buckley Oh, I see, sir.

Freddy Have his things packed and taken there.

Buckley Yes, sir. (*Opens door*) Mrs Orlock! The master'll see you now.

He admits Mrs Orlock and goes out

Freddy Good evening. I'm sorry to hear about Orlock.

Mrs Orlock What about me, pray? I've been waiting to see you for hours!

Freddy What about?

Mrs Orlock Well, about my husband. I don't like him stopping away all night.

Freddy It wasn't my fault.

Mrs Orlock Then whose fault was it, sir? You sent him.

Freddy Don't you speak to me like that or *you'll* get sent somewhere.

Mrs Orlock *And* I mightn't mind.

Freddy That'll do. Now listen to me. I'm sending one of the gentlemen from here to the Lodge.

Mrs Orlock What for, sir?

Freddy For the night. You've got a spare room there.

Mrs Orlock No, thank you. I prefer not.

Freddy You don't understand. I'm telling you what I *wish*.

Mrs. Orlock My husband isn't there. I shan't feel comfortable with a strange gentleman in the spare room.

Freddy Oh, nonsense! You flatter yourself. You'll be safe enough. Go and do what you're told.

Mrs Orlock I can't do it, sir. The sheets aren't aired.

Freddy That doesn't matter. He won't know until afterwards.

Mrs Orlock There's always something happening here what I don't like.

Freddy What do you mean by that?

Mrs Orlock What I say. Always comings and goings—and strange events.

Freddy Strange events?—explain yourself.

Mrs Orlock Well, look at what I've put up with these last few days. The Lodge all higgledy-piggledy—workmen here, workmen there—nothing but pails and buckets. I hate the place!

Freddy That's enough—that's your finish. Now you'll go.

Mrs Orlock Go?

Freddy Go, yes—you can take a month's notice and leave.

Mrs Orlock Leave the Lodge?

Freddy Leave my service.

Mrs Orlock But what about Bert?

Freddy Take Bert with you. I'm sorry for him, but he's either got to lose his job—or lose his wife.

Mrs Orlock So this is justice!

Freddy That'll do. For the month you're here, you'll do as you're told—beginning from now.

Mrs Orlock It's foul treatment.

Freddy Control yourself. If you're nervous tonight I'll send Cook over to sleep with you.

Mrs Orlock Cook! My God, no, thank you!

Mrs Orlock goes out very angry

Maid and Footman enter on landing. Footman walks round to bedroom door, opens it, switches on light and Maid exits through bedroom, and Footman follows her, closing door

Freddy Well, that's *your* funeral, anyhow.

Simon enters

Freddy Ah! You're the man I want. I hope you won't mind but I've had to move you to the Lodge tonight.

Simon Oh, indeed. And why?

Freddy Miss Hewlett's arrived, and we've had to give her your room.

Simon And who asked *her* here?

Freddy Well, who asked you, if it isn't a rude question, or even if it is? And furthermore, I regret to say that after tonight there'll be no room for you even at the Lodge.

Simon I see what you mean. I know who's at the bottom of all this —my sister-in-law. I'll have something to say to her.

Freddy Well, you'll have to say it from the Lodge.

He goes off

Simon remains on stage moodily. The drawing-room door opens

Oswald peers out, then seeing Simon, closes the door, which makes a slight noise

Simon hears it close and opens it again

Simon (*seeing Oswald*) Oh, it's you, is it? Come out.

Oswald Oh! Goodnight.

Simon (*follows him, stops him*) Where's your mother?

Oswald Gone to her room. (*Following as Simon makes for the stairs*) No, no. Don't go up after her.

Simon I warned her. Before you get engaged I want that cheque.

Oswald But I'm not engaged that I know of.

Simon No. Not till she's got me kicked out of the place tomorrow. And sent to the Lodge tonight.

Oswald She'll settle it when we get home.

Simon She'll settle it tonight—or I tell. Now then!

Oswald No, no, no! Don't keep harping on that. You wouldn't do yourself any good by telling.

Simon Yes, that's always her cry. It isn't only a threat.

Oswald Isn't it? I'd like to know what it is then.

Simon Hold your tongue! I'll call back here later. You get that cheque from her and meet me with it here.

Oswald When?

Simon When they're all asleep. Three o'clock.

Oswald Oh, I don't think I'd better.

Simon I think you had.

Oswald Oh! (*Going up the stairs*)

Simon Three o'clock. Sharp. Here. By this front door.

He goes out

Oswald remains for a moment, then hearing others coming—exit upstairs

Maid followed by Footman, carrying a bag, re-enter from bedroom. They exit slowly off landing

Enter D'Arcy and Joan from dining-room

D'Arcy Here we are, darling. Here are the stairs. Now I'm sure you're ready for bed.

Joan But I don't know where it is.

D'Arcy Well, the bed's in your room. I'm not quite sure where the room is, but we can easily find out.

Goes up to ring and—meets Simon, who enters

Hallo, I want to find out where this young lady's bedroom is— you ought to know, you've been in it.

Simon Yes. (*To Joan, who is standing at foot of stairs*) I'm much obliged to you, I'm sure.

D'Arcy Well, where is it?

Simon There. First room at the top of the stairs. (*Indicates door up the stairs*) Goodnight.

Exit

D'Arcy Yes. (*Then to Joan*) And goodnight to *you*, darling.

Joan You seem in an awful hurry to send me to bed. I'd like to sit up and talk a while.

D'Arcy I mustn't talk tonight. I've got work to do.

Joan Work, you! What sort of work?

D'Arcy Oh, about transferring some property. It's to do with a deed.

Joan Oh, nothing to do with me?

D'Arcy No. You go to bed.

Joan All right. Goodnight, darling. (*Kisses him*)

D'Arcy That's it.

And she goes upstairs

Oh, your coat. (*Handing it to her*) And I hope you won't wake up till tea. I mean early tea. (*He stands kissing his hand to her*)

Freddy and Prudence re-enter

Freddy What are you doing?
D'Arcy I'm goodnight-ing.
Freddy Well, have we got rid of them all?
Prudence Yes. Ozzy's gone. (*Puts out light in drawing-room*)
Freddy Now we must start business.
D'Arcy Well—I'm ready.
Freddy Good! Now, Pru. There's the old lady to see to.
Prudence Yes. I'll see her settled down nice and comfy. (*Goes to staircase*)
D'Arcy (*to her*) Well, goodnight.
Prudence Don't you worry, I'm coming back.

Goes upstairs

Buckley appears on stairs

D'Arcy Now look here, Freddy—
Prudence (*from stairs*) Goodnight, Buckley.
Buckley Goodnight, Miss. (*Comes down*)
Freddy Buckley, you needn't wait up. I'll lock up. Were Mr Simon Veal's things taken to the Lodge?
Buckley Yes, sir. William took them. He's back, sir. The gentleman didn't have very much. Goodnight, sir.
Freddy Goodnight to you.
D'Arcy And to you. (*To Buckley*)

Buckley goes off

Freddy (*to D'Arcy*) Now, what were you going to say?
D'Arcy Just that it makes it a bit difficult Joan being so trusting. Isn't she a darling?
Freddy Yes. The more I see of her the more I feel I may have been wrong in dragging you into it.
D'Arcy But you haven't. I walked into it.
Freddy Now look here, D'Arcy. If you think you'll have any regrets, now's your time to chuck it.
D'Arcy Chuck it? I'm going through with it, for her sake. She might think it's wrong, but I know it's right. I'm in it up to the —shins.
Freddy Good boy! I'll see you don't suffer for it, whatever happens.
D'Arcy Good!
Freddy Then now for it.
D'Arcy Yes. Splendid.

Freddy You can have one more drink if you like.

D'Arcy No. I don't want drinks. I've got no fear.

Freddy Haven't you? Then get some. That's where everyone falls down sooner or later at this game. They think it's easy.

D'Arcy What? But you said this *would* be easy?

Freddy That's just why you've got to be afraid. Afraid of the tiniest slip. One footprint might do it—one finger-mark.

D'Arcy I'll wear gloves. They always wear gloves.

Freddy Some people think the police are easily fooled. *Are* they?

D'Arcy Well, you've fooled them before now.

Freddy Never. What I've done is never to let 'em suspect. I've got a very high opinion of Scotland Yard.

D'Arcy Scotland Yard! But no one from Scotland Yard will come here?

Freddy Of course, they'll come tomorrow.

D'Arcy Why?

Freddy Why? We're not going to scrump apples. Do you know what we could get for this?

D'Arcy No.

Freddy Ten years.

D'Arcy Ten! I didn't think it would be as much as that. You didn't make this very clear to me.

Prudence comes downstairs quietly

Freddy Of course I made it clear.

D'Arcy looks over towards Prudence. Freddy sees her and stops talking

Prudence She's locked them all in that jewel-case. The key's under her pillow.

D'Arcy That's done it. You can't get the key from under her pillow.

Freddy Oh, keep quiet. I've been making friends with that jewel-case. I shan't require the key.

Prudence (*to D'Arcy*) He just says 'Open up, please,' and it does. You'll see. It's awfully cute.

D'Arcy But you're not going to open it in her room, with a loud click?

Freddy It'll click all right, but not loud. (*To Prudence*) Where's she put it?

Prudence She's left it on her dressing-table.

Freddy Oh, dear. Is *that* all? She's not doing me justice.

Prudence And she's going to bolt her door. I didn't suggest it, of course. She told me.

D'Arcy What! You've left a bolt on her door? Now you can't get in.

Freddy That's fine. That's just what I hoped she'd do. (*To Prudence*) Well, off you go. You know what you've got to do.
Prudence Yes. One moment. Here's Exhibit 'A'.

Hands Freddy a Chubb key

Freddy Yes. (*To D'Arcy, handing him key*) You'll want that.
D'Arcy (*taking it with diffidence*) Me? What for?
Freddy The key of the garage. I'll tell you about it.
Prudence (*giving Freddy a small glass bottle*) And this.
Freddy Right. (*To D'Arcy*) You may want this, too. But I hope not.
D'Arcy So do I. What is it?
Freddy Just a little bottle.
D'Arcy Scent?
Freddy No. Don't be inquisitive.
Prudence I'll go now. (*Turning to stairs*) Bye-bye. (*To D'Arcy*) Good luck!

She goes upstairs

D'Arcy (*to Prudence*) Yes, thanks—so do I, I'm sure. But how are you going to get into the room?
Freddy How I always meant to. From the conservatory roof.
D'Arcy What, you're going in through the window?
Freddy Yes, up a ladder. I shall go first.
D'Arcy Oh! and then—anyone?
Freddy I'll tell you. First of all, you meet me down here.
D'Arcy When?
Freddy A quarter to three. Sharp! You'll be wearing pyjamas, dressing-gown, soft slippers and a pair of gloves.
D'Arcy Yes, all right. I know about the gloves.
Freddy When we get in her room——
D'Arcy She may not be asleep.
Freddy I'll take care of that.
D'Arcy She may wake up.
Freddy You'll take care she doesn't.
D'Arcy Oh, you think *I'd* better do that. Yes?
Freddy When I've got the stuff I shall hand it to you and unbolt the door, let you out and bolt it again. You bring the stuff down here —out to the garage and hide it in your car.
D'Arcy Oh, *I* do. In *my* car? Is that a very good idea?
Freddy Very. Put it somewhere safe: in the tool-box or under the cushions. Lock the garage and bring me back the key.
D'Arcy But why in *my* car?
Freddy I shall get out down the ladder—and leave it there. Then, when we've finished, Pru will give the alarm.

D'Arcy Alarm? Is there going to be any alarm?

Freddy Yes. She's going to say she saw a man running down the drive. The old woman will wake up—miss her stuff and raise hell. I shall take charge—round up the whole house. The telephone will have been put out of order.

D'Arcy Who by?

Freddy By the burglar. I'll see to that.

D'Arcy Yes.

Freddy So I shall send you for the police—*in your car.*

D'Arcy But the stuff will be in the car. You want me to bring back a fat policeman in the car with the stuff?

Freddy Yes. The last place he'd expect to find it.

D'Arcy I won't put it under the cushions. He may have a sensitive seat.

Freddy As soon as I get the chance I'll take it off you. I know what to do with it.

D'Arcy But they may search the car.

Freddy What these local bobbies will search is the country-side for the burglar. I'll just see to that burglar right away. (*Takes gloves from his pocket*)

D'Arcy Ah, there are the good old gloves. This is fine. I feel like a real crook.

Freddy You *are* a real crook, and don't you forget it. Now the telephone.

Takes a pair of pliers from his pocket and cuts the telephone line

D'Arcy goes into room and comes back with a pair of gloves, putting them on

Now the window.

D'Arcy What about the window?

During the next few lines Freddy opens the window by the front door, removes a diamond of glass which he leaves lying on the floor, tests opening the window by reaching his hand through the hole, and leaves the window open

Freddy This window. The burglar's got to come in this way.

D'Arcy breaks the glass and puts it down, puts his heel through it. Freddy locks front door

D'Arcy (*watching eagerly*) By Jove, yes, this work is pleasanter than I thought. (*Pulling on gloves tightly*)

Freddy If they cop you, my God! your enthusiasm will wane. Well, there you are. Now you'd better go to your room.

D'Arcy Yes, but Freddy, there's something else. This little bottle. What is it?

Freddy Oh, that? That is for you, just in case she gets wakeful.
D'Arcy Why, what do I do with it?
Freddy Douse her with it.
D'Arcy Oh, douse! All right, if she looks like waking, I'll just pour some on my handkerchief and douse. Then I'll gag her with it.
Freddy Your handkerchief, your name on it. That's damn brainy. And be convicted of robbery with violence. That's Dartmoor and the 'cat'.
D'Arcy And the cat!
Freddy Go on. A quarter to three.
D'Arcy (*going upstairs*) You may have to call me.
Freddy By Gad! I'll call you something if I do!

D'Arcy goes upstairs, he waits halfway up, watching Freddy

Freddy switches out the standard lamp and crosses to D'Arcy

They are seen going upstairs

CURTAIN

SCENE 2

Mrs Hewlett's room, a comfortable and well-furnished room with a fire still burning brightly enough to throw some illumination. It reveals Mrs Hewlett asleep in bed L. The door is L. The window in the back wall has curtains over it which reach to the ground. Other usual bedroom furniture is about the room, including the chest of drawers on which rests the jewel-case

Mrs Hewlett, who is wearing a boudoir cap, is facing the light, sound asleep, and covered with a mass of bedclothes including a quilt. Only her face can be seen, her deep, regular breathing heard. The window curtains are cautiously parted and Freddy appears. He peers towards the bed, then silently enters. He takes a step or two to the bed and scrutinizes her; then turns again to the window and signals. D'Arcy arrives on the scene. They are both wearing dressing-gowns over pyjamas and their hands are gloved

Freddy indicates the bed and D'Arcy crosses towards it and takes guard over Mrs Hewlett, while Freddy immediately goes to the jewel-case. He brings it to the firelight. D'Arcy, engrossed in Freddy's actions, forgets to watch Mrs Hewlett who suddenly heaves restlessly and speaks in her sleep

Mrs Hewlett Where?

Freddy turns quickly and for a moment or two watches intently. D'Arcy produces the bottle and whispers to Freddy

D'Arcy Douse?
Freddy (*whispering*) Be prepared to.

D'Arcy takes out his handkerchief, then remembering, holds it doubtfully. Freddy, without apparently taking notice, puts out a hand and whips it away from him. D'Arcy crosses to the towel-horse and gets a face towel, which he brings back to the bed. He sniffs at the bottle and is almost overpowered himself by the effects. Freddy, who has been operating on the jewel-case with a small instrument, has now got it open. He puts it on a chair, takes a thin silk petticoat of Mrs Hewlett's which is hanging over the back of the chair, and placing this on the ground, empties the jewel-case and quickly wraps the petticoat round the jewellery. A distant sound is heard, like that of a chair being overturned on a parquet floor. Freddy stands motionless, listening. D'Arcy makes questioning gestures. Then comes a more definite sound of movement outside the window. Freddy turns, signs to D'Arcy to conceal himself, and himself quickly crosses the room to the window curtain, snatching a large bath towel from the towel-horse as he passes

After a moment the window curtains are parted. In the moonlight appears the face of Simon Veal peering in

Simon (*in a subdued voice but with challenge*) Margery!

Silence. D'Arcy stands half-hidden by curtain. Simon holding to the sill with both hands, leans a trifle farther into the room. With a lightning movement Freddy flings the bath towel over Simon's head, and putting one hand to Simon's mouth through the towel, twists the towel tightly and signals to D'Arcy who joins him. Mrs Hewlett gives a heave in bed and again groans loudly in her sleep

Freddy leaves the struggling Simon to D'Arcy and hurries to the bed. Freddy takes a glance at Mrs Hewlett; then unbolts the door and opens it. D'Arcy is struggling with Simon, who makes muffled sounds through the towel. Freddy returns and grapples with him, indicating to D'Arcy to go. D'Arcy makes for the door, forgetting the jewels. Freddy lets go with one hand to snap his fingers, which recalls D'Arcy, who catches up the petticoat and—darts from the room, shutting the door

But Simon has managed to release himself. He strikes out blindly, over-balances and falls back with a cry. There is a crash of glass and a thud. Freddy darts towards the door and just as he has bolted it Mrs Hewlett wakes with an exclamation

Mrs Hewlett What's that?

Freddy throws the bedclothes over her head as she puts up her bedside light. There is a great upheaval of the bedclothes. Freddy flies to the window and as she flings off the bedclothes slips behind the window curtain. Mrs Hewlett sees the empty jewel-case. She screams, and hugging the quilt round her, gets out of bed. She looks at the open window, then hurries to the door, unbolts it and— runs out screaming

Help! Help! Thieves and burglars! My joolry! Help! Help! Help!
(*Her voice grows more distant*)

Freddy flies to the door, looks out then follows her out, pulling off his gloves

Freddy (*heard in the passage*) Hallo! What's up? Who is it? What's the matter?

CURTAIN

SCENE 3

The hall is in darkness, except for the moonlight shining through the row of windows running along the back wall

Oswald comes downstairs stealthily with a lighted candle and emerges into this moonlight. He is in his pyjamas, dressing-gown and bed-slippers. He holds a cheque in his hand and as he advances he makes the mistake of looking back guiltily over his shoulder, with the result that he knocks over a brass tray with a crash

Oswald Oh, my God!

He puts it into place again, then listens for a moment and goes to the front door, which he opens. He looks out expectantly

Joan (*heard from the staircase—enters from bedroom*) What's that down there?

Oswald blows out candle, quickly and quietly closes the front door and slinks back—coming downstairs

Who is it?

Oswald gains the archway as Joan appears—he sneaks through this archway and off

Joan comes boldly down into the hall, crosses and switches on the lights. As she does so D'Arcy comes on landing, bolts downstairs, and runs right into her, he is still wearing his gloves and carrying the petticoat containing the jewellery)

D'Arcy!
D'Arcy Good Lord!
Joan What are you doing?
D'Arcy Let me go. I must get out.
Joan Where are you going?

D'Arcy To the post.
Joan What?
D'Arcy Parcel post.
Joan What d'you mean? What have you got there?
D'Arcy The parcel.
Joan Come here. What is that? (*Tries to get at the bundle*)
D'Arcy Don't! Dash! (*He drops a bracelet from the bundle*)
Joan What's this mean?
D'Arcy I've dropped it.
Joan D'Arcy! You've taken it.
D'Arcy Yes. For you.
Joan Good heavens! All her jewellery. You've *robbed* it.
D'Arcy Oh, darling, not that hard word.
Joan Well, what *have* you done?
D'Arcy I've removed.
Joan You mad fool! Take it all back.
D'Arcy I can't now. Even if I could, I couldn't.
Joan You must.

Mrs Hewlett's voice heard exactly as at end of Scene 2

Mrs Hewlett (*off*) Help! Help! Help! Thieves and burglars! My
joolry! Help! Help!
D'Arcy Listen. Quick. I must get out. Good-bye.

Hurries out

Freddy (*heard off*) Hallo! What's up? What is it? What's the
matter?
Sir George (*heard off*) Hallo, Freddy, what is it, what's the matter?
Freddy (*off*) Here! George! Harry! D'Arcy! Everyone! Quick.
Sir George (*off*) Someone's been burgled.
Mrs Hewlett Yes. I have.

She comes downstairs

Joan quickly slips the bracelet up her arm, under her sleeve

Freddy (*heard off*) Buckley! Everyone! Get up! Come out, damn it!

Mrs Hewlett coming downstairs

Mrs Hewlett All my joolry. I've been thieved.
Joan Did you see anyone?
Mrs Hewlett No. He stifled me with me quilt.

Freddy, Sir George and Harry come hurrying downstairs

Freddy (*coming downstairs—to Mrs Hewlett*) Calm now. Did you see
him?

Mrs Hewlett No, he got away out of the window.
Freddy How do you know that, if you didn't see him?
Mrs Hewlett Because my door was still bolted on the inside.
Freddy (*to the two guests*) Run round quick and have a look.

Sir George and Harry go out

*A Footman and two scared Maids in overcoats over their nightdresses enter.
Lady Chudleigh runs downstairs. The two male guests go to front door*

(*To Servants*) Come on, you! Everyone! Where's Buckley?
(*Shouting*) Buckley!
Sir George (*just inside—at front door*) This door was unlocked.

Mrs Hewlett sits in a state of collapse

Joan D'Arcy opened it.
Freddy D'Arcy?
Joan Yes. When the row started he ran down and dashed out.

Ruth comes downstairs—stands at foot. Buckley enters with Maids

Buckley Yes, sir?
Freddy (*to Buckley*) Come on! I want everyone. The whole lot.

Buckley goes out

She nods and goes up

*Mrs Hewlett sits on chair and another Footman, two more Maids and a
Cook are brought in by Buckley*

Lady Chudleigh (*to Joan*) Hallo, who are you? When did *you* come
here?
Joan Late tonight. I'm D'Arcy Tuck's fianceé.
Lady Chudleigh Oh, I see.
Freddy (*interrupting*) Yes. Don't interfere please. Sorry.

Freddy switches on lights

*Sir George and Harry run in from front door. Oswald slinks in unnoticed—
cross back of table to Mrs Hewlett*

Sir George It's old Veal.
Freddy What?
Harry There's a ladder up to the window. He's fallen through the
conservatory.
Mrs Hewlett Simon?
Sir George He's knocked out. Unconscious.
Mrs Hewlett But my joolry?

Harry No sign of that. Only a towel.
Freddy A towel?

Prudence appearing hurriedly on the stairs

Prudence Freddy! Freddy! A man! I saw a man!
Freddy You did? Where? Quick!
Prudence Running down the drive. I saw him from the landing window.
Freddy When?
Prudence Just now. He went past the lodge and out of the gate.
Sir George It may be Tuck.

D'Arcy enters at front door

D'Arcy No, it isn't me.
Freddy Where've *you* been?

Prudence comes downstairs stands at foot

D'Arcy To the gar-ounds.
Harry Did you see him too?
D'Arcy See who?
Prudence A man! I saw a man escaping.
D'Arcy No. That's why I went out. To look. But I didn't.
Freddy Well, it's too late now. Quick! Telephone the police.
D'Arcy Yes. Good idea. (*Goes to telephone*)
Freddy (*turning to Servants*) Everybody here?
Buckley Yes, sir. All my lot.
D'Arcy Hallo! Hallo!
Freddy Did any of you see anything? Come on. Speak up.
D'Arcy Hallo! Hallo!
Freddy Here! Let me do it.
D'Arcy All right. I can 'phone. I've done it before. (*Suddenly holding the 'phone up*) Hallo! Here! Look!
Sir George The wire's cut.
Freddy By Gad! Then he got in her room.
Harry This window's open.
Freddy (*cross to window*) Where? Yes, and broken.
D'Arcy Yes. Into pieces.
Freddy Here! You! D'Arcy! Don't stand looking like that! Go for the police. In a car! Quick! Take any car.
D'Arcy Oh, I'd better take mine, hadn't I?
Freddy Well, go on, take it. Hurry up. Wait a moment. (*Cross to sideboard*) The garage key.
D'Arcy I don't want that, do I?
Freddy (*at drawer of table*) Yes. Here. Take it. (*Hands D'Arcy key*)

D'Arcy That'll do splendidly. Yes. Where's the police station? Oh, never mind. That doesn't matter.

He goes out of front door

Freddy (*to Footman*) You, William. Go with Mr Tuck. Show him the way.
William Yes, sir.

Footman hurries out after D'Arcy

Freddy And Harry. You take another car for the doctor. Doctor Turner—you know where he lives.
Harry Yes, right, Freddy.

Exit

Mrs Hewlett What about Simon?
Freddy We'll see to him. You go and wait in the dining-room. Pru, take her there.

Prudence crosses to Mrs Hewlett and—takes her off

Mrs Hewlett I want my dressing-gown.
Freddy Then you'd better stick to your quilt.

Prudence and Mrs Hewlett exeunt

Lady Chudleigh Shall we go with them?
Freddy Yes, you two go.

The two ladies go

Joan is about to follow

Not you for a minute, please. Now, Buckley, go to Mr Veal. You, (*To Oswald*) you go too. You're his cousin or nephew or some damn thing. You (*To a Maid*) Brown, open the French window into the billiard room. Carry him in there, Buckley.

Maid (Brown) exits

Buckley Yes, sir.

Goes with Oswald out by front door

Freddy (*to the other Maids*) You go in the kitchen and wait there till the police come. Go on, Cook, not the first time you've done it.

Only Freddy, Joan and Sir George remain. Freddy turns to Joan, who is at foot of stairs

You were the first down here, it seems?
Joan Yes, the man was here when I came down.

Freddy (*keenly*) Who, the burglar?

Joan Yes. He knocked something over. That's what disturbed me. He got away just as I came down.

Sir George You've got some nerve.

Joan Yes, p'raps I have. Anyhow, I turned on the light—

Freddy Then the row started, and you say D'Arcy came running down?

Joan That's right. He dashed out.

Freddy Did he say anything?

Joan Well, simply—'Did you see anyone?' or 'It's a burglar' or something—I forget what he said now.

Freddy (*to Sir George*) Well, the fellow can only just have got away.

Buckley returns at front door

Buckley Sir!

Freddy Well?

Buckley Here's Mrs Orlock, sir. Wants to see you.

Freddy Well, what the Hell does she want?

Buckley disappears

Mrs Orlock enters at front door. She is in day clothes but evidently hastily thrown on. She is without a hat and her hair is dishevelled

Mrs Orlock I saw it happen. I saw it.

Freddy *What* did you see? From the start. Let's have it.

Mrs Orlock The gentleman sleeping in the Lodge came and knocked at my door. 'Get up,' he says, 'and come out'.

Freddy What time was that?

Mrs Orlock Just before three. I went out to him. He had all his clothes on.

Freddy Never mind what he had on. What did he say?

Mrs Orlock He says, 'I've seen a ladder,' he says, 'up against a winder at the house,' he says. 'I'm going to see what it is,' he says. 'You foller in case you're wanted,' he says. With that he made off.

Freddy And did you follow?

Mrs Orlock I 'ad to put on some shoes and a coat. Then I did. Sure enough I saw the ladder and him on top. He was strugglin' with a man in the winder. He 'ad a sheet over 'is head.

Sir George Who had? The man inside?

Mrs Orlock No, my gentleman.

Freddy What did the man inside look like?

Mrs Orlock I couldn't see. 'E was in the dark, in the room. I was over there by the bend of the drive.

Freddy Well—go on.

Mrs Orlock Suddenly he waved his arms, like as if he got a blow, and crashed through the conservatory roof.
Freddy He was knocked down. You're sure of that?
Mrs Orlock Positive. He was flung down. I screamed out. I watched for a minute than I went back into the Lodge.
Freddy Why?
Mrs Orlock What else could I do, like I was? I put on what clothes I could and came up 'ere.

D'Arcy hurries in at front door

D'Arcy We got a Bobby, just up the road.
Freddy What's the good of *one*?
D'Arcy It's all right. He sent the footman for another.
Freddy What have you done with him?
D'Arcy He's here. He's gone to see the—accident.
Freddy I'll see him. Come on, George. (*To Mrs Orlock*) You'd better come too.

Freddy goes off with Sir George

Mrs Orlock remains for a moment, looking at D'Arcy, who dislikes it. Then she turns and—also goes out

D'Arcy (*looks round to see the coast is clear, coming to Joan, who has turned from him*) Joan—darling——
Joan (*facing him, almost with anger*) Do you understand what you've done?
D'Arcy Do you understand why I did it?
Joan Yes, I think I do. Is *that* what you really wanted?
D'Arcy No, but this was my idea of how to get it back.
Joan You came here on purpose to do this. You planned it all—all this—this window—telephone—everything you did.
D'Arcy Yes, I did it all on my own. It was your property that's why. It was for you.
Joan For me! You know I'd never touch it even if I got it. You were never going to tell me.
D'Arcy P'raps not. But I was going to give it to you.
Joan Yes. How much of it?
D'Arcy Well, half.
Joan That's candid, anyhow. It was that you wanted, not me.
D'Arcy You'll be sorry you said that—when you think of me doing 'time'—a long sentence, I expect. Dartmoor and the 'cat'.
Joan All our happiness ruined just for this beastly money.
D'Arcy If you've finished with me I may as well be in gaol—But—one day—you'll realize—it was all done for your sake. Honestly. (*Taking her by the arm*) Joan!

Joan Oh, don't. (*She steps away. Almost cries*)

D'Arcy Well, what are you going to do?

Joan If I speak now you'll be arrested.

D'Arcy But you *can't* speak, you can't. Because you still love me.

Joan (*after a struggle with her emotion—turning away*) Yes, but don't you see how terrible this is for me. (*Crying*)

She turns quickly to the stairs as—

> *Freddy busily re-enters. He hurries down to the servants' door and speaks into the kitchen quarters*

Freddy (*to D'Arcy*) The Inspector's here. Now, please, in the dining-room—all of you.

The four Servants enter and go off with Buckley

Keep them standing by, Buckley, till the Inspector's done with them.

Mrs Orlock has entered and they pass her. About to speak to Joan when he sees Mrs Orlock

What do you want now?

Mrs Orlock There's something I haven't mentioned. Maybe I should have done.

Freddy Well, mention it now.

Mrs Orlock Before I went back into the Lodge, I saw the lights in this hall go up.

Freddy Quite right. This young lady put them up.

Mrs Orlock Then I saw someone run out. That gentleman, if I'm not mistaken.

D'Arcy No, no. No, you're not.

Freddy We know all about that.

Mrs Orlock Yes, sir, but I know *this*. Between the time Mr Veal was knocked down and the time these lights went up——

Freddy Well?

Mrs Orlock Nobody else got down that ladder. That I *do* know.

D'Arcy Well, Freddy—he may have—hidden somewhere——

Freddy In that case he must have hidden before he ran down the drive.

Mrs Orlock But that's not correct, sir. Nobody *did* run down the drive. I'd have seen him.

D'Arcy But he might have slipped by you. While you were dressing.

Mrs Orlock No, I kept a sharp look-out. Nobody don't slip by *me* as easy as all that.

Sir George enters

Sir George Freddy! Where are you?
Freddy I'm here.
Sir George Can I speak to you a moment?
Freddy Yes. (*To Mrs Orlock*) You can go through there to the others.

She goes

(*Turns to Joan*) I'm sorry, but the Inspector wants everyone there —to hear all they know.
Joan I've told *you* all I know. I know nothing else—nothing whatever.
Freddy Well, you might go and tell the Inspector that, will you?
Joan Certainly.

She goes off

Freddy D'Arcy, you, too.
D'Arcy Yes. (*To Sir George. Turns to Freddy*) Oh, what a thing for someone to have done.
Freddy (*to Sir George*) Well, what is it?

D'Arcy goes out

Sir George I say, old man. This is serious.
Freddy Well, I know that.
Sir George Yes, but now it's damned serious.
Freddy Why?
Sir George That man—old Veal——
Freddy What about him?
Sir George He's dead.
Freddy He's dead. Are you sure?

D'Arcy appears at door and is coming in but steps back when he sees that Freddy is not alone

Sir George Yes.
Freddy All right. I'll come.

Sir George goes off

Freddy is at the same moment going. Closes door

D'Arcy enters at front door

D'Arcy Freddy! One word. He's dead.
Freddy Yes. This is the very devil. We know it was a fall, an accident. But in the eyes of the law it's murder.
D'Arcy Murder? Who by?
Freddy Both of us. And you know what that means?

D'Arcy What?
Freddy The rope.

He goes off

D'Arcy remains

D'Arcy Rope. (*Cross to table supporting himself*)

CURTAIN

ACT III

Scene i

The Office of Chief Constable Grierson, Scotland Yard. Door down L. *Two writing-tables, one downstage* R., *one up* R. C.; *the latter having a large album and some files on it. A small armchair and several smaller chairs set to face the* R. C. *writing-table, also a chair down on the other side of the writing-table*

Chief Constable Grierson is sitting at the writing-table. He is an elderly and quite benevolent-looking man of ordinary class. He is examining two towels—a bath towel and a face towel. While he is doing so Chief Detective Inspector Sibley enters with a sheet of paper. Sibley is a sharper type, a few years younger than Grierson and rather more aggressive in his methods. A PC in undress uniform is at door without belt or helmet

Sibley Here's that statement, sir.

Grierson Oh. The one made by Mrs Orlock.

Sibley Yes. The later statement.

Grierson (*talking and looking at it*) Yes. It was this point I wanted to check—when she saw Tuck run out of the front door.

Sibley He made for the garage. He had the stuff with him then.

Grierson She didn't see that. That's just your idea.

Sibley I shall prove it. Unless I'm mistaken. And very shortly.

Grierson Have you got 'em here?

Sibley Yes. They've both turned up.

Grierson Tuck and Malone?

Sibley Yes.

Grierson They're nicely up to time.

Sibley No reason why they shouldn't be. We haven't let them know they're under suspicion.

Grierson Think you can get 'em to talk?

Sibley Oh, I think so. Tuck, anyhow.

Grierson H'm. About time, too. Three weeks gone by, you know. Pity *you* weren't on it at the start.

Sibley Thank you, sir. It's clearing up nicely now. You see the job *must* have come from inside the house. This statement's correct. Nobody *did* follow down that ladder. And nobody did run down that drive.

Grierson Well, then the bolted door?

Sibley Malone stayed in the bedroom while the old lady woke up.

Grierson Nerve.

Sibley Yes. But if what Marchant thinks about Malone is right, he doesn't suffer from lack of nerve.

Grierson No. By the way, we'll have Marchant in here for this.

Sibley Yes, sir. (*To Constable at door*) Davis! Sergeant Marchant.

Davis Yessir.

Disappears

Grierson What date was it Malone went abroad?

Sibley Fifteenth. The day after the inquest was adjourned. Came back on the twenty-first.

Grierson Too bad you know. No doubt he got away with the pickin's.

Sibley That's his game, according to Marchant. Look here now. (*Crosses round back of table to Grierson, places notes on table, referring to notes*) Malone goes to Africa, September 1925. That was just after that Brook Street Hotel case. And we never got down to that.

Grierson Doesn't follow. Here's his last trip—about the fifth of February to Monte Carlo. There was nothing at that time.

Sibley There was—a big job out there—at Monte Carlo, soon after he got there.

Grierson There's always big jobs *there*. It's a public hobby.

As Sibley is about to speak

Oh, I'm not going against you. Just making sure.

Davis opens door as Marchant appears

Yes, come in, Marchant.

Marchant is a quiet, thorough type of man. At the moment his manner is pleased and eager

Marchant I was just coming to see you, sir. I've hit on something else.

Sibley About Malone?

Marchant Yes, sir. I knew I'd seen him before somewhere. That's what made me so confident.

Grierson Well—who is he?

Marchant You remember that Leatherhead case—the Honourable Mrs Trelawny's stuff. I was on that.

Sibley Was he there?

Marchant One of the house-party. Not only that. Ten days after it happened he went to Paris.

Grierson How d'you know that?

Marchant Mrs Orlock, sir. You'll find it there. (*Indicates notes*) Excuse me. Yes. (*Looks over notes on table*) Here he goes. End of last June—to Paris.

Grierson How does Mrs Orlock know these dates?

Sibley Why, because her husband had to forward things—reports from the stables and so on. There's a book with all the dates in.

Grierson I see. Oh, yes; it looks quite promising.

Sibley (*to Marchant*) Well—anything else for me, before I see them?

Marchant No sir. Nothing I haven't given you. (*Looking at notebook*) His mode of living—extravagance and that, and no occupation.

Sibley Yes, yes——

Grierson But you told me he'd got a private income.

Marchant His father left him twenty thousand pounds.

Grierson That's a thousand a year.

Sibley Yes, and he lives at the rate of ten and earns nothing.

Grierson Well——

Marchant Then the sister. Only had one sister and she died in South Africa nineteen-eighteen.

Sibley Yes. Ethel Vera Malone.

Marchant Correct, sir. This Prudence isn't his sister at all.

Sibley Yes. I've got all that.

Grierson Of course, there again. That's highly suspicious—but not in itself a crime. If you could hang a man for saying a girl's his sister when she isn't—maybe some of *us* wouldn't be where we are.

Sibley (*slightly impatient*) Well, are you ready for them, sir?

Grierson D'Arcy Tuck—nothing known?

Marchant No sir. Looks like his first job. But with *him* of course there's the *motive*—this Hewlett property.

Grierson Quite so, quite so. Yes, all right—go ahead. Send for Bryant.

He rises and Sibley takes his place at the table. Grierson goes to chair apart from the others. Marchant to door, where he speaks to Davis and returns. Grierson puts towels away

Sibley (*as he takes Grierson's place*) Thank you, sir.

Marchant (*to Davis*) Tell Bryant to come along.

Grierson It looks to me as if you might find this Malone a pretty tough nut to crack.

Sibley Yes, quite possibly. But you wait till you see his pal.

Bryant, a Sergeant-writer, in plain clothes, enters with his materials

Grierson I shall want you to take this down, Bryant.

Bryant (*quite used to this*) Yes, sir. (*Sits at other table*)
Sibley I'll have Malone first. (*To Marchant*)
Marchant Yes, sir. (*Cross to door, opens it and tells Davis to call Malone*)
Sibley (*turning, rather abruptly, to Grierson*) Of course, there's to be no question what we're out for here?
Grierson Certainly not—not if you can land 'em with it.
Sibley If I can bring home the robbery to them, we're going to run them for murder.
Grierson Absolutely.

Freddy is shown in. He is serious, but without any apprehension whatever, it appears

Freddy Good evening, Mr Sibley.
Sibley Good evening. This is Chief Constable Grierson.
Freddy How d'you do?
Sibley And Sergeant Marchant you know. (*Over left shoulder*)
Freddy (*to Marchant*) Yes. Funny thing—when I met you the other day I couldn't place you. You came to the Trelawny's at Leatherhead when there was that burglary there. I was staying there at the time.
Marchant (*non-committal*) Oh, yes, sir? (*Exchange looks with Grierson and Sibley*)
Grierson Take a chair, Mr Malone. That's a comfortable one.
Freddy (*sitting in armchair*) Thank you. (*Looks round room with interest*)
Sibley Well, we're still very busy on this case.
Freddy I'm glad of that.
Sibley We're trying to eliminate. We get hold of all those who—possibly—might be guilty; and make quite sure they're not.
Freddy Oh, I see. Oh, then I'm here to be eliminated?
Sibley (*without a change of manner*) We hope so.
Freddy (*with a laugh*) So do I, I'm sure. Really, this is quite an interesting experience.
Sibley This man is here to take notes. Have you any objection?
Freddy None whatever.
Sibley Now—about yourself, please, a few details. You're very well off?
Freddy Very. I've made a lot of money.
Sibley How?
Freddy Stock exchange. Speculating, mostly. I've made a fortune. Well—two—(*To Bryant*) Make it two.
Sibley H'm. You travel a lot?
Freddy Yes. All over the shop—shooting, you know. I go to the Continent, too. I was there last week—Paris.
Sibley What did you go to Paris for?

Freddy (*hesitating a moment*) Has that got to be taken down?

Sibley smiles

Well, I had a business excuse. I went to see some people who deal in big game trophies—Mornay and Co., Rue Suisse.
Sibley Did that business take you a week to do?
Freddy No. But once in Paris—it usually takes me a week.
Sibley Besides, you haven't been big game shooting lately.
Freddy No, but I'm going again next month.
Sibley That is, if you're through with this affair.
Freddy You mean, if *you* are. You won't want me.
Sibley Oh, we might. (*Short pause*) How many sisters have you got?
Freddy One. Prudence. The one you've met.
Sibley (*a statement, not a question*) Just the one.
Freddy (*after a pause*) I had another. Ethel. She died in South Africa ten years ago. So I haven't got *her*, have I?

Grierson looks at Freddy, then

Sibley (*quickly*) Is this one really your sister?
Freddy Who—Pru?
Sibley Yes.
Freddy Yes, of course—why not? Both my parents were entirely respectable.
Sibley Her birth was never certified.
Freddy (*looking genuinely surprised*) Wasn't it? That's odd. Still, I'm afraid I can't answer for that. I was at school at the time.
Sibley And she was never mentioned in your father's will.
Freddy No. My father died before she was born. He died in nineteen hundred—(*Sees Sibley glancing at a note*) February, wasn't it?
Sibley Well?
Freddy Yes—and Prudence was born in June. Still, you can take it from me. Prudence is certainly my sister. I don't know why you should think she wasn't—or what that's got to do with it. However —go on.
Sibley Unfortunate that you should have had workmen's ladders about when there was this valuable jewellery in the house.
Freddy There's often valuable jewellery in my house.
Sibley Someone knew the ladder was handy and the right window to put it to. Who would have known that?
Freddy Oh, lots of people.
Sibley Right. Now to narrow it down. Who, in addition, could have known which was the jewel-case, and whereabouts it was in the room?

Freddy Yes, who?

Sibley Your sister was with Mrs Hewlett while she undressed.

Freddy My sister was, yes. But—look here, you keep on about my sister—what are you——? (*Pauses*)

Sibley Yes?

Freddy Are you suggesting that my sister told somebody where this jewel-case was?

Sibley Yes. (*His tone is quite quiet and conversational*)

Freddy What!

Sibley (*as before*) Yes. If it points to that.

Freddy (*jumping up*) Look here——!

Sibley Well?

Freddy (*subsiding*) Oh, I—suppose I must control myself, but this is ridiculous.

Sibley Did your sister tell *you* where the jewel-case was?

Freddy Me? Oh, it's me now? Oh, don't be so damn silly.

Sibley I've told you I must eliminate. Can I eliminate you on the evidence?

Freddy What evidence? A man broke in. He burst the window. He cut the telephone wire.

Sibley Couldn't you have done that?

Freddy Oh—yes, I suppose so. I don't quite know what with.

Sibley The broken window was a blind.

Freddy Oh, was that me, too? I'm an ingenious bloke, aren't I? Then I broke open the jewel-case without disturbing the sleeping beauty?

Sibley Well, somebody did.

Freddy Look here. That bedroom door was bolted on the inside. Whoever did it got away down that ladder. Surely to goodness you don't need to be told that.

Sibley Can you produce anyone who saw you come out of your own bedroom when the alarm was given?

Freddy No, I was the first out.

Sibley Oh, I understood Mr Tuck was the first out.

Freddy Well, he says so—yes. I didn't see him, he didn't see me. But all this is absolute waste of time. The burglar was seen by my sister.

Sibley I don't believe that.

Freddy What?

Sibley shakes his head

Oh! Well, I suppose you're entitled to say what you like in here. But you seem to have forgotten, as well as being seen by my sister, the man was heard in the hall by Miss Hewlett.

Sibley I hadn't forgotten. The man was detected by two persons— *your* sister and the fiancée of Mr Tuck.

Freddy Exactly.

Sibley Exactly. And this job was done by two men.

Freddy Two. (*Suddenly seems amused*) Excuse my smiling. I don't think I should shine as a burglar, but I should love to see D'Arcy Tuck being one.

Sibley (*rather more intensely*) Tell me this, please. Why did you ever make friends with Mrs Hewlett? She's not your class at all.

Freddy Her son wanted to marry my sister.

Sibley Did you approve?

Freddy No, I did not. (*To Bryant*) Underlined, please.

Sibley Mrs Hewlett says you *did* approve.

Freddy I temporized, that's all. You know what sisters are. If you say to your sister, 'You're not to marry that man,' what happens? She goes up like a rocket, and next time you see her she's looking at bassinet catalogues.

Sibley (*after a brief pause, with finality*) Mr Malone, as you may have realized, we know a good deal.

Freddy No, I can't say I've realized that at all.

Sibley One of the things we know is that you're not telling the truth.

Freddy Thank you. I'm almost sorry to say I can't lose my temper with you. It's all too damned ludicrous for that.

Sibley It may be found that the death of Simon Veal was accidental. I can't hold out any promise, but it's possible. Now you've got an idea of how much we know, don't you think it might be worth your while to make a statement? Think carefully.

Freddy I don't need t.o Here's my statement. If you think I've got anything whatever to do with this affair, you're wrong. (*Looking at Bryant*) That'll do. Put that down.

Sibley (*to Marchant*) Send for Mr Tuck.

Marchant (*to Davis*) Mr Tuck.

Davis exits

Sibley again turns to Freddy—Grierson passes note to Sibley—Sibley grunts satisfaction

Sibley I ask you this. Why did you invite Mrs Hewlett and Mr Tuck together to your house?

Freddy Knowing Mr Tuck I thought that was the best way to annoy Mrs Hewlett.

Sibley With Mr Tuck's full knowledge and cooperation?

Freddy Yes.

D'Arcy is shown in. His manner is effusive in order to hide any apprehension. The door is closed

D'Arcy Hallo, Inspector—how's everything?

Sibley Mr Tuck. Before we go any further, answer me this question.

D'Arcy Which one?

Sibley The one I'm going to ask you.

D'Arcy Oh, that one? Rather. Anything I can do to help.

Sibley With what motive did you arrange to meet Mrs Hewlett at Mr Malone's house?

D'Arcy He asked me to.

Sibley Why did he?

D'Arcy Well, you'd better ask him.

Sibley I want to know what reason he gave for asking you.

D'Arcy I asked him to ask me.

Sibley You've just said he asked *you.*

D'Arcy Well, he did. I asked him to ask me, so he asked me.

Sibley Why did you ask him to ask you? That's what I want to know.

D'Arcy Well, say so. It makes it so much easier. (*Pause*) So that's that.

Sibley Oh, no, it isn't. Answer my question, please.

D'Arcy Which one?

Sibley Why did you want to be there at the same time as Mrs Hewlett?

D'Arcy I didn't want to be. He wanted me to be.

Sibley But you distinctly said you requested him to invite you.

D'Arcy Well, of course. He said, 'I want you to be there,' so I said, 'Then ask me'—so he asked me.

Sibley Mr Tuck—this is Chief Constable Grierson.

Grierson Sit down, Mr Tuck.

D'Arcy sits

Sibley Sergeant Bryant is here to take notes. Have you any objection?

D'Arcy Have I?

Freddy I don't suppose so—why should you have?

D'Arcy No!—of course not.

Sibley Mr Tuck. You and Mr Malone have been sent for because you're suspected of knowing something about this crime. Now, do you wish to make any statement?

D'Arcy Yes.

Sibley Ah! Well, think it over. Don't be in a hurry.

D'Arcy It won't take long. It's only one syllable.

Freddy Now, D'Arcy. Don't be vulgar.

D'Arcy I don't care. I'm going to say it. Rats!

Sibley You'd be well advised to be a *little* less discourteous.

D'Arcy Very well then—mice!

Sibley I must put some questions to you, that's all.

D'Arcy I warn you—I may not answer.

Sibley Any refusal to answer may be brought up in court.

Short pause

You don't seem at all surprised at being suspected.

D'Arcy Don't I? (*off his guard*) I thought I did. I meant to be.

Sibley Come, come, Mr Tuck. Everything will be taken into account. Why don't you tell us all you know?

D'Arcy I can't. It's impossible. You know what I mean? I don't know anything, so its impossible.

Sibley (*resignedly*) All right—if you won't take my advice—(*Consults papers*)

A brief menacing pause

D'Arcy takes an obviously careless glance at Freddy, who remains absolutely stolid

Your motive in running round to the garage that night was, I suppose, to see if the burglar was there?

D'Arcy (*turning to Grierson*) Naturally, I thought he might be trying to pinch a car.

Sibley I see. So you admit you *did* run round to the garage?

D'Arcy Yes, I did.

Pause

When?

Sibley Directly the alarm was given—if not before.

D'Arcy Ah! Yes. No. I went there but when I went there—wasn't—

Sibley Wasn't what?

D'Arcy Wasn't when you think.

Sibley What?

D'Arcy Our whens are different. I went there afterwards. With a footman for the police. To get a car with a footman. For the police—I—with a footman went.

Sibley You just said you went because you thought a car might have been stolen.

D'Arcy (*to Grierson, ignoring Sibley*) I did. I *said* to the footman, I said, 'Footman, I shouldn't be surprised if we find a car has been stolen.'

Sibley And he replied what?

D'Arcy No. He didn't. He didn't hear not even enough to make him say what.

Sibley I can prove you ran downstairs, out of the house and straight to the garage. Now, definitely, did you or did you not?

D'Arcy I did not. (*Pause*) Unless——

Sibley Unless what?

D'Arcy Unless you mean when I did.

Sibley In any case why were you down in the hall so soon?

D'Arcy So soon as what?

Sibley Well, so soon as you *were*?

D'Arcy But that's ridiculous—I mean, if I was there as soon as I was there—I mean—naturally—there I was.

Sibley (*tapping the table impatiently*) Don't trifle with me. Mrs Hewlett came straight downstairs. By the time she got to the hall you'd run down and outside. Explain that.

D'Arcy She was screaming. Her sounds travel a great deal faster than she does.

Sibley Why did you run downstairs so quickly and out of the house?

D'Arcy To look.

Sibley To look for what?

D'Arcy To look to see. To see the man.

Sibley How did you know there was a man?

D'Arcy I didn't. If I'd known there was a man I shouldn't have had to look to see.

Sibley So this was it—you were asleep. You were awakened by a scream. Immediately you jumped out of bed, ran downstairs, unbolted the front door, and dashed out after some imaginary burglar. Very brave of you, wasn't it!

D'Arcy I'm a Tuck.

A pause. D'Arcy thinks he is doing pretty well and takes a self-satisfied glance at Freddy

Sibley (*deliberately*) Even before you got downstairs—Miss Joan Hewlett—was already there.

D'Arcy Yes, and why? Because *she* had heard someone in the hall. Which only *proves*—something.

Sibley Why didn't she express surprise at seeing you?

D'Arcy She did.

Sibley Oh, very well then—why *did* she? (*Pause*)

D'Arcy What? I don't know—I mean—why ask about *her*? This had nothing to do with *her*. (*Losing a good deal of his confidence*)

Sibley How d'you know it hadn't?

D'Arcy What? Well—good Lord—are you saying it had?

Sibley When she saw you in the hall—did she know *then* you had the jewels with you?

D'Arcy Of course she didn't.

Sibley Oh, she found that out later?

D'Arcy She—she didn't know at all. Of course she didn't—I mean, because I hadn't. How dare you? (*Anxiously looking at Freddy for inspiration*)

Sibley The jewels were wrapped in Mrs Hewlett's petticoat which has been missing since. They were taken out of the house. You were the first out of the house. You were seen returning from the garage by Mrs Orlock. A few minutes later Mr Malone deliberately sent you back to the garage. We know all that. (*Rising*) But *now*, what about Miss Joan Hewlett's position? Very much depends on what you say.

D'Arcy (*looks at Freddy*) I—I absolutely refuse to—to have her lugged into this.

Sibley Well, I make no conditions—but if she can be cleared, so much the better.

D'Arcy (*rising*) Cleared? She? What are you trying to make out about her?

Sibley She was standing there in the hall with the lights up. How could you have passed her and opened the front door, carrying those things in the petticoat, without her seeing?

As D'Arcy hesitates

Come on, show me. Demonstrate to me how you could have. If you want to state her innocence now's your chance.

D'Arcy Well, if I—if I—if I carried them like this——(*With his hands in front*)

Sibley I'm her. Standing here. There's the staircase, where you come from—there's the front door. Now, show me.

D'Arcy Well—these are the stairs—if I had them like this (*Hands behind his back*) would you notice?

Grierson looks at Freddy and D'Arcy during this

Sibley H'm—possibly not—if you went out like that. Is that how you did carry them?

D'Arcy No, I didn't. Because you know quite well if I'd had them at all she must have noticed. (*D'Arcy regains confidence and sits*) Pooh! Of course she'd have noticed. A great big bundle like that.

Sibley And how do you *know* it was a big bundle?

D'Arcy (*nonplussed; then suddenly inspired*) Well, it *must* have been a big bundle, you've just said yourself—it was in Mrs Hewlett's petticoat.

Sibley shrugs and resumes his seat

Freddy May I say something?

D'Arcy Yes.

Sibley Well?

Freddy The garage was locked. The key was in a drawer; only the butler, my sister and myself knew which drawer. I took the key out of the drawer and handed Mr Tuck the key in front of the whole household.

Sibley (*in contempt*) Duplicate.

Freddy (*with greater animosity*) Duplicate be blowed! Where is another key? Who made another?

Sibley (*to Freddy, waiving him*) Excuse me, please. (*To D'Arcy*) Mr Tuck, this involves a man's death. If you want to clear yourself about that man's death, I warn you again, you'd better tell us all you know.

D'Arcy Why ask me about it? It's *you* who know things. There's only one thing about the whole concern you *don't* know—and that is who did it.

Freddy Yes, now look here, Mr Grierson. The time has come to speak out. You're casting around pretty desperately for a—a victim. You've rigged up some plausible sort of a case against us. You could have made out just as likely-sounding a case against any member of the household, from Sir George Chudleigh down to the scullery-maid.

D'Arcy Yes. What was the scullery-maid doing that night? Do you know? No! Nor do I. So there you are.

Freddy (*to D'Arcy*) Shut up. (*To Grierson*) It's not without its funny side to a man in my position. Only a few weeks ago I was playing bridge with your Chief Commissioner.

D'Arcy And in my position too. I play bridge with all sorts of people.

Freddy (*rising*) There were some questions you *had* to ask, I admit. But your zeal has led you into making the most ridiculous accusations. Against me and against my friend, Tuck—a nervous man.

D'Arcy I'm not. Not very.

Freddy Now, look here. You think it over carefully—as you're fond of saying. You're worried; you're groping. You see a line of queer little possibilities leading to us. You follow blindly along that line and you'll hit up against a stone wall.

D'Arcy And break it. The wall, I mean, not your head.

Freddy Don't be rude. No occasion for that. But time's getting on. Three weeks gone by. You're snapping at any clue like a trout at a fly. This woman Orlock lets fall some little malicious hint and you grab it and swallow it. Three hours before this affair took place I gave that woman the sack. Did you know that?

Grierson (*to Marchant*) Have you any information about that?

Marchant She's still there, sir.

Freddy She was under notice at the time for cheek to me. And that's the woman whose word you take against the word of my sister and Miss Hewlett.

D'Arcy Yes—we don't mind your accusing us—well, not so much.

Freddy No, but when you try and worm some false admission out of us by making hasty threatening little innuendoes against those ladies—my God, you must be pretty hard up for a case.

D'Arcy Yes, I quite agree. (*To Bryant*) Put me down as saying that.

Freddy You've *no* case. Where's the jewellery? Where's the smallest particle of evidence? I want your help. This damned thing happened in my house. Instead of which, this is what we get. I can't answer for Tuck, of course——

D'Arcy I can. Anything you like.

Freddy I'm not trying to pull any bluff or any nonsense of that sort. I couldn't do it. It isn't in my nature. But I say this. If after what's happened we stay here at all, we stay here under arrest.

D'Arcy Or not. Which?

Grierson (*standing—after a pause*) I think you'd better bid the gentlemen good evening. (*Goes up to windows, looks out*)

Sibley (*very subdued*) Certainly sir. Thank you, Mr Malone. You must understand I was merely trying to do my duty.

D'Arcy That's all right. We don't want to be nasty about it.

Freddy Very well then. Good evening. If I can be of any assistance to you, I shall be at my house at Walton Heath. So will Mr Tuck. Won't you?

D'Arcy Yes, old boy, thanks, for the present. I like the golf.

Freddy Good evening. (*Goes to door*)

D'Arcy (*following him. Nods to each in turn—finally to Bryant*) Good evening, and thank you very much.

They go, closing the door

A brief pause

Sibley Well sir. (*To Grierson*)

Old Grierson, smiling, nods his agreement looking over notes on table

Grierson You'll get 'em all right, they did it.

Big Ben strikes half-hour. Marchant crosses to Bryant, looking over his notes

CURTAIN

SCENE 2

At Freddy's house next day. The scene is the same as in Act II

The front door bell rings and Buckley enters and crosses up to open it. Mrs Hewlett and Oswald are the visitors. Their mourning for Simon is not very conspicuous

Mrs Howlett Is Mr Malone at home?
Buckley Yes, Madam.
Mrs Hewlett He 'phoned and asked us to call here.

She enters followed by Oswald

Buckley Yes, madam. If you'll take a seat I'll tell him you've arrived.

Goes off

Mrs Hewlett (*seating herself and turning to Oswald, who is standing about nervously*) Can't you take a seat?
Oswald I don't care to.
Mrs Hewlett (*sits on settee*) Go on. Take it. Standing there looking goosey.

Freddy enters

Freddy Oh! (*in an unfriendly manner*) Good afternoon.
Oswald (*trying to appear genial*) Hallo! How are we?
Freddy How are we? I think some of us are going to feel a bit off-colour. (*Calls*) D'Arcy! Come on.

D'Arcy enters

Mrs Hewlett What, are you here, too?
D'Arcy Yes, no thanks to you.
Freddy (*to D'Arcy*) Leave it to me. Now then. Are you aware that I've been sent for by Scotland Yard and practically accused of this crime?
D'Arcy What about me?
Freddy Oh yes. Him too. And all owing to you.
Mrs Hewlett To me?
Freddy Yes. You made insinuations to the police. They said so. Just think of it. Think of the insult—to a man like me.
D'Arcy And another man—like me. Sending me through life with a blotted copy-book.
Mrs Hewlett (*to Freddy*) I never said anything against *you*, Mr Malone.

D'Arcy (*cross to Mrs Hewlett*) There you are. You admit you *did*
against me.

Freddy That's how it started. You accused Mr Tuck. They looked
at him and said, 'Oh, *he* couldn't have done much without help.'
So they picked on me.

Oswald (*to Mrs Hewlett*) I told you you'd gone a bit far, you know.

D'Arcy There! Did you hear that admission? Straight from this
horse's mouth.

Mrs Hewlett Well, they came along and said, 'Tell us the truth,
the 'ole and nothing but.'

Freddy The two girls are suspected as well.

Oswald What—Pru? (*To Mrs Hewlett*) Oh, what have you done?

D'Arcy (*to Oswald*) If you'll just listen, you're being told what she's
done.

Freddy I know this. You're going to withdraw any insinuations
against anyone.

Mrs Hewlett I am certainly not! What I said I stand to and stick
by.

Oswald No, Mother. (*To D'Arcy*) I'm sure at heart she regrets and
withdraws.

D'Arcy Never mind about that. Let her say it.

Oswald What do you want her to say?

D'Arcy Say this—'I don't accuse D'Arcy Tuck.'

Freddy Hi! Steady! I'll tell her what to say.

Mrs Hewlett (*rises*) You may tell me, but say it you won't catch
me do.

D'Arcy (*to Mrs Hewlett, taking Oswald across*) This is your son. That
is a drawing-room. Take him in and hear him out.

Mrs Hewlett Even so, I'll speak nothing truthless!

She goes into the drawing-room with Oswald

Freddy There you are—I told you. Pru's our strong card, I'll get
her here.

D'Arcy But why all these precuautions? We're clear, aren't we?

Freddy You never know. There's no harm in having that ace in your
shirt! (*Exit*)

Joan comes downstairs

Joan D'Arcy, does Mrs Veal suspect you?

D'Arcy I don't know. I don't care. I'm free now. They dismissed
me with flying colours.

Joan I've been so nervous about you these three weeks. D'you know
why I came here today?

D'Arcy Of course I do. Because you thought I was in danger.

Joan Yes, darling. But are you sure you're safe now?

D'Arcy Of course. I've got them baffled.

Joan Well, then, let's go away somewhere and get married. And we'll forget all about it.

D'Arcy Yes, darling, and only remember other things.

Joan But what have you done with what you took? Where is it?

D'Arcy That's so like a girl. You say 'Never speak of it again' and in the next breath you say 'Tell me the lot'.

Joan But I want it to be given back.

D'Arcy I can't. If I give it back they'll run me in for pinching it.

Joan You needn't put on a card 'With compliments from D'Arcy Tuck'.

D'Arcy Well, do you want it or not?

Joan No, I wouldn't touch an ounce of it.

D'Arcy Then why worry where it is?

Joan I believe there's someone else in it you're sharing it with.

D'Arcy Joan! You'd hate to think a thing like that of me.

Joan Yes, I should.

D'Arcy Then don't.

Freddy and Prudence enter

Freddy (*to Prudence*) Ozzy's in there with the old woman. Pop in and tick them off.

Prudence I should think so. The idea of Freddy being accused.

Joan And D'Arcy.

D'Arcy Thank you, darling. Yes, and me.

Prudence Well, *that* of course, is a scream.

She goes into the drawing-room

Joan Well, *I'm* not going to see the Veals. I'll come back when they've gone.

D'Arcy Yes, darling. I shall look forward to seeing you again.

Joan goes off

Oswald enters from drawing-room

Oswald I say—re this. You don't think any the worse of me, do you?

Freddy I couldn't. D'you know that Pru herself has been accused?

Oswald What?

Freddy Yes. The police say Pru never saw the man and that Joan never heard anyone in the hall.

Oswald Here! What if I can prove there *was* someone in the hall?

D'Arcy What d'you mean?

Oswald It's quite true. There was someone down here.

Freddy How d'you know?

Oswald I was down here myself.

D'Arcy What, at the time of the burglary?

Oswald Yes. Now tell Pru that.

Freddy That doesn't prove Pru saw the burglar. That only confirms Joan's story.

Oswald Oh—yes—I didn't think of it that way.

Freddy And anyhow, what were *you* doing down in the hall at that hour?

D'Arcy And why have we only just heard of it?

Freddy Were you down here when your uncle fell?

Oswald I—I can't say.

D'Arcy You've got a mouth, haven't you?

Oswald Yes—but——

D'Arcy All right. I don't want to see it. Just use it.

Freddy Answer my questions. Were you down here when your uncle fell?

D'Arcy (*as Oswald hesitates*) *Were* you?

Oswald Yes—I—suppose so.

Freddy and D'Arcy exchange a look and turn up stage. They hold a brief consultation and return down-stage

D'Arcy Would you care to make a statement?

Oswald No, thanks. (*Cross between them*)

D'Arcy All right. If you won't take my advice I shall have to ask you some questions, that's all.

Freddy Take a chair, Mr Veal. That's a comfortable one.

Oswald (*subsiding with a murmur*) Thank you.

Freddy Now then. Your uncle was wandering about the place at night. So were you. (*To D'Arcy*) There's something at the back of this.

D'Arcy Yes. Put it in front.

Oswald It was only I—I said I'd see him. (*Facing them*) Just—to give him something. He wanted something.

D'Arcy But what could he want at three in the morning?

Freddy That *you* could give him, anyway?

Oswald I'd rather not say.

D'Arcy Any refusal to answer may be brought up in court.

Oswald (*uncomfortably*) Court?

Freddy Oh, yes. The inquest's only been adjourned, you know. What was it your uncle wanted?

Oswald Well—money. Some money.

Freddy Money? What money? What for?

Oswald He—was going next morning, you see.

Freddy Now, look here, Veal. Your uncle wouldn't go until you or your mother had come across with some money. You had to agree. You were meeting him to pay him the money when he met his death.

D'Arcy Very brave of you, wasn't it?

Freddy He's a Veal. This man was blackmailing you, wasn't he?

Oswald I absolutely refuse to say another word.

D'Arcy Right, then think carefully before you speak.

Freddy (*behind Oswald to D'Arcy*) D'Arcy, ring up Scotland Yard and ask Chief Inspector Sibley to come down here at once. (*Signs to him to hold down telephone-spring*)

D'Arcy (*cross to 'phone*) Right you are. I shall very, very much like to see old Sibley again.

Freddy crosses to Oswald

(*On 'phone, obviously disconnected with exchange*) Hallo. Give me Scotland Yard. Thanks very much.

Freddy (*to Oswald*) You'd better speak up. By gad, if Sibley gets hold of you in that room of his he'll soon have it out of you.

D'Arcy Hoo! Rather! I'd hate to be a man with a guilty conscience among those devils. (*Speaking into 'phone*) Hallo! Is that Scotland Yard? How are you? Never mind about that. Give me Chief Inspector Sibley.

Freddy (*to Oswald*) You'd much better throw yourself on our mercy than on his.

D'Arcy His? He's got none. Sibley's an absolute swine. Hallo, is that you, Sibley, old boy? It's D'Arcy Tuck speaking.

Oswald (*agitated*) No, I say—hold on a moment.

D'Arcy (*on 'phone*) D'you hear that? Hold on a moment.

Oswald It's to do with my mother. You wouldn't wish her any harm.

D'Arcy Who wouldn't? (*On 'phone*) I'm at Freddy Malone's. If you care to come at once——

Freddy Tell him to hold on a minute.

D'Arcy (*on 'phone*) No. Hold yourself again.

Freddy (*to Oswald*) Why should your mother be afraid of a man who's dead? Is it something your mother's done?

Oswald What? Well—Oh, give me time to think.

Freddy Tell us or the Inspector. Which?

D'Arcy (*on 'phone*) Keep on holding yourself but be ready to start.

Oswald It's nothing to do with my uncle's death, nothing.

Freddy (*to D'Arcy*) All right. Have him along.

D'Arcy Start.

Oswald No, no.

D'Arcy Hallo? Too late. He says he's started. (*Puts down receiver*)

Freddy Then now you *are* for it. Speak up. What did Simon Veal know about your mother?

Oswald If I tell you, swear you won't tell the police?

Freddy I won't do anything that isn't honest.

D'Arcy But as your friends, we shall do our best to save you.

Oswald Well, it's only—Simon Veal was my father's brother you see. He knew something about Dad.

D'Arcy What's the matter? Dad's dead, too, isn't he?

Oswald Oh—I—ah——

Freddy (*feet on chair—as Oswald hesitates*) Is your father still alive?

Oswald Oh, I believe he is. Yes, he still is.

D'Arcy What? And when she married old Hewlett, was dad alive then?

Freddy Has your mother been divorced?

Oswald looks up at Freddy

We can easily find that out.

Oswald No. She hasn't.

Drawing-room door opens

Mrs Hewlett appears with Prudence

D'Arcy Dad's alive. They've not been divorced. She married old Hewlett——

Freddy By Gad! She's a bigamist.

D'Arcy and Freddy shake hands

Mrs Hewlett Ozzy! What have you been saying?

Freddy and D'Arcy resume their attitude as inquisitors. Mrs Hewlett is shown to a chair

D'Arcy (*crosses to Mrs Hewlett*) Now! *Your* statement, please.

Mrs Hewlett It's all a lie. I don't know he's alive. I haven't seen him for years.

D'Arcy Then he's all the more likely to be alive.

Freddy (*cross to Mrs Hewlett*) Stop all that flap-doodle. Where's your husband now?

Mrs Hewlett I don't know where he is or even *if*.

Freddy Simon Veal knew.

D'Arcy And so does Osram.

Freddy Yes. And he came to *you* to get money for Simon! Ugly!

D'Arcy Oh, very ugly. Both of them.

Mrs Hewlett I feel queer.

Prudence I'll get you some water.

Mrs Hewlett No thank you. This is no time for water. It's all a lie.

Freddy Anyhow, they can give you a good stretch for bigamy.

D'Arcy Mind you, Freddy, we may take a lenient view of this.

Freddy I think we ought to tell the police.

Mrs Hewlett No, no. You wouldn't do a think like that on me.

Freddy (*pointing to drawing-room*) Well, go back in there.

Mrs Hewlett crosses to door

I'll think it over. (*To Oswald*) You too.

Mrs Hewlett (*to Oswald, who has crossed to door* R.) A nice son you've turned out.

Oswald I couldn't help myself. They dragged it out of me.

Mrs Hewlett And to think of the trouble I once took to keep you alive.

She goes indignantly into the drawing-room R. *with Oswald*

D'Arcy This is fine. Quick! Where's Joan?

Freddy Hold on! I want you.

Holding D'Arcy's arm

(*To Prudence*) *You* tell Joan.

Prudence All right. (*To D'Arcy*) Seems almost a pity you ever pinched the jewellery at all.

She goes off

Freddy Now you can get your own back if you like. But you'd better let me handle it for you. You'll muck it up if I don't.

D'Arcy Really! Let me tell you, regarding this partnership, I wish to resign.

Freddy Don't you worry. I wouldn't have you as a partner at clock-golf. If it hadn't been for me, you'd have been in gaol by this time.

D'Arcy Gaol! Freddy, I won't boast but it was I who saved the situation at Scotland Yard. All that bluff of yours was no good. Look at the way you sneaked out, as if you'd just escaped—like this.

Freddy If they didn't arrest you it was only because you looked such a prize ass.

D'Arcy Oh no. It was my light and airy manner that did the trick. Didn't I creep out like you? No I stayed and jollied them. They liked me very, very much. I said 'Well, boys——'

Knock at door

D'Arcy goes up to door, opens it and discovers Sibley, Marchant and another plain-clothes man. D'Arcy immediately turns and goes off. Sibley enters. The other two remain behind him in the doorway

Freddy What do you want here?

Sibley That man, D'Arcy Tuck. I've a warrant for his arrest.

Freddy (*coolly*) Oh! Going to arrest *him*, are you?

Sibley Yes, only him for the present.

Freddy Oh! Got some fresh evidence?

Sibley I *have*.

Goes towards door

Freddy Hold on. I've something to tell you.

Sibley (*pausing*) Ah! You think *you'd* better speak?

Freddy Yes. *Now* I can tell you who stole that jewellery.

Sibley Well, I caution you——

Freddy Caution your grandmother. Mrs Hewlett has come here to see me. She admits the burglar was Simon Veal.

Sibley Indeed!

Freddy She saw him take the stuff and throw it out of the window in the petticoat.

Sibley Is she here now?

Freddy Yes. In the drawing-room. She'll tell you all about it. Leave her to me. I'll bring her along.

Freddy goes out slamming door

Sibley (*to Marchant*) He's up to something. Keep an eye outside the house.

Marchant Right, sir.

Goes out

Sibley (*to other man*) You—drawing-room window. I'll see to Tuck.

Man goes out at front door. Sibley goes out at door down L.

D'Arcy reappears at head of stairs. He steals down and seeing the hall empty sneaks through door up R. *and comes out again next moment with his hat and overcoat in his hand. As he turns to front door Marchant reappears. D'Arcy crosses down* L. *and Sibley reappears from there. D'Arcy starts going upstairs again*

Mr Tuck.

D'Arcy Oh! Come in.

Sibley I shall want you.

D'Arcy Well, I'm very, very busy. What?

Sibley Mr Malone has just told me who committed the crime.

D'Arcy Oh no, he hasn't. I know him too well for that. He wouldn't say anything against anybody unless it was false.

Sibley If *he* knows who did it so do *you.* I've a warrant for your arrest. Now. Your last chance. Who did it?

D'Arcy Ah, I see. Oh, no, you don't. He thinks I did it, so he's told you *he* did, to save me. And you're trying to make me say *I* did it, in case I think *he* did, to save him. Well, the answer to you is a stuffed tomato.

He goes out again quickly

Sibley (*as he attempts to run after D'Arcy, to Marchant*) All right. I'll get him. You stay outside.

Marchant goes out at front door, Sibley goes off after D'Arcy

Freddy enters from drawing-room with Mrs Hewlett

Freddy Good! He's not here. Now remember. Your one hope, if we're to keep quiet about that bigamy. You'll say exactly what I told you.

Mrs Hewlett I must. You've got me.

Freddy Yes. And you remember what you might get.

Sibley returns with D'Arcy. Marchant and his Partner in front doorway

Oh, here you are, Mr Sibley. (*To Mrs Hewlett*) Now then, out with it.

Mrs Hewlett I saw Simon Veal in my bedroom take my jewellery and throw it out of the winder in me petticoat.

D'Arcy Oh, this is the first I knew of it. Go on!

Freddy gives him a look

Mrs Hewlett I got out of bed. He saw me and fell into the conservatory.

D'Arcy I'm not surprised.

Freddy You told me he had the big towel over his head.

Mrs Hewlett Yes. So as I shouldn't see who he was, I suppose.

D'Arcy Ah! And he had the little towel no doubt in case she had to be doused.

Sibley Why haven't we heard all this before?

Mrs Hewlett Because I was afraid you'd say I shoved him off the ladder.

Sibley But you told me you suspected Mr Tuck.

Mrs Hewlett I never. You made me say that, the way you questioned me.

Freddy Hallo! I don't like the sound of that, Mr Sibley.

Joan appears on stairs. Comes to foot

Sibley (*to Freddy*) That's ridiculous. Are you prepared to sign a statement that this story's true?

D'Arcy Yes. (*To Mrs Hewlett*) Aren't you?

Mrs Hewlett Yes.

Sibley H'm. I see. Yes, this throws a very different light on it.

D'Arcy (*to Sibley*) Yes. Well, now we shan't really want you any more.

Sibley (*Turning to D'Arcy*) Oh, won't you? Then account for this bracelet marked on the clasp Mary Hewlett. And found in your room in town this morning.

Joan That's mine.

Sibley Oh! Yours?

Joan Yes. I gave it to Mr Tuck to have copied.

Freddy That's quite true. I was at Marvin Court when she took her own personal possessions away. That bracelet was among them. She showed it to me.

D'Arcy And to me. (*To Mrs Hewlett*) And to you, too, I think?

Mrs Hewlett Perfectly true. It's hers.

Sibley Oh, confound this.

Freddy Why confound it? When at last you've discovered the truth.

Sibley Well, but this case has all gone to blazes.

D'Arcy Then follow it.

Sibley (*to Marchant*) We can't make this arrest.

Joan Well, I shall be obliged if you'll give me back my bracelet.

Sibley Oh, you may take it (*Hands it to Joan*)

Joan Thank you. (*Turns to stairs*)

D'Arcy That's right, darling. Take it somewhere safe, away from all these people.

Joan goes upstairs

Sibley Well, I can't proceed any further with this, of course. (*To his men*) Get along. (*They go. He turns to Mrs Hewlett*) I'll call on you tomorrow for that statement. You've run a very grave risk, keeping this back about Simon Veal.

D'Arcy goes up stage to door

Mrs Hewlett Yes, but if you say I did him in, I'll have the law on you.

Sibley Well—good-day.

D'Arcy Oh, very.

Sibley goes out leaving door open

Oswald (*opening drawing-room door*) Oh, Mother!

Oswald enters

Freddy (*speaks to D'Arcy*) Shut the door.
D'Arcy (*to Oswald*) You hear? Shut the door.
Oswald Oh, certainly. (*Goes and shuts door*)
Freddy Now. You'll have to come to some arrangement about this
    property. You'll hear about that.
D'Arcy You'll hear a lot.
Freddy And—I don't want to preach. We can't all be perfect. We
    each have our little shortcomings.
D'Arcy Some shorter than others.
Freddy But do let this be a lesson to you in future. Be honest. It
    pays in the end.
D'Arcy (*to Oswald*) Are *you* listening to this?
Oswald Yes.
Freddy Be honest. It pays in the end. That's all.
D'Arcy (*to Oswald*) That's all. Stop listening.
Freddy And now—get out.
D'Arcy (*to Oswald*) Open the door.

He does so

Mrs Hewlett Well, anyhow I had a run for my money. If I'd known
    it'd end like this I'd have blown the lot. (*Pushes Oswald*) Get out!

She goes out with Oswald, bangs the door

Freddy Be honest. It pays in the end. I suppose, that applies to you,
    too.
D'Arcy You bet it does. I've done with this sort of thing. Never
    again me.
Freddy Then you won't want to know what I got for the stuff?
D'Arcy What! Did you sell it?
Freddy Of course I sold it.
D'Arcy Oh! (*sitting as he speaks*) Would you care to make a state-
    ment?

CURTAIN

THE BED BEFORE YESTERDAY

A Comedy

CHARACTERS

First presented by H. M. Tennent Ltd in association with Eddie Kulukurdis at the Lyric Theatre, London, on December 9th, 1975, with the following cast:

Victor Keene	John Moffatt
Alma	Joan Plowright
Mrs Holley	Gabrielle Daye
Aubrey	Frank Grimes
Ella	Helen Mirren
Lolly Tucker	Patsy Rowlands
Felix	Leonard Fenton
Fred Castle	Royce Mills

The Play directed by Lindsay Anderson
Setting by Alan Tagg

The action takes place in Alma's house in Brompton Mews

ACT I
Scene 1   4 o'clock on a late spring afternoon
Scene 2   Four months later; a morning in August
Scene 3   Tea-time the same day

ACT II
Scene 1   Shortly after 10 o'clock that night
Scene 2   About 11.30 the next morning
Scene 3   10 o'clock at night, three weeks later

Time—1930

ACT I

SCENE 1

Alma's house in Brompton Mews. Four o'clock on a late spring afternoon in 1930

The front door to the street opens into a very small recess between it and the room, with just space for a hat-and-coat-stand with umbrella-stand and doormat. Beside the front door is an oblong window with permanent lace curtains and practical side curtains. Other doors lead to the kitchen and the dining-room. A short staircase leads to a landing on to which open three further doors. The furniture, with some period pieces, and decoration of the room are in keeping with the taste of an owner who is precise and houseproud as well as being very well-to-do. The whole action of the play is during spring and summer, and the chintzes, etc., are in keeping with this. The pieces of furniture essential to the action are a sofa, a writing-table with telephone either on the writing-table itself or on a smaller table close by, complete with the fat, one-volume London Directory of the period. There is also a tea-table in two of the scenes, but this can be folded and placed aside during the rest of the action. This tea-table is in evidence at the opening, with two upright chairs placed on either side in readiness. It is set for two with everything ready, including a lidded muffin-dish and a cake-stand. Only the teapot and hot-water jug are missing (See set plan at end of book)

Victor Keene is standing up-stage of the table. He is in his late fifties, a gentleman fallen on evil days. He has made his well-worn suit and shoes look as presentable as possible for the occasion. His manner and attitude are self-conscious and rather intimidated; on his best behaviour and anxious to please. Alma enters from the kitchen, carrying a little tray on which are the teapot and hot-water jug. She is forty-five to six. She too has made the best of herself for the occasion, though she is always well-dressed. She is by no means a beauty and very conscious of the fact. She has a most difficult temperament, being liable to fly into uncontrollable fits of anger. At the opening her nervous efforts to face an important, self-imposed situation make her appear possessive and petulant, as she herself explains later on

Alma (*as she comes to the table and deposits the teapot and jug*) There we are. Sit down, Mr Keene.

Victor Oh—thank you.

He waits until she sits, then seats himself. A brief pause. Then Alma gives a little nervous, meaningless laugh

Alma (*with this laugh*) Her-her . . .
Victor (*responding in like fashion*) Her-her . . .
Alma Milk?
Victor Please.
Alma Before or after the tea?
Victor Oh—whichever you—do.
Alma (*decisively*) After. If you put the milk in first you have to guess how much tea. (*Sharply*) Don't you?
Victor Oh, I see, yes. But surely if you put the tea in first you have to guess how much milk?
Alma No, no. Tea first lets you judge the right blend from the colour you get from the milk.
Victor (*giving way*) Ah. Yes. I—see your point.
Alma Sugar?
Victor Please.
Alma One lump or two?
Victor Oh, whichever—one will do, thank you.
Alma I never think one is enough to sweeten the tea.
Victor Oh, very well; if you take two——
Alma I don't take any. Well? One or two?
Victor Two, please. I mean one. One. Thank you.

She hands him his cup

Thank you.
Alma (*pouring her own cup*) It's very kind of you to come and have tea with me.
Victor It's very kind of you to ask me.
Alma I got your address from your sister.
Victor Yes. She wrote to me too.
Alma (*sharply again*) About me? What did she say about me?
Victor Oh, just—she thought I'd like to keep up the acquaintance sort of thing.
Alma (*lifting the muffin-dish lid and offering*) Have one of these. Do you call them scones or scons?
Victor (*guardedly*) Which do you?
Alma Scons.
Victor (*as he takes one*) Yes, I knew it was one or the other. Thank you.
Alma (*starting the genuine conversation*) Mr Keene . . ?

Victor Yes?

Alma When you came to that hotel at Southbourne a fortnight ago . . ?

Victor Yes?

Alma Why did you come?

Victor (*obviously*) Why? To visit my sister. Just for a few days. She thought the change might do me good.

Alma When she invited you, did she say anything about *my* staying there?

Victor (*surprised*) No. Why should she? I mean—I'd never even heard of you.

Alma Because she went out of her way to tell me about *you*. Before you arrived, that is.

Victor About me? What about me?

Alma About—well—your past history.

Victor Past history? I haven't got one. (*A little chuckle and he takes a bite of his scone*) Why, what did she tell you?

Alma That you were a widower and—not doing anything and . . . (*She pauses*)

Victor (*with a little frown*) And what?

Alma Well—living on a very modest income, she said.

Victor (*resentfully*) That's true enough. But why should my sister want to tell you that?

Alma (*with nervous irritation*) Do please eat your scon over your plate, do you mind.

Victor Oh. (*Taking the plate*) Sorry.

Alma Scons make the worst kind of crumbs because they have butter in them.

Victor (*examining his scone innocently*) Oh, have they?

Alma I remember when I first saw you in the hotel. You and your sister were having tea with my step-mother in what they call the sun-lounge.

Victor Yes. You came in from giving your little dog a run on the leash.

Alma My step-mother's little dog.

Victor (*resignedly*) Step-mother's little dog.

Alma Personally I dislike little dogs.

Victor So do I. Oh, your step-mother's is quite a nice little dog . . .

Alma It's a horrible little dog.

Victor Oh, is it? I didn't get to know it at all well. (*Amiably*) But if you dislike it why take it for a run on the leash?

Alma Because my step-mother was having one of her bad feet days. (*With nervous irritation*) Besides, it wasn't a run on the leash. How can anybody give a dog a run on the leash?

Victor Oh, a little dog like that, surely? It could run even on the leash. Sort of patter, patter, patter.

Alma You stood up to say how-do-you-do still holding your teacup in your right hand.

Victor (*innocently*) Did I? I suppose I was taken aback or something.

Alma You got in a terrible muddle putting the teacup down and slopping it and having to wipe your hand before you shook with it.

Victor (*fighting resentment*) I don't know why you should remember that.

Alma It gave me time to take a good look at you.

Victor (*jokingly*) Did you want to?

Alma Yes, I was interested after what your sister had told me.

Victor Why, what more had she told you?

Alma About your first marriage.

Victor My first? I've only had one.

Alma Then it was your first, wasn't it? She said your wife died about ten years ago.

Victor Yes, in nineteen-twenty. Soon after I got back from the war.

Alma I know. Your sister told me all about her.

Victor (*genuinely annoyed*) She had no right to.

Alma You needn't think I asked her. She just told me.

Victor Told you what?

Alma That your wife ruined you by her extravagance. And that's why you're so badly off now.

Victor I'll have something to say to my sister.

Alma Well, it's true, isn't it?

Victor Whether it's true or not . . .

Alma Don't be snappish with me, Mr Keene. I'm only sympathizing.

Victor (*relenting somewhat*) Oh. Then it's very kind of you and all that; but I really don't see . . .

Alma That it's my concern?

Victor No. Yes.

Alma Don't you want it to be? (*A moment's pause*) I sympathized because I had much the same experience myself. In a sort of way.

Victor Really? But nobody ruined *you*, surely?

Alma Not in that way. (*Pause*) Aren't you going to drink your tea?

Victor Oh. Yes. It's still quite hot. (*He drinks for the first time*) I prefer it cool.

Alma You must find life very depressing. Because you were so well off at one time, weren't you?

Victor (*with a sudden change to candour*) Well, since you know so much about me, Mrs Millet, yes, I was. I had quite a good private income but—it all went.

Alma Your wife gambled, didn't she?

Victor This is my sister again, I suppose? Well, yes, it's true enough. My wife was a born gambler. It was just part of her nature.

Alma (*sincerely and bitterly*) Yes, I know what a curse one's nature can be.

Victor *You* do?

Alma Never mind about me yet. What happened about your wife?

Victor Well, there she was—at it the whole time. Stock Exchange—horses—she used to take trips to Monte Carlo. It was her whole life. She was Australian, you see.

Alma Oh, how sad.

Victor By the time I came back from the war I was pretty well ruined. I'd never done any sort of a job and I felt too old to start.

Alma (*pleased*) Yes. How old *are* you? Never mind, I can guess.

Victor I don't mind your knowing. I'm getting on for sixty.

Alma Oh, is that all?

He does not know quite how to take this. There is a brief pause

  More tea?

Victor No, thank you.

Alma There's some cake if you . . .

Victor No, thank you. I don't as a rule have any tea at all.

Alma Poor Mr Keene. (*Rising*) Well, let's sit over here. (*She moves to the sofa*)

Victor (*rising*) I'm afraid I mustn't stay too long.

Alma (*with sudden vehemence*) You've only just finished your tea—not that you've had any. Of course, if you *want* to go . . .

Victor (*anxiously*) No, no—if you really wish to talk to me . . .

Alma (*as before*) What do you think I asked you here for? (*Checking herself*) No, I'm sorry. I mustn't be like that. I promised myself I wouldn't.

Victor (*appeasingly*) Like what?

Alma Like I am. Like I've been ever since your came. Nervous and edgy and abrupt. I did so want to be pleasant. It's sort of over-anxiety. Do forgive me.

Victor That's all right, Mrs Millet. It's best to be oneself.

Alma Not in my case. (*She sits on the sofa*) Do sit down.

Victor sits in the armchair. Alma goes on evenly but always with impatience just below the surface

  Yes, I do want to talk to you. About myself. I've led an unusual sort of life. I had a very peculiar childhood to begin with. I was born a Bull.

He looks blankly puzzled. She notices this and takes him up, impatiently

  One of the Bull family. Bull's potted meat.

Victor (*to himself*) Good Lord.

Alma My mother died when I was born. They did that half the time in those days. My father wanted a son. He detested me for being a girl. Besides, I was hideously ugly. I always have been.

Victor Oh, come come . . .

Alma Please don't interrupt me all the time. Oh, there I go again. I'm sorry. But that was your fault.

Victor makes a reassuring gesture

I never saw much of my father. He married again. That old Southbourne hotel one. Poor thing, she's got very old and silly. I try to be nice to her; not that I'm nice to anybody for long. Then my father died too. I was brought up by an aunt. Very strictly. I was sent to a convent school. They wanted me to become a nun. (*Angrily and scornfully*) I soon saw to that. Insidious gammon. They were after my money, of course. (*With challenge*) You're not a Roman Catholic, I hope?

Victor Me? No. I'm just a common-or-garden C. of E. sort of thing.

Alma My father left most of his fortune to my step-mother—in trust for me, that is. At the time I only got a hundred thousand pounds.

Victor (*involuntarily*) Gosh!

Alma (*sharply*) What?

Victor Nothing—I wasn't interrupting.

Alma I was a very innocent young woman. I never thought of getting married.

Victor Why not? I'd have thought—(*checking himself*)—no. Please, go on.

Alma Then, when I was nineteen, a young man came along—an absolute scoundrel. Oh, of a very good family—heir to a title, and so on. And I married him. But he was as bad as the nuns—he only wanted my money. Oh, I had a shocking experience. Thank goodness it didn't last long. He very soon got drunk and fell out of an aeroplane.

Victor What a happy release. I hope he didn't spend too much of your money before he—fell out.

Alma He didn't have long enough. (*With a shrewd look at Victor*) So that's still all right, Mr Keene.

Victor So what did you do then?

Alma What could I do? A widow of twenty. My aunt was dead by then, thank goodness. I wasn't going to live with my step-mother. A little of her went a very long way; it still does. So I decided to try again—with George Millett. He was my official guardian. He was twenty-five years older than I was.

Victor Twenty-five? No?

Alma (*in a minor flare-up*) What do you mean 'no'? When I say twenty-five I mean twenty-five.

Victor (*hastily*) Yes, yes; I only meant fancy.

Alma (*calming down*) We lived at Reigate for twenty-odd years. He died six months ago.

Victor Oh, I'm sorry.

Alma No, you're not; why should you be? I'm the only person entitled to be sorry and I'm not either.

Victor (*stung into retaliation*) Was he?

Alma (*unconscious of any sarcasm*) No; I think he was glad to die. He'd got old and crotchety and he had bad feet.

Victor Oh, these bad feet.

Alma (*sharply*) Why? Don't tell me *you* have bad feet?

Victor No; I meant your step-mother.

Alma Oh, hers are just bunions. George Millet's feet had got past belief. It was all this ridiculous golf. Do you play golf?

Victor Good heavens, no. I can't afford anything like that.

Alma So then I sold the Reigate house and came to live here in London, in this mews.

Victor That's a bit of a come-down, isn't it? Oh, it's very nice and all that. But you say you've still got—well, ample means . . .

Alma You seem very concerned about that, Mr Keene.

Victor I? No. I only meant—is this house big enough for you?

Alma Quite big enough, thank you. It's got two bedrooms.

Victor So I should hope. You surely must have a spare room for a friend.

Alma I have no friends. (*Rising*) I'm a friendless woman. Or, rather, unfriendly. Aren't I?

Victor rises

Victor (*guardedly murmuring*) You're being very friendly to me.

Alma I've got this dreadful sort of nature—hostile to people— almost, oh, I don't know—rancorous. I've had it ever since I grew up, since my first marriage anyhow. I'm embittered. I look for opposition everywhere; I anticipate it. You needn't think I want to be like it. I struggle against it sometimes. But it's difficult to fight against what's—(*she thumps her chest*)—there, inside you; part of you.

Victor (*after a thoughtful pause*) But your husband . . . ? I mean, while he was alive—did he—come in for it?

Alma He learnt to turn his back and ignore it.

Victor D'you know what I'd have done? I'd have known you didn't really mean it and tried to make *you* see that too. Sort of laughed it off.

Alma (*thoughtfully*) No-one has ever done that.

Victor Then it's time they did.

Alma But I get like it with shopkeepers and servants. People like that can't laugh at me. All the same, I think you've been very clever.

Victor (*with a chuckle*) First time I've ever been accused of that.

Alma I'll try laughing at myself instead of hating myself. Poor Mr Keene, I'm sorry to inflict myself on you like this. I know the impression I've made on you and oh, I wanted so much not to. You think I'm an absolute shrew, don't you?

Victor Indeed I don't.

Alma (*angrily*) Oh, don't lie to me.

Victor (*reprovingly*) Now, now . . .

He gives a little laugh. Alma doesn't join in the laugh but pulls herself together and speaks quietly

Alma You *must* think I'm a shrew.

Victor No. Well—perhaps I may have, a tiny bit, to begin with. But against that, I think you've got . . . (*He pauses*)

Alma (*rather challenging*) Got what?

Victor (*very tentatively*) Well, charm . . . (*Hastily*) In a funny sort of way, of course.

Alma (*greatly softening*) You really mean that?

Victor I do. I daresay it's hard to believe.

Alma (*sharply again*) Why is it?

Victor No, I shouldn't have said that.

Alma Shouldn't have said I had charm?

Victor No; shouldn't have said it's hard to believe.

Alma Why not, if you really think so. (*A moment's pause*) Well? Shall I go on?

Victor Oh, please do.

Alma (*gentle again and appealing*) Well, what do you suppose I get like, here alone and like I am? I'm lonely. Wretchedly lonely.

Even this rather stupid Victor is wise now to what's up. He decides to play it cautiously

Victor No-one to visit you? No relations?

Alma My only relation is some sort of distant cousin named Lolly Tucker. She's divorced and lives at Ealing and takes lodgers. I'm afraid she's not quite our class.

Victor Oh. Well, what about a companion?

Alma (*suddenly fierce again*) Companion? You mean a female one? Some vicar's daughter with chronic adenoids?

Victor (*meekly*) Couldn't you find one without?

Alma No. They all have them. (*Sitting in the armchair*) In any case, another woman? No, thank you. (*Getting down to it forcibly*) I want two things, Mr Keene. I want someone to help me overcome this accursed disposition and I want company; agreeable company. A man.

Victor (*sitting on the sofa*) What—sort of man?

Alma Don't pretend you don't understand.

Victor Mrs Millett, what is this leading up to?

Alma And don't pretend either that you didn't come here to day hoping that this might happen.

Victor (*in protest*) Oh, Mrs Millett . . .

Alma Because of my money.

Victor Oh, but I had no idea that you were so prosperous.

Alma Your sister knew.

Victor (*more boldly, in self-defence*) She didn't. She gathered that you were well-off but neither of us had an inkling that you were Bull's potted meat.

Alma Oh, I know that my money is the only possible attraction . . .

Victor No, but . . .

Alma What do you mean 'no'? Of course it is.

Victor (*appealingly*) Oh, please—you don't want me to pretend I've fallen in love with you?

Alma No. Any more than I have with you. It's simply that you happen to be the right sort of man. A gentleman. And of the right age.

Victor But, Mrs Millett . . .

Alma Alma, my name is. Yours is Victor, isn't it? Very appropriate too.

Victor No, but hold on . . .

Alma (*incredulously*) Hold on?

Victor No, but please listen (*He rises*) Here I am, living on a piffling little annuity—two hundred and thirty a year—in a miserable basement flat off the Earl's Court Road. No decent clothes, no decent food. Hardly enough for tobacco. None of the old pleasures of life—no clubs, except my membership of the M.C.C.; I've always stuck to that. Then suddenly this incredible thing happens. *You* come along. I'm given my choice between carrying on the way I am—and you.

Alma You needn't make it sound like a choice of evils.

Victor No—I expressed myself badly. I only mean—ought one to get married just for money and nothing else; well, nearly nothing. Would it be ethical?

Alma What does that matter?

Victor Oh, so long as you don't think it does. (*He sits on the sofa*)

Alma I want your company; you want a share of my money. What has being ethical got to do with it?

Victor Well, if you put it like that how can I refuse?

Alma (*rising*) Then don't refuse. (*Softening greatly*) Oh, please— please, Victor. (*She sits by him on the sofa*)

Victor After all, I don't suppose it would be so—I mean it might turn out wonderfully. I did mean that about your having charm.

Alma (*eagerly, and growing quite emotional*) I can stop myself being like I am; morose and lonely and—blank. I can be happy; we both can. I can get rid of my flying-up and be pleasant and gentle. I'll try so hard to be.

Victor Perhaps I may be able to help about that.

Alma Oh, you will; I know you will. The money won't be the first thing with you for long.

Victor No, it's beginning not to be already. I'm sorry I said I wanted you only for the money.

Alma At least it showed you're honest.

Victor But the way I put it—I made it sound as if you were revolting.

Alma (*almost coyly*) And I'm not?

Victor Good heavens, no; of course not. Not really.

Alma You make me feel happy already. Kiss me, Victor.

Victor What? Oh, yes. I forgot that.

He kisses her formally and briefly on the cheek. She becomes gay and enthusiastic

Alma (*rising*) We can get married at once. In a registry office. I'm not going to be gawped at coming out of a church. We won't need a honeymoon. We can come straight back here and settle down. Oh, Victor—how soon can you be ready?

Victor I can give up my flat anytime. (*Rising*) Oh. (*The 'oh' is because he suddenly realizes that there is a snag which he has entirely overlooked*) Oh, Lord. There's something else. Oh, confound it— I got so carried away.

Alma (*shocked, challengingly*) Why, what do you mean?

Victor There's someone I'd forgotten about.

Alma Another woman?

Victor No, no. Aubrey. Oh, gosh.

Alma Aubrey? Who is Aubrey?

Victor My son.

Alma Oh, you have a son.

Victor Yes, I'm afraid so. He's dependent on me.

Alma Why? He can't still be an infant.

Victor No, he's quite grown-up—twenty-two, in fact. But he's never—how can I put it?—He's never quite developed.

Alma A midget.

Victor No, I mean developed mentally.

Alma (*less aggressively*) Oh, dear—an imbecile.

Victor Yes. (*Hastily correcting himself*) No, no. No. You couldn't put him away or anything like that. He's just—silly.

Alma You mean he can't feed himself or——

Victor (*cutting in*) —Oh, yes; he's quite active. In fact he's often a great nuisance.

Alma Does he work?

Victor He has worked. In little odd jobs. But never for long.

Alma Well, he can find somewhere to live and look after himself, I take it?

Victor He'll have to, won't he? (*Tentatively*) I mean, he can't very well come along here too.

Alma (*threatening to flare up*) What?

Victor No, I'm saying he can't. But you see, I'm his father. I feel responsible for him. Besides, I'm very fond of him in a way. Don't worry; I'll do something about him. We can't let anything interfere with our—future.

Alma (*very decisively*) Nothing's going to interfere with mine so you needn't think so.

Victor Quite, quite.

Alma pulls herself together with an effort and becomes amiable and practical

Alma Very well then—do you want to be shown your new home?

Victor Oh, please, yes.

Alma (*pointing*) Through there is the kitchen and back door.

Victor Oh, yes?

Alma (*going up and opening the dining-room door*) And this—this is my dining-room.

Victor (*glancing into the room*) Oh, that's very nice and compact.

Alma points upwards at the door nearest up-stage

Alma That front room up there—that will be your bedroom.

Victor Oh, that's very nice, I'm sure. You mean—all to myself?

Alma (*ignoring this; indicating the middle door*) In the middle there, that's the bathroom. (*Pointing to the third door*) And that's *my* bedroom. There's no point in my showing you that.

Victor (*with one of his little chuckles*) Her-her. Not yet, anyhow.

A pause. Alma turns and looks at him, deliberating. He notices this and his jocular manner leaves him immediately. After taking thought Alma speaks as if to herself

Alma I'd better tell you now and get it over and done with.

Victor Oh, please don't say anything you don't want to.

Alma *(half flaring)* I *never* say what I don't want to.

Victor *(appeasingly)* No, no. I think I can guess what you have in mind.

Alma *(still angrily)* What, then?

Victor Well, the—shall I say—the bedroom side of it?

Alma Well?

Victor hesitates

Alma What *do* I have in mind?

Victor All I mean is—a woman like yourself—a widow and still fairly young—that is, compared with women who are a bit older and past it . . .

Alma *(impatiently)* What are you trying to say?

Victor Simply that no doubt one of your reasons for wanting to get married again is that you may still be feeling—how can I put it nicely?—feeling the need of a husband not only in the day time.

Alma reacts with a little shudder. He compromises quickly

Occasionally, anyhow.

Alma And is that what is in your mind, too? As well as the money?

Victor No, no. With me it's entirely the money. I mean it was to begin with.

Alma *(softening again)* Come and sit here.

She sits on the sofa and pats the seat beside her. Victor obeys

I told you about my first marriage, when I was nineteen. I went into it without the slightest knowledge of what happened to a girl on her wedding night.

Victor Oh, I say. You mean nobody had told you?

Alma They didn't tell brides in those days. They observed the Victorian tradition that it wasn't a respectable thing to talk about. Girls had to find out for themselves. *(Bitterly)* I found out. My husband had no consideration or compassion or restraint.

Victor The rotter.

Alma I was forced down and outraged and terribly hurt. Oh I resisted, of course. I had a will of my own already. I scratched his face so badly that he couldn't show it in public for the rest of the honeymoon. But that wasn't for long. He went away almost at once.

Victor (*guardedly*) Well, don't be afraid that *I'd* try to do anything—unpopular—no, what's the word?—discourteous.

Alma (*greatly relieved*) I'm so glad you feel like that, Victor. That was my one and only experience of it; but that was enough.

Victor (*also relieved, perking up*) Oh, well; if that's how you feel, that suits me. But how about your husband—I mean the other, golfing one—Millett?

Alma He was quite willing not to from the first. With me, anyhow. I know he consoled himself here and there. I didn't mind.

Victor There'll be nothing like that with me. I don't want to have anything more to do with a woman even if she isn't you.

Alma You only say that to please me.

Victor No, I don't.

Alma Because, judging by George, quite elderly men still hanker for it.

Victor Not in my case.

Alma (*hardening suddenly and rising*) Because I'm so undesirable?

Victor rises

Victor No, no. That isn't the reason at all. It's simply I've—shot my bolt.

Alma You needn't be sordid. I can't think how any man could ever want to go through that disgusting rigmarole but apparently they do.

Victor (*meekly*) It's his nature. Besides, the world has got to be populated.

Alma (*defiantly*) Why?

Victor Oh, please; there's nothing to argue about. We're in perfect agreement. You don't want to sleep with me; I don't want to sleep with you.

Alma Only because I'm like I am.

Victor You said that before. It isn't true.

Alma (*flying up*) If you're going to contradict me the whole time we'd better not start at all.

Victor (*boldly*) Oh, yes we had. I'm not going to give you up in a hurry.

Alma That's for me to say, not you.

Victor (*holding up a warning forefinger*) Now, Olga . . .

Alma (*in a horrified tone*) Olga?

Victor I mean . . .

Alma Al-ma.

Victor Alma, yes, of course. Now, Alma . . .

He wags the forefinger at her and laughs a false laugh. After a moment she relapses completely and laughs too. She takes him by the shoulders

Alma Oh, Victor—I *knew* you were the one I was looking for. (*She releases him and turns towards the staircase*) Come along: I'll take you and show you your own little bedroom.

Victor Oh, *rather;* yes—thank you.

Alma leads the way upstairs. Victor follows her, his hands decorously clasped behind his back, as—

the CURTAIN falls

SCENE 2

The same. Four months later; a morning in August

The room is just as it was before. When the Curtain rises, Mrs Holley, a daily woman of about fifty, is using a carpet-sweeper and singing as she works. After a moment the doorbell rings, she goes and opens it

Aubrey is at the door. He wears an old suit and no hat. His manner is furtive. Aubrey's silliness takes the form of being offensive with the pleasantest of natures and accepting reproach with a fatuous grin. He enjoys using expressions and words which were in those days considered obscene. Beneath his slovenly appearance he is well-bred and not altogether an unsympathetic character

Aubrey (*secretively*) Is she out?

Mrs Holley (*who dislikes Aubrey*) Do you mean Mrs Keene?

Aubrey Yes, of course. Is she?

Mrs Holley She's gone shopping.

Aubrey (*advancing confidently*) Oh, good egg. What about the old man?

Mrs Holley I beg your pardon?

Aubrey My father. I suppose he's had to go, too. To carry the parcels, poor old sod.

Mrs Holley You'll kindly not use words of that sort to me. If you wish to see Mr Keene he's in his bedroom.

Aubrey What, isn't he up yet?

Mrs Holley Of course he's up. (*Dusting the desk*) Long ago. It's jest he likes to sit up there of a morning and smoke his pipe.

Aubrey (*laughing*) I get it. Not allowed to smoke it down here. (*He sits in the armchair*)

Mrs Holley (*aloof*) That don't concern me and it's not for me to say even if it do.

Victor comes from his room upstairs on to the landing. He is wearing a much better tweed suit. He speaks as he opens his door

The Bed Before Yesterday

Victor Who's that down there? My God, Aubrey! (*He comes down-stairs, speaking as he does so*) That's all right, Mrs Holley; thank you.

Mrs Holley I was jest about to go, sir, unless there's anything else.

Victor Nothing I know of. Only don't say I said so.

Mrs Holley (*with an amiable smile for Victor*) Not me, sir. I know better than that.

Mrs Holley goes off to the kitchen with the cleaner

Aubrey (*as Mrs Holley goes*) Bye-bye, Pussy.

Victor Will you stop behaving like that?

Aubrey Like what? (*He rises*)

Victor And I told you not to come here, didn't I?

Aubrey Not when she's in, you said.

Victor How were you to know?

Aubrey Know what?

Victor That she wasn't in, of course.

Aubrey Well, is she?

Victor No, thank goodness.

Aubrey Then what are you bellyaching about?

Victor I told you always to find out first.

Aubrey (*pitiably*) But I have found out, haven't I?

Aubrey's tone softens Victor, whose affection for Aubrey is never far from the surface

Victor All right, all right, my dear boy. But you know what it is.

Aubrey What what is?

Victor I'm being careful not to put her out. She's been considerate and cheerful; in fact quite gay at times, especially since her step-mother died. So long as she doesn't see *you* everything's fine. I'm absolutely in clover.

Aubrey Well, I'm bloody well not. (*He sits*)

Victor Now steady with that language. And don't be ungrateful, either. I've spent a lot of my own money in helping you along. I got you a decent room to live in. I found you a good job.

Aubrey I've chucked that.

Victor What? Aubrey, you haven't got the sack again?

Aubrey No, I tell you; I chucked it. It was a lousy job, Dad— buggering about trying to sell cars.

Victor (*losing patience*) My God, Aubrey, I don't know how I stick you. You are the biggest chump I ever . . . So what are you doing now? Nothing, as usual.

Aubrey I *am* doing something.

Victor You are? What?

Aubrey I'm an extra.

Victor An extra what?

Aubrey At that film studios. It's a damn good job. I get a quid for every day I'm there.

Victor And how often is that?

Aubrey (*gloomily*) Not frightfully often.

Aubrey's depressed tone softens Victor again

Victor Oh, my dear boy, I'm sorry I spoke like that. (*He pats his shoulder*) I know you do your best. I think about you a great deal, you know. Anyhow, you've got your room. I've paid your rent on that a month ahead.

Aubrey I know. I wish you hadn't, Daddy.

Victor (*heartily*) No, that's all right. I'm glad to.

Aubrey No, but I've quit.

Victor (*reacting again*) You've what?

Aubrey (*rising*) I've got another room pretty nearly as cheap.

Victor Where?

Aubrey The room you got was a lousy one anyhow, and the bloke who kept it is a frightful shit.

Victor But he was paid in adv . . . (*He gives up*) Oh, well, where are you now?

Aubrey Just along there. In Eaton Place. (*He jerks his thumb*)

Victor (*incredulously*) Eaton Place?

Aubrey It's a top room, a sort of attic. I think it's really meant for a skivvy but it's quite all right. It's got a basin and all that.

Victor But Eaton Place? How did you come to go there?

Aubrey That's really what I came to see you about. A girl found it for me.

Victor (*alerted*) A girl?

Aubrey She's got a flat on the floor below me.

Victor What girl? What's all this? Haven't I told you to be careful about women?

Aubrey You speak for yourself, old feller me lad.

Victor That'll do. Now—what have you been up to?

Aubrey Nothing. You can see for yourself. She said she wanted to meet you so I brought her along.

Victor What? Where is she?

Aubrey Outside. She was waiting while I had a look-see. I'll call her in. (*He opens the front door*)

Victor is anxious but curious

Victor Well, we mustn't be too long . . .

Aubrey (*calling*) Hi—come in—it's okay.

Victor Still I'd better find out about this.

Ella comes to the front door

Aubrey (*as Ella appears and passes him*) She isn't in. Only the old man.

Ella comes down to Victor. Aubrey closes the front door. Ella is an attractive and sexy girl of twenty-one. She is of provincial middle-class but bright and confident. She wears a neat and becoming but inexpensive summer dress and hat. Aubrey announces her from the doorway as she enters

Here she is, Papa.

Victor (*surprised by Ella's appearance*) Oh. How-do-you-do? (*He shakes hands with Ella*)

Ella How do you do, Mr Keene. My name's Ella—Ella Reed.

Victor Well, well. You mean to tell me you're a friend of Aubrey's?

Ella (*with a little laugh*) Yes. Why not?

Victor I'm very glad to hear it. Fancy poor old Aubrey getting off with a girl like you.

Ella (*seriously defensive*) It depends what you mean by getting off.

Victor Oh, no, no, no. I expressed myself badly.

Ella We're just friends, that's all. And I'm very glad we are. Aubrey's different from the others.

Victor I can well believe that. But where did you meet each other?

Ella At a Lyons tea-shop, actually. It was full-up and we shared a table and got talking.

Victor H'm. That was a bit forward, wasn't it? On somebody's part?

Ella Mine. I suppose I'm rather a forward girl. (*She smiles briefly*)

Victor begins to smile back but checks himself

Aubrey Well, come on, Pop.

Victor What d'you mean, come on?

Aubrey What you're always telling me—manners. Ask her to sit down.

Victor Yes, but you'd better not be here for too long. Very well; just for a minute . . . (*He indicates a chair*)

Ella Thank you. (*She seats herself*)

Victor (*sitting*) So you met and talked at Lyons. (*To Aubrey*) You must have got to know her very quickly.

Aubrey (*patting Victor on the shoulder*) I'll bet you would have too. (*He laughs, then sits*)

Victor What did you talk about?

Ella Oh, jobs and things. I'm by way of being an actress; or wanting to be.

Victor Are you, though? Have you been in anything lately?

Ella I've never been in anything at all. I get an odd day's crowd-work at Elstree or somewhere.

Victor Ah—on the films—an extra. So that's how Aubrey got on to that.

Ella Yes, I gave his name to my agent. But he's only done it about once. Poor Aubrey simply can't manage to get there early enough.

Victor (*beginning to get definitely hostile*) If you'll tell me something that poor Aubrey *can* manage . . .

Aubrey It isn't me we're talking about. (*He rises*)

Victor Yes, it is. (*To Ella*) He was in a perfectly good job . . .

Aubrey It was a lousy job . . .

Victor (*still to Ella*) You've taken him to a new room too, I hear. In Eaton Place. As if he could afford to live in this part of the world.

Ella Well, I couldn't either. But I know the man who owns the house.

Victor Oh, so that's it?

Ella No, it's not. There's nothing like that about it. (*With a quick smile*) Not with him, anyhow.

This brings a sharp glance from Victor. Ella goes on resignedly

And I'm being turned out of the flat, in any case.

Victor Oh, and why's that?

Ella It's just the old story, Mr Keene.

Victor What old story?

Aubrey Wake up, Dad. She's broke.

Ella (*reprovingly*) Aubrey . . .

Aubrey Well, he's got to be told sometime. And he's not very quick off the mark.

Victor Ah, now we have it. (*To Aubrey*) So that's why you brought her here?

Aubrey Yes.

Victor Have you been taking money off Aubrey?

Ella No—well—we sort of help each other out when we can.

Victor (*rounding on Aubrey*) That twenty pounds I gave you the other day for a new suit and shoes and things? Where's the new suit? Where is it? That isn't it.

The front door opens. Victor turns with an alarmed exclamation

Oh, good Lord. (*He rises*)

Alma enters, carrying a shopping bag of the period. She wears a dress of good quality but of quiet taste and a hat. She shuts the door

Alma There. I'm back in good time.

Victor Yes, dear; better than I . . .

Alma (*seeing Aubrey*) What's he doing here?

Victor He brought this girl.

Alma Oh? Who's she?

Ella rises. She does not appear in awe of Alma

Ella Good morning, Mrs Keene. My name's Ella. I'm a friend of Aubrey's.

Aubrey moves slowly towards the front door whenever Alma is not looking

Alma Really? I'm surprised to hear he's got one.

Ella Aubrey wanted me to meet his father. Actually, we were just going.

Alma You looked to me to be sitting pretty squat. (*Controlling herself*) No. But why did you want to meet my husband?

Victor All right, dear. I'll tell you when they've gone.

Alma But I'd like to know now.

Victor Well, you can guess—any friend of Aubrey's. They came to try and get some money.

Alma I see. (*To Ella*) And what's Aubrey to you, may I ask?

Ella (*boldly*) Someone to be with, that's all. (*She goes and takes Aubrey's hand*) I'm fond of Aubrey. I look on him as a sort of pet.

Alma Well, that's honest enough, but you must have very unwholesome tastes.

Ella I don't think so. Besides, he's such a pleasant change.

Alma What from? (*She puts her shopping bag on the table below the sofa*)

Ella Oh, never mind. Come on, Aubrey, we'll go.

Victor No, wait a minute. (*To Ella*) I'm afraid this has got to be put a stop to.

Ella (*challenging*) What has?

Victor I'm sorry, but I don't think you're the right friend for Aubrey.

Ella That's exactly what I am. And he for me.

Aubrey (*laughing*) I believe poor old Popsy thinks you're a tart.

Victor Aubrey—will you?

Alma (*genuinely puzzled*) A tart? What does he mean, a tart?

Victor It's a common term, dear—for a prostitute.

Alma (*in a shocked tone*) Victor . . .

Victor Well, you asked.

Alma (*to Ella*) And is that what you are?

Ella (*mildly*) No, I don't think so. No, of course not. I mean, I don't get paid for it, or walk out on the streets or anything like that.

Alma Then what *do* you do?

Victor Yes, well, never mind, dear. She told me she was trying to be an actress.

Ella That was the idea six months ago when I first came to London.

Alma Where from?

Ella Gloucestershire. My father's a house agent. My mother died and he married again. To a woman I hate. I had a terrible row with my father and left home. I wanted to go on the London stage because I'm good at acting. I played the lead in all the local amateur shows. (*To Alma*) You know—*Paddy-the-next-best-thing.* (*Dramatically*) *All-of-a-sudden-Peggy.*

Alma (*recoiling*) Good gracious. (*She sits on the sofa*)

Ella But I never realized how hopeless it would be. (*She sits in the armchair*)

Alma And so now you've come here trying to get help?

Ella Oh, if only you'd let me tell you all about myself—but I suppose I'd only shock you.

Alma You've done that already. Because so far as I can understand you are telling me that you allow men to seduce you.

Ella Yes, well . . .

Alma It's a very distasteful subject and one which I know very little about . . .

Aubrey *I'll* bet. (*He sits*)

Victor (*in a savage aside to Aubrey*) You keep your mouth shut.

Alma But is that true?

Ella Yes. Well, no. Not seduce me exactly, because . . .

Alma Because what?

Ella Well, I don't object, you see. Well, to be perfectly honest with you, I enjoy it like everybody else. So long as it's with somebody I like.

Victor Alma, I don't want you to listen to this.

Alma (*snubbing him flat; with a trace of the flare-up*) Do be quiet. Go on.

Victor is so squashed by Alma that he lets this go. Ella is anxious to be allowed to tell her story

Ella It all began when I had a terrible disappointment. I got spotted in the film-crowd by a very well-known actor. He sent for me to see him in his dressing-room on the set.

Victor Who was he?

Ella I don't know that I ought to tell you.

Aubrey It was Fred Castle.

Ella Aubrey.

Victor (*impressed*) Fred Castle, good Lord. (*To Alma*) Even you have heard of Fred Castle.

Alma (*indignantly*) What do you mean, 'even I'? I've seen him several times. George never missed one of those farces he's always doing. He's supposed to be very attractive to women. (*To Ella*) So you went to his room, did you? What did he say?

Ella (*with a little laugh*) I remember his first words. I'd better not tell you what *they* were.

Alma You'll tell me what I ask you. What did this Castle man say to you?

Ella He just sat and pointed at me and said, 'You look to have a very good pair of charlies.'

Alma (*again puzzled*) Charlies? What did he mean?

Aubrey Tits.

Alma Charlies? Tits? What are you talking about?

Victor Tits, dear; short for teats—or rather the same thing. (*Illustrating with cupped hands*) You know . . .

Alma Don't be so disgusting, Victor.

Victor (*roused*) Don't go on at me—it's not *me*. (*To Ella*) Keep it clean, can't you?

Alma (*to Victor*) Don't keep interrupting. (*To Ella*) What did you do then? Walked out, I should hope.

Ella Walked out? On Fred Castle? Oh, Mrs Keene, how could I? I thought my career was made. Naturally I did what he wanted.

Alma But do you mean to say *you* wanted to too?

Ella Of course. Well, I mean—Fred Castle—who wouldn't want to? Wouldn't you?

Victor Don't you speak to my wife like that. *She*, of all people.

Alma That'll do, Victor. (*To Ella*) What happened then?

Ella He took me out that night to Eaton Place to a house run by a man called Mr Morris.

Victor And what goes on there? (*Quickly and guardedly*) No, steady —I mean if it's anything too near the knuckle . . .

Ella Oh, it's nothing improper.

Aubrey (*confidentially to Victor*) Gambling, Papa.

Victor (*in a sudden shock*) What?

Ella Chemmy and roulette and things.

Victor can only glare

Mr Fred Castle doesn't really care for gambling. He's never been there since.

Victor But you have?

Ella Mr Morris asked me to come back to entertain his men friends; and he rented me this little flat next door.

Alma To entertain the men friends there as well?

Ella (*nearly losing control*) *Yes*.

Alma And you tell me you enjoy doing that?

Ella Well, I can pick the men friends I like, can't I? (*Turning impulsively*) Come on, Aubrey; it's no good; we'd better go. (*She rises*)

Alma We haven't yet heard why you came here trying to get money.
Ella (*sitting*) Well, I owe Mr Morris for the flat. He wants it all by tomorrow morning or he'll turn me out.
Alma And how much do you owe him?
Ella And I've had to get food and stockings and everything.
Alma How much, I asked?
Aubrey I'll tell you. (*Rising*) She wants a hundred and seventy quid.
Victor A hundred and seventy—it's past belief.
Alma (*rising*) I'm afraid you're a very weak and immoral girl.
Ella (*gently*) I don't think I'm *weak*.
Alma (*beginning to get worked up*) There's no denying that you're immoral, is there?
Ella (*rising*) No, not if you're old-fashioned, I suppose.
Alma These men you take to your flat—don't they give you money?
Ella (*shrugging*) They mostly seem to think I do it for pleasure.
Alma And that's exactly what you do, or so you say. Why can't you take yourself in hand and resist?
Ella Mrs Keene, why should anybody try to resist a thing like that?
Alma (*still angrier*) But you *can* resist if you put your mind to it. You can fight against anything and overcome it. You can change your whole nature.
Victor By gad, that's very true, dear.
Alma (*at the flying-up stage*) I didn't ask you to comment.
Victor No, but if anybody's got a right to say that, it's you. You've proved it yourself. You've been wonderful.
Alma (*in a complete outburst*) How dare you talk like that in front of people? My goodness, Victor, it's incredible sometimes how stupid you can be.
Aubrey (*delightedly*) Wow.
Alma Take that creature away out of my sight and keep him there. Go on, go away, go out and take him with you. (*She picks up Victor's hat and opens the front door*)
Victor Now steady, Alma . . .
Alma Go on, do what you're told. Go away, both of you. Go on. Go for a walk. And only *you* come back.
Victor I don't want to go for a walk. Now, Alma . . . (*He attempts his 'laughing at her' stunt, laughing falsely himself and pointing a fore-finger*)
Alma Stop that nonsense and it isn't what *you* want. (*To Aubrey*) Go on. You too.
Victor (*looking out of the door*) I think it's going to rain.
Alma Then take your umbrella. (*She throws an umbrella at Victor*)
Victor You'll be sorry for this, you know. Come along, Aubrey.

Victor takes his hat and umbrella and goes out

Aubrey follows Victor to the front door

Aubrey (*to Ella*) I'll see you later.
Alma You will not. I'll see to that.
Aubrey I wasn't talking to you, Honeybum.

Aubrey goes out

Alma closes the door, then goes through a little spasm of remorse, shaking her shoulders as though to shake the anger from her. She speaks as if to herself

Alma Oh, why do I have to get like that—I haven't been like it for so long. (*To Ella*) It's that ghastly Aubrey. Why did he have to bring you here?
Ella I'm sorry you dislike Aubrey so much.
Alma Dislike him—he makes me positively shudder.
Ella (*sharply*) You don't think I go to bed with Aubrey, do you?
Alma Oh, don't be so revolting and disgusting and shameless.
Ella Aubrey's just . . .
Alma (*cutting in*) Never mind Aubrey. These other men. Apparently you go with them right and left. And like it.
Ella But, Mrs Keene, doesn't everybody like it?
Alma (*emphatically*) No.
Ella But surely they ought to?
Alma (*with challenge*) Ought to?
Ella Well, if Nature tells you . . .
Alma Nature can be a savage and brutal thing. Look at tigers.
Ella I'm not talking about tigers.
Alma I am. And some men too, for that matter.
Ella But it isn't only that Nature urges you on to do it. It's so gorgeous when you do do it. I don't see how it can be wrong.
Alma I'm not talking about rights and wrongs. It's this finding pleasure in it. (*She sits in the armchair*)
Ella Well, if you don't, Mrs Keene, I'm very sorry for you. And for myself too. Because I've got in this awful mess and I was hoping for sympathy.
Alma (*severely*) Don't you tell me that I'm unsympathetic.
Ella No, but I took it for granted that you still went in for it like everybody else.
Alma That'll do, thank you. (*She rises*)
Ella There are heaps of other girls like me, you know.
Alma I do not know and don't want to.
Ella I think most unmarried girls will soon be doing it as a matter of course, like men do.

Alma I keep telling you I am not interested. (*She sits on the sofa*)

Ella (*sincerely baffled*) Honestly, you're awfully different from everybody else about it. (*Sitting on the sofa*) I mean, for instance, look at my grandmother.

Alma Why should I look at your grandmother?

Ella She had a boy-friend in Bordighera, an Italian boy, a gigolo. She used to spend every winter out there with him in Bordighera. Right up to the time she was seventy.

Alma (*incredulously*) Seventy?

Ella Over seventy.

Alma Poor thing. She must have had a particularly nauseating type of aberration.

Ella *I* don't think she was a poor thing at all. I think she got the best out of life. I only hope *I* live to be seventy.

Victor enters at the front door. He has regained his self-confidence and his manner is rather bossy. He closes the door and speaks while hanging up his hat and disposing of his umbrella

Victor Aubrey made off somewhere so I've come back.

Alma Is it raining?

Victor No, but I'm not going to hang about out there. Besides, I want a word with this girl.

Ella (*hopefully*) Oh, Mr Keene, do you? (*She rises*)

Victor Yes. About Aubrey. I'll find him somewhere to go. In fact, I've had a very good idea about that. But please understand I won't have you going about together.

Ella (*with spirit*) But you don't understand—I'm good for Aubrey. I stop him from doing silly things.

Victor Such as chucking his job and becoming an extra and getting mixed up with a gambling hell.

Ella (*turning to Alma*) Oh, Mrs Keene, do please make him understand. I've got to get this money right away.

Alma It's no good your looking at me like that. This is entirely my husband's concern.

Victor (*decisively*) Come along, now; I think you'd better go. (*He moves up and opens the front door*)

Ella goes up to the door

Ella (*in the doorway*) Yes, very well. But what a pity. Because I'm sure you're both such kind people really.

Ella goes out

Victor closes the door and comes down

Victor There goes a minx if ever there was one.

Alma (*effusively penitent*) Oh, Victor, I flew up at you. I'm so sorry. I won't ever do it again.

Victor Oh, well. It may have been my fault.

Alma What do you mean 'may have been'? Of course it was your fault.

Victor You can make amends, anyhow. I've got to find Aubrey somewhere else to live.

Alma (*sharply*) You're not going to bring him near *me*.

Victor No, listen; I've had a brainwave. I had it while I was waiting out there. Mrs Tucker.

Alma Mrs Tuck—you mean Lolly?

Victor Yes; that cousin of yours. When she called here that day she said she still had that house at Ealing and took lodgers. She might take Aubrey.

Alma Not if she knew him beforehand.

Victor (*moving to the desk*) She might. And in a nice healthy domestic atmosphere like that he might reform. He's very weak-minded. Try her, do. (*He picks up the telephone directory*)

Alma It wouldn't be fair on her.

Victor (*hastily*) She could find out for herself. Please, Alma. For my sake. You said you were sorry for flying up. Look up her number.

Alma accepts the book

Oh, thank you, dear.

Alma I won't have Aubrey coming in here to meet her.

Victor (*picking up the shopping bag*) Well—we'll see. I'll just take this through to the kitchen. I must get him away from that girl. Mustn't I?

Alma (*with a deep breath*) I never knew such girls existed. And there are numbers of others like her she says. What are we coming to?

Victor Oh, I dunno. This younger generation—all unsettled and restless.

Alma slowly turns the pages of the telephone directory as they speak

Alma These young women going to bed with men and—whatever the word is for it. What *is* the usual word for it?

Victor What? Oh, I—don't think we want to go into that.

Alma (*on a sharper note*) Why not?

Victor The er—the polite term for it is sexual intercourse.

Alma Oh, rubbish. And as if there could be a polite term for that.

Victor escapes with the shopping bag into the kitchen

Alma flips the pages more quickly to discover 'Tucker' in the directory as—

the CURTAIN *falls*

Scene 3

The same. Tea-time the same day

The tea-table is back in the same position as Scene 1, with three places laid, and a large tray with teapot, etc.

Alma dressed as in the previous scene, is seated at the table on one side. Lolly is seated behind it. A third chair has been occupied and is now back against the wall. The cakestand remains alongside the table. Lolly, who is drinking tea, is a plump, jolly, outspoken woman of Alma's age. She is a good stage lower in the social scale than Alma, good-looking, well-dressed and evidently prosperous. Besides the tea-cup, she is holding a little napkin, with which she gives her mouth a quick wipe

Alma Would you like a piece of seed cake?

Lolly No, thank you.

Alma You didn't have much tea. I hope you had all you wanted?

Lolly Oh, more than enough, thank you. It was Victor who didn't. He was hardly here a minute.

Alma (*taking Lolly's cup*) He's looking for this—son of his. (*She collects the tea-things on the tray*) He's been trying to find him all the afternoon. Not that it matters. I wouldn't let you take him in, even for a night. That was Victor's idea. (*She rises and moves to the kitchen*)

Lolly Yes, well, I'll wait and see him, anyhow; just for Victor's sake.

Alma Would you mind opening the door?

Lolly Of course, dear. What am I thinking of?

Alma exits with the tray

Alma Thank you.

Lolly (*finding her lipstick and using it with a hand-mirror*) Anyway, it's nice to see you again and have a bit of a pow-pow. It was sad about your old step-mother popping off like that.

Alma enters with a crumb-brush and tray

Alma Was it?

Lolly Oh, well. I daresay it was one of those merciful releases. (*Producing a cigarette-case and lighter*) D'you smoke, Alma?

Alma No. I never have. Victor smokes his pipe sometimes. In his own room.

Lolly (*lighting up*) Ah, a pipe-smoker. Yes, I thought he looked that sort. Tweedy-suited kind of chap. Shall I sit here? (*She indicates the sofa*)

Alma Where you like.

Lolly (*sitting on the sofa*) He's nice, Alma. You make a good pick.

Alma He's been very kind to me, and considerate. (*With deeper feeling*) He's made me quite a different woman.

Alma takes the cloth from the table and folds it during the dialogue. She is in no hurry about it

Lolly Well, marriage can't have meant much to you before. Oh, not that I can talk. Fifteen years ago it is now since I bade farewell to Archie. Let's see—did you ever know Archie?

Alma (*coldly*) I saw him once; but I never had anything to do with him.

Lolly You must be about the only woman who didn't.

Alma puts the folded tea-cloth over her arm and picks up the cake-stand and crumb-brush

(*Continuing in a sympathetic manner*) And your old George Millett— he was another of them, wasn't he?

Alma I don't quite know what you mean.

Lolly Well—another like Archie.

Alma But did you know George?

Lolly Yes, of course. Didn't you know I did? (*She quickly adds*) Oh, I didn't know him as well as he wanted me to. Don't think that.

Alma He was never very particular.

Alma goes into the kitchen

Lolly (*talking on during this*) Mind you, I'm not saying anything against your old George. He was a dear old boy. I don't blame you for sticking to him despite it all. But I *was* a bit surprised when you told me you'd gone and taken another one on.

Alma returns

Alma I wanted companionship. A man's companionship. I hate women. (*She resets the desk chair*)

Lolly (*readily*) Oh, so do I, dear. And this has turned out really well?

Alma (*with reserve*) Perfectly, thank you. George did everything he liked. Victor does everything I like.

Lolly Aren't you lucky? Oh, well; it's never too late.

Alma (*as if just for something to say*) I wonder *you* never married again. (*She sits*)

Lolly After what I'd been through with Archie? No, thank you. I've done better than that.

Alma How do you mean?

Lolly Archie was all right to begin with—as a lover and all that. That was his trouble, women. Like it is with all of 'em. Goodness knows he got all he could want from me.

Alma (*fighting shy of the subject*) You needn't go into any details.

Lolly (*oblivious*) Oh, I don't mind your knowing. He was one of those chaps that just have to have variety. Quite soon after we were married, off he went, fornicating all over the shop.

Alma Lolly, you're spilling ash on the carpet. (*She rises*)

Lolly Oh, sorry, dear. Even at home he was at it. I had to sack two of the parlour-maids. He even had a crack at the cook.

Alma There's an ashtray here somewhere. (*She takes an ashtray from the window table to Lolly*) There. (*She sits*)

Lolly Oh, thank you. So after I'd divorced Archie I said to myself, 'Oh, all right, my lad. I'll take a leaf out of your book. I've got this house, plenty of rooms and no-one in them. I'll take lodgers— nice, attractive gentlemen bachelor ones.' (*Laughing*) And that's what I've been doing ever since. I've got three there now. Life's one long razzle.

Alma has listened to this with growing resentment and incredulity. She exclaims almost involuntarily

Alma You too? You do that?

Lolly (*taken aback*) Well, of course. Why not?

Alma (*incredulously*) You keep men in the house and go to bed with them in turns?

Lolly Well, you needn't put it quite like that. It makes it sound a bit insincere.

Alma (*more and more worked up*) Insincere? I think it's horrifying.

Lolly Oh, come off it, Alma. You ought to be the first to sympathize. Your marriage was much the same as mine—sitting there alone at home listening to the wireless while your husband was off on his own, chasing every woman in sight. Why shouldn't I make up for lost time and enjoy myself?

Alma That's what I can't understand—your enjoying it.

Lolly (*catching some of Alma's vehemence*) But—God Almighty— haven't you always enjoyed it and don't you still?

Alma Very well, I'll tell you. I never let George touch me. He was quite willing not to. As for Victor, I told him from the start—no. And he doesn't mind either.

Lolly But why? What put you off it? Were you raped as a kid or something?

Alma Yes. On the first night of my first marriage; when I knew nothing about anything.

Lolly (*genuinely enlightened*) Oh-h, yes. I remember hearing now.

Well, of course—if you get a shock like that when you lose your virginity . . .

Alma Didn't you?

Lolly Shock? (*Laughing*) I went into absolute transports. I remember how I made Archie laugh. I will say for him, with all his faults, he was a marvellous hand at it.

Alma Transports! It's beyond me. I met another one today who's—like you about it. And she's still only a girl.

Lolly (*quietly and kindly*) Darling, you're the only one I've ever heard of who's like *you* are.

Alma I shrink from the very thought of it; from the whole revolting messy awkwardness of what you have to do. I think the whole thing's disgusting and nauseating and that Nature or Providence or whoever is responsible ought to be thoroughly ashamed of themselves. They might at least have thought of something nicer *looking* for it to be done with. I can't think of anything more repulsive than the sight of a man with nothing on. All that hideous bundle.

Lolly (*honestly sympathetic*) Oh, you poor darling.

Alma You needn't pity me. I'm only too glad to have avoided all that side of life.

Lolly Life—you don't know what life means. You poor dear, you were scared and horrified at the start and went and cut yourself off from the loveliest thing in the whole of existence.

Lolly's kindly manner and words have their effect on Alma. She softens a little

Alma I know I'm different but I'd rather you didn't tell me any more.

Lolly It's my duty to tell you and your duty to listen. Your duty to yourself. To say nothing of your duty to Victor.

This really makes Alma sit up and take thought. There is a note of uncertainty in her reply

Alma Victor's quite contented. He never thinks of that sort of thing.

Lolly Oh, rats. All men do. Especially at his time of life; a man gets his second wind. Oh, dear. I hope he's not doing an Archie on you.

Alma A what?

Lolly Having a bit of his own on the Q.T.

Alma Don't you dare say such a thing about Victor.

Lolly No, of course not. Then all I can say is he's being very unselfish.

Alma Unselfish? Do you really imagine that?

Lolly I don't imagine it; I know it. It means more to a man than it does even to us; though for meself I don't see how that's possible. Oh, Alma dear; if only you'd let yourself find out what it's like to be a woman. To be clasped tight to a man with him absolutely part of you and with that lovely urge growing in you all the time —on and on, more and more, nearer and nearer until ooo—it happens and you hear a glorious burst of bells and you're in Paradise—if ever Paradise could be such Paradise as that.

Alma (*after a moment or two; half-heartedly*) I know most people do find it attractive.

Lolly I can't bear to think of you missing it all your life. Try it while you've still got plenty of time. And think what it would mean to Victor.

Pause

Victor enters at the front door

Victor No good. Not a sign of him. (*He hangs his hat up and comes down*)

Alma Did you go to his room?

Victor Yes. The front door was open so I went right up there Nobody about at all.

Alma Well, it wouldn't have mattered in any case.

Lolly Oh, I'd have liked to have seen the boy.

Alma You wouldn't.

Lolly (*preparing to leave*) I'll be getting along now. (*Rising*) Thank you for the nice tea, dear.

Alma Not at all. (*She picks up the ashtray and takes it to the kitchen door*)

Victor Must you go so soon?

Lolly Yes, I really must. My lodgers will be getting home. Goodbye, Alma.

Alma Good-bye. (*Opening the kitchen door*) And—thank you for coming.

Alma exits to the kitchen

Victor escorts Lolly to the front door and lets her out

Victor Yes, it's been good to see you again.

Lolly Well, it's nice to do each other a bit of good when we can. Ta-ta.

Lolly exits

Victor closes the door and comes down

Alma enters from the kitchen

Victor What did she mean by that? I don't want any doing good to.

From this point Alma's whole manner shows a marked change. She has come to a decision and is amicable, eager and persuasive; with only an occasional brief moment of impatience and irritation

Alma Victor . . .

Victor Yes, dear?

Alma I want to speak to you.

Victor (*apprehensively*) Oh? Well—yes?

Alma I've been meaning to tell you. I saw you in a new light this morning. I was very pleased with you.

Victor (*puzzled*) Why? When? What?

Alma The way you dealt with that girl. It showed how strong-minded you can be if you choose.

Victor Rather too much so, I'm afraid. Poor little fool. I didn't mean to be too aggressive.

Alma But I like you to be aggressive. I want you to be more aggressive.

Victor I've no reason to be, Alma.

Alma Yes, you have. Aggressive with me too. Especially with me. I've always been the one to lay down the law. You've been so gentle and—giving-in.

Victor No, no. I've tried to be helpful and—considerate.

Alma Yes, and I haven't.

Victor Oh, you have, Alma.

Alma I have not. You're my husband. The husband should be the one to dictate.

Victor I've had no reason to . . .

Alma Instead of which I've always been the one to dictate: 'Do this; do that. I don't want you to do this. (*Meaningly*) I don't think we should do that.'

Victor Well, but we've got along very happily. There's Aubrey, of course; but apart from him—I'm perfectly contented, Alma.

Alma Oh, I'm sure you're not.

Victor I am.

Alma No. In one way—in particular—I know I've been very remiss.

Victor (*suddenly enlightened*) Oh, that? Well, dear, that's been up to you. But perhaps now that your step-mother's dead and you've got all that much more, it may seem a trifle squinny.

Alma (*put out of her stride, annoyed*) What are you talking about?

Victor What *you* are. You mean my allowance.

Alma (*almost flying up with impatience*) I do not mean your allowance.

I give you your whole board and keep and three pounds a week to say nothing of paying the whole of the rates and electricity and telephone . . .

Victor Yes, all right, all right . . .

Alma And *gas* . . .

Victor Yes, yes, all right. Now, Alma, don't begin . . .

A brief pause. Alma recovers herself, biting her lip

But if it isn't my allowance, what is it?

Another brief pause. Alma becomes gentle and almost pleading in her manner

Alma Victor . . .

Victor 'Mmm??

Alma Victor, I think I've been very behindhand in showing you affection.

Victor Oh, nonsense, dear; you've always been very affectionate.

Alma I mean affection in its deepest sense.

Victor Your affection has always been as deep as it can go.

Alma (*a flash of annoyance*) Oh, don't be dense. (*Recovering and becoming alluring again*) Deep. (*She moves close to him*) Deep. (*Her face close to his*) It.

Victor (*staggered*) It?

Alma It.

Victor (*incredulously*) Oh, not it?

Alma It. What Nature intended for a man and wife. Part of each other. In and in. Up and up. On and on. Nearer and nearer. Bells and Paradise.

Victor Good god. (*He sits on the sofa*) But, Alma, from the very start you said . . .

Alma (*sitting beside him*) I was prejudiced and—ignorant and dreadfully unfair to you. (*She kisses him suddenly*) *Now!* I am going upstairs to my bedroom. (*On the move*) You come, too.

Victor is utterly unprepared for this and very uncertain of his own desires and capabilities

Victor (*rising*) Now, hold on, Alma.

She halts and turns

This is something that Lolly has been gassing about.

Alma She made me realize—and she was quite right to.

Victor But I'd put all thoughts of that behind me.

Alma So had I. But now—oh, come along, I'm so inquisitive and stimulated.

Victor Yes, but I mean—in the middle of the afternoon and everything . . .

Alma (*hardening*) Don't you want to? Aren't you eager to?

Victor Yes, of course, if you are. But it's so unexpected.

Alma Doesn't that make it all the better for both of us?

Victor Yes, but it's a thing you have to . . .

Alma (*still more challenging*) Have to what?

Victor Well, sort of—have to think yourself into.

Alma Why? Because I'm undesirable and off-putting?

Victor No, no, no; of course not; it isn't only that . . .

Alma Then what is it? Have you been doing an Archie on me?

Victor A what?

Alma Going with other women behind my back?

Victor Alma—how can you speak like that?

Alma Then why aren't you running upstairs after me? *Bounding upstairs?*

Victor I am. Only give us a chance.

Alma (*seizing his lapels and shaking him*) Then come on, will you?

Victor (*making the best of it*) Rather—you bet I will.

Alma changes again to glad excitement. She relaxes his lapels; puts her hands on his shoulders for a moment

Alma Oh, Victor . . . (*She goes quickly upstairs*)

Victor follows slowly. Alma turns half-way up the stairs

Come on, Victor!

the CURTAIN *falls*

ACT II

The same. Shortly after ten that night

The lights are on and the curtains drawn, though it is still dusk outside

Victor, in a darker suit and tie, is sitting in an armchair reading the evening paper, and, for the first time in this room, smoking a pipe. There is a small table beside his chair.

Alma, in a stylish semi-evening dress, enters from the dining-room armed with a poured-out drink on a tray. She is in a very amiable mood. Victor's attitude at the opening is self-assured, and indeed rather patronizing

Alma Here, dear.

Victor (*glancing up*) Mm?

Alma A whisky and water for you. I thought you might like one tonight.

Victor Oh, thanks. Put it down there, will you?

Alma puts the tumbler on the little table. She stretches her limbs and then goes and reclines on the sofa. She smiles at her thoughts for a moment or two, then speaks

Alma Oooo—I feel so radiant, Victor. Wasn't this afternoon wonderful?

Victor (*looking up from the paper with a short smile*) I'm very glad you found it so.

Alma Well, you did too.

Victor (*with a brief chuckle*) M-hm.

Alma Oh, Victor; it can go on and on now, can't it? There's still a long time for us ahead.

He is reading again; she speaks rather more pointedly

Isn't there?

Victor takes a sip of the drink and replaces the tumbler

Victor Yes, dear, but . . .

Alma But what?

Victor It's not a thing you want to have a—well, a set time-table about.

Alma (*ignoring this*) After all these years, suddenly to discover—and you were so considerate.

Victor Oh. Thank you, dear. (*He gives another brief chuckle*)

Alma I mean it was so thoughtful of you to take so long about it. (*Brief pause; then, rhapsodically*) I got the bells. Did you get the bells?

Victor What bells?

Alma When it happens you seem to hear bells.

Victor Do you?

Alma Don't *you*?

Victor Well, I dunno—that sounds a bit high-falutin to me.

Alma Dear Victor, I know you were thinking only of me. I could tell that from what you said.

Victor (*apprehensively*) Why, what did I say?

Alma You said, 'Thank God I brought it off'.

He takes another sip, puts the tumbler back and rises

Oh, Victor, isn't it wonderful to know that we possess such a treat?

Victor (*putting the newspaper on the table*) My dear Alma, I'm very glad for you; especially now when you're getting on in life. But it's not a thing you want to overdo.

Alma I don't see how one could possibly overdo it.

Victor Oh, one can, you know.

Alma I can quite understand Lolly going on as she does. That girl this morning too—even at her age.

Victor What I mean is it's apt to take it out of you.

Alma Oh, yes; but only for that lovely minute with the bells.

Victor Yes, but quite apart from these bells . . .

Alma (*with a note of anxiety*) But, Victor; you do love it. Don't say you don't.

Victor I don't. I mean I don't say I don't. I do. Love it I mean.

Alma (*stretching out her arms to him*) Well, then . . .

The front-door bell rings. They are both very surprised

Who on earth can that be?

Victor I can't think. Somebody from outside wanting something.

Alma Someone come to the wrong house. You'd better see.

Victor (*going to the front door and calling*) Who is it? (*He opens the door*)

Aubrey appears. He is dressed just as before

Aubrey Oh, hallo, Pop.

Alma (*rising*) Send him away.
Victor (*to Aubrey*) What do you want?
Alma I won't have him in here.
Victor No, hold on, Alma. I've been trying to find him ever since this morning.
Alma It's my house, isn't it?
Victor Yes, but dash it he *is* my son.
Alma (*indignantly*) Very well, see him. So long as I don't. I'm going to my room.

Alma goes upstairs, but remains on the landing, listening. Victor admits Aubrey and shuts the front door

Victor (*bluntly*) Come in, then.

Aubrey comes down and picks up Victor's drink

Aubrey Hallo, what's this?
Victor (*following him down*) Leave that alone. That's my drink.
Aubrey Good for you. I'll bet you don't often get a piss-up.
Victor (*taking the tumbler from Aubrey and putting it back on the table*) What have you come for? And at this hour of night.
Aubrey I had to come. It's about Ella.
Victor That girl? No, thank you. I'm through with her.
Aubrey It's frightfully urgent. She's had an offer.
Victor Thank goodness for that.
Aubrey She's in a frightful mess, and wants your advice.
Victor She's had all the advice she'll get from me.
Aubrey Oh, don't be bloody about it, Dad. She's brought a bloke along.
Victor What? She's not here again, is she?
Aubrey Yes. Outside.
Victor Send her away.
Aubrey But this bloke's here, too.
Victor What bloke?
Aubrey A bloke named Felix. He comes from Morris's place.
Victor (*indignantly*) What are you talking about?
Aubrey He's Morris's stick-man.
Victor Stick-man?
Aubrey You know, the bloke who rakes in the doings. (*He imitates a croupier*)
Victor (*very incensed*) You mean you've brought some damned hanger-on from that gambling-den to this house?
Aubrey Ella got him to come along to show you she was on the level. (*He turns towards the front door*) I'll let 'em in.
Victor (*taking a step to prevent him*) No. I won't have it.

Alma (*from the landing*) Yes, she can come in.
Aubrey Oh, good egg! (*He opens the front door and calls*) Come right in.

Alma comes downstairs. Victor turns to her, protesting

Victor But, Alma . . .
Alma I want to see her again. She interests me more than she did.

Ella, entering, hears this last line and responds gladly

Ella Oh, thank you, Mrs Keene.

Ella is followed in by Felix and Aubrey. Felix comes right in. Alma speaks as Aubrey follows

Alma But not you. You can wait outside.
Victor (*to Aubrey*) You hear that? You wait out there.
Aubrey No, thanks.
Victor (*changing to sympathetic persuasion*) Go on, Aubrey, there's a good chap.
Aubrey (*disgustedly*) Oh, shit.

Aubrey exits

Victor closes the front door

Ella I'm awfully sorry to trouble you again, Mrs Keene, but something ghastly has cropped up.
Alma What is it now?

Ella presents Felix. Her manner towards him is aloof and unfriendly

Ella I've brought this man . . .
Alma I heard about him, thank you. What's he got to do with it?

Felix is about thirty-five. He is dark—he looks as if he were a Cypriot, but if so he has lived in England most of his life, for his English is perfect, in fact profuse, with a common and just very slight accent

Ella His name's Felix.
Felix Pleased to meet you, madam.
Ella I don't know whether he's got any other name.
Felix (*jokingly*) Oh, a large selection.

Alma sits on the sofa

Ella And this is *Mr* Keene. (*She indicates Victor*)
Felix Pleased to meet *you*, sir.
Victor (*glaring at him*) You won't be for long. You help to run this gambling-den?

Felix That is so, yes. I'm what you might call a junior partner. Like I understand you are here.

Victor If you're going to start by being insulting . . .

Alma (*quietly*) No, don't be aggressive, Victor.

Victor (*in a hurt tone*) Oh, it's *don't* be aggressive now.

Alma (*calming him*) Just until we've heard . . . (*To Ella*) Do you want to sit down, my dear?

Ella Oh, thank you. (*She sits beside Alma*) Shall I tell you what's happened?

Alma I'd like to do some talking first. (*To Felix*) You gave this girl a flat next to your building . . . ?

Felix Not me. I didn't. That was Mr Morris. It's him that owns the property.

Alma But why is she being turned out now without proper notice?

Felix There again, that's Mr Morris. But he considers she's had ample time to settle her losses and her back rent and that. He told her so six weeks ago.

Victor (*to Alma*) But there's something about an offer, dear, I don't know what it is.

Ella I can tell you that. Felix has offered me another flat to go to. (*Angrily, to Felix*) Go on—*you* tell them.

Felix I haven't offered—not me in person. It's just I have a friend who's willing to give her accommodation.

Victor (*scornfully*) A gentleman friend, no doubt?

Felix A perfect gentleman. He moves in the highest circles.

Alma (*optimistically*) Oh, well . . . (*To Ella*) Is he somebody you know and like?

Ella shakes her head: Alma is disappointed

Oh.

Victor (*challenging Felix*) What you mean is some man wants to keep her?

Ella No, it isn't that. If it was that I might . . . (*To Felix as before*) Tell them.

Felix (*to Victor*) It isn't he wants to keep her, sir; not in the sense you mean, speaking no doubt from your own vast experience.

Victor is about to protest violently; Felix beats him to it and continues

More like—maintain her. In a swankey way and at a very high-class address.

Ella (*with emphatic scorn*) Yes, Duke Street, St James's. They want me to become a whore.

Victor (*to Felix*) You unutterable swine.

Alma No, Victor . . .

Victor But damn it . . .

Felix (*politely*) Again, it is not me, sir. I don't mind what she does. I am the mere mouthpiece for my friend.

Alma (*amicably to Felix*) I expect you're really my friend himself.

Felix I only wish I was, madam. He's in very much better off circumstances than me. Or Mr Morris, either. No, my friend picked on her principally by reason of her being a girl of class. Oh, looks as well, granted; but class, that's what they go for my friend's clientele. They're very high-class themselves; guards officers and the like. Two or three M.P.s in their time off—Conservative ones, needless to say. Men of title even.

Victor Alma, I don't like you listening to this.

Alma Why on earth not? It's most interesting. Quite a revelation. (*To Felix*) Men of title, you say?

Felix (*warming to it*) Oh, yes, madam. (*Sitting*) In that quarter of the West End; all top-notchers.

Alma (*genuinely interested*) Goodness.

Felix (*encouraged; concentrating on Alma*) And then country gentlemen in town for the night and rich American visitors and so on. Oh, it's a very fruitful field.

Alma I'd no idea of all this. Really, it's quite fascinating.

Victor (*barely audible in protest*) Alma . . .

Felix And not only nights, of course. There's a very sizeable afternoon clientele.

Alma (*for her own benefit*) Afternoon—Oh, yes—I can quite believe that.

Felix Yes, there's quite a number of respectable old middle-aged-customers show their preference for matinée performances.

Victor That's enough. Get out of this house!

Alma (*to Victor*) Oh, do stop interfering. This is something I've never heard about and I want to. (*To Felix*) And do you mean she'd simply live in this smart flat and sit there waiting to be called on?

Ella, who has been sitting bottling up her indignation, now butts in angrily

Ella (*rising*) That's what they like to make out. It doesn't mean that at all. It means walking the streets at night with the police after you, and goggling at every vile man you meet. Doesn't it? (*She prods Felix*)

Alma Does it? (*To Felix*) Would she have to do that?

Felix Yes—it would mean she would have to walk around . . .

Ella There—you see?

Felix But round there, up and down Jermyn Street, it's a very exclusive beat; so long as she steers clear of the cheaper sister'ood. Some of those foreign ones can be very nasty with their handbags.

Victor Now, that'll do. Alma, I simply won't . . .

Alma Wait a moment, Victor. (*To Felix*) Now, you.

Felix At your service, madam.

Alma Oh, not at mine too, I hope. But tell me this. If she did this, would she still have to pay what she owes at your gambling place?

Ella (*vehemently*) Yes. That's how they want me to raise the money—this filthy way.

Alma (*to Ella*) Oh. (*Rising*) I thought perhaps you *wanted* to do it?

Ella Wanted to? Would you want to? Having to give yourself to the first brute of a man who came along.

Alma (*still quite intrigued*) Oh, but you could always choose only nice-looking ones.

Ella That's just what you can't do. (*To Felix*) Can you?

Felix (*to Alma*) No, madam. (*Rising*) With all his good qualities my friend would hardly stand for that. Outside of her own clientele she'd have to accommodate whatever comes along.

Ella (*to Alma, anxiously*) There you are! You see? After what you said this morning you must be horrified?

Alma Never mind what I said this morning. I was hasty and inconsiderate. There is that actual pleasure you spoke of.

Ella (*sitting*) Well, Mrs Keene, I don't want to be rude, but I just can't make you out.

Felix Of course, she'll have to face up to some formidable unpleasantness . . .

Victor That's enough from you.

Alma sits

(*Moving to the front door*) You get out.

Felix (*to Ella*) Well, there it is—Mr Morris says he's got to have the money tomorrow morning. (*To Victor*) That's O.K. I have no desire to outstay my hearty welcome.

Victor (*opening the front door*) I ought to inform the police about you. You'll be lucky if I don't.

Felix No, sir. I think you will be the lucky one.

Felix goes out

Victor shuts the door on him quickly and comes down, speaking as he does so

Victor God, what skunks there are in the world. (*He quickly finishes his drink, clamps the tumbler on the table and rounds on Ella*) How dare you bring a man like that into my wife's house?

Ella I had to bring him; to make you believe the trouble I'm in.

Victor You're in no trouble whatever, or needn't be. You can easily get a respectable job . . .

Ella Well, you've seen for yourself what may happen to me if you don't give me the money.

Alma All of these other men you've been so friendly with—won't one of them . . .?

Ella (*cutting in*) I don't know where they are. Or even who they are.

Alma Ask your grandmother—the one that goes to . . .

Ella Bodrighera?

Alma Bordighera.

Ella (*sarcastically*) I can't very well do that; she's dead.

Alma (*thoughtfully*) Oh, yes; I suppose she very likely is.

Victor (*in an aloof, rather sneering tone*) Why not the fellow who started you off? The man who first *took* you to this ghastly gambling place?

Ella (*startled*) Who?

Victor Your friend Fred Castle.

Alma Of course. Victor, how clever of you.

The suggestion has flabbergasted Ella. She does her best to hide this

Ella Oh, but, no really—I couldn't possibly do that.

Alma Of course you can. And taking you to the place wasn't all he did to you, was it?

Ella I don't think he liked me much. He never did anything else for me. I think I disappointed him.

Alma (*rising*) Well, if you won't tell him I'll tell him myself.

Ella (*rising*) Oh, Mrs Keene, you mustn't.

Victor No, steady, Alma.

Alma (*rounding on Victor*) Why? It was you who suggested him. Where is he acting now?

Victor At the Leicester Theatre, I suppose. He always is.

Alma Well, he'll be there now. If we go at once we can catch him.

Victor What? No, Alma, hold on. We can't do this.

Alma Well, if she won't go by herself we'll go with her.

Ella, who has been taking thought, now chimes in readily

Ella No, all right; I'll go. After all, he can't kill me.

Alma No, you kill him. Be firm with him. You don't know how to treat men. Except, I suppose, in bed.

Victor Alma, Alma . . .

Alma Don't keep on 'Alma, Alma', and wasting time. (*To Ella*) Go at once and catch him. You'd better take a taxi. (*To Victor*) Give her the money for a taxi.

Victor resignedly searches in his pocket

Victor Probably get there quicker by tube. Still . . .
Ella I'll do my best with Mr Castle but if he won't help me, Mrs
Keene, can I come and see you again?
Alma (*sitting on the sofa*) Not tonight.
Victor No, we've done what we can. You've had your chance.
Here's for your taxi. (*He gives her some money*)
Ella (*quietly*) Thank you.

Victor opens the front door

Alma Now go along quickly.

Aubrey appears in the doorway. Ella passes him and goes

Aubrey Cuckoo.
Victor You go away too. Go on.
Ella (*from outside*) Come along, Aubrey.
Aubrey Gosh. D'you mean he's coughed up?

Aubrey disappears quickly

Victor shuts the door

Alma Bolt the door.
Victor You bet I will. (*He bolts the door*) I've had enough of that
young woman. As for her bringing that swine of a fellow . . .
Alma Yes, but it was interesting to hear about prostitution. What a
pity there's such a disagreeable side to it.
Victor (*sitting beside Alma*) Alma—honestly, I don't know what's
come over you. It's that Lolly. Ever since she came you've been a
different woman.
Alma (*at her gentlest*) Yes, bless her for it. Oh, Victor; I wish I'd
known about it all along.
Victor Oh, well, better late than never, or whatever the saying is.
(*He pats her hand and turns away. He wants to get off the subject*) I
wonder whether that girl will find a taxi. (*He rises*)
Alma (*changing to the practical*) Why? You mean she won't be in time
to catch Fred Castle?
Victor (*unconcernedly*) Oh, I should think so.
Alma He ought to be told to wait and see her. (*She rises*)
Victor (*rather more anxiously*) No, no; he'll still be there.
Alma (*moving to the desk*) I think I'll just make sure. (*She sits and
picks up the directory*)
Victor (*alarmed*) No, Alma; steady. What are you up to? (*As she
begins to search the pages*) No, Alma; think what you're doing. We
don't want to get involved in this.

Alma (*as she turns the pages*) Well, it was you who sent her to him.

Victor But there's no need for him to know that. Do be careful, Alma.

Alma Leicester Theatre, Stage Door. (*During the next lines she dials, moving her eyes to and from the book*)

Victor Wait, will you. Listen, Alma. We can't get mixed up——

Alma (*cutting in*)—Will you stop interfering.

Victor No. You told me to assert myself and I'm damn well going to.

He tries to get at the receiver. She pushes him back. He half stumbles and by the time he has recovered himself she has dialled and is listening

It may lead to some hideous row.

Alma (*with a violent gesture at him*) Quiet, will you? (*On the telephone*) Are you there? . . . Yes. I want to speak to Mr Castle, please . . . Still what? . . . On stage? You mean he's still acting?

Victor Thank God for that.

Alma (*on the telephone*) Well, give him a message, please.

Victor No.

Alma (*flapping at Victor and continuing*) He's to wait there, please, until a young lady gets there to see him. . . No, I can't remember her name but it's important he should see her because she's in trouble and it's really Mr Castle who's responsible.

Victor (*horrified*) Alma. Oh, my God.

Alma (*with another quick flap at Victor*) What do you say? . . . Never mind all that; just . . . Certainly, it's Mrs Keene. . . Yes; twenty-nine A Brompton Mews. Keene, with an 'e' on the end. Keene . . . K—double e—n—e. Keene. . . (*Sharply*) I beg your pardon?

Victor (*in a last desperate effort*) Here, give me that. Let me speak to him.

Alma (*not yielding the receiver*) Are you there? . . . (*To Victor*) It's no use; he's rung off.

Victor I'm not surprised.

Alma He seemed a very ill-mannered man.

Victor Do you realize what you told him to tell Castle? That the girl's in trouble and he's responsible?

Alma Well, so he is. (*She rises*)

Victor But, Alma, that can only mean that he's put her in the family way.

Alma Oh, rubbish. And what does it matter, anyhow? The girl will soon tell him if it isn't that.

Victor (*relieved*) Oh yes, that's true. But he'll want to know what *you're* up to.

Alma She can tell him that too. (*She goes to the window table and pours a drink*) I'm a friend who's trying to help her.

Victor (*half-heartedly*) Well, let's hope so. (*He sits*)

Alma Of course. (*With a benign smile*) Stupid.

Victor But listen, Alma. This is the end of it about this girl. I'll get Aubrey away from her somehow and then that's done, finish.

Alma (*giving Victor the drink*) I suppose she'll have to go to Duke Street.

Victor She'll get there sooner or later—you said so yourself. (*Accepting the drink*) Thank you, dear. I'm sorry for her in a way but I'm not going to have you upset. (*Thinking aloud*) We've had enough for one day.

Alma (*affectionately*) Dear Victor—you don't call *today* upsetting, do you? (*She sits*)

Victor (*responding*) Oh that. I'm delighted about that. Anything to make you happy. (*In a practical tone, with a glance at his watch*) Come on, dear; it's time we went to bed.

Alma Oh, rather! (*She rises*)

Victor After all that I'm feeling pretty fagged out. (*He rises*)

Alma Oh, I'm not. I'm feeling quite gay. You go and get into your pyjamas and then come along to my room.

Victor What?

Alma Well, what do you suppose?

Victor Oh, but Alma dear, don't . . .

Alma Don't what?

Victor Don't—don't please have any ideas about now—again.

Alma (*in a hurt, not angry tone*) You mean you don't want to?

Victor Tonight? Alma, it isn't possible. I mean a man of my age, it absolutely whacks him. For quite a time.

Alma (*rather mischievously*) Listen, I had a lovely hot bath this afternoon—you know, afterwards. It made me feel so wonderful, so exhilarated. Why don't you go and have a bath?

Victor (*firmly*) I fully intend to have a bath, but not with any idea of exhilaration. I mean to have a good long soak.

Alma Well, do. Soak as long as you like and then come and tell me how you feel.

Victor I'm sorry, Alma. Definitely not tonight.

Alma Oh, Victor.

She looks suddenly fiery and he anticipates her volubly

Victor It's just that you've had this experience now suddenly late in life or rather, in middle-age or whatever it is, and you've found it very agreeable and exciting and all that and you want to go right ahead and carry on with it all the time—I believe women can do

that much more than men. I don't know. But men can't—at any
rate *I* can't. I never could.

Alma (*still fiery*) After all this time—and I came round to it—
chiefly for your sake because of what Lolly said about your being
unselfish about it—and now I find how wonderful it is and what
I've been missing—(*pointedly*)—and *you too* . . .

Victor (*aggressively*) That's no reason to turn it into a sort of smash
and grab thing. (*More appealingly*) It's meant for people who feel
deeply for each other at the right time.

Alma Right time? When? When next?

Victor Alma, it isn't a thing you can have a regular set schedule
for. (*Compromising*) Well, I don't know—I believe the working
classes do sort of earmark Saturday nights . . .

Alma What? Only once a week?

He shrugs

I must be very mistaken in my idea of the working classes.

Victor I mean—people at our time of life. I think once a week is
supposed to be—about it.

*Alma makes no reply. She turns and sits on the sofa with a quick impulsive
sitting action. Victor deliberates for a moment and decides not to continue
the argument*

Well, I'm going up now. (*He goes to the stairs*) Are you going to bed,
dear?

Alma (*dully*) Not yet. You go to your bath. I'll do the lights.

Victor Oh, right you are. (*Turning on the stairs*) Goodnight, dear.

Alma does not reply

Victor goes upstairs and into his room

*Alma remains on the sofa as though deliberating a desperate problem. Her
lips move to her thoughts and she is scarcely heard murmuring the words
'Once a week'. Her body makes a slight swaying movement as she sits. Then
comes a sudden sweeping change. She gets as intense a 'flying-up' fit as ever
before. She rise, picks up a cushion, flings it to the floor. Then she kicks it, and
strides upstairs, as—*

the CURTAIN *falls*

SCENE 2

The same. About 11.30 the next morning

Mrs Holley is standing in the middle of the room looking at a shopping bag. She calls up towards Alma's bedroom

Mrs Holley Madam! I'm going . . . I say I'm going, madam! Huh. None so deaf as them that doesn't want to.

Mrs Holley exits to the kitchen. Victor enters from his bedroom, with binoculars. He calls to Alma's closed door

Victor Well, I'll be off to Lord's, dear.

Mrs Holley enters

Good morning, Mrs Holley. (*He comes downstairs*)

Mrs Holley Good morning, Mr Keene.

Victor Why, what's up, Mrs Holley? Why have you got your hat on?

Mrs Holley I'm off.

Victor Anything wrong?

Mrs Holley Yes, sir, not that there's often anything right. But this morning . . .

Victor Why, what's happened?

Mrs Holley Madam comes in here with her shopping; starts in on me—why hasn't this bin done, why hasn't that. Go on, then, she says, take this stuff into the kitchen, talking to me as if I was some sort of Native.

Victor Yes, well, listen, Mrs Holley. Don't take it to heart. Between you and me, she's rather upset about something that went wrong.

Mrs Holley What went wrong, sir?

Victor I've no idea.

Mrs Holley I done nothing to upset her.

Victor No, no, she was like it before you got here. Now please, Mrs Holley, do all you can to make her, you know, like she generally is.

Mrs Holley Like she generally is who to?

Victor Please, Mrs Holley, for me. (*He hugs her*)

Mrs Holley Just for you, sir.

Victor Tha-at's better.

Mrs Holley Thank you, sir.

Mrs Holley exits to the kitchen with the basket. Alma enters from her bedroom with a travel brochure

Alma What were you saying to Mrs Holley?

Victor Oh, nothing, dear. She was just messing about in here. I'm going to Lord's now. Is that all right?

Alma (*coming downstairs*) Why shouldn't it be all right?

Victor Yes, well, have a nice day, dear. (*Pausing as he goes up*) Alma . . .

Alma Yes, what?

Victor Alma, is anything the matter?

Alma The matter? What do you mean?

Victor Only you seem rather, well, distant to me this morning.

Alma Do I?

Victor Mrs Holley seemed a bit put out. Did you have a row with her?

Alma One doesn't have rows with servants. I had occasion to speak to her.

Victor When I came down she was leaving.

Alma If she wants to leave she can. (*Calling into the kitchen*) Mrs Holley . . .

Mrs Holley (*off*) Yes, madam.

Alma You can go if you wish.

Mrs Holley Oh, thank you, madam.

Victor Just for the day that is.

Alma Well, of course for the day. What do you suppose?

Mrs Holley enters and moves towards the front door

Mrs Holley Good day, madam, Good day, sir.

The front doorbell rings. Mrs Holley opens the door

Ella is standing there

Ella Is Mrs Keene in?

Mrs Holley She is if you want her.

Mrs Holley exits

Ella Thank you. Oh, Mrs Keene.

Alma Yes. Come in. Shut the door, Victor.

Victor closes the door

Ella I hope you don't mind my coming here again.

Alma No, I want to hear what happened with that Castle man. (*She sits*)

Victor Did you see him?

Ella Yes, of course.

Victor What did he say about my wife?

Ella About who?

Victor About my wife. What did he say?

Ella Nothing. Why should he? He doesn't know you does he?

Alma Never mind about me. What did he say about you?

Ella Oh, need you ask. (*She sits*) He said what I knew he would. He said I was a fool to get mixed up with Morris and it was nothing more to do with him.

Alma So what are you going to do now?

Ella What can I do?

Victor I told you that yesterday. Go and get yourself a respectable job.

Ella Oh, Mrs Keene, please make him understand. I've got to get this money right away.

Victor No you haven't. Just clear out and leave. Morris can't do a thing.

Ella Oh, very well then, you've got to be told the whole truth.

Victor I've been told all I want to hear.

Alma No you haven't.

Victor What? Why not?

Alma Because I haven't. Go on.

A car is heard to drive up outside and sound its horn

Ella You're not going to like this.

Victor Oh, that'll be a nice change.

Alma (*interrupting*) Wait a moment. What's that car doing there?

Victor Car?

Alma (*pointing at the window*) There. Outside.

Victor It can't be coming here.

Alma Then why has it stopped outside my house?

Victor Half a tick—I'll see. (*He steps to the window and lifts a corner of the lace curtain. He looks out then reacts violently*) Good God; it's Fred Castle.

Ella (*in sudden panic*) Oh, no. (*She rises*)

Alma (*in a satisfied tone*) Then he did get my message.

Ella Your message?

Alma (*rising*) About you. Last night. I telephoned him.

Ella But I didn't see him. I lied to you. Oh, don't let him know I'm here.

The doorbell rings

I'll tell you everything when he's gone. I was just going to. Oh please don't tell him. I'll wait in here.

Ella scoots into the dining-room. The dining-room door remains a crack open

Victor (*in a dither*) Oh, good Lord, Alma . . .
Alma (*calmly*) Let him in, can't you?

Victor opens the door, revealing Fred Castle. He is about forty—very trim and well-turned-out. He is autocratic, completely the boss and not to be argued with; but with a sense of humour and a candour which are entirely sympathetic. He is at first in a very challenging mood

Fred Is there a Mrs Keene living here?
Victor Yes. I'm her husband.
Fred *Are* you though?
Victor Please come in.
Fred You bet I'll come in.

Fred walks in. Victor closes the door

Alma I am Mrs Keene.
Fred Really. My name is Fred Castle.
Victor (*gushing*) Yes, yes. You need no introduction.
Fred (*to Alma*) Was it you sent me that telephone message last night?
Alma Certainly it was. Why?

Fred looks slightly puzzled but is still on the offensive. He turns and looks at Victor

Fred That's an M.C.C. tie you've got there.
Victor That's right, yes. I'm a member.
Fred Oh. I didn't know they admitted blackmailers.
Victor (*more alarmed than affronted*) What? Really, Mr Castle—blackmail—that's a very ugly word.
Fred Ah. I see you know the right dialogue, too. Yes, it *is* an ugly word. (*Looking at Alma*) And it applies to some very ugly people.
Victor My wife didn't mean what she said on the 'phone.
Alma Victor, how dare you say that? Of course I meant it.
Victor Oh, do shut up.
Alma (*angrily*) What?
Victor (*to Fred*) I heard what she said about your getting a girl into trouble. Of course to you that can only mean one thing.
Fred Oh, thank yer.
Victor She didn't mean it that way at all.
Fred Then why didn't you stop her saying it?
Victor (*with desperation*) Have you ever tried to stop a telephoning woman?
Alma (*sitting on the sofa*) I'll tell you what I meant, Mr Castle. You took a girl to a gambling place kept by a man named Morris.
Fred Did I? When? And why shouldn't I, I'd like to know?

Alma Did you or did you not?

Fred Don't you question me. I've come to do that to you. You said this girl was coming to see me last night.

Victor Yes, but now she says she didn't.

Fred I know she didn't—why not?

Victor There's something very fishy about this.

Fred (*indignant*) I'll say there is. Why d'you think I've come here?

Victor (*passing Fred to get to the dining-room door*) Excuse me.

Fred *Excuse* you—that's a good one. Come on, what *is* this little game?

Victor (*opening the dining-room door*) Come out here.

Ella comes in

Ella and Fred face each other in silence for a moment; Fred with a frown as if searching his memory.

Ella I don't suppose you remember me?

Fred Eh? Oh, yes. I do. It wasn't so long ago.

Alma You saw her in a film studio and told her she had a nice pair of charlies.

Victor (*alarmed*) No, Alma—really.

Alma Well, that's what began it; according to her.

Fred Yes, I daresay I did. And I don't think I was far wrong.

Alma Then you took her to this Morris's and then took her home and had social intercourse.

Fred (*with a glance at the despairing Victor*) I'm glad I was so refined about it. (*Indignantly again*) And what the devil has that got to do with you? Are you her parents or something?

Ella No, they're only trying to be kind. Only I'm desperately wanting some money and they thought I'd better ask you first. Only I didn't dare.

Fred No, but it seems you get around telling people about me.

Ella No, only them. It's not a thing I boast about. Because I'm afraid I must have been rather a flop.

Fred (*more amicably*) You needn't think that. I like to mix it, you know. I don't go in for permanent attachments.

Alma That's true of all the men who have made reputations as great lovers.

Victor Alma, be careful what you're saying. You can't talk to Mr Castle like that.

Alma But it's a compliment. Everyone knows that Mr Castle is very attractive to women. Aren't you?

Fred Well, that's my good fortune, isn't it? (*Guardedly*) In some cases. (*Breaking off, to Ella*) What's all this, this trouble you're in? What happened to you?

Ella That night Mr Morris asked me to come back. So I did. Then he sort of took me up and rented me a flat next door, to entertain his men friends. So I did that too. But not for money. And I got awfully into debt.

Alma So now she's being turned out of the flat.

Fred (*not over-concerned*) Oh, dear.

Alma But she has got an offer to go to Duke Street and become a tart.

Victor Prostitute, dear.

Alma Oh, don't be so pernickety. (*Fred sits*)

Ella I only told you that as a sort of last effort to get the money. I got Felix to come along and help.

Victor You're the most unscrupulous girl I've ever heard of.

Ella Yes, I expect I am. (*She sits*) Because, if you must know, I don't need the money for the flat, I paid Mr Morris a week ago.

Victor and Alma are open-mouthed

Victor Paid him? How could you?
Alma Paid him with what? } (*Speaking together*)

Ella is silent for a moment; then speaks as though against her will

Ella Aubrey got the money for me.

Victor (*incredulously*) Aubrey?

Ella From the car place he had a job at.

Victor You mean to say they let him have it?

Ella No. Some customer paid a hundred and forty pounds for a car in cash. And Aubrey kept it.

Victor Stole it?

Ella Yes.

Victor Oh, my God.

Fred Who's Aubrey?

Alma His abominable son. Not mine, thank you.

Victor He's simple-minded.

Fred He sounds pretty capable to me.

Ella His boss was away at the time. He came back two days ago. I knew he'd find out so I went and talked to him.

Victor Walker?

Ella Yes. He was very angry of course. But I got him to give me till today to pay him back. But he's going to run Aubrey in if the money isn't paid this morning.

Victor But, good heavens, it's nearly twelve now. (*In a great flap*) Hold on—I'll phone Walker. No, that's no good; he calls himself something motor depot. The what motor depot? Oh, damn it, I've forgotten. Do you remember?

Ella I'm afraid not. I wrote it down but I haven't got it here.

Victor Why not? Oh, hell.

Fred (*rising and taking Victor aside, confidentially*) Steady, now. You seem to be in what is commonly known as a bugger's muddle. You know where this motor place is, anyhow?

Victor Yes, very close to here, thank God. End of Brompton Road by the Oratory. I'll go there are once.

Alma (*who has been regarding Victor's flap rather disdainfully*) Take your cheque-book.

Victor Yes, yes; I have it on me; but . . . (*He pulls up, faced by a snag*)

Alma (*with quiet command*) Pay the man.

Victor (*effusively*) May I do that? Oh, thank you, Alma.

Alma Then don't waste any time.

Victor No fear. I'll run all the way.

Fred You can take my car if you like.

Victor Oh, thank you, but it's no distance.

Fred It'll save you getting apoplexy. Come on; I'll tell my feller.

Fred goes to the front door. Victor hurries after him

Victor (*as he goes*) This is immensely kind of you.

Fred Oh, that's nothing.

Fred and Victor disappear leaving the door ajar

Ella turns to Alma. Ella does not appear very penitent

Ella (*rising*) Oh, Mrs Keene, I hardly know what to say.

Alma You don't often have that trouble, do you? Tell me this, did you ask Aubrey to steal it for you?

Ella Well, it was sort of—between us . . .

Alma All these lies—that other nonsense about Duke Street . . .

Ella (*with great assertion*) No, that was true. I did get that offer. It still holds good.

A car is heard starting up and driving away

Alma Then that's where you'll finish, I should think. Wretched girl. (*She turns aside angrily*)

Ella tries a bit of blarney

Ella Oh, Mrs Keene, if ever it looks as if I might really have to go to Duke Street, do you think I could come and see you again then?

Alma turns as if to rend her. She glares at Ella and speaks angrily

Alma Yes.

Fred enters through the open doorway and comes down

Ella (*to Alma*) Shall I wait until Mr Keene comes back?
Alma No, certainly not. (*She rises*)
Ella Then I'll go now. Thank you, Mrs Keene. Good-bye. Good-bye Mr Castle.
Fred (*airily*) Oh, good-bye, my dear. Glad to have seen you again.
Ella (*without any sarcasm; rather artificially coy*) Oh, I'm so glad you're glad. Good-bye.

Ella goes

Alma (*as Ella goes*) Go on: go on and close the front door, please.

Fred closes the front door

Thank you for lending my husband your car. It was very thoughtful.
Fred Well, he seemed a bit het up. I don't mind waiting a few minutes. This is all a rather unusual experience for me.
Alma It certainly is for me—to have a little while alone here with you of all people. (*Pointedly*) With your reputation.
Fred (*quite sincerely*) I just happen to be what I am. One thing, thank goodness—I don't need flattery. I never flatter *myself*. In fact, it gets rather a bore at times being so much better than anyone else.
Alma Oh, I didn't mean your reputation as an actor.
Fred (*with instinctive resentment*) Why, what more d'you want? (*Quickly urbane again*) Ohh, you mean the horses? (*Surprised*) Why, are you a race-goer?
Alma No, no, Mr Castle; I mean what I said before—your reputation as a ladies' man.
Fred (*laughing*) Oh, so that's it? Well, I'm not supposed to have many rivals in that field either. (*Leg-pulling*) So that's where your tastes lie, is it?
Alma (*dead seriously*) Yes. That's why it's so helpful to be able to consult an expert. You see, I've only just become interested in the physical side of it.
Fred Why, have you been in a nunnery or something?
Alma Yes. For over twenty-five years. In a nunnery of my own making.
Fred Pity you left it so late to come out.
Alma (*sitting on the sofa*) Not too late. But I don't suppose a man like you would want to be bothered with my case; odd though it is.
Fred I like oddities. I didn't know there were any left.
Alma Please don't laugh at me. I know I'm middle-aged and undesirable.
Fred I didn't mean it that way.

Alma Yes, you did. It serves me right for talking to you like this.

Alma is genuinely upset with herself. Fred sees this and becomes gentle and sympathetic

Fred Now, now—don't upset yourself. (*Confidentially*) I'll tell you something. I've had pretty nearly every desirable young woman who's available and quite a few who aren't. I don't say I get tired of them, but just now and then, there's something about a middle-ager—well, say forty-odd—which offers a new sort of kick.

Alma A beautiful woman though . . .

Fred Doesn't follow. As a rule the lovelier a woman looks the dumber she comes. It's personality that counts.

Alma Oh, Mr Castle. I think it's wonderful of you to be so versatile. Do you think I've got personality?

Fred You bet you have.

Alma (*brightening*) You mean I might possibly be one of these middle-agers who could offer a new sort of kick?

Fred (*slightly compromising*) Well, let's say—I didn't think there was much novelty left. But if there is you're certainly a starter.

Alma You're really laughing at me the whole time, aren't you?

Fred Not at all. I'm always ready to encourage an enthusiast.

Alma Then you're just being kind to me.

Fred Well, why not? Come on—snap out of all this droopy stuff. It's a thing to be bright about and—sporty.

Alma Oh, Mr Castle. You're making me feel more optimistic every moment.

Fred I'll tell you something else. (*Sitting beside her*) Women who are past the early stages have got another consolation.

Alma Oh, what?

Fred (*putting his arm round her*) They're always the most passionate.

Alma Oh, Mr Castle, are they?

Fred Always.

Alma Oh, Mr Castle; you've got your hand on my charlie.

Fred It's just making itself at home. (*Removing his hand and sitting up*) But I don't quite get this—have you been married long?

Alma A few months.

Fred Is that all? It seems a bit soon for you to be on the general rampage like this. Isn't he up to the job?

Alma (*rather incoherently*) No. Oh, yes. At the time it was wonderful and I got the bells and he brought it off thank God and everything. But he's no good about wanting and enthusiasm and oftenness enough.

Fred A bit past it it, eh? Poor devil. I hope I never get that way. You must have a heart, you know. Don't tick him off about it.

If you want to bring him up to scratch do it gently and fondly—
you know—a little monkey business.
Alma Monkey business? Oh Mr Castle; what do monkeys do?
Fred (*laughing to himself*) Oh, good Lord, we're back in the kinder-
garten. Here—turn your face here. (*Taking her face he brings it to
his*) Open your mouth a little.

Alma opens her mouth

No, just a little crack.

*A silent scene follows in which he plays on her lips with his tongue. She opens
her mouth and he inserts his tongue. Alma works herself up into a passionate
state. She grips his hand and takes it to her breast. At length, with an effort
he frees himself and laughs*

There you are. That's what's generally referred to as the guzzle.
Does it give you ideas?
Alma (*wildly exclaiming*) Ideas. (*She seizes him*)
Fred Steady now.
Alma Guzzle me again. Guzzle me.

They kiss

Fred (*getting himself disengaged*) My word. You're that novelty all
right.

*A car horn is heard. The shadow reappears on the window. Fred turns his
head towards it.*

But you'd better return to normal. (*Rising*) Your old man's back.
Alma Bolt the door.
Fred No, thank you.
Alma Oh, how exasperating.
Fred Your hair's a bit wonky.
Alma I don't care. (*Nevertheless she tidies it as she goes on*) Well, at least
I can say I've been guzzled by Fred Castle. (*She rises and goes to the
mirror*)
Fred (*with assumed severity*) Now, don't *you* start.

Victor enters hurriedly, leaving the door open

Victor It's all right—it's settled. He was pretty nasty about it but
he took my cheque. (*To Fred*) I'm very grateful to you, Mr Castle.
Fred That's O.K. I've got to get along now.
Victor Thank you for waiting. I'm sure it's been a great treat to my
wife.
Fred For me too. (*He gives Victor a mischievous dig*) You don't realize
how lucky you are.

Victor Oh, I do indeed.
Fred (*to Alma*) You keep him up to that. Good-bye.
Alma (*almost inaudibly*) Good-bye.

Fred turns to the door

Victor I'm sorry I've been such a bad host. I ought to have offered you something.
Fred Your wife did that.

Fred goes

Victor follows into the porch and gives him a wave of the hand. Then closes the door and turns, as the car is heard going and the shadow disappears

Victor My word, what an awfully nice chap.
Alma How much did Aubrey steal?
Victor A hundred and forty pounds.
Alma I'll tell the bank to pay it to your account.
Victor Oh, thank you, dear Alma. Doing this for my sake—it's wonderful.
Alma So long as you guarantee that I never see Aubrey again. (*She sits on the sofa*)
Victor Absolutely. What a business all round. To think that Fred Castle would ever come to this house. I must say he was awfully agreeable and helpful, wasn't he?
Alma (*flatly*) Very.
Victor How did you get along with him?
Alma We just chatted. He was very pleasant. Aren't you going to your cricket?

Alma is only half-listening; she is trying to decide whether to tell him something

Victor Righto then. (*Picking up his binoculars*) I'll be off. (*Getting up*) Good-bye, dear, and thank you again for what you did.
Alma (*as he gets to the door*) No, Victor. (*Rising*) Wait a moment.
Victor (*turning back*) Yes, what?
Alma You were quite right about me this morning, I was in a very bad mood. It was because of last night—your not wanting to—go on.
Victor Well, never mind that now. That's all . . . (*He breaks off with a gesture*)
Alma Let's be honest about it. You don't really ever want to do that, do you?
Victor Well, Alma, we were very happy together before it—cropped up.

Alma But don't you really ever have any sort of—(*making an urging gesture*) feeling that way?

Victor Well, I'm a normal man, of course. One occasionally—thinks about it.

Alma Haven't there been any times since we married when you wanted?

Victor Oh, yes, I suppose—mildly.

Alma But you've never done it? I mean with anybody else?

Victor Of course not.

Alma Why of course? I would have, if I'd been you.

Victor (*nettled*) I don't mind telling you I nearly did once.

Alma (*keenly enthusiastic*) Oh Victor, when?

Victor I was on top of a bus. It came over me unexpectedly, like a sort of itch. It happens that way. Expecially on the tops of buses.

Alma Poor Victor. But you resisted?

Victor Oh, it passed off. I forgot it when I got to Lord's. I saw Duleep make a hundred.

Alma You're quite right about how we were getting to be happy together. I don't want to upset that. So I've decided something. I'm going away.

Victor (*in great surprise*) Away? Where?

Alma I don't know where. Just for three or four weeks perhaps.

Victor But why on earth—what's the id . . . ? (*With sudden challenge*) Alma—what's the idea?

Alma (*decisive and practical*) Mrs Holley will see to you—I'll arrange all that. And I'll give you quite enough to keep you going.

Victor What's behind all this? I can't help suspecting something and I don't at all like it.

Alma I can't help that. I've got to do something about myself.

Victor Now listen, Alma. If this is what I think I won't stand for it.

Alma Are you the one to say? (*Brief pause*) Go on—go to your cricket. (*She sits on the sofa*)

Victor again turns towards the front door; pauses in thought. He takes a step down towards Alma and speaks gently

Victor Alma, just sit and think it over quietly. Don't go and ruin our whole life together. You don't seem to realize how fond I am of you.

Alma rises

Alma (*flying up*) Do you suppose I'm not fond of *you*?

Victor gives up. He takes his hat and walks out, closing the front door

Alma deliberates for a moment, then goes to the desk with the travel brochure. She picks up the telephone, sits, finds a number in the brochure, and dials

Alma (*after listening for a moment*) Are you there? . . . Is that Messrs Thomas Cook and Sons?

the CURTAIN *falls*

SCENE 3

The same. Ten o'clock at night, three weeks later

All the lights are on, and the curtains are drawn

Victor, wearing a dressing-gown and pyjamas, is standing by the window table drinking a glass of brandy. He pours another glass. A taxi is heard approaching. Victor looks out of the window, then finishes his drink hurriedly, moves down to a table and empties the ashtray into a wastepaper basket. He replaces the ashtray, then takes the drinks tray into the dining-room. The taxi door slams. Victor hastens to the stairs, switches off the lights, then runs upstairs, switches off the landing lights, and goes into his bedroom

Alma enters from the front door carrying a coat and vanity case. She switches on the lights by the front door, then puts the case by the window. A Taxi-driver enters with a hatbox and suitcases

Alma Just put them down there, please.

He puts the cases by the window. She pays him

Thank you.

The Taxi-driver inspects what she has given him, gives a slight jerk of the head, and goes

Alma shuts the front door and draws the bolts

Victor enters on to the landing and switches on the landing light

Victor Alma—good Lord—you've come back home again. (*He starts down the stairs*)
Alma That's fairly obvious, isn't it? Well, Victor?
Victor Good Lord, this is beyond anything.
Alma What is?
Victor Your suddenly turning up after all this time.
Alma It's only three weeks and a bit.
Victor Yes, but I'd have come and met you. If only you'd have let me know you were coming.

Alma It's just as well I didn't. I'm about three hours late. Something went wrong with the cross-Channel boat. They had to go and get another.

Victor Poor Alma, you must be fagged out.

Alma No, not in the least. I just sat and waited.

Victor Have you had any dinner?

Alma Oh, yes; a very good one. They saw to all that.

Victor Oh, good. But will you want something else before you turn in? A cup of tea or anything?

Alma (*casually removing her hat and coat and laying them aside as they talk*) No, thank you. And I'm not going to turn in just yet.

Victor Well, I'd better take your things upstairs, anyhow.

Alma No, leave them alone for now. I want to sit and hear all about you.

Victor Me? Oh, I've got along all right—as best I could.

Alma You've been looked after properly? Has Mrs Holley been behaving herself?

Victor Oh, fine. I've been going out for my evening meals. I did tonight. Then I came back and was reading in bed and heard you arrive.

Alma And Aubrey? What have you done about him?

Victor Nothing. That girl's still looking after him. I've just let it rip. I don't know what else to do.

Alma (*sitting on the sofa*) Well, now about *my*self—I've decided to tell you everything. I want to tell you all that happened to me straight away. I feel I should sleep better.

Victor (*sardonically*) I wonder if I will.

Alma No, I'm afraid you won't.

Victor For heaven's sake, let's keep it till tomorrow.

Alma No. Now sit down, Victor.

Victor (*greatly against his will*) Oh, all right then. (*He sits on the armchair*) Let's have it.

Alma You can smoke your pipe if you like.

Victor No, no; I've finished with all that for the night. I've cleaned my teeth and everything.

Alma Then just listen and don't keep fidgeting. Well, you know what my motive was in going abroad, to Bordighera.

Victor Yes, but—go on.

She glances at him sternly

Alma I didn't like it at first.

Victor Why only at first?

She gives a quiver of impatience at him. He makes a gesture of apology

No. All right. Carry on.

Alma There weren't many people in the hotel. A few American married couples and one old permanent Englishman. It was hopeless for me there, hopeless. I thought I'd come on a wild goose chase. I got almost frantic . . .

Victor Oh, Alma, do you have to tell me all this?

Alma Yes. I want you to realize what happened to me, and to try to understand. Just to show you the sort of—turmoil—I was in; there was a valet in the hotel who did the shoes. A regular valet, quite a smart, well-mannered young man. I got him to bring my shoes into my room in the morning. On the second morning he brought them in, I came out of my bathroom by mistake on purpose with nothing on.

Victor (*staring and shaking his head*) It's beyond me. What happened then?

Alma He ran away, screaming.

Victor I expect he thought *he'd* surprised *you*, and was screaming in apology.

Alma Don't try to be kind, Victor. It made me despair of myself. Then suddenly, ten days ago, it came my way—the complete fulfilment I was looking for.

Victor (*rising quickly*) That's enough. I don't want to hear any more. A wife coming home and telling her husband——

Alma (*cutting in sharply*)—Well, you knew what I'd gone for. You must listen.

Victor I will not.

Alma You must.

Victor (*moving to the cases*) I'll take these things upstairs and go to my room. And you too. To yours.

Alma (*rising*) Not yet, Victor, until I've told you everything—I want you to take pity on me and help me to decide.

Victor (*with challenge*) Decide what?

Alma What's going to happen to me now. And to you. Please, Victor.

He gives in without saying anything. She goes on as before

I hired a car to have a drive round the country. The driver was a young Italian, very bronzed and handsome and speaking very good English. I asked him whether he was married and he said no, he had too many girl friends to want to get married. I told him he ought to try going with a plain, middle-aged woman because I'd heard from a friend of mine who was a great connoisseur, that they were the women who were the most exciting and passionate and gave kicks.

Victor Alma, this is incredible; it simply isn't you. What in God's name has happened to you?

Alma He took me for miles to an empty farmhouse he knew of. It was all locked up but there was a nice clean barn.

Victor A barn? (*He sits on the sofa*) Good God, Alma, this is the most degraded thing I ever heard of. Like a dirty French farce.

Alma (*sitting in the armchair*) I couldn't help that. I'd found what I'd been longing for and it was more wonderful even than I'd hoped. I left the hotel and rented a little furnished villa by the week. He came in his car every afternoon. It was—(*closing her eyes*)—oh—beyond all words. (*Opening her eyes*) The great thing was he appeared to be quite inexhaustible.

Victor Thank you; it's bad enough without any sarcasm. I wonder how much you had to pay this bastard.

Alma I gave him what he wanted—I didn't care. But that was really the trouble; that's what led to it.

Victor Led to what?

Alma It was three days ago—it seems like weeks . . .

Victor What does?

Alma He came to the villa as usual, all gay and debonair and paying me compliments. He started to undress me . . .

Victor You can spare me the details . . .

Alma Then he began whispering about how he'd got into money trouble, and would have to sell his car and wanted me to give him a great deal more and when I said no he began shouting and threatening me; I thought he was going to kill me. And it was all so shaming because besides being frightened I had nothing on above my waist. I was like one of those Greek women from some vulgar piece of old statuary, struggling with some heathen male creature who is trying to get at her handbag.

Victor (*rising, forgetting himself in indignation*) The stinking Dago brute—by gad, I wish I'd been there.

Alma Oh, Victor, I wish you had. He threw me on the bed and got my bag and threw my traveller's cheques at me and took all my Italian lire and dashed off in his car. So I went straight to the telephone—that is, directly I'd got my camisole on again . . .

Victor And phoned the police . . .

Alma Police? No, of course not. I gave up the villa and booked to come back here today. (*Brief pause*) So here we are. (*Sharply*) And don't go on being angry with me; that won't do any good.

Victor Oh well—I don't suppose I've any right to be.

Alma Yes, you have. But please keep it to yourself, because if you're going to stay on with me after this . . .

Victor We'll thrash all that out tomorrow. (*Going up to the cases*)

Now, for goodness sake, go to bed. (*He takes up the two suitcases*)
I'll take these up.

Alma But, Victor, I want to get things settled about ourselves.

Victor Yes, but not tonight.

Alma You're ashamed of me, aren't you?

Victor No. What you do is up to you. It always has been. Don't
forget your coat and things. (*He goes to the bottom of the stairs*)
Don't bother about the lights; I'll see to them.

Alma (*picking up her coat and hat*) You needn't think I'm ashamed.
Yes, I am. But I'm only ashamed of being so vain as to think that
any man would really want me like that.

She starts upstairs, Victor following

I suppose my bed's made?

Victor (*on the landing*) Oh Lord, I hope so. Yes, I expect Mrs Holley
will have seen to that.

Alma (*opening her bedroom door*) It looks to be all right.

Alma goes into the bedroom

Victor (*speaking into the room*) Well, there you are. (*He puts the cases
inside*) Don't be too long getting to bed. Goodnight. (*He turns
away*)

Alma comes out of the bedroom

Alma Leave the landing light on. I'm going to the bathroom.

Victor Oh, are you? Yes, of course. Right you are.

Alma goes into the bathroom and shuts the door

Victor starts downstairs and stops half-way, looking anxious

*Lolly, fully dressed and carrying a hat and handbag, comes quickly, and
in a very surreptitious manner, from Victor's bedroom*

*There is some dumbshow, Lolly wanting to escape and Victor signalling that
Alma is only in the bathroom and for Lolly to go back to his room. Lolly,
despite this, comes impetuously down, pushing past Victor and making for
the front door. She unlocks this, but does not realize that it has been bolted.
She then tries to unbolt it, but finds it difficult. Victor goes to her aid, getting
Lolly out of the way and pulling back the bolt*

*Alma comes out of the bathroom, her toothbrush in her hand, and stands
watching*

Victor opens the front door

Lolly hurriedly escapes

Victor finishes bolting the door. He looks over his shoulder, and sees Alma.
She comes downstairs slowly and calmly and does not speak until she is at
the bottom and face to face with Victor

Alma Was that Lolly?

Victor Yes.

Alma Has this been happening often?

Victor No, this is only the second time. Soon after you went away
Lolly rang up. I said you'd gone abroad for a little change. So she
asked me to take her out to dinner. And—oh, well . . .

Alma Why did you say yes?

Victor Well, dash it, I was lonely. I wanted company and she was
very friendly and we had rather a lot to drink at dinner and there
it was.

Alma And now again the second time.

Victor She invited herself again. I couldn't very well say no. You
wouldn't want me to hurt her feelings.

Alma What about my feelings?

Victor (*boldly*) Well, think what you were doing.

Alma You didn't know what I was doing.

He makes a helpless gesture. She continues volubly

I've been completely open with you—poured out my troubles.
You weren't going to tell me a word about yourself and Lolly.

Victor (*lamely*) The husband isn't supposed to.

Alma You're really just as bad as I am and even worse.

Victor You began it.

Alma Never mind who began it. Can't you see what this means? I
come home to you and make a clean breast of all that happened to
me, half expecting you to turn away in disgust and leave me. And
now what do I find? That you're as bad as I am and even worse
and we're back where we were before.

Victor (*hopefully*) Oh, Alma; can we be?

Alma It isn't can we be, it's what we're going to have to be. Of
course it will be much easier for you than for me. You only did
what you did out of silly weak-mindedness. You never think of
that sort of thing as a rule. You said so yourself.

Victor Now and then, I said. (*Meekly*) Well, but we've still got
affection. At least, I have.

Alma Haven't we both? Are you accusing me of not being affectionate?

Victor No, no. But that'll help, won't it? Because affection really
counts for more than the other thing, doesn't it?

Alma I daresay it *does*. Yes, of course it does. Except at the actual
time.

Victor Try to overcome this other thing, Lolly.

Alma (*fiercely*) What?

Victor I mean Alma. Try to overcome it.

Alma I'm going to. I've got to, haven't I—if there's nothing else for it?

Victor And if there's anything I can do . . .

Alma The only thing you can do is never never to let the subject be mentioned between us again.

Victor No. We'll be like we were before any of this ever happened.

Alma I've said so already, haven't I? (*Moving to the stairs*) Now—I'll go and start my unpacking. You go to bed. I'll bring you your tea in the morning as I always used to.

Victor (*relieved and pleased with himself*) Thank you, dear Alma.

Alma mounts two stairs and turns

Alma Just one thing.

Victor (*amiably*) What is it, dear?

Alma Don't ever let Lolly know that I know.

Victor Know what?

Alma Don't be stupid, Victor. Don't ever let Lolly know that I know what you did with her tonight.

Victor Of course not. As a matter of fact, I didn't. You came barging in before we'd even started.

Alma (*with slow, joyful surprise*) Ohhh—oh, then you're still . . .

She runs down at him, throwing her toothbrush in the air. He catches her in his arms

Oh, Victor—how splendid. Come along.

They both run upstairs, Victor leading Alma. As they disappear into his bedroom—

the CURTAIN *falls*

Alma's bedroom

table

bathroom

Victor's bedroom

street backing flat

umbrella stand

front door

window seat

table

pillar

dining room

screen

large armchair

mirror

radio gram

table

shelves

standard lamp

waste paper basket

desk chair

small armchair

sofa

pillar

kitchen

desk

cake stand

tea table

table

Stage Plan